PENGUIN BOOKS

CASSANDRA'S DAUGHTER

Joseph Schwartz is a psychoanalytic psychotherapist and writer. Born in New York, he grew up in Los Angeles and was educated at the University of California, in Berkeley, where he received a B.A. in both physics and sociology and a Ph.D. in elementary particle physics. He worked for fifteen years in mental health research before becoming a clinician. He is the author of *Einstein for Beginners* and three other books. He currently lives in London with his partner, Susie Orbach, and their two children.

D1016225

JOSEPH SCHWARTZ

Cassandra's Daughter

A HISTORY OF PSYCHOANALYSIS

PENGUIN BOOKS

PENGUIN BOOKS
Published by the Penguin Group
Penguin Putnam Inc., 375 Hudson Street,
New York, New York 10014, U.S.A.
Penguin Books Ltd, 27 Wrights Lane, London W8 5TZ, England
Penguin Books Australia Ltd, Ringwood, Victoria, Australia
Penguin Books Canada Ltd, 10 Alcorn Avenue,
Toronto, Ontario, Canada M4V 3B2
Penguin Books (N.Z.) Ltd, 182–190 Wairau Road,
Auckland 10, New Zealand

Penguin Books Ltd, Registered Offices:
Harmondsworth, Middlesex, England

First published in the United States of America by Viking Penguin, 1999
Published in Penguin Books 2001

1 3 5 7 9 10 8 6 4 2

THE LIBRARY OF CONGRESS HAS CATALOGED
THE HARDCOVER EDITION AS FOLLOWS:
Schwartz, Joseph.
Cassandra's daughter: a history of psychoanalysis / Joseph Schwartz.
p. cm.
Includes biographical references (p.).
ISBN 0-670-88623-8 (hc.)
ISBN 0 14 02.9859 2 (pbk.)
1. Psychoanalysis—History. I. Title.
BF173.S387 1999
150.19'5'09—dc21 99–19938

Printed in the United States of America
Set in Sabon

To Susie
For her generosity of spirit
and depth of understanding

Cassandra, a princess of Troy, was given the power of prophecy by Apollo. But when Cassandra spurned Apollo, he decreed she should never be believed. Apollo, to whom the great temple at Branchidai was erected, was the patron god of the Pythagoreans, a grouping of rich industrialists and merchants. So too was science the patron god of the rich industrialists and merchants of the late nineteenth century. And so, too, did science give psychoanalysis the power of prophecy. And, as it is told, psychoanalysis has spurned the discipline that gave it birth and has not been believed.

But unlike the newly prosperous bourgeoisie of the nineteenth century who sought to invent roots for itself by appropriating the myths of antiquity, we are now too mature to rely on the Greeks for our narratives. The story of psychoanalysis is not the story of Cassandra, but the story of Cassandra's daughter, a strange, not entirely welcome newcomer on the world stage. We do not know the story of Cassandra's daughter. We have to write it ourselves.

Contents

I

Boundaries

Psychoanalysis is arguably the single most important intellectual development of the twentieth century. Comparable to the theory of evolution in the controversy it has caused and continues to cause, psychoanalysis informs part of our daily discourse in a way that evolution has never done. Terms such as unconscious, repressed, ego, ambivalent, complex, projection, denial and double-bind enter into conversations in every walk of life whenever people talk about mental states and the reasons for human actions. Psychoanalytic language and concepts have been integrated into Western culture through novels, poetry, drama and film, literary and film criticism. But a precise definition of the field remains elusive. What is psychoanalysis, really? How does it differ from psychology or psychiatry?

Psychoanalysis is a systematic attempt by many workers over the last 100 years to understand the structure and dynamics of the inner world of the experiencing human being. Simultaneously a theory and a therapy, psychoanalysis shares a boundary with literature, a boundary with psychiatry and medicine and a third boundary with academic psychology. These three boundaries define the concerns and methods that are uniquely psychoanalysis.

With literature, psychoanalysis shares a concern with the human subject, with the complexities and contradictions of human actions and with the richness of human emotional life. But whereas literature could be considered a means of describing – or symbolizing – human inner experience, psychoanalysis differs from the expressive world of literature in that psychoanalysis aims not only to facilitate a description of the human inner world but to understand it. Although psychoanalysis has many literary antecedents, the origins of psychoanalysis do not lie with literature. Historically psychoanalysis is located within the traditions of Western science as a systematic attempt to understand an aspect of human experience of the world – in this case, our experience of our own personal inner world.

Psychoanalysis shares a second boundary with psychiatry and medicine, the attempt within the medical traditions of the West to heal what the nineteenth-century Romantic psychiatrists called the sickness of the soul (Reil, 1803). The unconscious, before Freud, has an extensive medical history (Whyte, 1960; Ellenberger, 1970). But the intellectual traditions of psychiatry and psychoanalysis are entirely different. The origins of psychiatry lie in medicine, whose traditions are informed by trial and error, improvisation and the slow accumulation of practical clinical experience. Psychoanalysis shares with psychiatry a common goal of finding effective treatment for human mental pain. The early history of psychoanalysis is dominated by the engagement of two Viennese scientists turned physicians with the puzzle of the ancient medical condition of hysteria – the presence of physical symptoms such as paralysis, tics and anaesthesia with no organic cause. Psychoanalysis differs from psychiatry in that psychoanalysis offers a way to understand hysteria as the conversion of painful emotional experience into bodily symptoms. In offering this understanding, psychoanalysis introduces the possibility of a treatment – through talking – of causes, not of symptoms, causes that are located in human relationships as they have come to be represented in the individual's inner world, rather than in biological malfunctions of brain and central nervous system.

Psychoanalysis shares a third boundary with academic psychology. Here the intellectual traditions are similar. Psychology and psychoanalysis are both offshoots of the scientific sensibilities of the late nineteenth century: psychoanalysis as development of late nineteenth-century neuroscience and psychology as a development of physics in the psychophysics of Gustav Fechner and Hermann Helmholtz, the study of human perception of the physical signals of sound and light. But academic psychology identifies closely with the techniques of the physical sciences while psychoanalysis has developed its own technique of the spontaneous self-report – the free association – as the raw data of human subjective experience.

The three boundaries fluctuate in the intensity with which they are guarded. At present, a relative lack of interest on the part of academic psychologists in psychotherapy, and a relative lack of interest on the part of psychotherapists in the quantitative measurements that dominate psychological research, make for a live-and-let-live atmosphere. Within psychology more questioning attitudes have developed towards the allegiance of academic psychology to nineteenth-century models of successful scientific research based on physics (Barker, Pistrang and Elliot, 1994; Bem and de Jong, 1997). Within psychoanalysis there is an increasing interest in neuropsychology, the physiological substrate of human emotional response (Solms, 1996).

On the boundary between psychoanalysis and psychiatry and medicine there are increasing hostilities. In the United States, psychiatry has reacted to the past dominance of psychoanalysis within the mental health profession with an offensive based on the new discipline of molecular psychopharmacology. Targeting the many different molecules involved in the transmission or inhibition of nerve impulses across the synaptic cleft, cocktails of new psychopharmacological agents have proved, at least temporarily, effective in relieving symptoms of mental disturbance. From its new base in molecular psychopharmacology, psychiatric medicine has made deep raids into psychoanalytic territory, attacking both the efficacy and theoretical basis of the talking cure.

Attacks on psychoanalysis are an integral part of the history of psychoanalysis. From its inception in turn-of-the-century Vienna, psychoanalysis has inspired strong feelings. Early positive reviews of Freud's and Breuer's account of their novel treatment of hysteria emphasized the humanity of the talking cure, the intriguing methods it offered for exploring the inner world of human emotional life and for re-establishing the connections between the mind and the body (Ellis, 1898):

[Breuer and Freud] have succeeded in presenting clearly, at the expense of much labour, insight and sympathy, a dynamic view of the psychic processes involved in the constitution of the hysterical state, and such a view seems to show that the physical symptoms laboriously brought to light by Charcot are largely but epiphenomena and by-products of an emotional process, often of tragic significance to the subject, which is taking place in the most sensitive recesses of the psychic organism (p. 605).

At the same time, the negative reviews were hostile to the point of dismissal, attacking the subjective, unverifiable nature of the analyst's report as well as ridiculing the emphasis that Freud placed on the sexual origins of mental distress. A parody of psychoanalysis, based on Molière's *The Imaginary Invalid*, staged in the early 1900s by the Viennese Medical Society, had the new psychoanalytic doctor saying: 'If the patient loved his mother, it is the reason for his neurosis; and if he hated her, it is the reason for his neurosis. Whatever the disease, the cause is the same. And whatever the cause, the disease is the same. And so is the cure: twenty one-hour sessions at fifty kronen each' (Barea, 1966).

In the 1990s, the attacks on psychoanalysis from psychiatry have been joined by literary snipers along the border between psychoanalysis and literature. The mini-furore raised by an attack on Freud by a Berkeley literary critic in the pages of the *New York Review of Books* in 1993 reprised the critique of the *Imaginary Invalid* parody – psychoanalysis did not know what it was talking about.[1] The British novelist Fay Weldon entertained London audiences in the early 1990s with her scathing polemics against psychotherapy, in this case depicting a marauding therapist who subverts the real wishes of the patient. These literary critics invariably found it necessary to conclude their critiques by denouncing psychoanalysis as unscientific.

Border disputes between psychoanalysis and its neighbouring disciplines tend to be characterized by a lack of engagement with substantive issues in favour of playing on prejudice and received ideas about scientific work. Explicitly informing literary critiques of psychoanalysis and implicitly informing medical and psychological critiques as well, is a comparison of psychoanalysis to a mythologized natural science, a presumed paragon of precision whose language and methods all statements about the world must copy in order to be valid. What can an appeal by literary critics, of all people, to the presumed certainties of natural science be about?

When psychoanalysis is accused of being unscientific the charge is really that it is subjective, an accusation that raises loud alarms in the

Western mind. We learn from an early age, especially if we are men, that we must strive to be objective, that feelings are not to be trusted, that, in some renderings, to be subjective is a peculiar weakness of the female of our species. The fear that psychoanalysis is 'only subjective', and therefore that it is unreliable or even dangerous, has provoked four distinct responses. The first is to accept as fair the charge that psychoanalysis is unscientific with an ensuing attempt to reconfigure it to produce the controlled studies that have proved so effective in biology. A second response is to accept the characterization of psychoanalysis as unscientific but to insist that scientific criteria are not useful because what is important about psychoanalysis is that it creates meanings in ways that are completely different from the natural sciences. A third is to insist that psychoanalysis is in fact a science, with clinical evidence being a form of evidence valid in its own right. And a fourth reply to the criticism is to argue that the problem lies not with psychoanalysis but with a fallacious concept of science and scientific success.

The fourth response is the response we will explore here because a fallacious concept of science lies at the heart of the critiques of psychoanalysis and the responses to them.

Consider the following definition of science. Following John Berger (1972), we can define painting as a way of seeing. Literature and poetry then become ways of telling, dance becomes a way of moving, architecture a way of building. Science is a way of understanding. As a way of understanding, science has only one competitor – which it has effectively supplanted – and that is religion. The superior efficacy of scientific ways to understand the world by locating causation in the world of matter rather than in the world of spirit has been demonstrated over the past 400 years. Psychoanalysis is a science in the sense that it is an attempt to understand human subjectivity in material terms – it locates its understanding of human subjectivity in the world of lived experience rather than in the spirit world of Western religious traditions.

But in every generation the dead hand of past successes lies over the efforts by the human race to make sense of our experience of the world. All the sciences have at some time felt dwarfed by the past successes of physics with its often quite beautiful ability to establish the unity of apparently unrelated phenomena. Newton, in the most celebrated example, united celestial and terrestrial motion into a common framework – the falling apple and the revolving moon are acted upon by a common gravitational force emanating from the earth, the differences in their motion due only to the fact that the moon is falling sideways and the apple straight down. For 300 years, the achievements of physics served as a model for success in all of science. Only fifty years ago biology was belittled for its lack of precision, for its 'stamp collecting' of specimens, for its lack of generality, for its apparent lack of the (mathematical) rigour of physics. But the spectacular results of molecular biology over the past thirty years offer quite a different model for scientific success, inviting an examination of our previous attitudes.

Beginning in the 1930s as a gleam in the eye of two former physicists at the Rockefeller Foundation, who felt that the mathematical precision of physics was necessary to bring order and structure to the perceived inadequacies of the descriptive biology of the nineteenth century, molecular biology has since confounded its patrons. Among the many important results produced in the 1950s and 1960s was the identification of the genetic material of living organisms as the macromolecule DNA, the discovery of the genetic code, the discovery of the detailed step-by-step process by which a bacterial virus replicates itself and the discovery of the detailed steps by which the metabolism of a bacterial cell is regulated.

The successes of molecular biology are descriptive. Our understanding has been advanced, not by the statement of precise quantitative laws of motion, but by describing in detail the specific structures and sequences of events occurring in the biological processes of interest. The original intentions of the grant-givers of the Rockefeller Foundation have been turned on their head. Instead of creating a quantitative biology in the image of the mathematical models of physics, the essential descriptive nature of biology has been confirmed.

There is a reason why the fundamental successes of molecular biology are descriptive. The phenomena of biology are historical phenomena. The genetic material of living organisms is the complex result of millions of years of accumulated evolutionary changes. Such complexity cannot be understood in terms of frameworks erected for simpler forms of matter dealt with by the physics and chemistry that appeared earlier in the history of the universe. Complexity is not a complication of otherwise simple basic laws of nature. Complexity generates new phenomena that need to be understood in their own terms. An identification of the fundamental constituents of matter and the nature of their interactions is not enough to tell us either how the biological structures of the world came to exist or how they function. There is nothing in the timeless laws of mechanical motion, the laws of thermodynamics, the laws of the electromagnetic field, or the laws of quantum motion that predicts the existence of DNA in its cellular environment.

Biology is not simply applied physics and chemistry, because although the properties of atoms and molecules make life possible it is their organization, not their properties by themselves, that produces the phenomenon of living matter. Similarly, there have been many vain attempts to reduce the phenomena of human psychology – consciousness, memory, human emotions – to no more than a (complicated) manifestation either of the molecular events taking place in the living cell or of events occurring in the individual neurones of the human central nervous system. But just as molecular biology is not simply applied physics and chemistry, psychology is not applied molecular biology or applied neuroscience. The phenomena of psychology emerge from the organization of the physiological and molecular substrate of the human organism and, like the phenomena of molecular biology, need to be understood in their own terms, not in terms of the successes of other disciplines.

At bottom, the critiques of psychoanalysis, no matter how accurately they may pinpoint real problems in theory and practice, carry as a subtext the nineteenth-century story about science being precise, neutral and objective. And since psychoanalysis is plainly subjective not objective, and is not only contaminated by human subjectivity but is in fact the study of the complexity and ambiguity of the human subject, the slightest comparison to this mythologized objective science is sufficient (and indeed necessary) to establish the point.

Within the definition of science as a way of understanding based in the material world, psychoanalysis is indeed a science. As the British historian of science, John Forrester, has emphasized, what else could it be? Psychoanalysis is the search for understanding of our experience of our inner world, an exploration of what we might perhaps call inner space. The claim that psychoanalysis is unscientific is a distraction, sometimes maliciously intended. What we need from an account of psychoanalysis is not a sterile debate about whether psychoanalysis conforms to the criteria of past scientific successes but an analysis of the problems of human subjectivity that psychoanalysis has set itself to solve and an evaluation of its successes and failures.

Psychoanalysis is a creature of the twentieth century, the century that has magnified the successes and disasters of the Industrial Revolution a hundred-fold. The conflicts, promises, dangers and instabilities of the nineteenth-century Industrial Revolution have been carried forward through the twentieth century and into the twenty-first century, not diminished but greatly amplified as a modern, privately owned, mass production civilization has taken over the globe.

Vast increases in wealth have produced a historically unique global consumer culture of dazzling promise. Goods and spectacles radiate out from the centre in the form of clothes, music, movies and sport, offering the world population the promise of participation in the advancing prosperity of the North. Vastly increased overall wealth has been matched by vastly increased inequality and vastly increased poverty. In the early nineteenth century, the wealthiest English landed families – then the richest in the world – had 1000 times the annual income of a day labourer. The gradient of wealth has now increased to the point that the wealthiest industrial and commercial families in the US can have annual incomes in excess of 100,000 times that of a modern blue-collar worker. In the first three years of the Clinton administration, 1992–5, the wealthiest 0.5 per cent of US families saw their assets increase by $1.6 trillion – an average of $3.2 million per family – a combined increase greater than the increase of the remaining 99.5 per cent of the US population. Worldwide, in 1998, 358 billionaires had assets equal to the combined income of countries with 45 per cent of the world's population. In Tanzania, the average annual income is less than the cost of a single mammogram in Britain. Of the world's wealth, 98 per cent is owned by men, 2 per cent by women.

Along with the increase in the scale and gradient of wealth has come an increase in the scale of violent disaster, precipitated by the instabilities generated by such steep gradients of wealth – millions killed in the trenches of the First World War, the Nazi death camps and extermination campaigns, the nuclear bombing of Hiroshima and Nagasaki, the pogroms in the 1990s against ethnic minorities in Europe, Central Asia and Africa, and the routine use of torture as a means of social control by governments throughout the world. In 1998 the United States had troops stationed in 100 countries of the world.

The anxieties created by the instability of global political and economic arrangements are augmented by anxieties about the effect of corporate-dominated economic activity on the global environment. Global warming has threatened the stability of the West Antarctic Ice Sheet. Recent best estimates conclude that unchecked emission of greenhouse gases over the next 100 years could cause a collapse of the Sheet that would take 10,000 years to restore. The release of this volume of ice (3.8 million km^3) to the ocean would cause a rise in sea level of four to six metres and a flooding of the world's port cities.[2]

Psychoanalysis has developed in close relation to the events of the twentieth century. As opposed to the natural sciences – the pride and joy of a triumphant bourgeois culture of the nineteenth century – psychoanalysis has been charged not with participating in the glory of the Industrial Revolution but with cleaning up the mess it left behind. As we enter the twenty-first century, we have still not fully digested how much of a mess is caused by our world system. Sometimes the news is indigestible.

In the spring of 1987, I met colleagues Sally Berry, Margaret Green, Susie Orbach and Tom Ryan at the Institute of Contemporary Art off Pall Mall in London to hear a first-hand report about the work of the Internationalist Mental Health Team in Nicaragua. Along with other politically concerned London psychotherapists we had heard by word of mouth that – unusually for post-revolutionary movements – the Sandinistas were interested in mental health. We knew that the Sandinistas had been impressed by accounts of what had been achieved in Argentina and had invited exiled Argentinian psychoanalysts, then living in Mexico City, to make up a team to come to the city of León to help in the reconstruction of Nicaragua.

The meeting was crowded, lively, buzzing with optimism. Clear, straightforward descriptions of previous work at the Centre for Teaching and Research in Buenos Aires, details of the organization of the twelve-member Internationalist team in Mexico City, and outlines of the types of problems experienced by Nicaraguans in their post-revolutionary situation, including emotional withdrawal, anxiety and especially the widespread problem of frozen grief, moved us as we took in a tiny particle of what the Nicaraguan people had experienced in their civil war.

With the wisdom of twenty years of experience, team member Nacho Maldonado was careful to include in his account the many difficulties associated with the work, some of which were without historical precedent. Fifty years of terrorist rule by the ruling families of Nicaragua, led by the Somoza family, had produced many unusual practices. Foremost among these was the training of children in the arts of torture. When the Sandinistas came to power they inherited the problem of children aged seven to ten years old who had been trained by the Somocistas to pluck out the eyes of prisoners.

The problem of the rehabilitation of the child torturers of Somoza's Nicaragua is probably insoluble with present knowledge. Certainly an exploration with these children of the abuse they themselves may have been forced to endure would be a beginning. But the injuries inflicted on and by these children are the injuries of the entire century. Psychoanalysis has been called upon to treat the psychological consequences of the mess created by the social relationships of our time, as symbolized by the child torturers of Nicaragua. The twentieth century has created an urgent need for a therapy that can understand and treat injuries to the human psyche.

The history of psychoanalysis can be told in many ways. But in any telling there are certain markers in the historical timeline.

The first marker is the role of Sigmund Freud. Like all other aspects of human history, antecedents of the talking cure associated with the name of Sigmund Freud can easily be found – earlier in the century in moral cures practised by the medical profession, in the confessional practised for centuries by the Catholic Church, in literature, in practices in ancient Greece.

But tracing historical antecedents does not do justice to human originality. There are, after all, things that are new. Locating the roots of controlled heavier-than-air flight in the drawings of Leonardo da Vinci does not do justice to the achievement of the Wright brothers. There can be a kind of historical reductionism that weaves the threads of human activity into such a seamless web that one loses sight of those historical moments that are departures from, rather than extensions of, past human practices. Psychoanalysis is one of these.

Although it is true that genius is the mystification of accomplishment – that is to say, that the overall movement of human history produced by forces greater than any single individual creates the necessary conditions for the new to appear – the new must nevertheless be created and is created by human effort. In the case of psychoanalysis, there is a uniqueness to Freud's contribution to the creation of a discipline devoted to the exploration of the human inner world.

A second marker is the roots of psychoanalysis in natural science. The presenting problem of psychoanalysis was to understand the so-called nervous diseases of the time – hysteria, phobias, obsessions and paranoia. The origin of the approach to treating these conditions by concentrated listening lay in the great unifying premise of nineteenth-century science, that the world could be understood. Freud, who came to the problems of mental health as a neuroscientist trained in one of the most prestigious laboratories of Europe, approached traditional medical problems from the perspective of basic research: to learn and understand. Freud's sensibility as a man who sought understanding struck a powerful chord in the sufferers of nervous diseases. For, as Freud came to realize, the symptoms in question were in fact messages that could not be expressed in any other way. The appeal of a dynamic psychoanalysis reflects our desire to make sense of ourselves, to be understood.

A third marker is the invention of the analytic hour. When Freud initiated the early theory and practice of psychoanalysis based on the use of concentrated listening to what sufferers had to say about their lives, a listening informed by a belief that symptoms could be made sense of if the listening were done carefully and at length, he created both a method for the exploration of the human inner world and a theory for understanding what one might encounter there. Among the lasting contributions of psychoanalysis to human knowledge and practice is the analytic hour – repeated listening sessions, not as an ancillary part of medical treatment as in a kind of extended bedside chat, but concentrated extended listening for the express purpose of understanding the analysand's experience of life.

Like the microscope and the telescope, the analytic hour is an instrument that opens up a previously unseen world. For what was discovered in the early years of psychoanalysis was that powerful, difficult thoughts and feelings came into view in hourly sessions repeated over long periods of time. The analytic relationship made possible the systematic exploration of what has come to be called the transference relationship between analysand and analyst. As Freud cautioned early practitioners in a famous paper published in 1916 – it may seem so, but it is not you that your patient is in love with.

A fourth and final marker is the splits that have accompanied the development of psychoanalysis. Like the physical outer world, the human inner world has a structure. Workers in the field have been attracted to different aspects of the structure of the inner world, leading to the great, publicized splits between Sigmund Freud, Carl Jung and Alfred Adler in Vienna in the years before the First World War. What is central to the history of psychoanalysis is not so much the content of the disputes – disputes occur in every field – but the fact that they could not be contained within the discipline. What the splits in psychoanalysis demonstrate, in painful detail, is that paradigm shifts do not occur simply but are accompanied by great personal stresses, rivalries and the divisive phenomenon of winners and losers, all set in particular historical circumstances which can act either to further or to inhibit the development of new understanding.

A single dominant theme connects the markers along the historical timeline of psychoanalysis. From its very beginning psychoanalysis has been undergoing a paradigm shift involving one great generalization about human psychology: the fundamental conflicts in the human inner world lie not in our seeking a reduction in tensions caused by unsatisfied drives but are associated with difficulties in satisfying a fundamental human need for relationship. The historical circumstances informing the playing out of the paradigmatic tensions between a drive-instinctual versus a relational point of view were the highly traumatic social events of war and revolution in Europe – the introduction of mechanized killing in the First World War, the failure of the German revolution of 1918, the failure of the Hungarian revolution of 1919 and the catastrophic counter-revolution associated with the name of Adolf Hitler. In the inter-war years psychoanalysis's centre of gravity shifted from Vienna and Berlin to New York and London. The tension between instinctual and relational points of view of human inner conflict then developed in two distinct strands, American and British. In America, an interpersonal approach to the most extreme forms of mental distress by a group of workers in Washington DC, amongst whom the name of Harry Stack Sullivan stands out, located the source of psychic pain in ruptured, non-existent or abusive relationships. In Britain, the powerful theory of object relations, associated originally with the name of Melanie Klein, who took psychoanalysis into the nursery to treat childhood terrors and anxieties, led to relationship failure being identified as the source of mental disturbance, as was later articulated by the Scottish psychoanalyst Ronald Fairbairn.

As important as markers and themes are to guide our way through a complex story, they can also be a diversion from the main point of the journey. The concerns expressed about the safety of psychoanalysis are not just about its objectivity and reliability. At another level, when we question the safety of psychoanalysis we are questioning how safe it is to be interested in the world of human subjectivity and emotion, a subject that, in the sexual division of labour in the West, has been primarily the concern of women. Part of the fear and hostility with which psychoanalysis has been received is due to the fact that psychoanalysis is the formalization of work historically done by women in the male-dominated societies of the West. Emotions and the subjective life have traditionally been the province of women. Women's work has included performing the unrecognized emotional labour required to facilitate, establish and maintain the human interpersonal relationships without which we cannot live. The old saw – women's intuition – is a patronizing recognition of the sensitivity of women to the inner world of another's feelings. Our resistance to psychoanalysis – whether we are men or women – is in part due to our sense that what is being described is women's work, something, like the force of gravity, that we need not take notice of, unless of course we happen to fall. I have written this account as a guide to psychoanalysis, not only to show its strengths and weaknesses, but also to show just how interesting psychoanalysis really is.

2

Freud

At the turn of the nineteenth century, fame was defined by the Czech German poet Rainer Maria Rilke (1875–1926) as the sum of all misunderstandings that can gather around one name. But fame – however transient – and the universal recognition it brings in the mass society of the twentieth century is something qualitatively different from misunderstood accomplishments. Fame is now a powerful social force. At the end of the twentieth century, famous persons in their plenitude are not unlike Greek gods, each serving to represent in mythologized form different aspects of the fragmented social experience of twentieth-century life.

Famous pop stars – the Beatles, Madonna, Michael Jackson – have become worldwide cultural figures, their music and performance transcending national boundaries as representatives of an emerging world culture, born in the West to be sure, but the cultural equivalent of the transnational corporation. Hollywood movie stars – Theda Bara, Shirley Temple, Marilyn Monroe, Clint Eastwood, Leonardo DiCaprio – are now perhaps gods of success analogous to the American self-made millionaires of the nineteenth century. World politicians are famous because they represent in simplified form the complex politics of the global community. Assassins, adventurers and athletes achieve fame for singular actions: Lee Harvey Oswald, Amelia Earhart, Neil Armstrong, Yuri Gagarin, Pelé, Bjorn Borg are known for what they did, not for who they are.

Where then do figures like Sigmund Freud and Albert Einstein fit into the spectrum of the famous? Their fame seems of a different kind from that of other scientists or inventors such as Madame Curie, known for her investigation of radioactivity, the Wright brothers, pioneers of the airplane, or Bill Gates, the octobillionaire software whizz kid.

With Einstein, we have fame elevated far above accomplishment, a fame analogous to that of modern-day pop stars. The adulation showered on Einstein in his famous New York tickertape parade in 1921 was similar to the adulation accompanying a Michael Jackson world tour. Einstein was the first great international pop star, a cultural figure who transcended national boundaries.

The contrast between the universal fame of Einstein and our universal befuddlement about relativity can tell us something about the way we create famous figures without actually understanding their accomplishments. We know the human race creates mythic heroes. But why Einstein? Why should a theoretical physicist of German-Jewish origins with radical political views have become a cultural icon?

Today Einstein has come to stand for the abstruse and the difficult. Einstein is the genius no one can understand. In the 1920s, however, he represented something very different to the peoples of Europe and North America. The frequently cited front-page coverage of relativity in 1919 in the leading English-language newspapers was not actually excessive given the newsworthiness in Einstein's achievement – an entirely new theory of gravity confirmed with the help of a dramatic total eclipse of the sun witnessed on the exotic equatorial African island of Principe. Sir Peter Chalmers Mitchell, the director of the London Zoo and a science writer for *The Times* recalled in his memoirs that he had been to the meeting of the Royal Society to hear the preliminary report of the Principe expedition, thought it of major interest, and mentioned it to his editor who said, 'Well, you must write a leader about it' (Mitchell, 1937).[1]

Mitchell's interests – those of a man from what Eric Hobsbawm (1964) has called the *nouvelle couche social*, men who were displaced by cartels and monopolies from careers as owners of businesses into careers as journalists, scientists, and administrators – coincided with those of his boss Lord Northcliffe, Alfred Harmsworth. Harmsworth's newspapers routinely covered his many interests, including motoring, flying, wireless and exploration, activities that represented progress and the optimistic advance of civilization to the men of his social class.

A similar optimism, coupled more with hope than with conviction, informed the public reception of the news. Exhausted by the First World War, audiences responded to relativity with enthusiasm. The subject – the curvature of space caused by the presence of matter – was fascinating. That something new and different could be said about such everyday things as space, time and matter was exciting. And the news formed a welcome distraction from Europe's manifold post-war economic and political anxieties. But the complex social upheavals of the inter-war period in Europe – revolutions in Russia, Hungary and Germany; general strikes in France, Scandinavia, and Britain; fascist counter-revolution in Italy; the Great Depression; fascism in Germany – all took their toll on physics. The physics community itself failed to absorb Einstein's arguments; the understanding of relativity that was wished for did not materialize, and the world itself became an alien place after the First World War. Einstein became a symbol of the dumbing-down of Western culture.

If the processes of the twentieth century managed to turn the clarity of general relativity into its opposite, making the intimate relationship between matter and the shape of space unknowable, and have made of its inventor a godlike representative of the incomprehensible, what has the twentieth century done to Sigmund Freud?

The dominant image of Freud is Freud the Severe. His penetrating gaze sees deep into our souls. In his presence, any word, any gesture, betrays our secrets. If Einstein is the god of the incomprehensible, then perhaps Freud has become a god of judgement, an all-seeing father figure from whom nothing can be hidden. But Freud's fame, unlike Einstein's, is multi-faceted. Whereas everyone shares the same image of a long-haired, incomprehensible, genius Einstein, there are multiple Freuds – hero and villain, healer and charlatan, sexual liberator and sexual betrayer, revolutionary and reactionary. In the language of psychoanalysis, Freud is the target of the manifold projections of the feelings of disappointment, fear, love and longing that we can visit on the famous.

Freud's and Einstein's fame pose problems for anyone seeking an understanding of their contributions. One has only to recall one's own reactions to encountering a famous person to realize what powerful feelings can be aroused. Fame prevents writers from standing alongside their subjects to look at their work with them. Instead they stand opposite them in awe, often leaving room only for hatchet jobs or hagiographies, neither of which answer our questions about the work or about how these people came to be so well known.

Past studies of Freud have concentrated on the man rather than the work. Traditional biography, with its focus on establishing the human dimensions of the life, offers a useful approach to historical figures. But at the same time, because an account of how Freud and Einstein approached the leading scientific problems of the day has been lacking, the question of what these men actually did has not been fully addressed. Freud created a new way to comprehend the inner world of human experience. To appreciate how he reached this understanding we need to look at Freud's absorption in the scientific culture of his time.

Freud's life is exceptionally well documented. There are at least eight biographical treatments (Wittels, 1924; Puner, 1949; Jones, 1953; Ellenberger, 1970; Krull, 1979; Sulloway, 1979; Clark, 1980; and Gay, 1988). Much primary material has been published, including the teenage correspondence with Eduard Silberstein and Emil Fluss (Boehlich, 1990; E. Freud, 1969), the partial but still revealing courting correspondence with his fiancée Martha Bernays (E. Freud, 1960) and Jeffrey Masson's indispensable compilation of the complete letters to Wilhelm Fliess (Masson, 1985). In addition there is detailed historical research into Freud's surrounding circumstances, including the gonzo detective work carried out by Peter Swales in unearthing the identities and circumstances of Freud's early patients (Swales, 1986, 1987), an account of Freud's use of cocaine (Swales, 1989a), his relationship with his wife's sister (Swales, 1982, 1983) and his relationship with his best friend Wilhelm Fliess (Swales, 1989b). Swales enjoys tilting at the windmill of Freud's fame, playing the bad boy of Freud scholarship. But taken together his papers provide a refreshing, iconoclastic picture of Freud as a real man rather than as a cultural myth.

Sigmund Freud was born in 1856 in Freiberg (now Pribor, Czech Republic), an underdeveloped region of the 800-year-old Austro-Hungarian Empire, the son of an immigrant father from Galicia. The young Freud and his family were part of the great nineteenth-century wave of Jewish emigration to the West from the ghettos of the Pale of Settlement, the areas in eastern Europe to which the Jews were confined by law. Early photographs show Freud's father in the classic Galician ghetto clothes of long caftan and fur hat. Freud's mother was also born in Galicia but was raised in Odessa and Vienna. Both parents had Yiddish as their mother tongue. Freud's niece Judith Bernays recalled Freud's father during the years 1892–3 (Heller, 1956): 'I do know that my grandfather was no longer working, but divided his time between reading the Talmud (in the original) at home, sitting in a coffee house and walking in the parks. Occasionally he took me with him when others were too busy to occupy themselves with me. Tall and broad, with a long beard, he was very kind and gentle, and humorous in the bargain' (p. 418). Freud's son Martin Freud (1967) recalled Freud's mother: '[She was] a typical Polish Jewess with all the shortcomings that implies, full of life and vitality, had a lively temper and was impatient, self willed, sharp witted and highly intelligent' (p. 202). Marianne Krull (1979) gives a definitive account of the Jewish origins of the Freud family. In the Freuds' case, the final port of call was not Western Europe or the New World, but the nearby metropolitan centre of Vienna.

In Vienna, Sigmund, the eldest son, attended one of the new gymnasia of modernizing Austria, carrying the immigrant family's aspirations. Freud's sister, Anna Freud Bernays, three years his junior, recalled (Bernays, 1940): 'My mother as was natural hoped for great things from her first born' (p. 335). Ernest Jones (1953) recalls Freud's mother referring to him as 'mein goldener Sigi', even when Freud was in his fifties (p. 3).

Freud's entering class in 1865 was only the second entering class in the Leopoldstadt Communal-Real-und-Obergymnasium, then in Taborgasse 24 in the IInd Bezirk (district). The Leopoldstadt Real Gymnasium was part of an educational movement in German-speaking Europe with low fees and a curriculum that emphasized science and modern languages rather than the traditional Latin, Greek and the classics. The head of the Leopoldstadt Gymnasium, Dr Alois Pokorny (1826–86), a specialist on the flora of peat and moss of Lower Austria, had received his doctorate at the University of Göttingen and had been lecturer at the University of Vienna before becoming the school's first director in 1864. Pokorny's textbooks on botany and zoology were still in use a generation later (Knoepfmacher, 1938).

At the Leopoldstadt Gymnasium, Freud was head boy and through a friendship with the Jewish religion teacher, Dr Samuel Hammerschlag, gained entry into the educated Jewish community of Vienna. In his obituary of Hammerschlag Freud wrote (1904): 'Those of his pupils who were later allowed to seek him out in his own home gained a paternally solicitous friend in him and were able to perceive that sympathetic kindness that was the fundamental characteristic of his nature' (p. 255). Hammerschlag lived in the same house as Josef Breuer with whom Freud formed his famous collaboration. Freud named his daughter Anna after Hammerschlag's daughter and his daughter Sophie after Hammerschlag's niece.

At the Leopoldstadt, Freud also formed a close friendship with fellow student Heinrich Braun, who became a leading figure in the Social Democratic movement and founded the newspaper, *Die Neue Zeit*, with August Bebel and Karl Liebknecht. As Freud later wrote (E. Freud, 1960): '. . . we soon became inseparable friends. I spent every hour not taken up by school with him . . .' (Freud to Julie Braun-Vogelstein, 30 October 1927). Braun was a cousin of the Freud family's physician. Heinrich Braun's sister, Emma Braun, an accomplished linguist and writer, later married Victor Adler, a doctor and subsequent leader of the Austrian Social Democrats whose son Friedrich became a friend of Einstein, living in the flat below him during Einstein's married years in Zurich. Victor Adler, four years Freud's senior, had many of the same teachers as Freud including the Professor of Psychiatry Theodor Meynert, for whom Freud later worked. Adler also attended Charcot's lectures in Paris four years before Freud did, but he left psychiatry to pursue occupational health and safety work in Vienna's factories, becoming a doctor in general practice among the Viennese poor before devoting himself to full-time organizing for the Social Democratic movement (Barea, 1966). Victor Adler was a favourite of Eleanor Marx, Karl Marx's daughter, staying with her and Friedrich Engels in London in 1895 shortly after Adler's release from one of his many imprisonments in Vienna (Kapp, 1976). Victor Adler's unexpected death in 1918 at the age of sixty-seven deprived Austrian Social Democracy of the leadership that in Freud's opinion might have saved Austria from its subsequent fascism. Freud was invited by Heinrich Braun to Victor Adler's apartment at Berggasse 19, which Freud later bought and lived in for forty-seven years.

Adler's son Friedrich, a long-time militant in Social Democratic politics, made history on 21 October 1916 with a spectacular assassination, intended to galvanize the Social Democratic movement, of the Austrian Prime Minister, Count Karl Stürgkh, as he sat having Saturday lunch in the Hotel Meissl und Schadn in the New Market in Vienna. The following day Sandor Ferenczi, Freud's closest collaborator, wrote to Freud from Budapest: 'The case of Friedrich Adler shocked me. In spite of all the craziness that lies behind it (parricide) one feels a noble indignation, something genuine heroic in this act. Do you know any more about him, about his case? You do know his father. He is certainly very much to be pitied.' Adler's death sentence was commuted to eighteen years by the supreme court. He served only a year in jail.[2]

Freud's connections with the Social Democratic political community later brought him patients and students. Among them were Ida Bauer, famous as the case of 'Dora', the sister of Otto Bauer who was a leading Social Democratic politician; the socialist social worker Bertha Pappenheim, famous as 'Anna O.'; Emma Eckstein, whose sister Therese Schlesinger was a Social Democratic member of parliament; and in the second generation the analysts Otto Fenichel and Richard Sterba who heard about Freud from Kurt Adler, Friedrich Adler's brother.

Influenced by his friend Heinrich Braun, Freud toyed with the idea of law, but decided, like many Jewish immigrants on both sides of the Atlantic, on a career in science. On 1 May 1873, he wrote to his friend Emil Fluss about his decision (E. Freud, 1969):

Now I can speak freely. When I lift the veil of secrecy, will you not be disappointed? Well let's see. I have decided to be a Natural Scientist and herewith release you from the promise to let me conduct all your law-suits. It is no longer needed. I shall gain insight into the age-old dossiers of Nature, perhaps even eavesdrop on her eternal processes, and share my findings with anyone who wants to learn.

Freud worked hard for his coming Matura – the equivalent of the modern British A-levels or the French baccalaureate. Wilhelm Knoepfmacher, one of Freud's school friends and a founder of the Jewish organization B'nai B'rith, told his son about studying for the Matura with Freud (Knoepfmacher, 1938): 'The final examination for admission to the university was dreaded. My father remembered that he and Freud studied many nights together at the Freud apartment keeping awake with black coffee and grapes' (p. 289).

On 16 June 1873, in a letter to Fluss, Freud described his performance:

That I sometimes had good luck sometimes bad luck goes without saying. On occasions as important as these, kind Providence and the caprices of fortune always have a finger in the pie. Such events differ from the ordinary course of things. To cut a long story short, because I do not want to keep you in suspense about something so uninteresting – for the five papers I got excellent, good, good, good, satisfactory. Most annoying.

In October 1873 Freud entered the University of Vienna as a seventeen-year-old student of the life sciences. Although well to the east of the main centres of scientific research in France, Germany and Britain, the University of Vienna was a leading European institution with a distinguished faculty, many of whose names are known to students today.[3] Freud's principal interests were in evolutionary biology and physiology. In his first three years, half of Freud's 161 lecture and laboratory hours were spent with the professor of zoology Carl Claus and the professor of physiology Ernst Brücke and his assistants Ernst von Fleischl-Marxow and Sigmund Exner.

Claus, a specialist in the evolutionary biology of crustaceans was recruited from Göttingen to modernize the university's zoology department. His two-volume *Textbook of Zoology* went through ten editions and was translated into English by the noted English zoologist, Adam Sedgwick, in 1884. Claus visited Charles Darwin in 1871 when Claus was in London to marry for the second time, the visit being arranged by Darwin's younger colleague Sir John Lubbock (1834–1913). Lubbock's books, *Addresses: Political and Educational* (1879) and *Origins and Metamorphosis of Insects* (1876) were in Freud's library (Ritvo, 1972). Freud did his first research project in Claus' laboratory.

Brücke, Freud's teacher of physiology, is well known to students of psychoanalysis from Freud's often quoted remark written at the age of sixty-eight (Freud, 1925): 'At length in Ernst Brücke's physiological laboratory I found rest and full satisfaction – and men too, whom I could respect and take as my models' (p. 192).

Freud found in Brücke a man who embodied the great Romantic period of Western science in the nineteenth century. A student of the famed Johannes Müller in Berlin, Brücke's thesis on osmotic pressure in semi-permeable membranes, was one of the landmarks of modern biology. Brücke showed that the osmotic pressure in the living cell was not due to a vital force but was simply due to differing concentrations of salts on either side of a membrane, a fact exploited by the antibiotic drug penicillin which acts by interfering with the enzymes of the bacterial cell wall, thus weakening the wall and causing the cell to burst from the internal osmotic pressure.

Moving to Vienna from Königsberg in 1849 Brücke began research on the physiology of speech which led to the development of the first prostheses for damaged vocal chords. He was among the first to isolate the enzymes involved in digestion. He studied protoplasmic flow in the stinging nettle and the motion of pigment cells in the chameleon where he showed that the changing colours of the chameleon was simply due to the differing movement of yellow and black cells towards and away from the surface of the skin. Along with his friends, Hermann Helmholtz and Emil du Bois Reymond, Brücke was a central figure in the great advances in modern physiology originating in German-speaking Europe. The American psychologist G. Stanley Hall, who was later to invite Freud to Massachusetts, observed at the time (Hall, 1881): 'Physiology has been characterized as just now permanently *the* German science' (p. 108). Freud was to emerge from eight years in Brücke's laboratory with first-hand experience of how things were done at the very top of the scientific profession.

But Freud was not meant to be a natural scientist. From his auto-biography we know that he experienced two major disappointments at the University of Vienna in his first three years. One of them was due to the unexpected prevalence of anti-Semitism in an institution of higher learning (Freud, 1925): 'Above all I was expected to feel myself inferior and alien because I was a Jew' (p. 191). In 1876 Professor Theodor Billroth, Freud's teacher of clinical surgery, found it necessary to state his fears about Jews in his book about medical education in German universities (Billroth, 1876).

Those we call Jewish-German are just only by chance speaking German and are only by chance brought up as Jews in Germany even if they can write poetry and express their thoughts in the German language better and more beautifully than many of the purest Germanic race. They lose their national traits just as little as Germans lose theirs when they are scattered among another nation as in America. One must therefore neither expect nor wish the Jews ever to become German nationals, to expect that they would be capable of feeling the national struggle as Germans themselves feel it. They are lacking above all, that on which our German feelings, more than we might like to admit, are based, namely the entire medieval romantic. (p. 153)

In an open letter, the liberal jurist Ferdinand Horn (1876) warned of the dangers of declaring the Jews to be permanent potential traitors to the German people:

Completely ignored in your views – I repeat – especially cruel – is that you have undertaken to suddenly declare many hundred thousands of your fellow citizens stateless, that in the name of German science, of the spirit of liberating German science you undertake to renew the ancient curse that an unlucky people has suffered for a thousand years.[4]

In the streets, the anti-Semitic fears of the university found their counterpart in attacks on Jewish children in the neighbourhoods of Vienna. The father of the historian Ilsa Barea (1966) reported his experience as a schoolboy in Vienna at the same time:

The street urchins waged war against Jewish boys. In nearly every road there was a young hooligan who attacked and tormented the little Jew-boys he knew, and when we went home from our lessons in religion, still given outside the regular school hours, we were often ambushed by whole gangs. It was not so bad, it rarely meant more than some bumps, but it was terribly bad: to meet a hatred we couldn't understand, and were unable to combat, necessarily appeared to us as the most violent injustice and evil. (p. 305)

The anti-Semitic feelings expressed in measured tones by Billroth was endemic in the Vienna medical community. Nine years later, in 1885, Carl Koller, a Jewish colleague of Freud's working in Billroth's clinic, fought a duel over an anti-Semitic insult. Freud described the incident to Martha (6 January 1885):

In the confusion of the past few days I haven't found a moment's peace to write to you. The hospital is in an uproar.

On Sunday Koller, the man who made cocaine so famous and with whom I have recently become more intimate, was on duty at the Journal. He had a difference of opinion about some minor technical matter with the man who acts as surgeon for Billroth's clinic and the latter suddenly called Koller 'a Jewish swine'. Now you must try to imagine the kind of atmosphere we live in here, the general bitterness – in short, we would all have reacted just as Koller did, by hitting the man in the face. The man rushed off, denounced Koller to the director who however gave him a thorough dressing down and categorically took Koller's side. This was a great relief to us all. But since they are both reserve officers, he is obliged to challenge Koller to a duel and at this moment they are fighting with sabres under rather severe conditions. Lustgarten and Bettelheim (the regimental surgeon) are Koller's seconds.

I am too upset to write any more now but I won't send this off till I can tell you the result of the duel. So much could be said about all this.

. . .

All is well my little woman. Our friend is quite unharmed and his opponent got two deep gashes. We are all delighted, a proud day for us. We are going to give Koller a present as a lasting reminder of his victory.

The official report of the incident names Koller's opponent as Friedrich Zinner: 'All in all there were three thrusts (or rounds); during the third, Dr Zinner was wounded on his head and right upper arm. He was immediately bandaged and taken to the General Hospital . . . Dr Zinner received a severe wound on his head' (Becker, 1963). The anti-Semitism that Freud encountered has been minimized by some students of the period as being little more than relatively harmless prejudice (Ellenberger, 1970; Boyer, 1995). But the spoon has not been invented that lets one sup with racism with safety.

Freud's second major disappointment at the University of Vienna was his feeling that he was not talented enough to make a success of a career in science, a not uncommon reaction that can accompany the failure of members of marginalized groups to gain entry to the academic professions. As he later recalled (Freud, 1925): 'I was compelled moreover during my first years at the University to make the discovery that the peculiarities and limitations of my gifts denied me all success in many of the departments of science into which my youthful eagerness had plunged me' (p. 191). Freud's biographer Ernest Jones (1953) relates a story that indicates that Freud felt unequal intellectually to the company he kept in those years. 'I told [Freud] once the story of a surgeon who said that if he ever reached the Eternal Throne he would come armed with a cancerous bone and ask the Almighty what he had to say about it. Freud's reply was: "If I were to find myself in a similar situation, my chief reproach to the Almighty would be that he had not given me a better brain"' (p. 38).

He wrote to Martha from Paris on 2 February 1886:

There was a time when I was all ambition and eager to learn, when day after day I felt aggrieved that Nature in a benevolent mood hadn't stamped my face with that mark of genius which now and again she bestows on men. Now for a long time I have known that I am not a genius and cannot understand how I ever wanted to be one. I am not even very gifted; my whole capacity for work probably springs from my character and from the absence of outstanding intellectual weaknesses.

In 1898, he wrote apologetically to Wilhelm Fliess: 'I have an infamously low capability for visualizing spatial relationships which made the study of geometry and all subjects derived from it impossible for me' (4 January 1898). In 1915 he wrote to James J. Putnam at Harvard, a leading figure in the introduction of psychoanalysis in the United States (E. Freud et al. 1978): 'I think I ought to tell you that I have always been dissatisfied with my intellectual endowment and that I know precisely in what respects' (p. 191). And in 1926 he wrote to Princess Marie Bonaparte (Jones, 1955): 'I have very restricted capacities or talents. None at all of the natural sciences; nothing for mathematics; nothing for anything quantitative. But what I have, of a very restricted nature, was probably very intensive' (p. 443). Jones, who knew him very well, was unambiguous in his report of Freud's perception of his own limitations (Jones, 1953): 'One thing about himself he was always sure: that he had a poor intellectual capacity. There were so many things, e.g. in mathematics or physics, he knew he should never be able to understand where so many others could.'

As a schoolboy Freud had been attracted to Darwin's theory of evolution, a powerful theory that brought all of biology together in one great narrative strand. Through the concept of continuous evolution by natural selection, the common historical origin of life is made plain, eliminating the need for the separate creation, by divine intervention, of the different species.

At university, Freud followed up his original interest in evolution by taking six courses in zoology and comparative anatomy with Claus in his first three years and by becoming in the middle of his third year a research student in Claus's laboratory. Claus assigned Freud to investigate whether a certain lobe-shaped organ in the eel, found by a competing zoologist Simon Syrski, was capable of producing sperm and was therefore a testicle (Reidel-Schrewe, 1994). The problem of the apparent hermaphroditism of the eel, which dates from antiquity, had acquired relevance in evolutionary theory because of Darwin's speculation that the earliest vertebrate forms had both male and female reproductive organs – implying that sexual mating occurred later in evolution. But by 1873 evolutionary theory was too well established for a relatively minor dispute about the historical timing of sexual reproduction to be very interesting. The testes of the eel proved to be a tedious research problem relieved only by the opportunity to visit Trieste to obtain the hundreds of specimens he needed for the dissections.

Freud abandoned zoology in the autumn of 1876, after his second trip to Trieste, to become a research student in the far more interesting physiology laboratory of Ernst Brücke. Neurophysiology and neuroanatomy were hot topics and Freud did well to gain entry to one of the leading research laboratories in Europe. He was looking for something more important to work on, that in a careerist interpretation of his work would serve to make his name. In a more generous interpretation one might say that Freud, as the eldest son, responsible for the family fortunes, knew only too well the importance of good research in the making of a successful scientific career. One could also say that Freud as an intelligent and highly motivated student showed good judgement in his rejection of Claus in favour of Brücke.

Physiology in Vienna was a branch of applied physics and as such was frequently mathematical in its discussion and presentation, as in Sigmund Exner's mathematical analysis of the expansion of muscles in the intestinal wall, which appeared along with Freud's first published paper on the origin of the nerve roots of the river lamprey (Exner, 1877; Freud, 1877). To deal with his lack of mathematical competence, Freud, after joining Brücke's entourage in the winter semester of 1876, enrolled in Fleischl's three-hour-a-week course, Higher Mathematics for Medical Students. This was possibly a condition for entering Brücke's laboratory or perhaps something Freud felt he had to do for himself to improve his knowledge of mathematics. But the knowledge Freud would have gained in this course of lectures would not have been at Fleischl's level of competence, nor at Exner's or Brücke's or Breuer's.

Fleischl and Breuer, Freud's collaborator on hysteria, had both matriculated first in the Faculty of Philosophy, not the Faculty of Medicine, following, in Breuer's case, the advice of his educated father and, in Fleischl's case, the advice of Brücke himself (Hirschmüller, 1989; Lesky, 1976). Fleischl concentrated on laboratory work in chemistry and physics but also had private instruction in higher mathematics with Spitzer (Exner, 1893). Nine years after Fleischl, Freud enrolled directly in the Faculty of Medicine, possibly not realizing that further skills in mathematics, physics and chemistry were advisable prerequisites for a biomedical research career at the highest level.

Breuer had university-level courses of studies in analysis (differential and integral calculus) and mathematical physics; he had studied magnetism, electricity and heat with Professor Josef Stefan in the Faculty of Philosophy where the treatment was sophisticated and mathematical. Freud, in contrast, took Stefan's equivalent course in the Faculty of Medicine which was tailored to students with more limited mathematical skills. As a lecturer, Stefan was known for his ability to make the highly mathematized subjects of physics accessible to non-mathematically prepared students, especially to future teachers.[5] But nevertheless Freud found it difficult to get interested in what Stefan had to teach. In a later letter to Martha, Freud wrote (Jones, 1953): 'Astronomers tell us that there are stars whose gleaming we now see which began to burn hundreds of thousands of years ago and perhaps already are in the process of extinction, so far away are they from us and even for rays of light which travel 40,000 miles a second without becoming tired. I always found that hard to imagine . . .' (p. 126). Had Freud absorbed Josef Stefan's lectures he would have quoted the correct speed of light of 186,000 miles per second and would not have been mystified about its propagation. Freud's strengths were not in the physical sciences and mathematics.

In Brücke's laboratory Freud did as he was told, working as an apprentice on problems suggested to him by his professor. He published four papers in neuroanatomy during this period with Brücke; they were well-executed projects, stepping stones along the way to an independent career as a researcher. He worked first on the dissection of the nerve roots of the brook lamprey, a fish selected for its primitive nature, to explore the evolutionary antecedents of mammalian nerve and synapse. And he worked on the river crayfish in an attempt to elucidate the structure of the connections of single nerve fibres to the ganglia, the relay stations (to use a modern metaphor) of nerve transmission throughout the body.

But Freud's two ventures into physiology proper were failures. His work with Salomon Stricker in 1878 on the mechanisms of salivation did not produce publishable results. And his later 1884 attempt, using a dynamometer designed by Exner, to measure the sense of increased strength induced by the action of cocaine, was poorly executed (although he drew the right conclusion: the increased sense of strength given by the drug is psychological not physiological). Freud's strengths as a neuroscientist were in histology, the patient examination of tissues under the microscope. In this work Freud was in competition with members of other laboratories to be the first to chart the then unknown anatomy of the nervous system.

Many commentators have read into this early period of Freud's career the genius that Freud clearly must have been to have achieved his later fame (Brun, 1936; Jelliffe, 1937; Triarhou and del Cerro, 1985). But Freud was part of a team, working on leading problems to be sure, but still just part of a team. And he knew this better than many of his followers. His assessments of his early work are matter-of-fact recognitions of being a cog in the wheel of the research enterprise (Freud, 1897a). In a later letter to Rudolf Brun, the Swiss psychiatrist and chronicler of Freud's early neurological career who had requested copies of Freud's neurological papers, Freud's daughter Anna wrote (FreudP, B1): 'He wants you to know that he sends [them] to you with pleasure and remarks only that most of these small works collected there as separate reprints are worth very little. He thinks that you will be disappointed if you occupy yourself with them' (6 March 1936).

Freud was a competent research student. His later research, after he left Brücke's lab, is similarly competent, called publishable in the trade, but with little real originality except for the fine paper on organic and hysterical paralysis written with Charcot's encouragement, in which he argued that the symptoms of hysterical paralysis could not be due to real damage to the physical anatomy.

Although Freud came away with feelings of intellectual inferiority as a result of his failure to make a research career as a neuroscientist, the real problem was not mathematics. Freud lacked the deep interest in the problems of the natural world, the language in which they were expressed and in the details of their solution that are the prerequisites for a successful career in science. Freud lacked more than mathematical skills – he lacked inspiration. Freud's lack of inspiration shows most in what he does not say about his work. In his correspondence, there are no comments about the work of others that he admires, no comments about reading that excites him, no informed comments about the literature that he reads. There is little sense of personal enjoyment in Freud's writing, either about his work or studies. Although he worked very hard, something was missing. His remarks about research have the edge of a critical outsider rather than the enthusiasm of a man in love with his subject.

In a long review article on the state of play in mapping the anatomy of cranial nerves, Gustav Schwalbe, a senior researcher in the field, cited Freud's work on the spinal ganglion of the river lamprey (Schwalbe, 1879):

If, as is usually the case from these [ganglion] cells, only one process develops, then accordingly these nerves would be described as unipolar. But this single process sooner or later gives way to two separate nerve fibres in a similar manner, as Freud has recently shown, to the caudal spinal ganglion cells of Petromyzon. Freud found that all transitional forms of these cells exist, from unipolar cells whose process first divides into two parts at a great distance from the cell body (the T cells of Ranvier) to opposite pole cells which as is well known is characteristic of the spinal ganglion cells of most fish (p. 192).

Schwalbe used Freud's results to argue for the structural similarities between ganglion cells in the spine and in the brain (pp. 241, 243).

Any research student would be happy to be mentioned in this way by a senior figure in the field. But it would be an unusual student, one who was distanced and self-critical about their career, who would also make mordant observations on the competitiveness of scientific research and a recognition of publications as the currency of success. Freud wrote to his close friend Eduard Silberstein:

Last week I had the great scientific satisfaction of receiving a paper by Professor Schwalbe from Jena, who accepts the results of my work on the spinal ganglia, quotes me many times and calls me among other things 'the aforementioned research scientist', which among people who would take food from each other's mouths, must be considered a rare courtesy. Schwalbe incidentally is the man who writes the annual histology report and so this business has a practical advantage as well.[6]

The rare enthusiasm Freud expressed about a piece of scientific work was for Robert Koch's announcement of the isolation of the tuberculosis bacillus in 1882. In addition to infecting the lungs, the tuberculosis bacillus infected the intestines, the joints, and the lymphatic glands. These varying sites of infections displayed widely differing symptoms and were thought to be entirely different diseases. Now this varied symptomatology could be seen to be due to infection by the same bacteria, a classic simplification in understanding. Freud wrote to Martha (9 October 1883): 'Tuberculosis! Is it contagious? Is it acquired? Where does it come from? Is Master Koch of Berlin right in saying that he has discovered the bacillus responsible for it?' Freud's excitement about Koch's work was perhaps partly informed by the fact that both his mother and his friend Ignaz Schoenberg, the man who had intended to marry Martha's sister Minna, had pulmonary tuberculosis at that time. Freud's mother survived for fifty years but Schoenberg died the following year. Freud's close friend Josef Paneth died of the disease seven years later.

In 1882, Brücke told Freud that he should leave research. The accepted explanation is that Freud wanted to marry and Brücke knew that there would be little chance of Freud's earning enough money in the foreseeable future if he remained in basic research. There were only two possible permanent research positions in Brücke's lab and those were filled by the extremely capable Sigmund Exner and Ernst von Fleischl-Marxow. As the story goes, Freud was forced out of a research career by financial considerations and the limited opportunities existing for research in Vienna at the time, a symptom of the relative economic decline of the Austro-Hungarian empire in spite of modernizing efforts by the upper echelons.

But one always has an uneasy feeling when a professor advises a student to leave research. There is no evidence that Brücke was other than supportive of Freud. Nevertheless, if Freud had been as good as Exner or Fleischl one might have expected Brücke to turn over another stone in order to keep him. In the case of Exner, Brücke had sent him to Heidelberg to work with Helmholtz when Exner was a student; he then made Exner a lecturer a year after his graduation, when he was only twenty-five years old. In the case of Fleischl, Fleischl's uncle, Johann Czermak, was a famous physiologist and, as we have seen, Fleischl's mother had been in a position to be able to ask Brücke directly for advice on her son's career.

There are then the questions – probably unanswerable – about ethnicity and class in Brücke's decision. Both Fleischl and Exner came from well-established gentile Viennese intellectual families. Both had attended the elite Akademische Gymnasium, whereas Freud had attended the less-established, less-exclusive Leopoldstadt Ober-und-Real Gymnasium. Under conditions where academic advancement was difficult, Brücke may have drawn the line just short of Freud for any number of reasons unrelated to Freud's abilities and motivation. It the event, Freud endured feelings of inferiority for the rest of his life – that he was not good enough to make a successful career in basic research.

Freud's search for a problem that he could uniquely make his own was to last for twenty years. He considered a career as a dermatologist and even thought of moving to America as his sister Anna was to do. Instead he decided to try to make a career out of clinical neurology, clinical research and teaching – a not untypical career choice for biomedical researchers at the time. Josef Breuer and Benedikt Stilling (1810–79), two noted researchers of the time known to Freud, had both been forced into similar decisions.

He discussed his options with Martha by post. 'What I am going to do next I am not quite sure. I am considering dermatology, not a very appetizing field, but for general practice very important and interesting in itself. I intend on calling on that department tomorrow; if there are no *Aspirant* jobs vacant, I shall go to Meynert' (5 October 1882). Eighteen months later he wrote (15 April 1884) that he was considering taking 'a decisive step towards our union by starting, say a medical practice here or in the country or by emigrating to America'. In answer to her query about where 'here' was he replied (19 April 1884), 'By a German region ("here") I was of course thinking of Lower Austria, Moravia or Silesia. For the time being anyhow I am still quite ready to fight and have no intention of breaking off my battle for a future in Vienna. The "struggle for existence" still means for me a struggle for existence here.'

But if his enthusiasm for histology had not been fully fired his enthusiasm for clinical work was even less. For the next three years he was reduced to find publishable material out of the meagre pickings of part-time research and a clinical practice. He wrote to Martha (16 January 1884): 'I had a lazy day yesterday; my discovery evaporated in the chemical laboratory, and I was rather annoyed about it. It is hard to find material for publication, and it infuriates me to see how everyone is making straight for the unexploited legacy of nervous diseases.'[7]

Freud worked as a resident physician in the Vienna General Hospital and as a clinical researcher in the Institute of Cerebral Anatomy. He developed a gold-staining procedure for bringing into relief the unexplored fine structure of the nervous system, a tool that he felt would lead to the success he needed. In response to a query from Martha, he gave a somewhat patronizing, but not unsophisticated description of his histological research:

What my work, for which you so sweetly wish me luck, consists of, I cannot tell you without a terribly long explanation. One thing however I can divulge: it has to do with a method for the chemical treatment of the brain. Clear? No.

Well, 'as is well known', the brain must first of all be hardened (in spirits for instance) and then finely sliced in order to show where the fibres and cells lie in relation to one another, where the fibres lead to etc. The fibres are the conducting paths from the different parts of the body, the cells are in control of them, so respect is due to these structures. Now on the sliced segments of the hardened brain very little is visible, but more appears when they are coloured with carmine, because then the cells and fibres grow redder than the other less important parts. Even so it is very difficult to see all the fine fibres or even to get very clear pictures. It is well known that silver staining and gold staining produce beautiful pictures on other specimens – that is quite different colouring for the different elements – now this is being tried out on the brain. I believe that so far I have succeeded best. These are technical tricks which exist in every craft, but which science cannot do without. Is my darling princess satisfied now? (15 October 1883)

But in spite of the initial promise of gold-staining, the great histological successes were to go to others. The 'Method', as he called it, proved elusive, giving unreproducible results (Upson, 1888). The deft hands and quiet environments in Spain and Italy were to produce the detailed pictures of the synaptic connections that constitute our present picture of the structure of the nervous system. Camillo Golgi (1843–1926) in Italy perfected a method of prolonged immersion in a potassium dichromate–silver nitrate solution which yielded stable pictures. Santiago Cajal y Ramon (1852–1934) in Spain built on Golgi's technique to create our current picture of synaptic axon–dendrite connections. Golgi and Cajal received the 1906 Nobel Prize for their work on the structure of the nervous system. Golgi spent the better part of his Nobel acceptance speech attacking his co-winner Cajal and the synaptic theory (anon., 1967).[8]

Freud worked on other things. He studied the incompletely

myelinated nerve fibres of the human embryo as part of a project to learn about the nervous system in its early stages of development. He traced the origin and course of the principal auditory nerve and carried out clinical research on infantile cerebral palsies. In addition, he was among the first to explore the possible useful applications of cocaine in medicine. On 24 April 1884 Freud wrote to Martha about his intention to begin investigating it in the hope that it would lead to something important and accelerate their marriage plans.

I am also toying now with a project and a hope which I will tell you about; perhaps nothing will come of this, either. It is a therapeutic experiment. I have been reading about cocaine, the effective ingredient of coca leaves, which some Indian tribes chew in order to make themselves resistant to privation and fatigue. A German has tested this stuff on soldiers and reported that it has really rendered them strong and capable of endurance. I have now ordered some of it and for obvious reasons am going to try it out on cases of heart disease, then on nervous exhaustion, particularly in the awful condition following the withdrawal of morphine (as in the case of Dr Fleischl). There may be a number of other people experimenting on it already, perhaps it won't work. But I am certainly going to try it and, as you know, if one tries something often enough and goes on wanting it, one day it may succeed. We need no more than one stroke of luck of this kind to consider setting up house.

Freud missed making the discovery of his friend Carl Koller, the victor of the duel over the anti-Semitic insult, of the usefulness of cocaine as an anaesthetic for the eye. But he proceeded to use the drug himself, finding it particularly helpful for migraine, indigestion and for handling stressful social occasions.[9] Cocaine proved to be another project that did not work out.

Freud was bored. Clinical research held little appeal for him and the doors seemed closed to anything more interesting than what he had. That autumn he began to feel that 'the unexploited legacy of nervous disease' might be his only opportunity both for doing original research and augmenting his livelihood as a clinician. He had his eye on developments in France where the ancient syndrome of hysteria had become a hot topic under the intellectual and institutional leadership of the neurologist Jean-Martin Charcot at the Salpêtrière Hospital in Paris.

The symptoms of hysteria were spectacular. They included convulsions, disturbances of vision, deafness, loss of the sense of taste and smell, numbness of half the body, paralysis of the limbs, dumbness and contractures – permanent spasms holding an arm or a leg in a contorted position. In convulsions the so-called *grande mouvements* were, unlike movements in epilepsy, powerful, highly co-ordinated motions and contortions which frequently led to a loss of consciousness. Disturbances of sight included a loss of colour vision, selective colour blindness (particularly violet) double vision and seeing things at twice or half their normal sizes. The contractures, anaesthesias, paralyses and tremors were highly labile and could be transferred symmetrically to the other side of the body leaving the original area completely normal. Psychologically, patients could present as highly irritable or as melancholic and depressed. Heredity, in the form of an inherited hysterical disposition, was seen to be the ultimate cause of hysteria. Attacks could be brought on by early childhood experiences, trauma, strong emotional experiences including grief, or prolonged illness. Railroad accidents involving 'concussion of the spine' – so-called railway spine or railway brain – frequently produced acute hysterical episodes invariably after a delay or 'incubation period'. The course of the disease varied greatly according to the particular symptoms. Contractures and paralysis could last for years and suddenly disappear. Marriage could interrupt symptoms which could reappear in middle age. Hysterical symptoms could be rapidly exchanged for others.[10]

At the Salpêtrière, hysteria had become not only respectable, but the great unsolved puzzle of neurology. Charcot had liberated hysteria from the prejudice of the medical profession which had linked the distress either to a malfunctioning of the female sexual organs or to malingering and theatrics on the part of the sufferer. Charcot identified hysteria in men in 5 per cent of his cases and in addition had confirmed diagnoses of hysteria in women with no genitalia. Progress was being made in Paris. Freud felt he might be able to become part of it.

In the spring of 1885, Freud applied for a study grant to go to Charcot's clinic. On 19 June 1885 he wrote to Martha:

I dream about this grant every night; yesterday for instance I dreamt that Brücke told me I couldn't get it, that there were seven other applicants all of whom had greater chances!

The next day Freud learned that he had received the grant, apparently with the decisive intervention of Brucke. He was delighted. He wrote a high-spirited, optimistic letter to Martha:

Oh, how wonderful it will be! I am coming with money and staying a long time and bringing something beautiful for you and then go on to Paris and become a great scholar and then come back to Vienna with a huge enormous halo and then we will soon get married and I will cure all the incurable nervous diseases and through you I shall be healthy and I will go on kissing you till you are strong and gay and happy. (20 June 1885)

In addition to the good news about the grant, Freud achieved a long-sought academic appointment as Privatdozent. Things were looking up. Six days later, on 26 June, he wrote Martha a nostalgic letter about his inaugural lecture to be given the following day.

I am wondering who will turn up at the lecture tomorrow. Strange to think that I shall be standing in Brücke's auditorium where I did my first work and with an enthusiasm I have never known since and where I had hoped to stand at least as an assistant beside the old man.

As planned, Freud visited Martha in Wandsbek at her family's house on the outskirts of Hamburg, spent six weeks with her and showed up at the Salpêtrière on 19 October 1885.

The six months Freud spent with Charcot changed his life. On 11 November 1885 after he had been in Paris for a month, he wrote to Martha:

. . . when I come away from him I no longer have any desire to work at my own silly things; it is three whole days since I have done any work, and I have no feelings of guilt. My brain is sated as after an evening in the theatre. Whether the seed will bear any fruit, I don't know; but I do know that no other human being has ever affected me in the same way.

In Paris Freud became convinced by Charcot's argument that the neuroanatomical mapping of the nervous system was complete, that the theoretical basis of organic malfunctions of the nervous system was now sufficiently understood and that the frontier of neurology lay in the solution to the problems of the so-called nervous diseases, particularly hysteria.

To the possibility of contributing to research at the frontier of nervous disease was added an entirely new respect for clinical work. In opposition to trends in German medicine, where physiology took pride of place as being the location of all disease, Freud found that Charcot was willing to leave physiology to others while he concentrated on interpreting the clinical symptoms he observed at the Salpêtrière Hospital. Eight years later, when his transition to clinical work was nearly complete, Freud (1893a) described how formative was his experience of Charcot's way of working:

Charcot indeed never tired of defending the rights of purely clinical work, which consists in seeing and ordering things, against the encroachments of theoretical medicine. On one occasion there was a small group of us, all students from abroad, who, brought up on German academic physiology, were trying his patience with our doubts about his clinical innovations. 'But that can't be true' one of us objected, 'it contradicts the Young–Helmholtz theory.' He did not reply 'So much the worse for the theory, clinical facts come first' or words to that effect; but he did say something which made a great impression on us: 'La theorie c'est bon, mais ça n'empêche pas d'exister'. [Theory is good, but it doesn't prevent the existence of other things.] (p. 13)

In Paris in 1885, there was still a career to be made. After a frustrating first two weeks in which Freud was simply one of many lonely, unnoticed foreign visitors to the Salpêtrière, he broke through to Charcot's circle by offering to translate Charcot's famous Friday lectures into German. Charcot accepted. On 12 December, Freud wrote to Martha:

Charcot took me aside today and said: 'J'ai un mot a vous dire.' And then he told me he would gladly consent to my translating his volume III into German – what's more not only the first section which has already appeared in French, but also the second which hasn't yet been published. Are you pleased? I am. This is again something very gratifying. It is bound to make me known to doctors and patients in Germany and is well worth the expense of a few weeks and several hundred Gulden, not to mention the few hundred Gulden it will bring in. It will be of great advantage to my practice and moreover will pave the way for my own book when that is ready for publication.

Freud knew what he had to do to further his career. But he also had good judgement. Hysteria had become the leading problem of neurology; Charcot's clinical work was fascinating. Freud's expulsion from basic research, his marginalization and the necessity of making a living were driving him away from neuroanatomy into the calling that was to make him famous – the intriguing problems of human psychology.

3

Hysteria and the Origins
of the Analytic Hour

Breuer's and Freud's method of treating the ancient medical syndrome of hysteria stands out as a turning point in the long history of attempts to understand human psychology. Analogous to Galileo's use of the telescope to explore previously unknown structures in the night sky, the development of the analytic hour created an instrument that opened up an entirely new way to explore previously unknown structures in the human inner world.

In October 1886, Freud reported on his work with Charcot to the weekly meeting of the Society of Viennese Physicians, the leading medical society in Vienna. Freud chose to present a case of Charcot's that demonstrated that hysteria could be found in men as well as in women with very little difference in symptomatology. Freud was challenged by Theodor Meynert to present his own case of male hysteria that conformed to Charcot's description. Rudolf von Urban (né Urbantschitsch) was at the meeting and described it years later to Jones (Clark, 1980):

Everyone in that room knew that the highly emotional Meynert was subject to attacks of aphasia with palsy of the right arm. This was his defensive reason for finding an anatomical basis for hysteria and probably his incentive for mapping cerebral localizations generally. When the young Freud opened up on the existence of hysteria in males also, Meynert felt uncomfortable. Meynert's wild youth and unstable personality were proverbial; as a young man he had been repeatedly drunk and locked up by his grandfather, the police surgeon. (p. 91)

Freud responded to Meynert's challenge six weeks later with a presentation of a patient suffering from hemi-anaesthesia – a loss of sensation on the left side of the body – in a twenty-nine-year-old engraver (Freud, 1886b). The patient, August P., had come for treatment because of a loss of feeling and loss of a sense of location on the left side of his body. The family history was full of grief: his father had a violent temper; his mother suffered from headaches. There were six sons: the first had died of a cerebral infection associated with syphilis; the second son suffered from convulsions; the third son was an army deserter; and the fourth and fifth had both died at an early age. August P. was the sixth and youngest. He suffered fits at the age of eight as a result of being run over by a carriage. He was now a social isolate who suffered disturbed sleep and runaway thoughts and his present illness had been precipitated by a traumatic encounter with his eldest surviving brother who refused to repay a loan. The brother had run at him with a knife, threatening to stab him. The engraver ran home in terror, fell unconscious at his front door and for two hours suffered violent spasms.

Freud's demonstration of the patient revealed a loss of sensation on the skin on the left side of the head. Pricking, pinching or twisting the left earlobe gave no effect. Neither did the insertion of a small rolled-up piece of paper into the left nostril. Freud's finger inserted down the left side of the throat failed to produce a retching reaction. Freud demonstrated a similar 'absolute anaesthesia' lower down the body. When blindfolded the patient could not find his left arm or the parts of the left side of his face with his right hand. The sense of balance was disturbed, with the patient falling over if asked to stand on his left leg. In addition, there were the disturbances of the colour sense typical of hysterical patients. With the right eye, his colour vision was normal except for violet which was identified as grey. With his left eye, only yellow and light red could be identified correctly. There was hope for a cure in this case because the symptoms fluctuated dramatically in intensity, indicating the absence of basic neurological damage in all the affected areas.

This case typified the neurological problem of hysteria in the late nineteenth century: how to understand apparently severe disturbances of central nervous system function – pain, paralysis, loss of sensation – that had no obvious physiological origin.

When Freud entered private practice as a nerve specialist on his return to Vienna from Paris in the spring of 1886, he treated cases of hysteria by the accepted means of the day: physical exercise, proper food, avoidance of fatigue and stress, authoritative prohibition of the expression of hysterical symptoms, massage, electrical stimulation of the peripheral nervous system (faradization) and a hydrotherapy consisting of cold-water baths. But he also knew that hysteria was not an organic disease of the nervous system. With Charcot's approval, he had completed a study of the symptoms of hysterical paralyses in comparison to the symptoms of organic paralyses where real damage to the nervous system could be observed. The symptoms of hysterical paralysis did not conform to a real physiology (Freud, 1893c).

Organic paralyses fall into two distinct classes. The first class arises from damage to the peripheral nerve fibres. The second arises from damage to nerve cell bodies in the brain itself. In the case of Bell's palsy, identified in 1830 by Charles Bell (1774–1842), the fibre of the peripheral facial nerve becomes compressed, possibly due to inflammation arising from viral infection, as it passes through a narrow passageway in the temporal bone behind the ear. All the facial muscles on the affected side are incapacitated, causing the face to sag, difficulty in closing the eye, a heavy feeling in the face and problems with salivation and taste. In cases of only partial paralysis, recovery is spontaneous and complete in almost all cases. In cases of complete paralysis, recovery depends on the extent of damage to the nerve. If the electrical excitability of the facial nerve remains intact, complete recovery can occur in 90 per cent of cases.

As opposed to Bell's palsy, where a peripheral nerve fibre is affected, there can also be lesions in the brain itself that can have an effect on the facial nerve. Damage to the cell body of the facial nerve within the brain causes a progressive weakening in nervous transmission along the conducting fibre. The paralysis no longer affects all the muscles of the face. Instead, the nearer muscles around the eye are affected less than the muscles further down the face. This is a general rule in cerebral paralyses. In the case of the limbs, the shoulder is less paralysed than the hand, and the hip is less paralysed than the foot.

The case of hysteria fitted neither of these two patterns. In no case of hysterical paralysis had the paralysis of entire muscle groups characteristic of a failure of a peripheral nerve been observed, as in the case of Bell's palsy. And in hysterical paralysis the nearer shoulder muscles could be inert while the patient retained movement of the distant muscles in the hand, or the hip could be frozen while the person was able to move the foot. Such a pattern, as Freud observed, corresponded to an imagined not a real nervous system. In an article for a medical encyclopedia he wrote (Freud, 1888):

A further and extremely important characteristic of hysterical disorders is that they do not in any way present a copy of the anatomical conditions of the nervous system. It may be said that hysteria is as ignorant of the nervous system as we ourselves before we have learnt it. (p. 49)

With organic damage ruled out as the origin of hysteria, the question then, if one were going to make a serious attempt to solve the problem, was how to find a way to investigate it.

As early as 1883, before he had gone to work with Charcot, Freud had been deeply impressed by the success of his friend Joseph Breuer in talking to his patients about their symptoms. One of Breuer's early cases was that of a twelve-year-old boy who returned from school complaining of headaches and difficulty in swallowing. For several days the boy continued to refuse food, vomiting when being forced to eat. After five weeks, during which the boy was listless and bedridden, Breuer was called in. He questioned the boy closely for any upsetting experience he may have had. The boy finally mentioned a strong reproof he had received from his father. But Breuer was unconvinced that the reproof was the actual problem. Enquiries at his school produced no further information and Breuer was planning to try hypnotism. The boy's 'clever and energetic' mother intervened, however, begging the boy to speak. The boy then burst into tears and told his story. On his way home from school he had gone into a public toilet where a man had exposed himself, asking the boy to take his penis into his mouth. The boy had run away in terror but had been afraid to mention the incident to his parents. Breuer concluded (Breuer and Freud, 1895):

As soon as he made his confession he recovered completely. In order to produce the anorexia, the difficulty in swallowing and the vomiting several factors were required: the boy's innate neurotic nature, his severe fright, the irruption of sexuality in its crudest form into his childhood temperament and as a specifically determining factor, the idea of disgust. The illness owed its persistence to the boy's silence, which prevented the excitation from finding its normal outlet. (p. 289)

Inspired by Charcot and impressed by Breuer's results, on his return to Vienna from Paris in 1886 Freud actively collaborated with Joseph Breuer on the problem of hysteria. The collaboration between the two men was exceptionally close. As Breuer later recalled to the Swiss psychiatrist Auguste Forel (Ackerknecht, 1957):

. . . as cases came to me which I expected would greatly benefit from analytic treatment but which I myself could not treat I showed them to Dr Freud who had just returned from Paris and the Salpêtrière and with whom I had the most intimate personal and professional relationship . . . The cases, their course, the treatment and the theory they yielded, were naturally continuously dealt with between us; our theoretical views developed through this process, not without differences naturally, but so collaboratively that it is quite difficult to say what came from one and what came from the other. (p. 170)

Freud had returned from Paris with Charcot's message that hysteria was to be taken seriously as a disease entity, that it was not malingering, that it was not confined to women, and that the much maligned technique of hypnosis was a useful tool for its exploration. He knew that it was not organic in origin. And he knew that Breuer had used hypnosis not to suggest away symptoms but to explore with his patient the emotions connected with their first occurrence. Charcot had used hypnosis to observe hysterical symptoms, but Breuer had used it to listen for their origin. Observation was not enough; there was something far more important to learn by listening. As Freud wrote in his encyclopedia article (Freud, 1888):

[Hypnosis] is even more effective if we adopt a method first practised by Joseph Breuer in Vienna and lead the patient under hypnosis to the psychical prehistory of the ailment and compel him to acknowledge the psychical occasion on which the disorder in question originated. This method of treatment is new, but it produces successful cures which cannot otherwise be achieved. (p. 56)

Freud took up hypnosis as the tool that might yield the secret of hysteria – achieving what at first he felt to be small but promising successes (to Fliess, 28 December 1887). As part of his commitment, Freud undertook the translation of two books by the French neurologist Hippolyte Bernheim on hypnosis and its applications to psychotherapy, published in 1888 and 1890. In July 1889 Freud visited Bernheim at his clinic in Nancy for the purposes of improving his hypnotic technique, but was disappointed by his visit. He found that Bernheim, too, had trouble inducing hypnotic states, especially with non-hospitalized patients. The problem of the unreliability of hypnosis was endemic. In 1893, Dr Frederick van Eeden from Amsterdam described the difficulties in treating middle-class patients by hypnotism:

In poor house or hospital practice, suggestion is not difficult, and success remarkable. The simple theory is carried out in an authoritative manner, orders are given, few words are used, no explanations granted and with little trouble astonishing results are achieved.

But if the sufferers are more highly cultivated, it is soon evident that this system will not answer. Such patients are sceptical and independent; a tone of command irritates them and appears ridiculous to them; they refuse to be ordered about and will not submit without understanding why. (p. 242)

In 1892 Freud began experimenting with a new method. He had learned from Bernheim that after hypnosis patients only apparently forgot what had happened to them. If the physician insisted forcefully enough the patient would remember. Freud attempted to make use of this observation in his so-called pressure technique in which he placed his hand on the forehead of the patient and insisted they remember what had happened at the time the hysterical symptoms first occurred.

While Freud was experimenting with new techniques, his collaboration with Breuer became increasingly strained. From Freud's point of view, Breuer was a maddeningly hesitant colleague, reluctant to publish. As Freud later wrote to Fliess: 'I believe that he will never forgive that in the *Studies* I dragged him along and involved him in something where he unfailingly knows three candidates for the position of *one* truth and abhors all generalizations, regarding them as presumptuous' (1 March 1896). From Breuer's point of view, Freud was a man given to fixed ideas. As he wrote to Forel: 'Freud is a man of absolute and exclusive formulations; that is a psychic need which drives him in my opinion to huge generalizations' (Ackerknecht, 1957, p. 170). The irreconcilable differences in style between the two men ended their relationship.

Breuer was an excellent biologist with significant successes before his collaboration with Freud. Breuer knew that understanding in biology lay in the elucidation of detail not in the formulation of general laws. With Ewald Hering, he had unravelled the workings of the vagus nerve in regulating breathing. In his research on the mechanism of balance he used well-designed experiments on pigeons to show that the position of the head was sensed by the flow of lymph in the semi-circular canals of the ear. This work led to Breuer's discovery that the utricle, a membrane sac filled with lymph in the inner ear, was the organ that sensed orientation with respect to the earth's gravitational field (Lesky, 1976).

Freud had not had the successes of Breuer. His interest was in psychology and his taste was not for detail but for depth of understanding. Of his early research in neuroanatomy, by far his most interesting paper is his review of the structure of the nervous system (1884), an attempt to synthesize the current state of knowledge. In his work with Charcot, his most interesting paper is the theoretical paper on hysterical versus organic paralysis (Freud, 1893c). His often-cited monograph on aphasia was a theoretical effort (Freud, 1891). In his book on infantile cerebral palsies (1897b), Freud was both criticized for excessive theorizing and praised for an 'unsurpassingly clear and comprehensive presentation and critical appreciation of the entire clinical and anatomical material' (Ellenberger, 1970, p. 477; Masson, 1985, p. 267).

In their disagreements, Freud and Breuer were representative of two conflicting approaches to theory in biology known as the lumpers and the splitters. The lumpers emphasize the commonalities of the facts of life, the splitters the uniqueness. Successful collaboration between these two styles is rare. When one looks at the stakes Freud and Breuer were playing for – a major innovation in the treatment and understanding of hysteria – what impresses is not that their relationship ruptured but that it was able to contain the tensions of their conflicting styles through to publication.

Of the five cases that Breuer and Freud wrote up for *Studies on Hysteria*, Breuer's case of Fräulein Anna O. introduced the beginning of the technique that was to become the analytic hour. The identity of Anna O. was revealed by Ernest Jones, in his biography of Freud, as the famous social worker Bertha Pappenheim, in honour of whom the West German Government issued a commemorative stamp in 1953. The information we have about Bertha Pappenheim's illness comes from Breuer's write-up of her case in *Studies on Hysteria*, a lucky find in the archives of the Kreuzlinger Sanatorium in Switzerland of a lengthy case report written by Breuer, the associated correspondence between the sanatorium and Breuer, Pappenheim's mother and Pappenheim's cousin, in addition to letters written by Pappenheim herself, describing her illness (Hirschmüller, 1989; Appignanesi and Forrester, 1992).

Bertha Pappenheim was born in 1859 into a very rich, very orthodox Jewish family. She was a friend of Martha Bernays. The Bernays and Pappenheim families were close; after the death of Martha's father, Martha's mother appointed Pappenheim's father to be Martha's legal guardian.

Breuer was called in by the Pappenheim family in November 1880 because of a persistent racking cough and because the twenty-one-year-old Pappenheim was refusing food. Her distress had begun the previous spring, increasing in severity in July when her father became seriously ill with lung complications due to tuberculosis. At that point she was experiencing hallucinations, feelings of absence, facial spasms, pains in the left eye socket as well as contractions in the right arm and leg. In the following months, Pappenheim became increasingly disabled. Her neck muscles became paralysed; she had severe headaches, a convergent squint and disordered vision; she developed contractures and loss of sensation in her right arm and leg, which subsequently extended to the left arm and leg. On both sides, her fingers remained mobile, a classic symptom of hysterical paralysis.

Among other psychological symptoms were terrifying hallucinations of black snakes, and absent mental states, particularly in the afternoon when she would moan 'agony, agony'. She suffered a polyglot word salad where she spoke individual words in six different languages. From the beginning of March she could only speak in English.

Breuer saw Pappenheim every day for seven months. In June, because of fears of suicide, he had her forcibly transferred to a villa near a sanatorium in Inzersdorf, outside Vienna. Two months later, in August, worried about her condition worsening, Breuer took her back to Vienna for intensive evening consultations. He established an unusual rapport with his patient, a rapport that he protected by avoiding premature interpretations and diagnoses. As he described it to Forel (Ackerknecht, 1957):

The essential merits of my achievement are that I recognized what an unusually instructive and scientifically important case chance had assigned to me, and that I persevered with attentive and faithful observation, declining to ruin the simple interpretation of these important facts by preconceived opinions. (p. 170)

Breuer observed that Pappenheim's mood changed once she had described her hallucinations in what they came to call their evening story-telling sessions, and what Pappenheim called her 'talking cure' or 'chimney sweeping' (Hirschmüller, 1989):

The change in her was remarkable when she had given her account of these matters; she came out of her absence, was at ease, cheerful, set herself to work, spent all night drawing or writing, perfectly rational, went to bed at 4 o'clock – and the same process started all over again. (p. 285)

Even more interesting was his observation that certain symptoms vanished completely as a result of the evening story-telling sessions.

For several weeks Pappenheim had refused to drink fluids, dealing with her thirst by eating fruit (Hirschmüller, 1989):

... she complained quite naturally of the pain of thirst, but if water was brought to her lips, she could not be induced to accept any, without saying why. In the end she told one evening how she had seen her companion's dog, which she regarded with disgust, drinking out of a glass. She had said nothing about this because she did not want to seem coarse (many weeks before). Five minutes later she complained of thirst, drank a half flask of water, and after that she had no more inhibitions about drinking. (p. 288).

During the consultations begun in Vienna in the middle of August Breuer elicited three or more stories from her every evening in intensive listening sessions which, he later reported, relieved Pappenheim of her major symptoms (Breuer and Freud, 1895): 'It was clear from this work as a whole that each product of her abnormal activity . . . acted as a psychic stimulus and continued to do so until it was narrated, but with this it completely lost its potency' (p. 19).

Bertha Pappenheim is credited with calling the treatment she received from Breuer 'the talking cure' and the name has stuck. But mindful of the old medical saying 'doctors supply the treatment, God supplies the cure', it is more accurate to call the process, not the talking cure, but 'the listening treatment'. Pappenheim's talking cure occurred in the context of her relationship with Breuer. Simple talking was not enough; the talking must be heard and must be felt to be heard. Pappenheim had been talking to her family in a language that frightened and confused them. It was only Breuer, because of his skill as a physician and his discipline as a scientist to be free of preconceptions, who was able to be present to hear her. Through his listening Breuer formed the necessary relationship with Pappenheim through which the talking cure could take place. When Breuer had her forcibly relocated to Inzersdorf, Pappenheim refused to engage in the evening story-telling sessions with sanatorium staff (Hirschmüller, 1989):

Every attempt by Dr Breslauer to persuade her to tell her stories to him was a failure, even when he asked much the same questions as I did. Even I had to work hard, pleading, chatting and especially repeating the stereotyped formula: 'And there was a boy' [in English] until suddenly she 'caught on' and began to speak. She never began without first touching my hands to make sure it was really me. I found such resistance particularly when she was in a contrary temper, having been vexed by something or other; she knew that the 'talking cure' [in English] would rid her of all her malice and energy, and if she 'did not want to be good' she declined it. (p. 287)

Breuer stopped seeing Pappenheim in June 1882, an ending of treatment that has been a matter of some controversy. A year later, on 31 October 1883, Freud wrote to Martha about the gossip that accompanied Breuer's termination of his treatment of Pappenheim (Forrester, 1990):

But, Martchen, discretion *on all sides*. And be discreet, too, about what I am about to tell you. Breuer has a very high opinion of her, and gave up her care because it was threatening his happy marriage. His poor wife could not stand the fact that he was so exclusively devoting himself to a woman about whom he spoke with great interest. She was certainly only jealous of the demands made on her husband by another woman. Her jealousy did not show itself in a hateful tormenting fashion, but in a silently recognized one. She fell ill, lost her spirits, until he noticed it and discovered the reason why. This naturally was enough for him to completely withdraw his medical attention from B.P. Can you keep this to yourself Martchen? (p. 19)

Martha replied immediately on 2 November 1883.

It has often been on the tip of my tongue to ask you why Breuer gave up Bertha. I could well imagine that those somewhat removed from it were wrong to say that he had withdrawn because he realized that he was unable to do anything for her. It is curious that no man other than her physician of the moment got close to poor Bertha, that is when she was healthy she already [had the power] to turn the head of the most sensible of men – what a misfortune for the poor girl.

Albrecht Hirschmüller, Breuer's biographer, has made the most thorough study of the end of her treatment. Breuer was exhausted by the amount of time and energy his treatment of her required. As he wrote to Forel: '. . . it is impossible for a general practitioner to treat such a case without his activities and way of life being completely destroyed' (Ackerknecht, 1957, p. 170). Jones's famous story of Breuer being scared off by a phantom pregnancy of Pappenheim is unsupported by historical evidence. However, it does seem to be the case that Breuer encountered difficult feelings in his relationship with Pappenheim and his treatment of Anna O. may have been only partially successful because it was not yet realized that the doctor–patient relationship itself formed part of the treatment and that it needed to be resolved for the treatment to succeed.

Anna O. was the woman who introduced Breuer and Freud to the importance of listening. But it was the case of Cäcilie M. that taught Freud the technique of interpretation that was to become a major feature of his psychotherapy and was to lead to the famous applications in the interpretation of dreams, interpretations of slips of the tongue and interpretations of the hidden meanings in jokes. Freud's patient, Cäcilie M., taught him how to make sense of what he was hearing. These two women gave Breuer and Freud the analytic hour and the beginnings of psychoanalysis.

Freud repeatedly referred to Cäcilie M. in both his early and later writing as his teacher (*Lehrmeisterin*). To Fliess he wrote that her case was decisive. Peter Swales (1986), recognizing her central importance for the history of psychoanalysis, discovered her identity by matching Freud's description of Cäcilie M. as a poet with the books of poetry he found in Freud's library.

Anna von Lieben was born in 1847, the daughter of Sophie Gomperz and a wealthy Jewish banker, Baron Eduard von Tedesco. Following a privileged childhood, her teenage years were filled with physical and emotional problems. She was close to her maternal aunt, Josefine Wertheimstein, a famous Viennese hostess who had a nervous breakdown in 1866 following the sudden death of her son. At the age of twenty-four, Anna married Leopold von Lieben, a Viennese banker with whom she had five children. She was free from pain only when she was pregnant.

Breuer was the family physician to the von Liebens. He referred her case to Freud and from 1889 Freud saw her twice a day for three years. As he described the case to Fliess, he had been called in because the family did not know what to do with Anna. Swales writes that the family circle saw Freud, the eastern European Jew, as a pretender anxious to get his hands on the money that the intensive treatment of such a wealthy client provided.

Anna von Lieben suffered severe facial neuralgia (face ache), pain in her feet and a penetrating pain between her eyes. She had a regular pattern of attacks occurring twice daily. Over the period of three years Freud had the opportunity to treat 'several hundred of such cycles'. Freud found that under hypnosis the pain in her face was relieved when she remembered an argument with her husband, leading to an insult that she felt as a 'slap in the face'. Similarly, a shooting pain in her right heel was relieved when she remembered anxiety she felt as a newcomer to a sanatorium where she feared she might not be on 'the right footing' with strangers. A piercing pain between her eyes was relieved when she recalled a piercing look her grandmother had given her when she was fifteen. Also relieved were stabbing sensations in the heart, feelings of nails being driven into her head and feelings of choking in the throat ('I shall have to swallow this'):

Realizing the symbolic nature of her symptoms Freud began to interpret von Lieben's hallucinations in the same way. Instead of viewing her visions as incomprehensible derangements he accepted them as messages (Breuer and Freud, 1895):

[She] passed through a period during which she transformed every thought she had into a hallucination, the explanation of which called for much ingenuity. She complained to me at that time of being troubled by a hallucination that her two doctors – Breuer and I – were hanging on trees next to each other in the garden. The hallucination disappeared after the analysis had brought out the following explanation. The evening before, Breuer had refused to give her a drug she had asked for. She then set her hopes on me but had found me equally hard hearted. She was furious with us over this and in her anger she thought to herself: 'There's nothing to choose between the two of them; one's the match [Pendant in German] of the other.' (p. 255)

Freud needed to address one of the outstanding problems in psychogenic origins of hysteria. It was clear to researchers that hysteria was at least partially ideogenic in origin. But it was difficult to understand concretely how ideas could be transformed into physiology. One dominant idea was that there could be a kind of neural short circuit as in the well-known case of nausea due to motion sickness. Sensations of movement originating in the labyrinth of the ear were irreconcilable with sensations arising from the optic tract. The lack of co-ordination between the two bundles of nerve impulses caused the impulses to jump their tracts, so to speak, and to activate pathways leading to sensations of nausea that normally originated in the pathways of smell and digestion. But this argument merely illustrated that unusual connections in the nervous system were possible. In the case of Anna von Lieben, the question confronting Freud was how emotional experiences could produce the highly specific physical symptoms she exhibited (Breuer and Freud, 1895):

Everyone will immediately ask how it was that the sensation of a slap on the face came to take on the outward forms of a trigeminal neuralgia, why it was restricted to the second and third branches [of the trigeminal nerve] and why it was made worse by opening the mouth and chewing – although incidentally not by talking. (p. 251)

Freud resolved this for himself in two ways. The first was to propose a kind of Pavlovian response to emotional events. Von Lieben's first attack of toothache and facial pain had occurred, perhaps coincidentally, at a time when she had experienced severe self-reproach. Freud proposed that later in life von Lieben associated self-reproach with facial pain, the two always going together in a repeat of her earlier experience.

A second, more general, way to understand the effect of words on the body was to take the physiological metaphor literally as real bodily reactions to words (Breuer and Freud, 1895):

How has it come about that we speak of someone who has been slighted as being 'stabbed to the heart' unless the slight has been in fact accompanied by a precordial sensation which could suitably be described in that phrase and unless it was identifiable by that sensation? What could be more probable that the figure of speech 'swallowing something', which we use in talking of an insult to which no rejoinder has been made, did in fact originate from the innervatory sensations which arise in the pharynx when we refrain from speaking and prevent ourselves from reacting to the insult? (p. 254)

Although it is now well established that repeated psychological stress can cause permanent physiological injury, the mechanisms remain unclear and are under active investigation today (van der Kolk, 1987).

While Breuer and Freud were working hard to make sense of what Breuer had heard from Bertha Pappenheim and what Freud was hearing from Anna von Lieben, their medical colleagues were continuing to prescribe rest, regulation of diet, exercise, hydrotherapy, electrotherapy, drugs including cannabis and ergot – a natural form of LSD – massage, and travel to help their patients. A few physicians recognized that talking helped. W. Blair Stewart, writing on the treatment of neurasthenia, advised junior colleagues in 1901 (Gosling, 1987): 'Take time to sit by your patient and reassure in positive terms. Ten minutes quiet conversation will do much to relieve the worry, excitement, morbid fears and ideas of mental depression' (p. 130). Morris Benedikt in Vienna was experimenting with short-term psychotherapies to heal what he called the 'pathogenic secret'. The listening practised in the Catholic confessional and the Cure of Souls in some religious orders, as well as the 'moral treatments' offered by many nineteenth-century physicians, could be taken as both antecedents and parallels to the talking cure as practised in the analytic hour. But Breuer and Freud had turned the informal listening sessions routinely practised by physicians into a genuinely new therapy – long-term listening for the express purpose of therapeutic change.

Freud and Breuer were the first to permit the human subject to speak for him/herself. Rather than attempt to impose preconceptions on what he was hearing from Anna O., Breuer let her do her own 'sweeping' away of pain. And their joint exploration of the meaning of her experience represented the opening of a new chapter in the history of human understanding. For the first time, a space had been created where the meanings of subjective experience could be purposefully sought until they were found. Analyst and analysand could now equal the efforts of the poets and novelists with a new method, a day-to-day, week-to-week recapitulation of experience until it was revisited and understood at the necessary levels. The results in the successful cases enabled every individual to become the novelist or poet of their own experience.

Freud understood that he was encroaching on territory previously occupied by the writers and poets when, in his famous apology in the *Studies*, he said (Breuer and Freud, 1895):

I have not always been a psychotherapist. Like other neuropathologists, I was trained to employ local diagnoses and electro-prognosis, and it still strikes myself as strange that the case histories I write should read like short stories and that, as one might say, they lack the serious stamp of science. I must console myself with the reflection that the nature of the subject is evidently responsible for this, rather than any preference of my own. The fact that local diagnosis and electrical reactions lead nowhere in the study of hysteria, whereas a detailed description of mental processes such as we are accustomed to find in the works of imaginative writers enables me, with the use of a few psychological formulas, to obtain at least some kind of insight into the course of that affection. (p. 231)

The literary aspect of Breuer's and Freud's technique was appreciated by the theatre director Alfred Freiherr von Berger in his 1895 review of the *Studies of Hysteria* for the *Vienna Morning Press* (Kiell, 1988):

A scientist who sails the sea of the human soul cannot pretend to cool and sober objectivity no matter how hard he try. He cannot avoid poetical ways of conceiving and presenting. But then again he is compelled not by his subject alone. Something else stirs and moves in him. There is much wisdom in this book, much goodness, depth of feeling and psychological acumen which must have deep roots in the sensitivity of an all knowing heart. Both scientists want to concentrate on an accurate sketch of the subject of their study. Nothing could be further from their minds than allowing their individual personalities free play as a poet inevitably would. Yet if we delve into the tremors of a soul which lays bare the innermost nerves of a stranger's personality, our own personality will respond whether we intend it or not. (pp. 70–71)

Breuer and Freud were as concerned as other neurologists to understand the mechanism of hysterical conversion. But the relative ease with which many symptoms could be permanently relieved by talking, coupled with a recognition that the physiology of hysterical paralysis was an imagined not a real physiology, led Freud to abandon the search for a neurological mechanism in favour of a completely psychological understanding of hysteria. In taking this step Freud was forced to treat his previous experience as a neurologist as an irrelevance. As Jones (1953) recalled Freud's later attitude towards neurology: 'I must say I do not know of anything that seems more irrelevant for the psychological understanding of anxiety than a knowledge of the nervous paths the excitations follow' (p. 224).

Interestingly, in his abandonment of neurology, Freud may have been influenced by Carl Claus, his first research supervisor. Claus's sensibility was in conflict with that of Brücke, with Claus (1884) insisting that life was more than physics and chemistry and Brücke insisting that the *only* forces at work in an organism were those of physics and chemistry. As it turned out, both views were correct. The only forces at work in an organism are those of physics and chemistry, but the laws of physics and chemistry are not enough to account for the phenomena of biology, the forms of matter that are capable of self-replication. Similarly, Freud was led to see that the laws of biology and neurology were not enough to account for the phenomena of psychology, the forms of matter that are capable of morbid anxiety.

It is not difficult to understand why the talking cure became the method of choice for those who could afford it. Here is Freud's description of the medical treatment Anna von Lieben received for her facial pains (Breuer and Freud, 1895):

... since an abnormal excretion of urates was undoubtedly present and a not quite clearly defined 'acute rheumatism' played some part in the patient's history, a diagnosis of gouty neuralgia was plausible enough. This diagnosis was confirmed by the different consultants who were called in at each attack. Treatment of the usual kind was ordered: the electric brush, alkaline water, purges; but each time the neuralgia remained unaffected until it chose to give place to another symptom. Earlier in her life – the neuralgia was fifteen years old – her teeth were accused of being responsible for it. They were condemned to extraction, and one fine day, the sentence was carried out on seven of the criminals. This was not such an easy matter; her teeth were so firmly attached that the roots of most of them had to be left behind. This cruel operation had no result, either temporary or permanent. At that time the neuralgia raged for months on end. Even at the time of my treatment, at each attack of neuralgia the dentist was called in. On each occasion he diagnosed the presence of diseased roots and began to get to work on them; but as a rule he was soon interrupted. For the neuralgia would suddenly cease, and at the same time the demand for the dentist's services. (p. 249)

Teeth were not the only body parts routinely extracted by the practitioners of the period. In 1884, the neuropathologist Paul Flechsig reported the use in his clinic of female castration for the treatment of hysteria, with proposals for the further development of 'the indications for the use of castration as a treatment of neuroses and psychoses' (Flechsig, 1884).

The practices of psychiatry, as Freud observed in the extraction of Anna von Lieben's teeth, too often took the form of cruel, desperate measures. The pain and panic that trained professionals can feel when faced with behaviour and mental states of individuals so afflicted that they can no longer enter into conventional human relationships, can get translated into cruel and unusual forms of punishment. Electro-convulsive shock therapy, forced feeding, prefrontal lobotomies, forced restraint and the modern anti-depressant drug regimes, which can be used as chemical strait-jackets in understaffed, neglected mental hospital wards, often appear to be the punitive gestures of a frustrated medical establishment whose lack of understanding of the causes of mental pain created a need that was filled by psycho-analysis.

In Freud's time, Britain had 20,000 asylum admissions a year with an average stay of 4½ years, which resulted in a steady state asylum population of around 100,000 inmates, a population similar in many aspects of its organization to that of a prison. Those with the resources and social confidence to avoid the asylum sought alternatives. The prosperous, middle-class parents of Breuer's and Freud's patients preferred to give their daughters the private, extended individual attention offered by their doctors than to commit them to such asylums. The talking cure promised a humane alternative for the treatment of unfathomable mental states. A report on madhouses in

England in 1811 noted that the famous astronomer William Wriston had been lucky to avoid being incarcerated in an asylum (Porter, 1987): 'His friends judged rightly: to have committed him to a madhouse, would have in all probability fixed him with irremedial madness' (p. 325). The need for an alternative was there, as was the social class to support and protect it.

Classical psychoanalysis, in both form and content, was as much a product of the late stages of the Industrial Revolution as was the telephone and the wireless. Electricity had been an oddity for 2000 years until the railroads created a need for rapid communication which was satisfied by the exploitation of Oersted's discovery in 1820 that an electric current could cause a magnetic needle to deflect. Currents could be sent down wires and detected at the far end by magnets in a dot–dash form of signalling that was the Morse code. With real markets existing for rapid communication that could reward innovation, the translation of voice signals into electric currents could replace the Morse code. Similarly in psychoanalysis, a new form of human communication grew out of the need for an innovation that could translate previously incomprehensible messages from the human inner world, the wealth that could finance the work, and the physiologists who had the conceptual resources to transform the ancient syndrome of hysteria into a problem capable of yielding to modern methods of investigation.

If, as it proved, the time was right for the development of an alternative to psychiatry that offered practitioners and patients a way actively to engage with mental pain, a treatment that promised not only relief but understanding, one might ask why it was Sigmund Freud and Joseph Breuer who developed the analytic hour?

The history of knowledge disciplines includes numerous routinely cited episodes of simultaneous discovery: Newton in England and Leibniz in Germany simultaneously inventing the calculus; Darwin and Wallace simultaneously conceiving the idea of the evolution of species; Hertz in Germany narrowly beating Lodge in England for the discovery of electromagnetic waves; Poincaré in France losing out to Einstein in Switzerland for the theory of relativity; Watson and Crick in Cambridge winning a headlong race to beat Linus Pauling in Pasadena to the prize of the double helix. Key problems in any historical period are in the air and are worked on by a number of people simultaneously. Their solutions, although signed by individuals, have a sense of inevitability to them, summarized by an old saying: 'Great discoveries are made one year before they are absolutely inevitable.' Nevertheless there can be a quality of uniqueness to scientific discovery quite similar to the quality of uniqueness we are accustomed to assign to works of literature and art (Stent, 1972).

Contemporaries of Freud and Breuer clearly recognized that their *Studies on Hysteria* was different from other approaches to hysteria. Even the more grudging acknowledged the lead they had taken in understanding hysteria psychologically, as in the review by the German neurologist Adolph Strümpell (Kiell, 1988):

This collection of essays on the pathology and therapy of hysteria is welcome proof that the psychogenic theory of hysterical phenomena is increasingly accepted and appreciated among physicians. The authors possess great skill and exercise considerable psychological astuteness in illuminating the state of mind of the hysterical patient. Their discussions offer many interesting and stimulating insights. (p. 66)

Breuer and Freud were part of an international community of mental health workers dealing with a range of obscure mental states of which hysteria was the most famous. In Switzerland, Bleuler was trying to understand the communications of schizophrenic patients in an institutional setting at Rheinau. In Germany, Kraepelin was in the process of developing more accurate typologies of psychotic states. In France, Delboeuf, Binet and Bourru and Borot all were working on cathartic discharge of traumatic experiences through hypnosis, while Janet was working with his famous patients Lucie, Marie, Marcelle and Madame D. on what he called 'fixed subconscious ideas' as the source of their distress. In Vienna, Freud's old teacher Meynert was teaching that the origins of sexual deviations could be located in early experience, while Moritz Benedikt could be said to have anticipated Breuer and Freud with his formulation of the pathogenic secret, as well as developing a short-term psychotherapy for its treatment.

And so one could construct a scenario of a piecemeal creation of a psychoanalysis in which Benedikt might have begun to experiment with long-term talking therapies in very difficult cases, where a theorist such as Janet might have been tempted to understand the mechanism of catharsis and so be led to the formulation of causal agents of human mental pain, where Krafft-Ebing, in his attempts to understand sexual pathology, might have been led to early childhood experience, or where, across the ocean in the US, J. J. Putnam might have expanded his ten-minute talks with patients as a purely pragmatic attempt to solve medical problems that did not seem to yield in any other way. Meanwhile the psychiatric establishment would have been decrying the efficacy of talking cures as being due to suggestion, the psychologists would have been insisting on controlled experiments, as they were attempting to do with perception, while the neurologists would have been insisting that the patients really had an organic disease such as Tourette's syndrome.

But that is not how it went in psychoanalysis. It was Freud who used the instrument of the analytic hour to create the discipline of psychoanalysis – and not his contemporaries. And since it was Freud's interpretation of the events taking place in the analytic hour that shaped the subsequent development of psychoanalysis – one could say the history of psychoanalysis consists of a continuous conversation with Freud – one can ask about the uniqueness of Freud's contribution.

Certainly a significant factor was Freud's skill as a writer. He wrote with a forceful unfolding clarity characteristic of the great scientific stylists. The question here is not where Freud learned this style, or who were his sources, his so-called influences, but rather, what did the clarity of his arguments say about his understanding of the problems? Freud wrote with clarity because he had an exceptional grasp of the problems, a conviction in the depth of his understanding and, as it turns out, a deep psychological receptivity to human experience. Throughout his correspondence Freud's interest is most apparent, not about his work in neuroscience, but in his perceptive comments about his friends, family, colleagues and surroundings. Here is a part of his analysis, written when he was twenty-seven years old, of the suicide of his friend Nathan Weiss.

Weiss hanged himself in the public baths in the Landstrasse ten days after he had returned from his honeymoon. Freud's analysis of the cause of Weiss's suicide shows the same nuanced compassion that characterizes his psychoanalytic writing.

As an explanation the world is ready to hurl the most ghastly accusations at the unfortunate widow. I don't believe in them. I believe that the realization of an enormous failure, the rage caused by rejected passion, the fury at having sacrificed his whole scientific career, his entire fortune, for a domestic disaster, perhaps also the annoyance at having been done out of the promised dowry, as well as the inability to face the world and confess it all – I believe that all this, following a number of scenes which opened his eyes to his situation, may have brought this madly vain man (who in any case was given to serious emotional upheavals) to the brink of despair. He died from the sum total of his qualities, his pathological self-love coupled with the claims he made for the higher things of life. (To Martha, 16 September 1883)

The confluence of Freud's interest in human psychological motivation, his appetite for theory given shape by his training with Brücke, his ambition and his intellectual frustration, made him seize with alacrity the opportunities offered as a theorist of the talking cure. Freud took up the instrument of the analytic hour to become the analyst of human motive and feeling for which he so clearly had what we may call talent, a talent consisting of an intense but detached interest in people, coupled with a strong taste for the kind of theory that made sense of a wide variety of seemingly disparate experience.

In contrast, Breuer was far more interested in the particularities of medicine and biology. When Freud began to posit all neurosis as flowing from different varieties of sexual abuse, Breuer felt disinclined to follow. And Freud, with the bit between his teeth – a method, a field of study wide open for advances and a receptive public – did the rest. As he wrote to Fliess in 1896: 'As a young man I knew no longing other than for philosophical knowledge and now I am about to fulfil it as I move from medicine to psychology' (2 April 1896).

Freud's competitors could have slowly constructed a psychoanalysis piecemeal. But the depth of Freud's approach to human mental pain and his ability to express his understanding in powerful explanatory narratives gave his understanding a sustained persuasiveness that could only be challenged by a similar depth of vision. Rather than seeing Freud as the father of psychoanalysis it is more useful and more accurate to see Freud as the first, and most important, theoretician of the analytic hour.

A century later, it has become fashionable in New York and London to dismiss Freud's observations and understandings of what happened in his consulting room as being fatally flawed. These critiques, like those of Galileo's contemporaries, have questioned the instrument itself. As Paolo Gualdo described the objections of University of Padua philosopher Cesare Cremonini in a letter to Galileo of 6 May 1611: '[He] entirely ridicules these observations of yours and is amazed that you assert them as true.' To seventeenth-century intellectuals, objects that could only be seen with an instrument and not by the naked eye could be artefacts of the instrument itself. Seventy years after Galileo had created modern astronomy with his observations of the moons of Jupiter, the craters of the moon, and the phases of the planet Venus, John Flamsteed, the English Astronomer Royal, still found it necessary to argue that systems of lenses 'do not impose upon our senses' (Van Helden, 1989).

Similarly, 100 years after the invention of psychoanalysis, it is still necessary to argue that what happens in the analytic hour is interesting, important and real, and that suggestion, a supposedly fatal invalidation of the analytic exchange, is far from invalidating but is a part of human psychology and needs to be understood as such. Because these critics have dismissed the events that take place in the analytic hour as artefacts of the instrument, their critiques end up being fascinating, well-researched character assassinations or intellectually challenging philosophical discussions about the meaning of science, neither of which address substantive issues posed by the existence of the human inner world. Dreams, unconscious motivation, anxiety states, phobias, human mental distress and human subjective experience are real things. Prior to Breuer's and Freud's contribution of the analytic hour their exploration had been no more than guesswork. The question, as always, is not about Freud's character, or whether psychoanalysis is a science or not, but whether psychoanalysis, the theorization of the long-term listening that is the analytic relationship, tells us anything interesting, important and real about mental pain and about ourselves.

4

First Theories

At the end of the twentieth century, the romantic nineteenth-century belief that science and technology would provide a just world of plenty has turned into a far more cynical view. From a place of former glory as a force for the emancipation of the entire human race, science now is simply one of many vested interests in society making claims on the public purse in pursuit of objectives that are all too frequently remote from, or even threatening to, human existence.

One of the casualties of science's fall from grace has been the belief that the world can be understood. Information has replaced knowledge; explanation has replaced understanding. As we enter the twenty-first century, the comprehensive unifying schemes so satisfying to the scientists of the nineteenth century and to the educated classes of the period strike a ludicrous note to post-modern sensibilities hardened by the incomprehensibility of twentieth-century experience. We no longer believe that very much understanding is possible. Theory has become an exercise in mystification rather than a way to increase our understanding of a problem of concern. Most of us, including our intellectuals, do not know what it actually feels like to understand a problem of any complexity.

The problem of not knowing what constitutes understanding is particularly acute in theories of human affairs. Here theoretical fads – catastrophe theory, chaos theory, evolutionary psychology – and a mood of anything goes as long as it sounds good have become the norm. In such a climate, where the goal of understanding appears to be unattainable and where one feels ashamed to live in a time when theory is just a game, it can be difficult to evaluate properly Freud's first attempts to theorize what he observed in the analytic hour.

We must remind ourselves of something that should, after 300 years of the successes of modern Western science, be self-evident but is not, that theories are not truths *per se* but are constructions – ways of understanding. Theories are tools designed for a specific purpose at a particular time and place. In the case of psychoanalysis, the construction of the first theoretical tools for understanding the human inner world as revealed by the analytic hour was dominated by a particular theorist, Sigmund Freud.

Freud's style was to look for unifying threads in the array of symptoms located under the headings of hysteria, anxiety, obsessions and melancholia. In his early attempts at theory, Freud took as his starting point the idea that a quantity of neural excitation got detached from an original experience and went astray in the nervous system. His clue that detachment was crucial was in the things that patients said (Freud, 1894):

Something very disagreeable happened to me once and I tried very hard to put it away from me and not think about it anymore. I succeeded at last but then I got this other thing which I have not been able to get rid of since. (p. 52)

The idea of neural excitation was meant to symbolize neural activity in response to a specific experience. The central feature of the scheme was not excitation *per se* but its displacement.

Using the idea of displaced neural excitation, Freud was able to order neurotic symptoms according to whether the excitation originated in the mind or the body and whether it ended in the mind or the body. In hysteria, the excitation would have originated in the psyche as emotional trauma, the excitation becoming displaced into bodily symptoms. In obsessional neurosis, the displacement was from one idea to another idea, from a fear of going mad to an obsessional brooding – 'What if I don't want to breathe?' Paranoia became a special case of obsessional neurosis where a self-reproach, instead of remaining displaced into an obsession with the self ('I am dirty, I must wash'), got projected on to other people ('They hate me. They think I am dirty'). In anxiety neurosis, the excitation arose in the body as a frustrated sexuality, the somatic excitation remaining in the body, causing anxiety in the same way that unprocessed fright causes anxiety

– the organism knows a response is called for but is unable to make it. Finally, phobias could be seen as a form of anxiety neurosis – a displacement of the anxiety caused by unprocessed somatic excitation into a range of fears such as fear of heights, of going outside or of snakes, thunderstorms, birds or darkness. Thus conceptualized, the practitioner has a way to begin to treat otherwise incomprehensible symptoms by locating the origins of displaced excitation in prior experience.

The coherence of the scheme encouraged Freud to make a critique of the then blanket explanation of neurosis as inherited mental degeneracy (Freud, 1896a):

There has been too little research into these specific and determining causes of nervous disorders, for the attention of physicians has remained dazzled by the grandiose prospect of the aetiological precondition of heredity. (p. 146)

Heredity, while not being denied a possible concurrent role, was reduced to insignificance as being neither necessary nor sufficient in the face of the powerful influence of specific real-life disturbances of the nervous system. In place of the vague dictum of heredity, even today the theoretical court of last resort when distress, physical or mental, cannot be understood, Freud substituted a coherent classification of nervous disorders as arising from definite human experiences. To those with a taste for unification, it is a lovely scheme, a fine example of nineteenth-century scientific sensibilities.

But the sensibility of a scientist like Freud was not to be satisfied with simply classifying nervous distress. He wanted to understand its dynamics. What actually caused the displacements? In neurasthenia (a kind of mental fatigue), it was masturbation; with anxiety neurosis it was insufficient libidinal discharge due to coitus interruptus or sexual abstinence; and in the cases of hysteria and obsessional neurosis, it was childhood sexual abuse, passively in the case of hysteria, with active participation and the ensuing guilt in obsessional neurosis.

With his unifying framework of the sexual aetiology of neurosis, Freud thought he had found the solution to the puzzle of hysteria (Freud, 1896c):

I put forward the thesis that at the bottom of every case of hysteria there are *one or more occurrences of premature sexual experience*, occurrences which belong to the earliest years of childhood but which can be reproduced through the work of psychoanalysis in spite of the intervening decades. I believe this is an important finding, the discovery of a *caput Nili* [source of the Nile] in neuropathology. (p. 203)

Freud presented his developing theory of the sexual aetiology of the neuroses in a series of seven papers between 1894 and 1896, summarizing his views in an important lecture given to the Society for Psychiatry and Neurology on 21 April 1896. In combination with the letters and drafts to Fliess from the same period, one can obtain a picture of the clinical problems on which Freud based his theory of the sexual aetiology of neurosis.[1]

Freud described severe cases, some coming to him after long, unsuccessful institutional treatment, all of whom suffered trauma which had to be 'classed as grave sexual injuries; some of them positively revolting'. A man who, as a boy, was forced to stimulate the genitals of a woman with his foot developed a fixation with his legs which turned into an hysterical paralysis of both legs. A woman with anxiety attacks, occurring only at certain hours of the day and capable of being calmed only by the presence of a particular one of her many sisters, proved to have been assaulted by a man who, afraid of being interrupted, used to ask if this sister were at home. A little boy compulsively repeated with his little sister the same acts of abuse he had previously experienced by a governess. Frau P., who was suffering from fears of persecution, had had a sexual relationship with her brother between the ages of six to ten. A woman's twelve-year-old brother had sexually licked her feet and those of her sisters when they undressed at night, a sexual preference that the woman had inadvertently witnessed the father carrying out with her wet nurse when she herself was four years old. The father had then hit her on the head with his boot when he discovered her hiding under the bed. A male patient had been abused by an uncle in scenes in which a little sister less than a year old had also been involved. The patient had in his turn then abused his eldest sister with the result that she became psychotically overwhelmed.[2]

Freud's sympathy was strongly aroused by his cases. Of cases of oral and anal sexual acts with children, that produced symptoms including intestinal disturbances, choking and vomiting, sensations accompanying defecation, indigestion and disgust at food, he wrote (Freud, 1896c): 'People who have no hesitation in satisfying their sexual desires upon children cannot be expected to jib at finer shades in the methods of obtaining that satisfaction ... the grotesque and yet tragic incongruities reveal themselves as stamped upon the later development of the individual and of his neurosis in countless permanent effects which deserve to be traced in the greatest detail. Where the relation is between two children the character of the sexual scenes is of the same repulsive sort, since every such relationship between children postulates a previous seduction by one of them by an adult' (p. 215).

Writing to Fliess, Freud described his way of discussing these traumas with patients:

She came today and confessed that she had thought a lot about the treatment and had discovered an obstacle.

'What is that?'

'I can make myself out to be as bad as I must; but I must spare other people. You must allow me to name no names.'

'No doubt names are unimportant. What you mean are your relations to people. Here it surely will not be possible to conceal anything.'

'I really mean that earlier I should have been easier to treat than today. Earlier I was unsuspecting; but now the criminal significance of some things has become clear to me and I cannot make up my mind to talk about them.'

'On the contrary, I believe that a mature woman becomes more tolerant about sexual matters.'

'Yes you are right there. When I say that the people who are guilty of such things are noble and high-minded I am bound to think that there is a disease, kind of madness, and I must excuse them.'

'Well then let us speak plainly. In my analyses the guilty people are close relatives, father or brother.'

'Nothing has gone on with my brother.'

'Your father, then.'

And then it turned out that her supposedly otherwise noble and respectable father regularly took her to bed when she was from eight to twelve years old and misused her without penetrating ('made her wet', nocturnal visits). She felt anxiety even at that time. A sister six years her senior with whom she had talked things over many years later confessed to her that she had had the same experiences with their father. A cousin told that when she was fifteen she had to fend off her grandfather's embraces. Of course when I told her that similar and worse things must have happened in her earliest childhood, she could not find it incredible. In other respects it is a quite ordinary case of hysteria with the usual symptoms. (28 April 1897)

Finally, the controversial case of Emma Eckstein illustrates the magnitude of the difficult cases Freud encountered in his early use of the analytic hour.[3] Emma Eckstein came to Freud in 1895 as a twenty-nine-year-old unmarried woman who, because of severe pains in her legs, had been unable to walk since puberty. Her case has attracted intense attention from historians because of the appallingly botched operation Wilhelm Fliess performed on her nose for her nervous condition while she was in treatment with Freud.

Fliess, on a special visit from Berlin, operated on both Eckstein and Freud in Vienna in late January or early February 1895. Eckstein did not heal properly. She had swelling, a decayed odour coming from the nasal cavity, haemorrhages, and discharged bowlfuls of pus. In Fliess's absence Freud had called in his colleague and boyhood friend Ignaz Rosanes, an ear, nose and throat specialist and director of the Princess Royal Stephanie Hospital. On cleaning the wound Rosanes found a piece of thread, began pulling it and before they had time to consider what they were doing had removed a foot and a half of antiseptic gauze from the cavity. This initiated an immediate haemorrhage and further complications over the next month which nearly cost Eckstein her life.

The Eckstein operation has been a convenient stick with which to beat Fliess for medical incompetence and Freud for covering up for Fliess. But for this charge to hold, historians need to make a comparative study of medical practice. Freud himself reminded Fliess that such accidents were common and that their colleague Robert Gersuny, director of the Rudolfinerhaus Hospital, had had a similar experience and no longer used antiseptic gauze for that reason (8 March 1895).

Even though blood-saturated swabs were notoriously easy to leave behind in the operating wound, it was not until the 1940s, after a number of incidents occurred in close succession, that a system for numbering swabs was introduced (Fido and Fido, 1996).

Freud could barely restrain his dismay. On 11 April 1895 he wrote to Fliess that he was terribly shaken by the disastrous repercussions of what was to have been a routine operation. Judging from the subsequent pacifying letters Freud wrote to Fliess, Fliess was outraged at any imputation of wrongdoing on his part and the lack of sympathy that Fliess showed Freud for having to deal with such a mess undoubtedly undermined their relationship.

In spite of the botched operation, Eckstein continued in treatment with Freud. A year later, fuller details of her mental pain began to emerge. In a statement often interpreted as a further pacification of Fliess, Freud wrote, on 16 and 28 April 1896, that he had found an explanation of Eckstein's bleeding that let Fliess off the hook: her bleeding was a hysterical symptom caused by intense unsatisfied longing. Although this sounded like a cover-up of malpractice with the physicians engaged in an exercise of blaming the victim, on 4 May important clinical details of Eckstein's history emerged. As a child, she had had a history of severe bleeding from cuts and nosebleeds. She had had headaches that were not taken seriously and heavy bleeding when she began her periods, a symptom that was finally taken as a sign that she did have a medical illness. She told Freud that at the age of fifteen she had had a severe nosebleed when she wanted to be the patient of a particular young doctor. And she related that when she saw how concerned Freud was by her first haemorrhage she realized that she had always wanted to be loved during her illnesses instead of being accused of malingering, that in spite of the danger she felt a happiness she had never known before.

It can be difficult to accept that body and mind are so interconnected that actual bleeding can occur as a manifestation of an intense longing to be loved, as a symptom of mental distress. But Marie Cardinal's powerful bestseller *The Words To Say It* (1975) describes how her successful treatment by analysis cured her of hysterical bleeding. After years of unsuccessful medical treatment for haemorrhages and faced with the stark choice of suicide or permanent commitment to a psychiatric hospital, Cardinal consulted a psychoanalyst in the 14th Arrondissement of Paris. In the first session, the analyst confirmed her feeling that the pills she was taking were dangerous and told her she would have to stop taking all medication. To her question, 'What if I haemorrhage?' he replied 'Do nothing.' And when she persisted: 'But they already have put me in hospital for this, they gave me transfusions, curettages,' he said, 'I know it, do nothing. I will see you tomorrow.'

Cardinal relates that she awoke the following morning drenched in blood, filled with terrifying memories of past bleeding:

One time the blood had flowed in such large clots that it might have been said that I was producing slices of liver, one after another, with an absurd obstinacy; as they passed through me they caressed me gently, softly. They had taken me to the hospital for an emergency curettage. Another time, the blood had come out of me like a red thread which wouldn't stop unwinding – an open faucet. I remember the shock of seeing it, and how it terrified me: 'At this rate the blood will drain out of me in ten minutes flat.' Again, the hospital, transfusions, doctors and nurses covered with blood, throwing themselves on my arms, my legs, my hands, trying to find a vein, struggling through the night. Then, in the morning, the operating room and again, a curettage. (p. 31)

She waited the six hours until her appointment, arriving bundled up in cotton pads.

At last I entered and said right away, 'Doctor, I am bled dry.' I remember very well having chosen the words because I found them beautiful. I also remember that I wanted my look and my posture to communicate the pathetic. The doctor answered me quietly and calmly: 'Those are psychosomatic disorders. That doesn't interest me. Speak about something else.' (p. 32)

Cardinal was shocked. 'He did not want me to speak about my blood! But of what else did he want me to speak? What ELSE? Apart from my blood there was only fear, nothing else, and I could no more speak of it than think about it' (p. 32). This insistence on looking past the symptom of bleeding to 'something else' began a successful analysis lasting seven years.

We do not have the kind of document for Emma Eckstein that Marie Cardinal has provided for her treatment. But in the light of modern clinical experience it would appear that Freud, in relating to her bleeding as a symptom of further underlying distress, made it safe for her to speak to him about frightening scenes of childhood abuse (Sinason, 1994). On 17 January and 24 January 1897, Freud described these developments to Fliess. Eckstein told of scenes where a devil stuck needles into her fingers. She described a genital torture she had experienced, consisting of the cutting-off of a part of her labia, having her bleeding sucked and being given a piece of the skin to eat.[4]

Freud took this report seriously. He felt he was seeing in his consulting room a counterpart of the confessions made by women accused of witchcraft. He wrote to Fliess:

Do you remember that I always said that the medieval theory of possession held by the ecclesiastical courts was identical with our theory of a foreign body and the splitting of consciousness? But why did the devil who took possession of the poor things invariably abuse them sexually and in a loathsome manner? (17 January 1897)

Albert Hirst, Eckstein's nephew, felt that Freud's treatment of his aunt had been a success. For a period of twelve to fourteen years Eckstein ran her mother's household, coping efficiently with an open house and severe financial difficulties. She then suffered a relapse and became bedridden again, because, Hirst believed, a Viennese architect whom she loved married someone else. Freud visited her at that time but, as Hirst recalled, there was conflict between them and the treatment was not resumed. Eckstein lived out her remaining ten years as an invalid (Masson, 1984). Writing about her forty years later in 1937, Freud felt that Eckstein's early traumatic experiences had not been fully resolved by analysis lasting only a year. But he also felt that she might not have relapsed if she had not encountered a fresh trauma in the form of her unsuccessful love.

By 1896 Freud was halfway to creating a new psychology. He still had one foot in neurology with his conception of displaced excitation. But the breakthrough had already been made. Freud took seriously what his patients told him. Instead of referring to the existing texts, he permitted himself to learn from patients, to attempt to make sense of what he was told. Hysterics suffered from reminiscences. But their memories were repressed, pushed into a hypothesized unconscious, where they were transformed into symptoms which could be interpreted to reveal the hidden experiences that lay behind them.

Freud knew his theory of hysterical phenomena as arising from repressed experiences of sexual abuse was an advance on prevailing orthodoxy, an orthodoxy that, being Freud, he had no hesitation in attacking on a number of fronts. To the argument that hysterics were simply people who were psychically inadequate to meet the demands of sexuality, he cited the cases of two young women who had developed hysterical symptoms in adolescence, in one instance after the stroking of her hand by a boy, and in another by the telling of an off-colour joke. Freud understood these reactions not as examples of a psychical inadequacy but as the specific result of traumatic experience buried in the patient's past. Against the theory that hysteria seemed to run in families and therefore most probably had a genetic component, Freud argued that what was being observed was the widespread occurrence of inappropriate sexual conduct within the same family. In answer to the argument that the apparently exaggerated hysterical reactions were due to an abnormal sensitivity, Freud replied that the sensitivity was only apparently exaggerated and was perfectly understandable once one understood its origins in prior traumatic experience. Thus the mental 'sensitiveness' of hysterical patients, a 'high degree of readiness to feel hurt on the slightest occasion', could be likened to the sensitivities one might observe in a married couple where an apparently slight incident can ignite a powerful row (Freud, 1896c): 'You would certainly infer that the conjugal scene you had just witnessed was not solely the result of this trifling occasion, but that the inflammable material had been piling up for a long time and the whole heap of it had been set alight by the final provocation' (p. 217). Freud's concept allowed Charcot's notion of hysterogenic points – points on the body which, when touched, triggered convulsive attacks – to be recast. The hysterogenic points had nothing to do with the touch itself: the touch simply served to induce an unconscious memory of a past series of events.

And so the problem of hysteria had been effectively transformed from a problem in neurology to a problem arising in prior human experience, that is to say, to a problem of psychology – 'a psychology of a kind for which philosophers have done little to prepare us' (Freud, 1896c, p. 219).

The Freud of 1896 was convinced that he was on the right track. A single aetiological agent (like Koch's tuberculosis bacillus) – childhood sexual abuse – could be seen to be the causative agent in all the major neuroses. The agent worked through the repressed, strangulated affect associated with the original experience. There was now no need for special pleading in the form of abnormal sensitivities or genetic predisposition or inherited mental degeneracy. Neuroses could be understood as a result of lived experience. The order of the day would be to develop not the neurology of neurosis but an exploration of its psychology, in particular the puzzle of why repressed memories have a pathogenic effect, whereas unrepressed memories do not. The mystery of hysteria seemed close to being solved.

But a year and a half later, on 21 September 1897, Freud wrote the most famous letter in the Freud–Fliess correspondence, the letter in which he apparently renounced the sexual aetiology of the neuroses: 'And now I want to confide in you immediately the great secret that has slowly been dawning on me in the last few months, I no longer believe in my *neurotica* [theory of neuroses].'

Much has been made of Freud's so-called recantation of what has been called the seduction theory. At one end of the spectrum it has been seen as a profound betrayal of the sexually abused. At the other extreme it has been lauded as the real beginning of psychoanalysis. The issues are complex, and involve a confrontation with the reality of our society's abuse of children, feelings about Freud and his fame, and our general ignorance of the difficulties associated with the development of theory. Freud's so-called abandonment of the seduction theory was part of the struggle to create a theory of the neuroses. The actual story is not one of did he or didn't he, was he or was he not a betrayer, but can only be understood as a particular example of the kind of changing fortunes that occur in every attempt to create understandings of our experience of the world.

There can be no doubt about the prevalence of childhood sexual abuse in the late nineteenth century. The sexual abuse of very young children by wet nurses and servants had been widely reported by teachers and clergy at least from the mid-nineteenth century (Ellenberger, 1970). In France, the work of Ambroise Tardieu and Paul Brouardel in forensic psychiatry documented ubiquitous and horrific incidents of violence and sexual abuse against children (Masson, 1984). Brouardel was the only other lecturer in Paris besides Charcot who Freud felt had anything worthwhile to say and he rarely missed his lectures and demonstrations (Freud, 1886a; 1913a). Freud visited the Paris morgue on the day that Brouardel did an autopsy on a child who had been raped and murdered by her father (Masson, 1984). In the period 1880–1900 Richard Krafft-Ebing and Havelock Ellis, as well as Theodor Meynert, Albert Moll, and Charles Féré, routinely refer to early sexual experience as being the cause of later sexual deviations as well as warning about the sexualization of violence against the young. Moll (1912), in addition to citing cases current at the time, including those in which he was called as an expert witness (pp. 234–9), reported the effects of the widespread belief that venereal disease could be cured by sexual intercourse with children.

In a great many cases, sexual offences against children are brought to light only when, on examining the child, gonorrhoeal or syphilitic infection is disclosed. Many authorities hold that the superstitious hope of curing venereal disease by sexual intercourse with an innocent child is a comparatively frequent source of such infection in children. (p. 226)

The less severe sequelae of these traumatic events were seen by Breuer, Benedikt and other practitioners of the period. Benedikt reported six case studies at a conference described in the *Internationale Klinische Rundshau* in 1889, illustrating the effects of pathogenic secrets and their treatment, including a case of a young girl brought to him by her mother (Benedikt, 1906): 'I had the suspicion that her daughter had been sexually abused and from it had become somatically and psychically ill' (pp. 136–7). Indeed, it was proved that the girl had been sexually abused at the age of ten by a grown man, and had since then often suffered burning pains.

The history of child abuse extends back to antiquity, as amply illustrated in Greek and Roman art and literature (Kahr, 1991). Brutality against children in the form of child labour and the kidnapping of children from orphanages and workhouses, effectively child slavery, was a central feature of industrial capitalism. The photographs of Lewis Hine and the writings of Charles Dickens document the reality of the labour of children who were 'flogged, fettered and tortured in the most exquisite refinement of cruelty' (Fielden, 1836).

The practice of child abuse extends to the late twentieth century, as illustrated by almost weekly reports of the institutional abuse of children. A recent exposé of four Catholic orphanages, two in Dublin, one in Cork and one in Galway, revealed systematic physical abuse by the nuns of the children entrusted to their care. Women who had been children at Goldenridge orphanage in Dublin came forward to describe ritual beatings with chair legs, whippings with rosaries, being locked in spin-driers as punishment, being forced to eat their vomit when sick and being tied up like chickens and hung upside down on high doors as punishment for being 'bold' (Lennon, 1996). Paedophile rings involving the police, the clergy, government officials, academics and politicians have been exposed in the notorious Dutroux affair in Belgium, in the Kincora Boys' Home in Northern Ireland, the Bryn Alyn Home and Bryn Estyn Home in Wrexham, North Wales, and in children's homes in Cheshire, Leicestershire, Staffordshire and Merseyside in England and worldwide in the Catholic Church in the US, Canada and Australia. In Belgium, on 20 October 1996, 250,000 demonstrators, 3 per cent of the population, holding white balloons, lilies, roses and daisies, marched through Brussels in solidarity with the parents of the children who had died at the hands of the Dutroux gang and demanded a clean-up of the complicit government and police.[5]

One hundred years ago, Freud had ample evidence to suggest that widespread, pervasive cruelty to children – and, in the case of the neuroses, sexual abuse – could well be the universal aetiological agent behind the disease. Yet he was uneasy about his theory. In the spring and summer of 1897 he complained to Fliess that hysteria was not coming out as he wished. And this it could not do because sexual abuse is not the only form of violence of aetiological significance for hysteria.

By mid-September Freud was so unsure of himself that he wrote the letter of 21 September 1897 to Fliess saying that he no longer believed in his theory of sexual abuse as the universal origin of hysteria. He gave three reasons: a lack of what he felt to be the complete success necessary to clinch the case, along with the possibility that the partial successes could be understood in other ways; he had found that in all his cases, including that of his own father, the father was the guilty party and he felt that so much child abuse by the father was improbable; and finally he was not sure whether one could tell the difference between fact and an emotionally charged fiction that had been internalized in the unconscious.

Freud's feelings were muddled – a mixture of relief, elation and disappointment. Something had been resolved – he knew he had been chasing a theory that was not right. He wanted it to be true because it would be so conclusive, so definitive, so guaranteeing of fame and fortune. But there were too many doubts.

Nevertheless, in spite of his doubts, he still remained attached to his theory. In December he wrote to Fliess that his confidence that paternal perversion was the origin of hysteria had been boosted by further evidence (12 December 1897). Ten days later he wrote again, describing the experiences of a patient who had been raped by her father at the age of two:

The father belongs to the category of men who stab women, for whom bloody injuries are an erotic need. When she was two years old, he brutally deflowered her and infected her with his gonorrhoea, as a consequence of which she became ill and her life was endangered by the loss of blood and vaginitis. (22 December 1897)

On 27 April 1898, seven months after announcing to Fliess that he no longer believed in his *neurotica*, Freud wrote that the daughters of his sister Marie were all hysterics and that he suspected the father. But in the same letter he also corrected himself as not having given sufficient weight to what he called 'fantasy'. Four days later he wrote: 'I am completely involved in the dream book' (1 May 1898).

Three months later he wrote to Fliess that his doubts about having omitted other major factors in the aetiology of hysteria had now increased to the point at which they overwhelmed whatever value the work had had and he dreaded returning to it (26 August 1898). Freud was in the process of abandoning his work on hysteria and the sequelae of sexual abuse in favour of his work on the interpretation of dreams. His own self-analysis was underway. Fantasies and dreams became his main interest. The tool of interpretative free association offered a chance to make sense of unconscious processes, including the process of repression by which we 'forget' a name and make an incorrect substitute in its place (26 August 1897).

He was excited about creating an entirely new theory of dreams. If hysteria had not come out, dreams would. In the same letter in which he had accepted that his understanding of hysteria was insufficient he had written: 'In this collapse of everything valuable, the psychological alone has remained untouched. The dream[book] stands entirely secure and my beginnings of the metapsychological work have only grown in my estimation. It is a pity that one cannot make a living, for instance on dream interpretation' (21 September 1897).

Freud's interests had shifted decisively away from the extremes of psychopathology. When, two years earlier, Freud had written to Fliess that psychology was now his consuming passion, he had said he had two goals: to create a theory of mental processes based on a model of nerve forces and excitation, and to try to learn something about normal psychological processes from his study of psychopathology. Now he was abandoning the model of nerve forces in favour of direct insight into normal human psychology using himself and his self-analysis as his principal guide (to Fliess, 3 October 1897; 14 November 1897).

Central to his interest in normal psychology was his discovery of the Oedipal triangle. Freud mentions the Oedipus legend for the first time in a letter to Fliess of 15 October 1897. Despite feeling bogged down, he nevertheless felt he had found something of great generality: 'I have found, in my own case too, [the phenomenon of] being in love with my mother and jealous of my father, and I now consider it a universal event in early childhood.' From this insight Freud felt he could understand the universal appeal and power of Sophocles' play, *Oedipus Rex* – the play released repressed feelings as the males in the audience, to their horror, realize that they, too, in fantasy had wished their fathers dead because they wanted their mothers for themselves.

Two years later, in *Interpretation of Dreams*, Freud summarized the Oedipus story in the version used by Sophocles as a gradual unfolding of the evidence to reveal that King Oedipus had unwittingly murdered his father, King Laius, and had married his mother, Queen Jocasta. Successful resolution of the Oedipal triangle in which the boy child must learn to master his sexual feelings towards his mother and his murderous feelings towards his father is perhaps the most widely known feature of Freud's theory of human psychological development. Less well known is the fuller story of the Oedipus legend, a story of attempted filicide, a complex of the father not of the son – a Laius complex, not an Oedipal complex (Graber, 1952; Devereux, 1953; Kausen, 1972; Krull, 1979; Ross, 1982; Pines, 1983).

Laius' father, the King of Thebes, died when Laius was one year old. After years of struggles for the throne, Laius, still a youth, was banished to a life of wandering. On a visit to Pisa, Laius fell in love with the son of King Pelops, kidnapped and sodomized him. Furious at the rape of his son, Pelops, along with the Olympian gods Zeus and Hera, condemned Laius to remain childless for a long time and then to be killed by his own son who would marry his wife. Upon regaining the throne of Thebes, Laius married Jocasta but mindful of the curse avoided sexual relations with her. Jocasta, however, got Laius drunk and conceived his child. When the child was born, Laius had the infant's feet pierced with an iron pin and ordered a shepherd to abandon him on the mountainside. The shepherd took pity on the infant and entrusted him to a Corinthian shepherd. The Corinthian shepherd took the infant to the King and Queen of Corinth who, being childless, adopted him as their own, naming the baby Oedipus (the Greek word for swollen foot) in sympathy for his maltreatment. Upon reaching maturity and hearing that his parents were not his real parents, Oedipus consulted the Delphic oracle who told him that he was destined to murder his father and marry his mother. Fleeing Corinth to avoid the oracle's fate he encountered Laius in a chariot with a party of four men on a narrow road. Ordered imperiously to get out of the way, a fight ensued. Laius hit Oedipus on the head with his double goad and Oedipus, drawing on the strength the gods had given him, killed everyone in the party except one servant who escaped. Upon arriving in Thebes Oedipus solved the riddle of the Sphinx, thus rescuing the city from destruction, and was made king. He married Jocasta, who gave birth to four children, and the couple ruled together for fifteen happy years until the gods decided that the facts of the case needed to be made known and set a plague on Thebes.

Does the story of Oedipus symbolize universal incestuous desires genetically inherited, a psychology in which the conflicts are inner conflicts arising from biological drives inherent in every human being? Or is the story of Oedipus a story of parental relationships gone terribly wrong, a vicious cowardly father attempting to kill his infant son and then attacking a perfect stranger, who unwittingly kills his own father in self-defence?

The Oedipal triangle remains a powerful symbol for the complexities of the mother–father–child relationship. Within a framework of triangular relationships in general, the sexual dynamics can be considered a secondary effect – the primary question being the process by which the relationship becomes sexualized in the first place. Taking this view, Freud's observations of the apparent universality of the sexualization of the mother–son relationship can be seen as part of the dynamic of the Victorian patriarchal family. This family romance is dominated by an absent authoritarian father who, arriving home, asserts the priority of his own needs over his children's by making overt or covert sexual demands on his wife. The wife, resentful of abandonment by her husband and of his authoritarian attitudes, lavishes her attention on her son. And the son, perceiving rivalry for the mother's affections expressed in sexual terms, responds in kind.

Through Oedipus and dreams, Freud was following his trail where it was leading even though it was taking him away from his most severely distressed patients. By July 1899, as he neared completion of the dream book, he was getting cold feet: 'Such a child of sorrow! I have great difficulties with it; I cannot manage more than two hours a day without calling on friend Marsala for help' (to Fliess, 8 July 1899). By September the agony had increased: 'If only someone could tell me whether there is any value to the whole thing!' (6 September 1899). On 21 September he had the proofs in front of him. He was unhappy with his writing ('tortuous sentences'), a symptom of an insufficient understanding. He consoled himself that fate: 'simply did not turn out any better'. At the end of October he sent the first copy to Fliess. By mid-November sales were satisfactory and in December and January the professional reviews started coming in (Kiell, 1988). Although they were favourable, they were not ecstatic. Freud was not happy. But the book was done.

The elements of Freud's vision of human psychology were now in place: the unconscious as the recipient of repressed material; the importance of childhood sexuality; the interpretation of dreams and the conduct of therapy by the method of free association; a theory of dreams as expressions of repressed wishes; and the resolution of Oedipal tensions as the central feature of human psychological development.

Freud's shift to pure psychology was to end his friendship with Fliess. He had stopped relying on Fliess as a sounding board for the neural mechanisms that he was leaving behind. When chided by Fliess for abandoning his attempts to give a biological explanation for psychological phenomena, Freud replied that he was not in disagreement in principle but that, for reasons he could not understand, he found it impossible to do other than create a purely psychological theory to account for what he was seeing in his consulting room: 'But apart from this I do not know how to go on, neither theoretically nor therapeutically and therefore must behave as if only the psychological were under consideration. Why I cannot fit it together [the organic and the psychological] I have not even begun to fathom' (22 September 1898).

Three years later the break was nearly complete. Freud no longer found it interesting to try to understand Fliess's attempts to mathematize biology, pleading mathematical ignorance in his inability to follow Fliess's arguments. Fliess for his part had little time for Freud's interpretive efforts. As Freud wrote three years later: 'If as soon as an interpretation of mine makes you uncomfortable, you are ready to agree that the "reader of thoughts" perceives nothing in the other but merely projects his own thoughts you really no longer are my audience either and must regard my entire method of working as being just as worthless as the others do' (19 September 1901).

It is rare to have such a complete record of the behind-the-scenes events accompanying the arrival of a major human achievement as we have in the Freud–Fliess correspondence. Jeffrey Masson, now the black beast of the international psychoanalytic community for his critique of psychoanalysis and of Freud, deserves credit for his successful effort to persuade Anna Freud to release the letters and for his editorial work in preparing the correspondence for publication. Perhaps the only other comparable record is Einstein's notebooks from the years 1907–15, recently released by his estate after decades of embargo similar to the embargoes that have existed and continue to exist around Freud's papers. In the case of Einstein we may now get a serious analysis and a new understanding of Einstein's most remarkable achievement, his theory of gravity.

In the case of Freud, the presence of such a record has not been without its hazards. Investigators have approached this archive with a number of different agendas and have not always asked of it questions that could add to our understanding of the creation and subsequent development of psychoanalysis. Unlike the case of Einstein, where the record is being pursued in an attempt to unravel the mystery of Einstein's extraordinary originality, approaches to the Freud archive have been informed by covert and overt attempts to discredit psychoanalysis, to attack Freud for his sins or equally to preserve Freud as a hero of the psychoanalytic movement.

The controversy surrounding Freud's abandonment of the so-called seduction hypothesis illustrates the lack of discipline with which the historical record has been approached. Terry Johnson's fine play, *Hysteria*, used Freud's letter to Fliess in which Freud says he no longer believes in his 'neurotica', as a highly effective dramatic device. Here was the turning point where we could see history being made. But the actual record does not permit such a simple reading.

One contentious point has been whether Freud really did abandon childhood sexual abuse as a real event. The temperature of these debates has been such that quote and misquote have been fired back and forth in a yes-he-did, no-he-didn't exchange without a serious reading of what is in fact a contradictory and incomplete record.

An examination of Freud's references to seduction in his complete works from 1905 to 1938 – a span of over thirty years – shows clearly that Freud did not abandon the reality of childhood sexual abuse. Throughout this period, Freud's writing repeatedly mentions seduction in an unforced way as being a part of the aetiology of mental disturbance as follows: certain conditions occurring 'either as a result of seduction or masturbation'; children can be 'led by influence of seduction'; conditions can be caused by the 'external influences of seduction'; a boy's attitude towards women 'had been disturbed by an early seduction'; 'The effect of seduction has long been familiar'; 'A girl who was made the subject of a sexual seduction'; common enough events 'such as the sexual abuse of children by adults, their seduction by other children (brothers and sisters) slightly their seniors'. Freud added two notes to a later edition of *Studies on Hysteria*, saying that his patients Katharina and Rosalia H. had been sexually abused by their fathers, not their uncles as he had previously reported. And in his discussion of female sexuality Freud clearly states:

Actual seduction too is common enough; it is initiated either by other children or by someone in charge of the child who wants to soothe it, or send it to sleep or make it dependent on them. Where seduction intervenes it invariably disturbs the natural course of the developmental processes and it often leaves behind extensive and lasting consequence.[6]

However, along with Freud's preference for dealing more with fantasy than with the psychopathological sequelae of real events also came a point of view that, while acknowledging the reality of sexual abuse, also substantially denied the existence of incest by fathers. Towards the beginning of their correspondence, Carl Jung wrote to Freud from the Burghölzli clinic asking for Freud's advice: 'At the moment I am treating a six year old girl for excessive masturbation and lying after alleged seduction by her foster father. Very complicated! Have you had experience with such small children?' (13 May 1907). Freud had. He was sure it was fantasy, and wrote back (23 May 1907): 'In your six year old girl, you surely must have discovered in the meantime that the attack is a fantasy that has become conscious, something which is regularly disclosed in analysis and which misled me into assuming the existence of generalised traumas in childhood.'

Freud's teaching on this matter is clearly expressed in his introductory lectures on psychoanalysis given in the two winter terms 1915–16 and 1916–17 at the Psychiatric Clinic of the University of Vienna. While acknowledging the reality of abuse in some cases, he gives explicit instructions to students that reports by women of sexual abuse by their fathers at an early age are usually fantasies and, further, that the difference between fantasized and real events of early abuse may not matter (Freud, 1916):

The fantasy of seduction has special interest, because only too often it is no fantasy but a real remembrance; fortunately, however, it is still not often as real as it seemed at first from the results of analysis. Seduction by children of the same age or older is more frequent than by adults; and when girls who bring forward this event in the story of their childhood fairly regularly introduce the father as the seducer, neither the fantastic character of this accusation nor the motive actuating it can be doubted. When no seduction has occurred, the fantasy is usually employed to cover the childhood period of auto-erotic sexual activity; the child evades feelings of shame about onanism by retrospectively attributing in fantasy a desired object to the earliest period. Do not suppose however that sexual misuse of children by the nearest male relatives is entirely derived from the world of fantasy; most analysts will have treated cases in which such occurrences actually took place and could be established beyond doubt; only then they belonged to later years of childhood and had been transposed to an earlier time.

All this seems to lead to but one impression, that childhood experiences of this kind are in some way necessarily required by the neurosis, that they belong to its unvarying inventory. If they can be found in real events, well and good; but if reality has not supplied them they will be evolved out of hints and elaborated by fantasy. The effect is the same, and even today we have not succeeded in tracing any variation in results according as fantasy or reality plays the greater part in these experiences. (p. 379)

Freud was bothered by this model for it left unanswered the question of where, if there were no real events, the fantasy came from. His answer is clearly strained. Freud brings in a hypothesized collective memory of the human race as a whole, a memory of a time when such practices were presumed to be widespread:

Whence comes the necessity for these fantasies, and the material for them? There can be no doubt about the instinctual sources; but how is it to be explained that the same fantasies are always formed with the same content?

I have an answer to this which I know will seem to you very daring. I believe that these *primal fantasies* (as I should like to name these, and certainly some others also) are a phylogenetic possession. In them the individual, whenever his own experience has been insufficient, stretches out beyond it to the experience of past ages. It seems to me quite possible that all that today is narrated in analysis in the form of fantasy, seduction in childhood, stimulation of sexual excitement upon observation of parental coitus, the threat of castration – or rather castration itself – was in prehistoric periods of the human family a reality; and that the child in fantasy simply fills out the gaps in its true individual experiences with true prehistoric experiences. We have again and again been led to suspect that more knowledge of primordial forms of human development is stored up for us in neuroses than in any other field we may explore. (p. 380)

It is clear that a significant part of human experience is denied by a view that equates reality and fantasy. Real events matter. A therapy that denies the role of the father, stepfather or, less frequently, the mother, as instigators of sexual activity with their children is a diminished therapy. The clinical issues, however, are complex. The events of cumulative abuse are highly elaborated in the fantasies of survivors where they serve as survival mechanisms. These can include fantasies of rescue, fantasies of the survivor herself being responsible for the abuse, fantasies of the vulnerable child getting 'just what she deserved'. Furthermore, modern clinical experience indicates that treating the real events as *only* fantasy can be welcomed by a survivor as an alternative to fears of retraumatization. Such a therapy can have a certain kind of positive result where survivors are supported in a denial of the real events, and thus permitted to integrate aspects of the traumatic experience in such a way as to allow them to love and to work (Davies and Frawley, 1992).

Historically then we have a clear picture of Freud's interests shifting over the period 1895–1900 towards interpretation of dreams, towards the new-found power of interpretation that was able, astonishingly, to make sense of incomprehensible symptoms.

An eleven-year-old boy had developed an elaborate bedtime ceremonial (Freud, 1896b). The boy needed to give his mother an exceptionally detailed description of his day. He needed to be sure that there were no bits of paper or other rubbish on his carpet. He needed to have his bed pushed up against the wall and have it surrounded with three chairs. The pillows had to lie in a special way. On getting into bed he needed to kick out with his legs a definite number of times and then he needed to lie on his side. How was such a distressing obsessional ritual to be understood?

Freud analysed these symptoms to uncover that years ago the boy had been sexually abused by a servant girl. Once the abuse was revealed, the meaning of the ceremonial could be decoded 'point by point'. The position of the chairs and bed was for protection, the arrangement of the pillows was so that they would be different from the arrangement when the abuse took place. The movement with the legs was a kicking away of his abuser and lying on his side was to avoid lying on his back as he had done when the abuse occurred. And the scraps of paper needed to be picked up to avoid any reproach from his mother (p. 172).

But at the same time that Freud was learning how to make sense of symptoms through exploring the mechanism of the repression of childhood experience, he was also rejecting what is now known to be the dominant mechanism for dealing with cumulative trauma – dissociation. Breuer had learned about dissociated mental states from Bertha Pappenheim. But Freud had dealt with the dissociated states that his patient Fanny Moser had presented as delirium and not as states of distinct altered consciousness that Breuer had called hypnoid states and that Janet had called dual consciousness (Bromberg, 1996). Having rejected Breuer's conception of hypnoid states, a vertical splitting of consciousness into two or more non-communicating parts, Freud had, by 1895, two years before the famous letter to Fliess, already set himself along a clinical path which would concentrate on cases involving repression, the suppression of memory from above (Freud, 1914, pp. 67–8). Freud was now making the exploration of the repressed contents of the unconscious the cornerstone of his interest in mental life.

The reason for such a choice could be analysed. But the history of psychoanalysis was affected far more by Freud's later recollections about his early work than in the actual shift itself. If one follows Freud from a theory of the unitary cause of hysteria lying in sexual abuse to a shift towards an interest in interpretation culminating in *The Interpretation of Dreams*, one can accept that Freud was entitled to develop his understanding and clinical practice in a way that suited his taste and temperament. And one can understand that once the emphasis was on interpretation and the decoding of symptoms, then new cases of those who had been sexually abused coming for therapy would encounter an approach that would concentrate on fantasy, a potentially far less threatening form of treatment than to re-encounter traumatic real events. Freud's subsequent views then can be seen historically as a limitation. As the first theorist of the analytic hour he, for complex reasons, found it more congenial to deal with repression rather than dissociated states.

But there is a further complication. As many commentators have pointed out, Freud found it necessary, in his historical accounts of his work, not only to distance himself from his work of 1895–1900, saying that he underestimated the effects of fantasy in comparison to real abuse, but also to add that his patients had not told him the truth. In his history of the psychoanalytic movement he said (Freud, 1914): 'Analysis had led back to these infantile sexual traumas by the right path yet they were not true' (pp. 17–18). In his autobiographical study he said (Freud, 1925): 'When, however, I was at last obliged to recognize that these scenes of seduction had never taken place, and that they were only fantasies which my patients had made up or which perhaps I had forced on them, I was for some time completely at a loss' (pp. 33–4). And in the 'New Introductory Lectures' written nine years later he wrote (Freud, 1933): '. . . almost all my women patients told me they had been seduced by their father. I was driven to recognize in the end that these reports were untrue and so came to understand that hysterical symptoms are derived from fantasies and not from real occurrences' (p. 120).

Succeeding generations may be forgiven for taking the above sentences as evidence that Freud had renounced his earlier papers dealing with the reality of child abuse, that he denied the truth of what he had been told by his patients in the period 1895–1900 and that, for a variety of reasons, he had turned his back on survivors of incest perpetrated by fathers. Jeffrey Masson (1984) has been prominent in putting forth this view based on his reading of the Freud–Fliess letters,

Freud's complete works, and strong evidence that Freud was quite *au courant* with the reality of child sexual abuse from his visits to the Paris morgue during his time in Paris. Masson suggests that Freud lost his nerve and found a safer harbour in dealing with repression and fantasy.

Other commentators (Cioffi,1988; Israels and Schatzman,1993) have taken seriously Freud's remark from his autobiographical study (1925) – 'or perhaps I had forced on them'. From a close reading of *The Aetiology of Hysteria* they have concluded that Freud's patients did not actually report scenes of abuse to him but that he inferred their existence indirectly – in other words, that Freud did impose stories of abuse on his patients in the first place. Their conclusion is that Freud was a scoundrel. To them to accuse one's patients of lying in this way is unconscionable.

A third view is the well-researched analysis of Marianne Krull (1979) who ties Freud's turning his back on the realities of seduction to the death of his father in 1896 and his difficulty in confronting in self-analysis the hints that there was improper sexual conduct between him and his own father.

A fourth view is that of Peter Swales (1989c) who, in his inimitable style, has traced the one single but significant reference made by Freud in 1907 to Johann Weier, a sixteenth-century writer on the persecution of witches. The reference is in a letter to Hugo Heller, editor of a journal on art and literature, who had requested from Freud a list of 'ten good books'. In Freud's response he questioned Heller's request for 'good' books, saying (E. Freud, 1960): 'Neither do you say, "the ten most significant books", in which case I should have to mention such scientific achievements as those of Copernicus, the old physician Johann Weier on witchcraft, Darwin's Descent of Man and so on' (p. 278). Weier argued in defence of women persecuted as witches that they had not committed witchcraft but only fantasized about it and Swales suggests that it was from reading Weier, probably in connection with his treatment of Emma Eckstein, that Freud became interested in the power of fantasy.

A fifth view has been suggested by Valerie Sinason (1994) who, from her own experience of the extreme difficulties of treating survivors of ritualized abuse, has suggested that Freud was overwhelmed by the feelings he experienced in his treatment of Emma Eckstein and other severely abused patients and turned his attention to less difficult and painful cases and subjects while never abandoning his belief in the reality of childhood sexual abuse.

A sixth view, the view of traditional classical psychoanalysis, as argued by Freud's biographer Ernest Jones and reproduced in the subsequent accounts of Freud's life by Ronald Clark and Peter Gay, is the view that accepted Freud's own statements that he had not seen actual cases of child abuse in the period 1895–1900 but only fantasies primarily invented to hide the shame of childhood masturbation (Jones, 1953; Clark, 1980; Gay, 1988).

A seventh view, related to the traditional view, is that of Henri Ellenberger (1970) who argued that Freud showed many of the symptoms of a 'creative illness' in the years 1895–1900, an illness which permitted him to break through the constraints of neurology to create a new theory of fantasy and its interpretation (pp. 447–50).

An eighth view is that of David Smith (1991), who argues that Freud was indeed seeing fantasies of sexual abuse but that they were not fantasies to cover past actions. Instead they were fantasies of abuse stimulated by Freud's technique, the use of the pressure of his hand on a patient's forehead to aid the patient's memory. Smith supports his arguments with a number of interesting quotes from Freud's papers of the period indicating that Freud himself may have entertained this possibility.

A ninth view is that of Lloyd deMause (1991) who argues that Freud never denied the reality of the remembered stories of sexual abuse he had heard. Instead, because of his theory of repression as the causal factor in mental illness, he was led to pursue his patients for forgotten scenes of *infantile* sexual abuse. For deMause, one of the leading scholars of the maltreatment of children, Freud correctly abandoned his theory of infantile sexual abuse while never denying the reality of remembered abuse. In the Fliess letter of 28 April 1897 about the woman who 'was made wet' by her father, Freud indicates that he was routinely expecting to find earlier forgotten incidents. 'Of course when I told her that similar and worse things must have happened in her earliest childhood she could not find it incredible.' Leopold Löwenfeld, a colleague of Freud, reported in 1899 that a patient of his who had been in treatment with Freud had only fantasized the infantile sexual scenes he had told to Freud (Masson, 1984): 'The patient told me with certainty that the infantile sexual scene which analysis had apparently uncovered was pure fantasy and had never really happened to him' (p. 413).

Is it possible to synthesize these various viewpoints to form a definitive picture of Freud and his motivations?

The difficulties in forming a decisive analysis of what was going on for Freud in 1895–1900 should not be underestimated. First is the question of so-called palaeo-diagnosis, or trying to arrive at a modern understanding of what clinicians have seen in the past. Writers hostile to psychoanalysis have insisted that Freud was seeing purely organic disturbances such as Tourette's syndrome. With the exception of Anna O., whose sanatorium records were unearthed by Henri Ellenberger, we do not have detailed records of psychiatric treatments let alone records of psychoanalytic sessions. So it is difficult to know with the degree of certainty one might wish what Freud was seeing in his early cases. Nevertheless the explicit details of sexual abuse that Freud disclosed to Fliess would not seem to be plausibly accounted for by suggestion. It would seem, then, that deMause is closest to the mark – that what Freud later disowned were scenes of *infantile* sexual abuse.

But then the question arises of why Freud found it necessary later in life to deny quite so thoroughly the reality of the real scenes of abuse he had described to Fliess in the years 1895–7 without offering this important clarification – that he was referring only to infantile sexual abuse. Here again we are on uncertain ground. The forcefulness with which Freud later asserted that all the stories he heard in these years were not true seems bizarre. He could have written his account emphasizing his turning away from Breuer's hypnoid states, his interest in the possibilities opened up by what he learned about interpretation from Anna von Lieben, his excitement on realizing that dreams would yield in a new and exciting way to this technique, his growing interest in fantasy and in childhood sexuality, without giving such an ambivalent signal about the reality of the vignettes he actually reported. Such an account would be a sufficient story.

But that is not what Freud did. Freud rejected Breuer, not at the level of allowing differences between them, but by declaring Breuer's characterization of dual conscious states *all* wrong. It was not enough to develop an exciting new approach to the interpretation of dreams, *all* dreams had to have as their driving force an unfulfilled wish. It was not enough to investigate childhood fantasy and sexuality and in so doing bring the subjectivity of children on to the world stage, *all* child memories of sexual abuse by fathers had to be fantasies. It was not enough for some of the stories he had heard from clients in the years 1895–7 possibly to have been forced, *all* the stories he heard were untrue. This was Freud, a man, in Breuer's words, with a strong taste for 'absolute and exclusive formulations; that is a psychic need which drives him, in my opinion, to huge generalizations' (Acker-knecht, 1957).

Given that this was Freud, what is it that we would like to know from the historical record? One possibility would be to try to synthesize the conflicting views about Freud's motivations in the period of his first theories, 1896–1900. If one approaches this record without malice or hero worship, there does seem room to accommodate virtually every reading. Freud was an ambitious scientist with an exceptional interest in theory. Above all he sought understanding of what he was seeing. Although retaining an interest in the dissociated states characterized by Breuer as hypnoid, his theoretical interests moved more to understanding repression, an interest, as Krull emphasizes, that ran parallel to an effort to understand himself. Freud was now forty, and his grand theory of hysteria, based on the single aetiological agent of repressed memories of infantile sexual abuse, had not worked out. At the same time he had the highly intriguing method of interpret-ation before him, a method that was letting him make sense not only of symptoms but of slips of the tongue, forgotten names, dreams and, above all, his own psyche. This would be the promising new scientific direction to take. In addition, like Breuer before him with Anna O., he was exhausted by the emotional demands of his clinical practice in the period when Breuer was sending him the most difficult, unwanted cases of hysteria.

The pressures for change were there – a push out of clinical work with the most distressed, difficult patients and a pull towards an entirely new frontier of understanding dreams and normal psychology.

Did Freud possibly induce his sexually abused clients to fantasize scenes of infantile abuse under the influence of the pressure technique as suggested by David Smith? We cannot rule this conjecture out. Nor is it too much to believe that his desire for success and recognition might have been a factor in his move away from the dissociated states accompanying sexual abuse to, as he put it, more normal psychology. The question of whether this represented a failure of nerve, as argued by Masson, cannot be resolved without further documentation which we may never have. Was possible sexual abuse by his father a factor as suggested by Marianne Krull? Her insightful use of Freud's dreams to support her argument is highly suggestive but, without the support of the dreamer himself, must remain conjectural. Was Freud a scoundrel, as argued by Cioffi, Israels and Schatzman, for accusing his patients of lying to him about scenes of infantile sexual abuse that he himself had suggested? Well, yes, there would seem to be something less than attractive about Freud's later accounts of his early clinical experience, and he did substantially deny the role of fathers as perpetrators in his later writings.

In fact, the development of psychoanalysis was affected by the change in Freud's interests over the period 1895–1900. The psychological sequelae to the trauma of repeated childhood abuse – dissociated states, the importance of real events, the treatment of so-called borderline conditions and of psychosis – took a back seat to an exploration of fantasy life and a dynamics originating in sexuality and the Oedipal triangle. In addition, Freud's emphasis on trying to learn from psychopathology as much as he could about general human psychology meant that homosexuality tended to become pathologized and the psychology of women could not be approached with the openness necessary to address adequately the reality of women's experience in patriarchal society, an inadequacy well illustrated by the superficial anatomical metaphor used to describe female envy of male privilege.

All this is an integral part of the history of psychoanalysis. But it is a serious mistake to attribute the inadequacies of psychoanalysis in its early years to the personality of Freud. What we require from the historical record is help in understanding how Freud's leadership was exercised, how it was challenged, how those challenges were handled, how alternative strands to classical psychoanalysis originated and developed. It is not Freud's personality that is the issue in an attempt to understand the development of psychoanalysis but the responses to his personality in the settings in which they occurred. The history of psychoanalysis is not the history of Sigmund Freud. It is an institutional history shaped by Freud's leadership but not determined by it. We now need to consider how psychoanalysis dealt with its internal and external tensions in the years 1900–14.

5

First Splits

When the stakes are high enough, disputes in knowledge disciplines can attain mythological status. The trial of Galileo in 1632 and the Huxley–Wilberforce debate about Darwinian evolution in 1860 are legendary episodes in the grand forward march of science. At the other end of the spectrum, disputes rest as forgotten footnotes to history as in the century-long dispute over Newton's versus Leibniz's notation for the operations of the calculus. Or disputes can be remembered as a significant but not central branch of Western history as in the famous dispute over the nature of combustion – whether something was added (oxygen) or something was taken away (phlogiston) during burning.

The personalities of the disputants, differing access to or membership in the elites of the discipline, different degrees of perceived importance of the dispute to the society at large, and the role of special interests or larger class or institutional forces combine to give every dispute over knowledge claims a distinctive character.

In the case of the famous splits in psychoanalysis in the years 1911–13, associated with the names of Sigmund Freud, Alfred Adler and Carl Jung, a new element entered. For the first time the unconscious motives of the participants became an open part of the dispute. With varying degrees of sophistication, the participants analysed not each other's arguments but their reasons for making them. Jung criticized Freud's neurotic inability to acknowledge religious and spiritual feelings. Adler argued that Freud's emphasis on the fundamental role of sexuality in the aetiology of the neuroses was a product of Freud's own personal experience. Freud and his supporters understood both Adler's and Jung's defections as transference re-enactments to Freud:

in Adler's case he was seen as relating to Freud as a paranoid brother; in Jung's case he was seen as relating to Freud as a seductive son. As in most disputes of historical importance, the substantive issues between the three men reflected divisions in the society at large.

Dividing Freud and Adler was the fundamental question of human action: are we masters of our fate or do we act out of instinctual conflicts of which we are largely unaware? Adler, informed by his personal and clinical experience, felt certain that human beings do create their world. In his view, we do things not *because of* but *in order to*. Freud could not accept Adler's view of the centrality of human agency in light of his experience of the unconscious motivation in human affairs.

In the case of Freud and Jung, the fundamental disagreement was a re-enactment of the conflict between modern Western science and traditional Western spirituality. Jung in his recollections (1961) described Freud's passionate efforts to recruit him in the fight against 'the black tide of occultism'. Freud's strength of feeling indicated to Jung that Freud had closed his mind to anything that philosophy and religion, 'including the rising contemporary science of parapsychology', could offer about human psychology (p. 173). In 1929 Jung wrote that Freud refused to accept that God was his father, and in his autobiography characterized Freud's scientific outlook as a 'materialist prejudice'.

Jung took a classic position in opposition to the materialism of Western science by insisting that nothing could exist unless it was perceived (Jung, 1961): 'We are still a long way from understanding what it signifies that nothing has any existence unless some small – and oh so transitory – consciousness has become aware of it' (pp. 177–8). Such a sensibility is anathema to modern science which is based on the fact that the world exists whether or not there is any conscious awareness of it. To Freud, Jung's perspective smacked of the very superstitions that modern science had long since rejected, a legacy of the oppressive medieval doctrines that had persecuted scientists from Galileo to Darwin.

All three men were exceptional clinicians, in every account capable of sensitive attunement to the experiences of their patients. The forms their respective understandings took were outwardly irreconcilable, but the experiences on which they were based, the separate parts of human psychology to which each responded strongly, cannot be discarded without impoverishing our understanding of human inner life. Adler's defection left Freud's psychoanalysis without a way to understand how human beings could have purpose, a gap that was not addressed until the 1930s. Jung's defection left Freud's psychoanalysis without a way to understand the collective psychological experience of the human race and without a way to approach the social-psychological formation of the human subject – a gap that was not addressed until after the Second World War.

Alfred Adler was born in 1870 in Penzing, a rural northern suburb of Vienna, not far from Schönbrunn Castle. His paternal grandfather was a furrier, his father a grain merchant, his uncle a tailor. The family kept farm animals including horses, cows and goats. Adler was the second of six children; he had an accomplished older brother named Sigmund, a figure frequently cited as being important in the development of Adler's concept of inferiority. The family moved several times but except for four years from 1877–81, when the family fortunes declined and the family was forced to live in the Jewish quarter of Leopoldstadt, always lived in the northern and western suburbs of Vienna where there were few Jewish families.

The young Adler played with the gangs of gentile children of mixed class backgrounds in the vacant lots on the outskirts of Vienna. According to Carl Furtmüller (1946), Adler's close friend and colleague, Adler grew up unencumbered by the endemic anti-Semitism of late nineteenth-century Vienna. Adler converted to Protestantism in 1904. His younger brothers Max and Richard converted to Catholicism.

Adler attended the gymnasium and entered the medical school of the University of Vienna in the winter of 1888. His university records show that he took only the required subjects, passing his three Rigorosa with the grade of *sufficient* – the lowest passing mark. In 1895, in between his second and third Rigorosa he worked in the Department of Ophthalmology of the Vienna Poliklinik, founded in 1871 by Moritz Benedikt to provide free medical care for working-class people. He was an interested observer of the student political scene at the university, where he aligned himself with socialist groups whose inter-nationalism was in opposition to the anti-Semitic nationalism of the far right and the liberal pan-German nationalism of the centre-right. At these meetings he met Raissa Timofeyevna Epstein, daughter of a Jewish merchant from Moscow and Smolensk, and a former student at the University of Zürich. The couple married on 23 December 1897. Their first child was born the following August, their second three years later. Two other children followed in 1905 and 1909.

Adler was interested in social medicine and established his practice in the Praterstrasse, a Jewish, lower-middle-class neighbourhood. His patients included employees at the Prater amusement park – the acrobats and trapeze artists of the shows – who came to him with concerns about job-threatening physical ailments and perceived physical weaknesses.

In 1898 he published a popular monograph on the occupational health and safety of garment workers. The *Health Book for the Tailor Trade* was the fifth in an occupational health series edited by Dr G. Golebiewski in Berlin, a leading specialist in the field. Adler's contribution to the series showed first-hand knowledge of the conditions of garment workers at the time, perhaps gained from his uncle David, the tailor, and his grandfather Simon, the furrier, and called for new labour laws to bring relief to this unregulated sector, including provisions for sick leave, accident and unemployment insurance, pensions, a forty-eight-hour week, an elimination of piece-work, and adequate housing and eating places. In so doing, he aligned himself with working-class interests against a medical establishment that denied the presence of social and environmental factors as causal agents in the incidence of disease (Dembe, 1996).

Over the next six years he argued for increased medical care for the poor, for preventive medicine, for teaching and research posts for social medicine and social hygiene. He proposed an increased role for the physician as an educator for children and made suggestions for dealing with the perceived problems of masturbation, sexual excess and homosexuality, citing Freud on the importance of early experience and childhood sexuality (Ellenberger, 1970). And in response to the quite revolutionary advances in bacteriology that so impressed the young Freud, Adler stressed not prophylaxis against bacteria as in immunization but prophylaxis against the conditions which permitted bacteria to breed.

In the polemics surrounding the Adler–Freud controversy, Adler's political concerns have frequently been cited as having clouded his clinical judgement. The annotated edition of the Minutes of the Vienna Psychoanalytic Society states (Nunberg and Federn, 1962): 'Adler was a socialist and a member of the Austrian Social Democratic Party; in later life, his scientific views became greatly influenced by his political beliefs' (p. xxxiii). Jones stated years later in his autobiography (Jones, 1959): 'Like many Jewish doctors in Vienna, [Adler] was a Socialist by political conviction, and moreover of the type whose views were based on a sense of social inferiority, with consequent envy and resentment, than on more objective grounds. He came to psychoanalysis attracted by the stress it laid on the suppression of personal wishes, and hoping to get from it some scientific support for his Socialist strivings' (p. 217).

Adler's sympathies were with the working-class movement, but he was never politically involved. Compared to other psychoanalysts, such as the active Social Democrats Paul Federn and Carl Furtmüller, and the elected Social Democratic Vienna Councillor Josef Friedjung, Adler was actually apolitical. And in contrast to analysts of the younger generation, such as Otto Fenichel, who became the leader of the left opposition within psychoanalysis, Wilhelm Reich, founder in 1928 of the Socialist Society for Sexual Consultation and Sexual Research in Vienna, Ernst Simmel, president of the Society of Socialist Physicians and editor of the *Socialist Doctor* from 1926–30 in Berlin, or Edith Jacobson and Muriel Gardiner, who risked their lives in the anti-Nazi underground in the 1930s, Adler positively opposed organized political action.

Adler came to feel that solutions to political problems lay not in a struggle for power but in renouncing power in favour of educating the psyche to have social feelings. His motto was: 'Only a better individual can make a better system' (Bottome, 1939, p. 62). He opposed the Bolshevik revolution in Russia where his friend and former patient A. A. Joffe had become a major official. In 1918, Adler founded the famous free Child Guidance Clinics, which gained institutional support from the ruling Social Democrats in the Red Vienna of the 1920s. The experience gained in these clinics crossed the Atlantic Ocean in the flight from the Nazis notably to the Wiltwyck

School for Boys outside New York City, where Ernst Papanek, a leading Adlerian educator in Vienna, worked with the young Claude Brown whose book, *Manchild in the Promised Land*, about growing up in Harlem, was a US bestseller in the early 1960s.

Freud and Adler were polar opposites. Furtmüller (1946) recounts how Freud was always well groomed, with a neatly trimmed beard, 'masterful and elegant' in his speech and even in small groups having the ability to speak both informally and with great authority at the same time. In contrast, 'Adler was always the "common man", nearly sloppy in his appearance, careless of cigarette ashes dropping on his sleeve or waistcoat, oblivious of outer prestige of all kinds, artless in his way of speaking although knowing very well how to drive his points home' (p. 346). At university, Adler had been only a mediocre student with a strong interest in medicine. Freud had been a superior student with a strong interest in research. Adler immediately became a practising physician for the poor; Freud had an elite scientific training, working in a leading laboratory before being forced eventually to take up medical practice.

Adler's milieu was the socialists and revolutionary intellectuals of Vienna. He was a frequent visitor to the Sunday evening open house organized by Carl Furtmüller's wife, Aline Klatschko Furtmüller, the daughter of Russian revolutionaries. Ernst Federn, son of Paul Federn, a close member of Freud's analytic circle, remembered the pre-war Furtmüller Sunday evenings from his childhood (Adler, 1965): 'I remember these meetings, and Carl Furtmüller, who was a man of caustic wit and great intelligence. Aline Furtmüller was a close friend of my mother, but the split between Adler and Freud severed the relationship. We children did not carry on this feud. On the contrary we were very close until the Nazis separated us' (p. 325).

Freud's milieu was the intellectual and social elite of Vienna, whose social focus was the soirées at the aristocratic home of Josephine von Werthheimstein, Anna von Lieben's aunt. There Fleischl put chickens and crayfish into trances and Werthheimstein's brother, the philosopher Theodor Gomperz, entertained not only Meynert, Breuer and Fleischl, but also Freud's philosophy teacher, the famous Franz Brentano, the musician Anton Rubinstein, the playwright Eduard von Bauernfeld, and the poet Hugo von Hofmannsthal. Although liberal in sentiment, the Werthheimsteins found thoughts of the impoverished masses difficult to bear. As Emilie Exner, wife of Sigmund Exner of Brücke's laboratory and a Werthheimstein intimate, wrote in 1907 (Barea, 1966): 'The mere contact with sickness or misery caused them psychological and physical pain' (p. 298).

The elitism that can be said to have characterized Freud's milieu extended to his psychoanalytic practice and his inner circle. In a lecture for doctors about psychotherapy, Freud recommended refusing for treatment 'patients who do not possess a reasonable degree of education', stating (Freud, 1905b): 'It must not be forgotten that there are healthy people as well as unhealthy people who are good for nothing in life' (p. 263). In a textbook (1910), written in close consultation with Freud, Eduard Hitschmann expressed similar sentiments about who was suitable for psychoanalysis: '. . . a certain degree of natural intelligence and ethical development is necessary; with worthless persons, the interest of the physician which strengthens him for delving into the mental life of the patient soon wanes' (p. 206). In 1916, Freud dismissed his own introductory lectures on psychoanalysis as 'crude stuff meant for the masses' (Pfeiffer, 1972, p. 48). In a 1923 encyclopedia article he wrote (Freud, 1923a): '. . . since [psychoanalysis] necessitates the devotion of long and intense attention to the individual patient, it would be uneconomical to squander such expenditure upon completely worthless persons who happen to be neurotic' (p. 250). The analyst Richard Sterba (1982) recalled the value placed in Freud's circle on being a *gescheiter Mensch* – a clever person capable of deep insight into situations and relationships as well as having a wide knowledge of many subjects. An analyst such as August Aichhorn, with his lower-middle-class accent, who was 'only a school teacher', felt himself to be marginalized in Freud's group.

In contrast, Adler took on all comers from his base near the Prater, addressing himself to their concerns without reservation. A study of the class and status of Freud's and Adler's patients showed that out of sixty-seven citations in Freud's published cases 74 per cent were wealthy, 23 per cent were middle class and 3 per cent were poor. Out of forty-three citations in Adler's papers the figures were 25 per cent, 40 per cent, and 35 per cent respectively (Wasserman, 1950; 1958).

When Adler encountered Freud's work in 1899 he had well-developed interests in social medicine, nervous diseases and the psychology of physical ailments and perceived physical inferiorities. But although their interests and social surroundings were very different, the twenty-nine-year-old Adler found in the forty-three-year-old Freud a kindred spirit – an experienced physician who was exploring the psychological origins of physical ailments. As Adler recalled his first encounter with Freud's work (Adler, 1965):

I remember very well when as a young student and medical man I was very worried and discontented with the state of psychiatry and tried to discover other ways, and found Freud was courageous enough actually to go another way and explore the psychological reasons for physical disturbances and for neuroses. (p. 218)

On 2 November 1902, Freud wrote to Adler inviting him to join an informal discussion group to be held in his house in the Bergasse (AdlP):

Dear Colleague,

A small circle of colleagues and supporters afford me the great pleasure of coming to my house once a week in the evening (8:30 PM after dinner) to discuss interesting topics in psychology and neuropathology. I know Reitler, Max Kahane, and Stekel will come. Would you be so kind as to join us? We are meeting next Thursday and I await your reply whether you would like to come and whether Thursday evening suits you.

The discussion group that Adler joined was to be called the Wednesday Psychological Society. The first members of the group were Freud, Adler, Wilhelm Stekel, Max Kahane and Rudolf Reitler. Stekel had consulted Freud for a brief psychotherapy (Stekel, 1950). Kahane was director of an out-patient clinic for psychotherapy in the Bauernmarkt, and Reitler directed a thermal therapy centre in the Dorotheergasse (Shorter, 1992). To make the discussion egalitarian, members' names were drawn by lot from an urn so that everyone had an obligation to speak.

The meetings of the Wednesday Psychological Society enabled Freud to exercise his leadership. For interested parties it was a chance to explore with Freud an entirely new approach to questions and problems that had bothered clinicians for generations. In discussion of the much-argued-about harmfulness of masturbation the key question for the new psychoanalysis was not the possible physiological harm of the act but the psychic function it served. Freud pointed out sardonically that masturbation was taking the rap for the fact that the dominant culture viewed all forms of sex as dangerous (v. 1, pp. 560–7). In the case of men suffering paedophilic attraction to young girls, the frank acceptance of childhood sexuality meant that the question for psychoanalysis was not what caused some men to have a sexual interest in children but what fixed the development of the sexual interest of some men at an early age (v. 1, p. 88). In a discussion of childhood suicide, prompted by a major statistical survey that had absolved schools of any blame, the new psychoanalysis saw childhood suicide as an exit from an inner conflict about approaching adulthood. Schools could make a difference by recognizing that this transition period required attention to the student's need for understanding and love, as well as having a sympathetic understanding of the hostile transference reactions students could have towards their teacher (v. 2, pp. 479–506). Freud argued further that sadism became a feature of the teenage educational landscape because teachers felt themselves to be inadequate to the emotional demands of their students, an inadequacy that had its roots in the bigotry against homosexuality:

In suppressing the practice of homosexuality, one has simply also suppressed the homosexual direction of human feelings that is so necessary for our society. The best teachers are the real homosexuals, who actually have a benevolent superiority toward their pupils. If however a teacher with repressed homosexuality comes face to face with this demand he becomes sadistic toward the boys; these teachers hate and persecute the children because they make those 'sexual demands' thereby irritating the teachers' sexuality. Just as the homosexuals are the best teachers, so the repressed homosexuals are the worst, and the strictest. (pp. 495–6)

This new psychology in the making included analyses of hysterical vomiting, compulsive blushing, compulsive doubt, lying, the psychology of the only child and of mother love, as well as discussion of difficult cases such as those of functional impotence, spasms of the glottis, and of a man who as a child was forced to urinate into his tutor's mouth. Freud understood from his research experience the value of collaborative work and he succeeded in creating in the Wednesday meetings a laboratory where psychoanalysis could develop in a sustained and concentrated way.

His leadership was taxed by an intoxication with interpretation on the part of his junior colleagues which drove contemporaries to distraction and which, in spite of its impressive beginnings, laid psychoanalysis open to ridicule, disbelief and marginalization. In spite of Freud's efforts to restrain his junior colleagues from playing fast and loose with the new technique, they could not resist. Suddenly, through analytic interpretation, the whole world could yield its secrets. To interpret was to understand.

On 1 September 1906, the Russian revolutionary Tatjana Leontiev tried to kill Peter Durnovo, one of the most hated of vicious czarist officials, while he was holidaying in the Hotel Jungfrau in the Swiss resort town of Interlaken. By mistake she killed another man, Charles Müller, who resembled Durnovo (Baynac, 1985). At the meeting of the Wednesday Society of 10 April 1907, Fritz Wittels proposed an analysis of Leontiev's action that was a parody of psychoanalytic interpretation. The new dress that Leontiev wore was interpreted by Wittels as a preparation for a symbolic sexual act carried out with a Browning revolver – 'a well known symbol of the male genitalia' – ignoring the fact that her attempt was carried out at a luxury hotel where appropriate dress was required. When it was put to Leontiev that her intended target had different hair and beard from the man she killed, she responded that hair and beard can be changed. This was then interpreted by Wittels as an indication of paranoia. And when, subjected to a body search, she spat at the authorities, this action was explained as a symbolic attempt by Leontiev to be a virgin.

Freud strongly opposed the clever-clever reductionism of this kind of analysis.

One must not condemn the assassins so harshly and unmask them because of unconscious motives. The harshness of such a judgement would be repulsive.

Rather a certain tolerance is required towards these hidden emotions. The unconscious motive deserves forbearance. (p. 164)

At a previous meeting on 5 May 1909, Freud had had to deliver a scathing denunciation of Isidor Sadger who attempted to put the famous writer Heinrich von Kleist (1777–1811) metaphorically on the couch. Kleist, a dramatic poet concerned with the unreliability of reason, a prominent theme for Romantic writers and poets attempting to come to grips with modern science, had killed himself at the age of thirty-four. Freud rejected Sadger's overemphasis on sexuality, his intolerance of human affliction – 'a second repellent aspect of his paper', and his superficiality – 'All we can see is that Kleist, one of the most creative poets in our literature, was at certain periods of his life an awkward boy; aside from that, we were shown which sexual aberrations he had.' Mentioning similar weaknesses in a previous analysis of Franz Grillparzer by Stekel, Freud said: 'The general public is right in rejecting this type of analysis.' And in discussions of clinical work, Freud repeatedly urged caution, emphasizing that there was all the difference in the world between occasional and repeated symbols, that these matters were delicate and that interpretation as such required caution and tact.[1]

If Freud was exasperated by the lack of restraint of his Viennese colleagues in their private discussions, he had even less reason to be pleased with their public performances. Live debates about psycho-analysis were coloured by breathtaking insults delivered by the defenders of psychoanalysis. When the Hamburg neurologist Ernst Trömner read a paper about sleep at the 1910 Congress of the Inter-national Society for Medical Psychology, Leonard Seif rose and said that he had a piece of advice for Trömner – to read the *Interpretation of Dreams*. The following year, when Trömner read a paper on dreams, this time extensively quoting the *Interpretation of Dreams*, Seif rose again and said that he was glad that Trömner had taken his advice but that he had another piece of advice for him – to read it again (Jones to Freud, 17 October 1911).

At the International Congress of Medicine held in Budapest in 1909 the Frankfurt psychiatrist Adolf Albrecht Friedländer criticized psychoanalysts with a bill of particulars, citing Isidor Sadger as an exemplar, for their confrontational behaviour at conferences, their lack of courtesy, and their failure to acknowledge prior sources, all of which combined to produce what he not inaccurately called 'an orthodoxy freed from all timidity' (Friedländer, 1911).

But Freud found it difficult to impose discipline on his supporters. Feeling isolated and embattled in Vienna – professionally by colleagues who were repulsed by psychoanalysis in general and the sexual aetiology of the neuroses in particular, and socially as a Jew in the increasingly anti-Semitic climate of Vienna. He needed all the allies he could get. Anti-Semitism in Central Europe was to have an important role in shaping the development of psychoanalysis for the next two generations.

In 1902 over half of Vienna's population had not been born in Vienna, the result of a wave of immigration over the previous fifty years that had included Freud's parents. This grouping of immigrant workers, concentrated in the 16th district of Vienna, formed the social base of Austrian social democracy. On the other side of the political divide was the Viennese petit bourgeoisie who formed the lower-middle-class base of support for an elected anti-Semitic city administration headed by Karl 'The-small-man-must-be-helped' Lueger of the Christian Social Party.[2]

Anti-Semitism, as in the Viennese joke 'a book is simply what one Jew copies from another' (Steiner, 1997), was a routine part of Viennese life and, as it proved, easily exploited politically. Lueger simultaneously attacked both social democracy and the big capitalist enterprises as being Jewish conspiracies. The Christian Social Party and its militants attempted to divert city funds to construct Catholic churches; the Vienna Municipal School Board attempted to segregate Jewish and Christian children in a pilot programme in ten of the city's 399 public schools and in 1898 tried to make the Kaiser-Jubilaums-Stadtheater an Aryan theatre. The *Christian Family Society* had chapters numbering between 100 and 400 members in all nineteen Viennese districts and had organized a boycott of Jewish shops with Lueger's slogan 'Kauft nur bei Christen' [Only buy from Christians], a tactic keenly observed by the young Adolf Hitler and copied twenty years later in Nazi Germany (Boyer, 1995).

Freud was acutely aware of his anti-Semitic surroundings. In 1910 seven Hamburg neurologists, including Ernst Trömner the sleep specialist, announced that they were going to boycott sanatoriums that used psychoanalysis as part of their treatment. Even though they felt there was value in Freud's concepts of repression and abreaction and in a limited applicability of the sexual origins of hysteria, they justified their action by objecting to the exclusive sexual aetiology of neurosis, a belief they held to arise from the degenerate sensuality of the Viennese (anon., 1910). Freud wrote to Ferenczi about the anti-Semitic implications of this move:

Among the latest attacks, the letter about the session in Hamburg is note-worthy. There they make the argument I had wanted to deflect by moving to Zurich, namely that Viennese sensuality can't be found elsewhere! You can still read between the lines that we Viennese are not only pigs but also Jews. (24 April 1910)

Freud hoped to solve his problem of the superficiality of the Viennese analysts and his problem of anti-Semitism at one stroke by moving the centre of psychoanalysis away from what he saw as the Jewish-dominated Vienna group to Protestant Germanic Switzerland. The Swiss Protestant psychiatrist Carl Jung, working at the prestigious Burghölzli Mental Hospital in Zurich where he had earned an inter-national reputation for innovations in psychiatry, would be the man to take over the intellectual and institutional leadership of psycho-analysis. On 3 May 1908 Freud wrote to Karl Abraham in Berlin telling him to moderate his criticism of Jung because Jung was the only Christian in the movement: '. . . it was only by his appearance on the scene that psychoanalysis escaped the danger of becoming a Jewish national affair'. On 13 August 1908 Freud stated his intentions to Jung just before he was to visit him in Zurich:

My selfish purpose, which I frankly confess, is to persuade you to continue and complete my work by applying to psychoses what I have begun with neuroses. With your strong and independent character, with your Germanic blood which enables you to command the sympathies of the public more readily than I, you seem better fitted than anyone else I know to carry out this mission. Besides I am fond of you but I have learned to subordinate that factor.

Jung was flattered to have won Freud's confidence and his love. But more senior colleagues than Jung saw that the fight to establish psychoanalysis could only be led by Freud himself. On 19 October 1910, Jung's superior, Eugen Bleuler, the Director of the Burghölzli and a distinguished senior figure in Swiss psychiatry, wrote to Freud explaining his reasons for not wanting to join the newly formed International Psycho-analytic Association (Alexander and Selesnick, 1965):

For you evidently it became the aim and interest of your whole life to establish firmly your theory and to secure its acceptance. I certainly do not underestimate your work. One compares it with that of Darwin, Copernicus and Semmelweis. I believe too that for psychology your discoveries are equally fundamental as the theories of those men are for other branches of science, no matter whether or not one evaluates advancements in psychology as highly as those in other sciences. The latter is a matter of subjective opinion. For me, the theory is only one new truth among other truths. I stand up for it because I consider it valid and because I feel that I am able to judge it since I am working in a related field. But for me it is not a major issue whether the validity of these views will be recognized a few years sooner or later. I am therefore less tempted than you to sacrifice my whole personality for the advancement of the cause. (p. 5)

Freud had been aware of Bleuler's reservations for some time, but he was unable to see further than the tactical implications of Bleuler's reticence. Four days later, on 23 October 1910, he wrote to Jung that it would be worth an as yet unknown sacrifice to keep Bleuler's support in order to prevent a widening of the gap between psychoanalysis and the psychiatric profession. Freud and Bleuler met that Christmas in Munich where they argued amicably all Christmas Day and Freud succeeded in getting him to join the Zurich branch of the Association. But Bleuler had understood the dynamics of the psychoanalytic movement. In spite of the apparent reconciliation he formally withdrew from the Zurich Society the following November while still desiring to remain on friendly terms with Freud.

Another friend who wished to keep a certain distance was the French Swiss psychologist Edouard Claparède, successor to his cousin Théodore Flournoy as Professor of Psychology at the University of

Geneva and later supervisor of the young Jean Piaget. Claparède attended the 1908 International Psychoanalytical Congress in Salzburg but remained an interested outsider and relatively impartial to the internal and external disputes that accompanied the establishment of the new psychology. In his autobiography he described, without rancour, his unsuccessful attempt to relate his own work to that of Freud (Murchison, 1930): 'When Freud's work appeared, I thought that the best way to explain his libido would be to identify it with "interest". But Freud did not agree.' Claparède's introduction (1926) to the first French translation of Freud's *Five Lectures on Psychoanalysis* summarized, again without rancour and without adulation, Freud's importance for psychology:

Freud's doctrines, which were just then beginning to be widely diffused, and which Flournoy and I received with great sympathy, though without any exaggerated enthusiasm, confirmed in me my conviction of the importance of the years of childhood for the subsequent destiny of the individual. (p. 87)

On the question of the future of psychology Claparède asked: 'Will psychology have its Einstein? Anyhow it has its Binet and Freud' (p. 96).

The organizational problems Freud encountered in trying to create an institutional base for the development of psychoanalysis were similar to those faced by voluntary political groups. Leadership in voluntary groups is not supported by an established hierarchy, participation in the groups is optional and there are none of the usual sanctions that can be applied to impose discipline or assert prerogatives of authority. Unless the majority of the participants is unusually experienced and the aims of the project so compelling that personal disputes are easily managed by appeal to the common purpose, leadership becomes a stressful matter that rarely can be exercised with the necessary tact and understanding for more than a short period of time. The result is the well-known tendency of voluntary groups to oscillate between the extremes of a tyranny of leadership and a tyranny of leaderlessness.

In the case of psychoanalysis, the members of the Viennese Wednesday Psychological Society were drawn to a theory of human psychology that arose out of well-established problems of the time. Edouard

Claparède and Eugen Bleuer had little difficulty in appraising and accepting the results of psychoanalysis in the light of their own professional experience. It is, therefore, nonsense to argue that psychoanalysis was isolated from the mainstream.

But psychoanalysis lacked an institutional framework to support it. Indeed, as Henri Ellenberger has suggested, Freud's eventual success in creating such a framework – an international training and membership organization existing entirely outside conventional medical and educational institutions – is perhaps the most astonishing of his achievements. However, in the period 1902–14, psychoanalysis was a weak, voluntary organization united only by the interest of its members in the ideas of psychoanalysis, an interest which varied greatly in depth and intensity from one member to another.

Leadership in such a heterogeneous grouping is necessarily indirect. Freud was the professor, but he was a professor without department or clinic. Those wanting to work with him did so voluntarily for as long as it suited them. Potential members of the Wednesday Psychological Society could be screened, but once accepted neither Freud nor anyone else in the Society had the authority to discipline them for their interpretive excesses or for their antagonistic behaviour at conferences. Freud's cautionary admonitions to get on with the work and leave the rest of the profession alone fell on deaf ears.

The institutional weakness of psychoanalysis produced a defensive intolerance of opposing points of view in many, even the most able, while at the same time leaving other members chafing at the bit of what leadership Freud could exert. In the meantime, Freud wanted psychoanalysis to develop, not in a diversity of directions, that would have required an institutional security that was not available, but through personal loyalty to him and his vision of psychoanalysis. To Freud, a good leader was one who knew how to attract and bind people to him. Freud, in attempting to create a secure base for the development of psychoanalysis, could only hear ambivalence in Bleuler's reservations. There was not the depth of social experience available at the turn of the last century in the West that would let him hear Bleuler's withdrawal as a familiar symptom of problems that invariably accompany membership in weak or marginalized organizations.

Freud attempted to strengthen psychoanalysis by seeking acceptance outside the Jewish circles of Vienna from which he had drawn his first supporters. Jung's interest in Freud and psychoanalysis offered the possibility of transferring the base of operations from Vienna to Zurich, from a voluntary organization predominantly of Jews to an institutional setting led by Christians. Such a move might have succeeded were it not for the heterogeneity of the subject of psychoanalysis itself.

What informed the early splits in psychoanalysis was the difficulty in accommodating the variegated psychologies of human beings in society. We are still very far from an understanding of how our unconscious processes are formed through social experience. We do not even have a theory of language acquisition as an example of perhaps our most important unconscious learning process. In place of an adequate understanding of the effect of the social formation on conscious and unconscious processes, a problem far exceeding the resources of early psychoanalysis, Freud, Adler and Jung were forced to insist, above all else, on their own visions of human inner life. In so doing they re-enacted through their visions the class, racial and sexual tensions of the society in which they lived.

In the case of the split between Freud and Adler, class tensions were dominant, with Freud representing the isolated individual psychology of upper-middle-class Vienna, and Adler the collective psychology of the immigrant working class. In Jung's case it was both class and racial tensions that divided him from Freud. Jung embodied the collective psychology of the European peasantry, immersed in the powerful myths and symbols of the preceding 2000 years of Christianity; Freud, in contrast, represented the psychology of the cosmopolitan Jewish bourgeoisie.

The Viennese did not like Freud's fondness for Jung; they sensed his dissatisfaction with them and suspected that he was talking about them behind their backs. It was true. In the setting up of the 1908 Salzburg conference Freud wrote to Jung: 'If there is still time to do anything about the programme, I must ask you to do what you can to thwart my talkative Viennese; otherwise we shall all drown in a torrent of words' (17 February 1908). About Sadger, Freud wrote: 'Sadger [is a] congenital fanatic of orthodoxy, who happens by mere accident to believe in psychoanalysis rather than in the law given by God on Sinai-Horeb' (5 March 1908). About Stekel, Freud wrote: 'He is a slovenly uncritical fellow who undermines all discipline; I feel the same way as you do about him' (11 November 1909). In the same letter he wrote, 'I must own that sometimes I get so angry at my Viennese that I wish they had a single backside so that I could thrash them all with one stick.' A year later he was writing to Jung, 'If you do come [to Munich], I hope you will be nicer to me than my so-called oldest supporters here, who are finally beginning to get under my skin' (3 December 1910). The following March, just before Adler's resignation, he wrote to Ferenczi: '. . . there is only one of all the Viennese who has a scientific future and that is little Rank . . .' (12 March 1911) and 'Unfortunately they are a lot of rabble and I shall feel neither horror nor regret if the whole show here collapses one of these days' (30 March 1911).

At the Second International Psychoanalytical Congress at the Grand Hotel in Nuremberg on 30 and 31 March 1910, the Viennese analysts held a meeting without Freud to organize a protest against his choice of Jung as life president of the International, with extraordinary powers including the right to approve every lecture or article. As Wittels recalled, Freud broke into the meeting and told them (Wittels, 1924): 'Most of you are Jews, and are therefore incompetent to win friends for the new teaching. Jews must be content with the modest role of preparing the ground' (p. 140).

Freud knew how deeply his move towards Jung had antagonized the Viennese. Ferenczi wrote to him on 5 April: '. . . I was struck by the deep sadness which the transfer of the Central Office to Zurich produced in Adler.' To soften the blow, and to deliver the promised scientific freedom, at the next meeting of the Wednesday group in Vienna on 6 April 1910, Freud proposed Adler as president of the Vienna Society. Adler responded with further criticism of how things were being handled, but said that he was satisfied that discussions had 'eliminated the harshness' of the proposals. The power of the president had been limited and the term of office was to be for two years, not life. Adler insisted, however, that Freud retain the leadership of Vienna, although Freud's feelings were now only too apparent. Stekel noted that Freud seemed to have 'a deep hatred toward Vienna' while Sadger observed: 'Freud has been fed up with the Viennese for the last two years.' Nevertheless Freud was satisfied, writing to Jung on 12 April that although the group had been very upset they had treated him with affection and that he had agreed to continue to chair the scientific meetings.

In the background of this attempted shift of institutional power to Zurich were the increasing theoretical disagreements between Freud and Alfred Adler. In the language of the time, the split arose as a result of Adler's interest in the so-called ego instincts, that is to say, conscious willed behaviour, and Freud's exploration of unconscious conflicts. In Freud's view, expressed in the Wednesday meeting of 19 May 1909:

Adler now brings to our attention something quite worthy of note, which does not come to light in our presentations. We always follow the sexual drives and their effect on the psyche; a complete description requires the relationship of the ego-instinct, and Adler demonstrates this part of behaviour. This is the censorship that the ego exercises over the actual sexual situation; it is the real cause of repression.

Freud was sympathetic to ego considerations, the part played by conscious human agency, but in the excitement of discovering new ways to release material from the unconscious, he felt that the role of the ego was of secondary importance. In a discussion on the psychology of compulsive doubting on 19 January 1910, Freud acknowledged that every effect has numerous causes and that, up until then, ego processes had been neglected in favour of the exploration of repressed material. In the previous month, on 19 December 1909, Freud had written to Jung in a similar vein, that it was difficult to hold both points of view simultaneously and that he had slighted the ego in favour of repression because he felt it to be much less explored.

A year later, Freud wrote to Jung that he found Adler to be a 'very decent and intelligent man' but that his theories were virtually incomprehensible and that he had succeeded in forcing Freud to play a role of an authority figure preventing younger men from advancing (25 November 1910). A week later, Freud wrote that things were 'really getting bad with Adler', saying the situation reminded him of his falling out with Fliess. But he wasn't sure of himself.

Naturally in my attitude toward him I am torn between my conviction that all this is lopsided and harmful and my fear of being regarded as an intolerant old man who holds the young men down, and this makes me feel most uncomfortable. (3 December 1910)

Freud's ambivalence towards Adler was resolved as their disagreements played out in the field of sexuality. Freud wrote to Jung: 'The crux of the matter – and that is what really alarms me – is that he minimizes the sexual drive and our opponents will soon be able to speak of an experienced psychoanalyst whose conclusions are radically different from ours' (3 December 1910).

At the Wednesday meeting of 19 May 1909, Freud and Adler had tangled on the question of male sexuality. Freud saw the failure of a man to respond sexually as being only one of a number of possible outcomes of the way a boy's libido can become attached to his mother – in this case he had not been able to connect libido to a loved woman. Other scenarios – men who could only love unfaithful women where they could be jealous – were seen in terms of men whose libidos remained fixated on their mother. Or, in the case of men who could only love a woman whom they could rescue in some way, Freud saw the male libido being invested in a fantasy of themselves giving birth just as their mothers did.

Adler preferred a less interpretive approach. Arguing that Freud was effectively describing prerequisites to love, Adler cited the similar cases of men who needed to have a shorter woman, a taller woman or an older or a younger woman. For Adler, such prerequisites arose as a secondary expression of difficulties in the mother–son relationship itself. In the case of impotence, Adler identified what he called an excessive sensitivity, a fragility, traceable back to an early period when the boy's mother was inaccessible and did not 'turn her tenderness entirely toward him'. In Adler's clinical experience, male impotence 'most often' arose because of the perceived failure of the woman to come forward to meet the man. Adler concluded that this kind of anxious sensitivity in matters of love played 'an almost more important role than the normal sex instinct'. Adler did not see sex in the same way as Freud did, as a fundamental drive of childhood whose successful sublimation was the key to normal human development. Adler took the view that dysfunctional sexuality was a reflected symptom of relational conflict.

A year and half later, Adler had developed his analysis to understand childhood conflicts as attempts to overcome helplessness induced by unsatisfactory relationships. In one case, he argued that the male-identified sexual play of a little girl was simply an expression of her desire to be the one who was dominant. Freud was not at all happy. He wrote to Jung: '. . . here one can see clearly how he tries to force the wonderful diversity of psychology into the narrow bed of a single aggressive "masculine" ego-current – as if the child had rejected femininity and had no other thought than to be "on top" and play the man' (3 December 1910). On 22 January 1911, an astonished Freud described to Jung that Adler was seeing the adult sex act as not necessarily arising from the sexual drive at all but from a desire on the part of the man to reinforce his masculinity through the performance of the sexual act: 'Recently he expressed the opinion that the motivation even of coitus was not exclusively sexual, but also included the individual's desire to *seem* masculine to himself' (3 January 1911).

For Furtmüller, writing in retrospect in 1946, the disagreements between Adler and Freud were exciting (Adler, 1965): 'The weekly meeting of this group are among the most fruitful intellectual experiences I have ever had. The centre of interest was always to see how Freud and Adler would interpret in their different ways the factual material presented by members of the group' (p. 326). For others it was disruptive. Matters came to a head towards the end of 1910 when, on 16 November, Eduard Hitschmann moved that Adler's theories be thoroughly discussed to see if his departures from Freud's views could be resolved or, failing that, to see if their points of difference could be thoroughly understood.

The discussions were unsuccessful. Seven months later, Adler had resigned as editor of the *Zentralblatt*, the psychoanalytic journal, and seven members of the group had presented a formal protest at the way differences of opinion within the Society were being handled:

The undersigned, having heard about the approaching change in the administration of the Zentralblatt, consulted Dr Adler where we learned from him about the matter of the exchanged letters. We therefore conclude that Dr Adler, who is one of the two founders of the journal, has been pushed out of the editorship by the pressure of the publisher on the pretext of financial reasons. This is not an isolated case but the last step in a series of unfriendly acts directed against Dr Adler's person and his approach to science, the extent of which has now first become clear to us. In our opinion the Society and the Journal are weapons against the opposition to psychoanalysis. But since the Society and the Journal should be a place for free discussion for psychoanalysts themselves, these actions show more and more clearly an attempt to create positions of power inside psychoanalysis and to maintain them with all the thoughtless disregard that is usual in power struggles. We are utterly opposed to such a way of going about things. We are convinced that, with this action, both the internal development as well as the external reputation of psychoanalysis will suffer.

As such we have the deepest regrets that the departure of Dr Adler from the Psychoanalytic Association was formally provoked and we completely support his action in resigning. We lay the highest value in maintaining the fullest scientific exchange with him and we will find a suitable form for accomplishing this.

We have decided to give this explanation for two reasons: Firstly, in such an important matter it is our duty to the Society to be completely open. Secondly, although we place great value in remaining active, supportive members of the Psychoanalytic Association, we can do so only if our views are treated with respect. Should the Society be of the opinion that our standpoint and position impedes our duties to the Society in the slightest way, we request the Society to lay this matter before a general meeting of the membership for a decision.

Vienna, June 20, 1911.

Dr Carl Furtmüller
Dr Margarethe Hilferding
Franz Grüner
Gustav Grüner
Dr David Ernst Oppenheim
Dr Friedjung
Paul Klemperer[3]

After the summer break, on 11 October 1911, at a special plenary session held in the Café Arkaden, Freud announced to the group that Adler had resigned *in toto* from the Vienna Psychoanalytic Society. Then, speaking for the board, he requested that members belonging to Adler's circle, whose 'activities bear the stamp of hostile competition', must choose between Adler's new grouping, the Society for Free Psychoanalytic Investigation or the Vienna Society. Furtmüller expressed surprise at the exclusionary order and requested a full discussion on the question of incompatibility. After discussion, the group voted eleven to five that membership in the Society for Free Psychoanalytic Investigation was incompatible with membership in the Vienna Psychoanalytic Society.

Furtmüller then announced his resignation and the resignations of five others: Margarethe Hilferding, David Oppenheim, the Grüner brothers, and Paul Klemperer. Dr Peter Milford-Hilferding, the son of Margarethe Hilferding, recalled in 1996 (personal communication): 'My mother used to say that Individual Psychology in practice was far superior to psychoanalysis. She was on friendly terms with Adler and especially with his wife. She thought that Freud had behaved abominably to Adler and this was one of the reasons why she then took the side of Adler.'

After the split Freud was less inclined to acknowledge the validity of Adler's point of view. In his history of the psychoanalytic movement, he wrote (Freud, 1914): 'The truth is that these people have picked out a few cultural overtones from the symphony of life and have failed to hear the mighty primordial melody of the instincts.' Ernest Jones was delighted. He wrote to Freud on 25 May 1914: 'We have greatly enjoyed the third and last proofs of the "Geschichte". I find it superlatively good, *not at all* too strong and quite final – the last word in the matter. The passage about the "paar kulturelle Obertone" is magnificent.'

There is a much debated question of depth here. In a hierarchical model of the psyche, Adler's psychology of conscious life lies at the top of the psyche, Freud's psychology of repression and unconscious motivation lies underneath, and Jung's psychology of a collective unconscious lies still lower. As with all hierarchies, such a ranking inevitably introduced the invidious distinction of which psychology was more fundamental or profound.

The can of blame for the split has been tossed back and forth between the rival parties for over fifty years, in the process obscuring the importance of understanding, without prejudice, the differences in human inner life that the different scientific styles of the two men led them to emphasize. The fundamental difference in emphasis between them, as Freud himself recognized, was between the very real human capacity to act as symbolized by the ego and the very real effects on human actions of repressed material in the unconscious.

Freud's emphasis on exploring the processes of repression represented an appreciation of how deep-seated in the psyche are the impediments to action. In this sense he understood, where Adler did not, the limitations on human autonomous action. That this understanding came to be expressed in the language of drive, instinct and sexuality was an example of what Jung was to call Freud's knowing more than he understood.

But Adler also knew more than he understood. It is the human subject that is decisive in both personal and historical transformation, the human subject that both forms and is formed by social existence, and that confronts a world not in conditions of its own choosing. Adler responded to what he knew to be true, that there is an aspect of human subjectivity that is capable of autonomous action. But his theory was difficult to reconcile with the existence of human unconscious processes.

The unresolved Freud–Adler conflict anticipated the psychological dynamics of the devastating failures of the revolutions in Europe after the First World War. An inadequate understanding of the possibilities and limitations of human action and the deep-seated fears associated with personal and political change are obstacles that plague every new social movement. In countless practical, political situations following the war, the tension between what was possible and what was not possible and the tension between desire for change and fear of change could not, as in the theoretical disagreement between Freud and Adler, be held creatively. In the aftermath of the 1914–18 war this unresolved emotional difficulty – a lack of understanding of the ambivalences in all human action – was to produce horrific consequences.

The German revolution of 1918–23 was one of many mass political upheavals that took place throughout Europe during and after the First World War. Political systems buckled under the breakneck pace of late-nineteenth-century industrialization and the processes of economic concentration and monopolization. National political structures were unable to achieve the parallel concentration needed to regulate the emerging transnational economic realities. The world war created fissures in every national government through which pressures for change along class, sexual and colonial lines erupted. The individual national crises are well known. Put together they describe a world system in a state of collapse: the 1916 Easter rebellion in Ireland; the 1917 Russian revolution; the declaration of a workers' republic in Finland in 1918; Red Clyde in Scotland; the first social democratic governments in Scandinavia; female suffrage in Britain; the 1919 Hungarian Soviet Republic; the 1919 French general strike and revolt of the fleet; the 1919 Austrian social democratic government which introduced unemployment benefit, the eight-hour day, statutory vacations, and in the Army a right to trade union organization and elected governing bodies for soldiers; the 1920 general strikes and factory occupations throughout Italy; the 1926 general strike in Britain.

In Germany, anti-war protests throughout the war, culminating in the January 1918 strike of one million munitions workers in solidarity with the Russian revolution, preceded the German revolution of October. On 29 October 1918, facing certain defeat, the German High Command ordered the naval fleet in Kiel to launch an attack on the British. The Kiel sailors mutinied, took control of the base and on 3 November elected a soldiers' and sailors' council to run the city of Kiel itself.

Over the next week the revolution spread southward to cover the entire country. By 9 November thirteen out of sixteen major German cities – Bremen, Hamburg, Lübeck, Cologne, Frankfurt, Stuttgart, Leipzig, Dresden, Braunschweig, Magdeburg, Nuremberg, Munich and Berlin – were under direct working-class control. Six weeks later,

400 delegates to a national Congress of the governing bodies met in Berlin and called for a socialization of all industries, a reform of the army including removal of all badges of rank, election of officers and control of the army by soldiers' councils.

The problems associated with such a rapid dissolution of former political structures and the creation of new ones proved to be insurmountable. The seventeen-year-old Kurt Weill, present in Berlin as a student of music at the Hochschule für Musik, witnessed the events in amazement. On 12 November 1918 he wrote to his brother Hans (Schebera, 1995): 'The great revolution broke out with such elemental force and such fabulous speed on Saturday that it must be incomprehensible to people in the countryside' (p. 17). In Augsburg, the home town of Bertolt Brecht, the red flag was raised over the town hall and Brecht was voted on to one of the soldiers' councils. But as Brecht recalled ten years later (Münsterer, 1963):

We all suffered from a lack of political conviction. And I myself from that inability to get worked up about anything at all. I was given a lot of work to do . . . I was hardly different from the great majority of the other soldiers; of course they had had enough of the war but they were incapable of political thinking. I don't remember it with much pride. (p. 149)

Militant but unprepared action in Berlin resulted in the disaster of Spartacus week with the arrest and assassination of Rosa Luxemburg and Karl Liebknecht on 15 January 1919. In Bavaria, the popular leader Kurt Eisner was assassinated on 21 February 1919. Nevertheless the ruling Bavarian Council declared a doomed Bavarian Soviet Republic against the counsel of activists in the German Communist Party. Freud's son Ernst was studying architecture in Munich at the time. Freud wrote to Ferenczi, who was himself in the middle of the Hungarian revolution: 'About us privately, there is only the fact that we know by way of a telegram from Munich that Ernst, amidst the turmoil of the revolution has earned his diploma with distinction' (20 April, 1919).

Years later, in writing about the events of the failed German revolution of 1918–19, Rosa Leviné-Meyer reflected on the psychology of revolutionary situations (Leviné-Meyer, 1973):

Great masses of people suddenly awaken to political life. They become aware that things are not quite what they ought to be and that they can be changed. They are carried away by new experience and ready to storm heavens. And they naively believe that *everybody* has undergone the same transformation – a rare case of human vanity being prepared to forego the distinction of being ahead of the others. (p. 74)

With the sole exception perhaps of the work by the Jungian analyst Andrew Samuels (1993), the psychology of political participation remains a great unexplored frontier of psychoanalysis. It is only when these issues can be explored in a psychoanalytic way – in depth to expose and resolve the conflicting feelings of the participants themselves – that a proper balance between possibilities and limitations can be struck.

With Adler and his supporters expelled, Freud was drawn even closer to Jung. At the same time, Jung was beginning to experience his own difficulties with Freud. Jung's original attraction to Freud had been informed by his interest in what Freud was learning about unconscious processes. But whereas Freud felt that the point of psychoanalysis was to make repressed material in the unconscious conscious, to free the individual from the prison of neurotic misery, Jung's project was the celebration of unconscious processes, particularly as expressed in powerful myths and symbols. On 11 February 1910 Jung had written Freud an impassioned statement on the importance of religion as an expression of 'the deep instincts of the race', stating his vision of the role of psychoanalysis in re-establishing a modern equivalent of Christianity:

I think we must give [psychoanalysis] time to infiltrate into people from many centres, to revivify among intellectuals a feeling for symbol and myth, ever so gently to transform Christ back into the soothsaying god of the vine, which he was, and in this way absorb those ecstatic instinctual forces of Christianity for the *one* purpose of making the cult and the sacred myth what they once were – a drunken feast of joy where man regained the ethos and holiness of an animal. That was the beauty and purpose of classical religion, which from God knows what temporary biological needs has turned into a Misery Institute. Yet what infinite rapture and wantonness lie dormant in our religion, waiting to be led back to their true destination!

Jung's vision of 'ecstatic instinctual forces of Christianity' was a waking of the fundamental differences in thinking between the two men.

Yet Jung was still Freud's great white hope – the manly, accomplished Germanic Christian who would make psychoanalysis acceptable to the world. But from Jung's point of view, Freud became overbearing, power-hungry and intolerant of Jung's intellectual independence. It seemed to Freud that his heir apparent was in danger of abandoning the basic principles of psychoanalysis to pursue a theoretically barren spirituality. Their relationship eventually collapsed because it had slowly been taken over by an unstable emotional dynamic which neither was able to control.

Jung had read *The Interpretation of Dreams* in 1900, the same year that he took up his first professional appointment at the Burghölzli Hospital as an assistant physician. He was attracted to the technique of free association because of its close relationship to his own research on word association tests and in April 1906 sent his book on word association studies to Freud. In July 1906 he sent Freud a copy of his new book on schizophrenia in which he formally acknowledged Freud's 'brilliant discoveries'. In October the two men began an extensive correspondence similar in depth and intensity to the correspondence between Freud and Fliess that had ended two years earlier.

The Freud–Jung correspondence moves from the initial excitement of two professionals discovering the extent of their mutual interests to an intimacy about their respective family affairs, to Jung's increasing involvement in the organizational affairs of the psychoanalytic movement, to Freud's selecting Jung to be, as they were to call it, his son and heir. Unwittingly they had introduced a dangerous family dynamic that undermined whatever chances the two men had to contain their differences within the same professional organization.

On 17 February 1908, after two years of correspondence, Freud addressed Jung as 'Dear friend' instead of 'Dear friend and colleague'. In the very same letter Freud mentioned his failed relationship with Fliess. Jung replied in his next letter, three days later, with a proposal that the two of them might avoid a Fliess outcome if they treated each other as father and son:

Dear Professor Freud,

I thank you with all my heart for this token of your confidence. The undeserved gift of your friendship is one of the high points in my life which I cannot celebrate with big words. The reference to Fliess – surely not accidental – and your relationship with him impels me to ask you to let me enjoy your friendship not as one between equals but that of father and son. This distance appears to me fitting and natural. Moreover, so it seems to me, strikes a note that would prevent misunderstandings and enable two hard-headed people to exist alongside one another in an easy and unrestrained relationship. (20 February 1908)

Freud did not respond directly to Jung's suggestion. But later that year, after a rewarding visit to Jung at the Burghölzli, Freud addressed Jung as 'My dear friend and heir' (15 October 1908). The following spring the Jungs visited Freud in Vienna where an incident took place that was to come to symbolize the difficulties in their professional and personal relationship.

In a discussion in Freud's study about parapsychology there was the sound of a loud sharp crack coming from the bookcase. Jung announced that another one would come in a moment. And to Freud's amazement, one did. As he wrote to Jung after his visit: 'I don't deny that your stories and your experiment made a deep impression on me' (16 April 1909). Jung, for his part, felt some unease about whether Freud took his 'spookery' for stupidity. Freud evidently had told Jung that in spite of his loyalty to Fliess he had come to feel that Fliess was stupid with his theories of the nose and biological cycles. At the same time Jung, seeing a real gap between his sensibility and Freud's, felt liberated from Freud the father figure he had himself proposed. He wrote to Freud (2 April 1909):

That last evening with you has most happily freed me inwardly from the oppressive sense of your paternal authority. My unconscious celebrated this impression with a great dream which has preoccupied me for some days and which I have just finished analysing. I hope I am now rid of all unnecessary encumbrances.

By return post Freud commented wryly on Jung's pulling away from the parental relationship at the same time that he, Freud, was embracing it (16 April 1909):

It is strange on the very same evening when I formally adopted you as eldest son and anointed you – [in the lands of the unbelievers] – as my successor and crown prince, you should have divested me of my paternal dignity, which divesting seems to have given you as much pleasure as I, on the contrary derived from the investiture of your person. Now I am afraid of falling back into the father role with you if I tell you how I feel about the poltergeist business. Accordingly, I put my fatherly horn-rimmed spectacles on again and warn my dear son to keep a cool head, for it is better not to understand than make such sacrifices to understanding.

Freud concluded that superstitions are caused by unconscious obsessions seeking explanation that utilize chance occurrences – the 'compliance of chance' – in the same way that hysterics use the compliance of the body as an expression of symptoms.

At this point there might have been a relatively calm reflection between two 'hard-headed' colleagues about where their respective paths were taking them. But the father–son dynamic that they had played with made it impossible. The final breakdown of their relationship in the last two months of 1912 is profoundly sad – an intellectual and personal divorce accompanied by great intensity of feeling. Jung gained his freedom. Freud had his heart broken for the last time.

On 13 June 1912, Freud had written to Jung criticizing his new argument that anxiety did not arise from the incest taboo but that the incest taboo arose from a displacement of a primeval free-floating anxiety. To Freud it sounded suspiciously similar to Adler's rejection of the sexual aetiology of mental disturbance. Nevertheless he tried to preserve their relationship:

Even if we cannot come to terms immediately, there is no reason to suppose that this scientific difference will detract from our personal relations.

But Jung's trip to the United States in the autumn of 1912 – where he presented his rejection of Freud's sexually based libido theory – was, as in the case of Adler, the straw that broke Freud's back. On 11 November 1912, after his return from America, Jung wrote that he had found that his version of psychoanalysis had 'won over many people who until now had been put off by the problem of sexuality in the neuroses'. Jung defended his loyalty to psychoanalysis and to his friendship with Freud ('I feel no need at all to break off personal relations with you') and rejected Freud's claim that he was resisting the sexual implications of the libido theory:

I can only assure you that there is no resistance on my side unless it be my refusal to be treated like a fool riddled with complexes. I think I have objective reasons for my views.

After a meeting in Munich the air cleared slightly as each felt they understood each other. Jung wrote on 26 November: 'Now you can rest assured that I shall not give up our personal relationship.'

But then on 3 December, Jung protested that Freud's circle, instead of taking the trouble to understand his ideas, were interpreting them as expressions of neurosis:

I am forced to the painful conclusion that the majority of psychoanalysts misuse psychoanalysis for the purpose of devaluing others and their progress by insinuations about complexes (as though that explained anything. A wretched theory!). A particularly preposterous bit of nonsense going the rounds is that my libido theory is the product of anal eroticism . . . The pity of it is that psychoanalysts are just as supinely dependent on psychoanalysis as our opponents are on their belief in authority. Anything that might make them think is written off as a complex.

Freud responded in a quietly critical tone on 5 December:

You mustn't fear that I take your 'new style' amiss. I hold that in relations between analysts, as in analysis itself, every form of frankness is permissible. I too have been disturbed for some time by the abuse of psychoanalysis to which you refer, that is in polemics especially against new ideas. I do not know if there is any way of preventing this entirely; for the present I can only suggest a household remedy; let each of us pay more attention to his own rather than his neighbour's neurosis.

Jung took Freud's response amiss. He responded by return post on 7 December: 'Since you have taken so badly to my "new style", I will tune my lyre a few tones lower, for the present.' Freud answered on the 9th: 'I follow with interest through all the variations of the lyre that you play with such virtuosity.'

Matters came to a head in the exchange of the next two letters in which, united in their opposition to Adler, Jung made a slip of the pen. He intended to write: 'Even Adler's cronies do not regard me as one of theirs.' But theirs was written *Ihrigen* with a capital 'I', meaning 'yours' instead of a lower case 'i' meaning 'theirs'. On 16 December Freud used this slip to chide Jung: 'The habit of taking personal objective statements personally is not only a (regressive) human trait, but also a very specific Viennese failing. I shall be very glad if such claims are not made on you. But are you "objective" enough to consider the following slip without anger? "Even Adler's cronies do not regard me as one of *yours*."' Freud signed it 'Dennoch ganz der Ihrige, Freud. [Yours nevertheless, Freud.]'

This provoked an angry polemic from Jung, summarizing all his grievances against his senior colleague (18 December 1912). Freud, who showed every sign of being wearied by the relationship, might have expected that his remark would provoke such a response.

Dear Professor Freud,

May I say a few words to you in earnest? I admit the ambivalence of my feelings towards you, but I am inclined to take an honest and absolutely straightforward view of the situation. If you doubt my words so much the worse for you. I would however point out that your technique of treating your pupils like patients is a blunder. In that way you reproduce either slavish sons or impudent puppies. (Adler–Stekel and the whole insolent gang now throwing their weight about in Vienna.) I am objective enough to see through your little trick. You go around sniffing out all the symptomatic actions in your vicinity, thus reducing everyone to the level of sons and daughters who blushingly admit the existence of their faults. Meanwhile you remain on top as the father, sitting pretty. For sheer obsequiousness nobody dares pluck the prophet by the beard and inquire for once what you would say to a patient with a tendency to analyse the analyst instead of himself. You would certainly ask him: 'Who's got the neurosis?'

You see my dear professor, so long as you hand out this stuff I don't give a damn for my symptomatic actions; they shrink to nothing in comparison with the formidable beam in my brother Freud's eye. I am not the least neurotic – touch wood! I have submitted legis artis et tout humblement to analysis and am much better for it. You know of course how far a patient gets with self-analysis; not out of his neurosis – just like you. If you should ever rid yourself entirely of your complexes and stop playing father to your sons and instead of aiming continually at their weak spots took a good look at your own for a change, then I will mend my ways and at one stroke uproot the vice of being in two minds about you. Do you love neurotics enough to always be at one with yourself? But perhaps you hate neurotics. In that case how can you expect your efforts to treat your patients leniently and lovingly not to be accompanied by somewhat mixed feelings? Adler and Stekel were taken in by your little tricks and reacted with childish insolence. I shall continue to stand by you publicly while maintaining my own views, but privately shall start telling you in my letters what I really think of you. I consider this procedure only decent.

No doubt you will be outraged by this peculiar token of friendship, but it may do you some good all the same.

With best regards,

Most sincerely yours, JUNG

On 22 December, Freud responded in part to Jung's accusations:

I am sorry that my reference to your slip annoyed you so; your reaction seems all out of proportion to the occasion. In regard to your allegations that since I misuse psychoanalysis to keep my students in a state of infantile dependency I myself am responsible for their infantile behaviour and to the inferences you draw from this contention, I prefer not to judge, because it is hard in matters concerning oneself and such judgements convince no one. I wish merely to acquaint you with certain facts concerning the foundations of your theory and leave you to revise it. In Vienna I have become accustomed to the opposite reproach, to wit, that I concern myself too little with the analysis of my 'students'.

Freud had had enough. On New Year's Day 1913 he wrote to James Putnam in the US about the loss of Jung 'whom I overestimated greatly and in whom I had invested much personal feeling' (Hale, 1971). Two days later, on 3 January 1913, Freud wrote to Jung calling for an end to their personal relationship.

I can answer only one point in your previous letter in any detail. Your allegation that I treat my followers like patients is demonstrably untrue. In Vienna I am reproached for the exact opposite. I am held responsible for the misconduct of Stekel and Adler; in reality I have not said one word to Stekel about his analysis since it was concluded some ten years ago, nor have I made any use of analysis with Adler, who was never my patient. Any analytical remarks I have made about them were addressed to others and for the most part at a time when we ceased to associate with one another. – In building your construction on this foundation you have made matters as easy for yourself as with your famous 'Kreuzlingen gesture'.[4]

Otherwise your letter cannot be answered. It creates a situation that would be difficult to deal with in a personal talk and totally impossible in correspondence. It is a convention among us analysts that none of us need feel ashamed of his own bit of neurosis. But one who while behaving abnormally keeps shouting that he is normal gives ground for the suspicion that he lacks insight into his illness. Accordingly I propose that we abandon our personal relations entirely. I shall lose nothing by it, for my only emotional tie to you has long been a thin thread – the lingering effects of past disappointments – and you have everything to gain, in view of the remark that you recently made in Munich, to the effect that an intimate relationship with a man inhibited your scientific freedom. I therefore say, take your full freedom, and spare me your supposed 'tokens of friendship'. We are agreed that a man should subordinate his personal feelings to the general interests of his branch of endeavour. You will never have any reason to complain of any lack of correctness on my part where our common undertaking and the pursuit of scientific aims are concerned; I may say, no more reason in the future than in the past. On the other hand I am entitled to expect the same from you.

Regards,

Yours sincerely, FREUD

Their letters crossed. Jung's of the same date was angry but conciliatory: 'If I offer you the unvarnished truth it is meant for your own good, even if it may hurt.' Upon receiving Freud's letter Jung responded by postcard:

Dear Professor Freud

Küsnach-Zürich, 6 January 1913

I accede to your wish that we abandon our personal relations, for I never thrust my friendship on anyone. You yourself are the best judge of what this moment means to you. 'The rest is silence.'

Thank you for accepting Burrow's paper.

Yours sincerely, JUNG

Towards the end of the year, on 23 November 1913, Freud wrote to Stanley Hall in the US (E. Freud, 1960): 'The only unfavourable developments within the psychoanalytic movement concern personal relationships. Jung, with whom I shared my visit with you at that time, is no longer my friend, and our collaboration is approaching complete dissolution. Such changes are regrettable but inevitable' (p. 311).

Coincidentally, two days later, Jung wrote Jones a postcard in English, summarizing his perspective on the split (JJL):

I think it is necessary in science as well as everywhere in the world to give credit and to listen to each other's arguments. I am not worried with mere working hypotheses. I therefore cannot understand why a different view should not be carefully discussed. It is an extremely difficult and even unfair standpoint to reduce a different view to personal complexes. This is psychology of the 'nothing but'. It takes off all seriousness and human consideration and replaces it with personal gossip and suspicion. (25 November 1913)

Two years later Freud was angrier. In an exchange with James Putnam, Freud found fault with religious ethical conversions such as he felt he had witnessed in Jung: 'Then came his religious ethical crisis with higher morality, "rebirth", Bergson and at the very same time lies, brutality and anti-Semitic condescension towards me. It has not been the first or last experience to reinforce my disgust with saintly converts' (8 July 1915).

The loss of Jung cemented Freud's bitter sense of isolation and embattlement. In 1913, the tax authorities wrote to Freud querying his low reported income, saying 'everyone knows that his reputation extends far beyond the frontier of Austria'. As Jones (1955) reported, Freud replied:

Professor Freud is very honoured at receiving a communication from the Government. It is the first time the Government has taken any notice of him and he acknowledges it. There is one point in which he cannot agree with the communication: that his reputation extends far beyond the frontier of Austria. It begins at the frontier. (p. 435)

A year later Freud wrote to Ferenczi: '. . . it would be absurd to expect a sign of recognition when one has 7/8 of the world against one . . .' (31 October 1915).

On the threshold of the First World War, Freud's psychoanalysis was established as a new approach to the understanding of human psychology. It had provoked a spectrum of responses from passionate embrace to an equally passionate rejection. Within psychoanalysis itself there was a range of opinion. Having been active members of the movement, Jung, Adler and Stekel found it necessary to go their separate ways, accompanied by bitterness and dispute. Others attended briefly and went their own way quietly (Mühlleitner, 1992). Some passionately defended Freud and the cause of psychoanalysis. Ernst Federn (1963) reported that his father Paul Federn, along with Eduard Hitschmann and Ludwig Jekels, met Adler in a coffee house to attempt a last-ditch reconciliation. But Federn's father was unable to restrain himself and 'cut the negotiations quite short by opening the talks with: "Adler, admit you are a Judas"' (p. 81). Other early practitioners such as Hermann Nunberg, who initiated the practice of the training analysis, were able to find space within psychoanalysis to develop their own ideas about ego psychology.

The trifurcation of the Freud–Jung–Adler split would not, as Bleuler suggested, be resolved 'a few years later or sooner'. The issues expressed during the early years – to what extent are human beings masters of their own fate, how far does the participation in human culture require the mastery of basic human drives, to what extent does religious experience tell us important things about human psychology – are still unresolved. There will always be those who find their psychology in Adler's insistence on the human capacity for autonomous action, or with the fundamental conflicts represented by Freud's drive theory, or by Jung's evocation of symbol and myth and the intriguing question of the collective unconscious. The task for future theorists of the analytic hour is to restore the common ground of psychoanalytic exploration.

6

The Transference

What was new with the invention of the analytic hour was the opportunity to explore at length all the feelings that appeared in the course of treatment, a topic that produced extensive discussions in the Wednesday Psychological Society and in lengthy papers explaining analytic phenomena to wider medical audiences. In a theoretical article in 1912, Freud referred to the 'almost inexhaustible topic of transference', the now visible dynamics of the relationship between past and present as displayed in the patient–therapist relationship.

For the first time in the treatment of mental distress, the patient's responses to the therapist became an explicit part of the treatment. In hypnosis, rapport with the therapist was essential. But in analytic treatment the shape, texture and nature of the rapport, instead of being merely exploited in the service of a cure, was itself observed for symptoms of underlying distress capable of treatment. As Freud put it in 1908 to the Wednesday Psychological Society: 'The vicissitudes of the transference decide the success of the treatment' (p. 102).

But the appearance of transference reactions in the analytic hour was not necessarily obvious. In his recommendations to physicians practising psychoanalysis, Freud proposed a fundamental rule that physicians do nothing to censor the free flow of their own responses to their patient's communications (Freud, 1912b):

Just as the patient must relate everything that his self-observation can detect, and keep back all logical and affective objections that seek to make a selection from among them, so the doctor must put himself in a position to make use of everything he is told for the purposes of interpretation and of recognizing the concealed unconscious material without substituting a censorship of his own for the selection that the patient has foregone. To put it in a formula: he must turn his own unconscious like a receptive organ towards the transmitting unconscious of the patient. (p. 115)

The question remains then, how does it work? How does the analyst turn her unconscious to that of her analysand? At what point, one imagines, does an analyst say, 'You seem to expect that I will exploit you the way your older sister exploited you' or, 'You seem to think that you need to reassure me the way you needed to reassure your anxious mother'? In practice the process is usually less direct.

A woman in treatment with Freud (1913b) got into a routine of bringing him flowers. Finally, Freud felt obliged to ask her not to bring flowers any more. This rejection produced a deep depression. The exploration of her feelings led to memories of past events. At the age of seven the girl's father had refused her money to buy some paints for painting Easter eggs. Subsequently the girl took sixpence out of change from an errand, bought the paints and then hid them. Upon inspecting his change the father asked whether she had bought the paints with it after all. The girl denied it but her older brother gave her away. The father demanded severe punishment which was reluctantly administered by the mother. The punishment plunged the girl into despair. She described it as the 'turning point in my life'. She changed from being a wild and exuberant child into being shy and timid.

The exploration of a number of other incidents, involving giving and receiving, with Freud himself, led to an understanding of the origins of the woman's depression. As Freud recounted the story:

When she was three and a half she had a nursemaid of whom she was extremely fond. The nursemaid became involved in a love affair with a doctor whose surgery she visited with the child. It appears that at that time the child witnessed various sexual proceedings. It is not certain whether she saw the doctor give the girl money; but there is no doubt that to make sure of the child's keeping silence, the girl gave her some small coins, with which purchases were made (probably of sweets) on the way home. It is possible too that the doctor himself occasionally gave the child money. Nevertheless the child betrayed the girl to her mother out of jealousy. She played so ostentatiously with the coins that her mother could not help asking: 'Where did you get that money?' The girl was dismissed. (p. 306)

Exploration of the meanings involved in this early incident showed that the child had come to understand that money was a medium of exchange for love. Taking money from her father, in spite of his denying her the paints, was, for her, a way to declare her love for him. 'Her father's punishment was thus a rejection of the tenderness she was offering him – humiliation – and so it broke her spirit' (p. 307).

The key element in Freud's vignette is that the flowers were given in such a way that Freud felt obliged to ask her to stop. Here is where the transference made its visible appearance in the treatment. The flowers, instead of being given in a way that the two of them might make a joke of it, or given in a way that Freud might simply continue to accept them, or given in a way that Freud might ask her about it, were instead offered to Freud in such a way that he felt obliged to call a halt to her gifts, thus reproducing the despair caused originally by the father's rejection of the child. The subtlety lay in Freud acting on this feeling of obligation and the therapy then consisted of resolving with the woman her subsequent feelings in a way that had not been possible with her father.

Transference re-enactments as new editions of old experiences are accompanied by affect, mood and feeling. And it is these emotional phenomena that are the compelling feature of the transference.[1] The feelings that can be aroused in the analyst as he or she listens to, engages with and absorbs what the analysand is saying are very powerful and at times disturbing. Thus, there was the fear that analysts would substitute censorship of their own in reaction to the feelings that they had in response to their patients. As Freud put it in 1912: 'But if the doctor is to be in a position to use his unconscious in this way as an instrument in the analysis, he must himself fulfil one psychological condition to a high degree. He may not tolerate any resistances in himself which would hold back from his consciousness what has been perceived by his unconscious' (p. 116). The ideal analyst then would be the completely analysed person who had resolved all his own areas of conflict and would, in principle, be completely open to receive whatever conflicting feelings existed for the patient without having to deny or evade them. For this reason Nunberg's proposal of a training analysis for all analysts was taken up in 1910 and adopted in all psychoanalytic training programmes after the First World War.

It proved difficult, however, to come to a clear view on how to handle the complexity of feelings that the receptive analyst would inevitably experience with an analysand. Freud's view was that through the training analysis, analysts would attain a state of being in which they would reflect back only what they had received from the patient's unconscious (Freud, 1912b): 'The doctor should be opaque to his patients and like a mirror, should show them nothing but what is shown to him' (p. 118). Freud was specifically concerned that a certain kind of analytic receptivity called the rule of abstinence be observed. If normal conversational conventions were permitted to prevail, with one confidence deserving another – 'You know that happened to me once' – the asymmetry that is so necessary for analysis to work could be destroyed. The space, instead of being devoted to an exploration of the difficult and conflictual aspects of the analysand's experience, including their experience of the analytic conversation itself, could become a coffee house exchange between familiars that is collusive with past experience instead of offering the opportunity to examine unconscious patterns of relating.

It has taken two generations of work to realize that the ideal of the completely analysed analyst, reflecting to the patient only what she has received and nothing of herself – the so-called mirror model of psychoanalysis – is unrealistic. Beginning with Ferenczi's experiments with mutual analysis (Fortune, 1993), psychoanalytic psychotherapy has come to realize that analytic neutrality and the rule of abstinence, while a useful practical guide in the early period of psychoanalysis, is not a solution to the problem of maintaining the mutual but asymmetric nature of the analytic relationship (Aron, 1991). The mutual responses of analyst and analysand to each other in which the analyst's feelings, as in the example of Freud's feeling obliged to refuse the flowers, are not only recognized but are an essential part of the transference relationship without which the analysis cannot proceed. As Aron put it: 'Self-revelation is not an option; it is an inevitability' (p. 40).

The transference is a central issue in all psychoanalytic psycho-therapies, including those of Adler and Jung. Adler downplayed the formal significance of the transference in his theoretical writing. He denied the term while at the same time retaining an acute awareness of its importance. In a discussion of the therapeutic relationship he wrote (Ansbacher and Ansbacher, 1956): 'I expect from the patient again and again the same attitude which he has shown in accordance with his life-plan towards the persons of his environment and still earlier toward his family' (p. 356). For Adler the central dynamic leading to neurosis was relationship failure, 'the nature of which always turns out to be a lack of ability to make contact' (p. 328). Adler tuned into unconscious communications by not paying attention to the words of a patient: '. . . instead [I] read his deeper intention from his bearing and his movements within a situation' (p. 330). And Adler routinely accepted the importance of unconscious processes:

Not that the patient wants to lie to us but we have learned to recognize a vast gulf between a man's conscious thoughts and his unconscious motivations, a gulf which can be bridged by a disinterested but sympathetic outsider. The outsider, whether he is the psychologist, or the parent, or the teacher, should learn to interpret a personality on the basis of objective facts seen as an expression of the purposive, but more or less unconscious strivings of the individual. (p. 330)

What is of interest in Adler, in the light of later developments in psychoanalysis, is that the striving of the individual is a striving towards relationship by resolving the unconscious conflicts that have stood in the way of making contact: 'We refuse to recognize and examine an isolated human being.' In Adler's therapy the lack of ability to make contact is revealed to the therapist through the transfer-ence, the therapist playing a maternal role of helping the individual establish contact with his or her milieu. Adler, while not treating the transference with the same theoretical respect as Freud, used it in the same way – as an inevitable part of the treatment process, needing to be understood as an unconscious communication by the patient about the failures of past relationships.

Jung, meanwhile, with his intense interest in the unconscious in its own right, developed a number of important modifications and alternative theoretical interpretations of transference phenomena. Whereas Freud saw normal mental processes as simply taking place unconsciously, Jung envisioned the unconscious as a sea containing a vast multitude of life in which consciousness sits as an island (Jung, 1946):

Consciousness no matter how extensive it may be, must always remain the smaller circle within the greater circle of the unconscious, an island surrounded by the sea; and like the sea itself, the unconscious yields an endless and self-replenishing abundance of living creatures, a wealth beyond our fathoming. (p.14)

Jung's approach to the transference was far more circumspect than that of Freud because the contents of the unconscious for Jung contained potentially overpowering past experiences from the entire history of the human race. In this vision Jung attained a model of psychotic processes, long an interest of his, in which consciousness dissolves leaving the individual helpless in the face of a chaotic battering from his or her unconscious. That Jung should arrive at such a model where Freud did not may be related to a psychotic break Jung experienced in childhood, making him sensitive to the existence of terrifyingly chaotic mental states (Winnicott, 1964). Jung distinguished sharply between Freud's concept of the transference – a set of feeling states occurring in the analytic dialogue, and his own ideas of transference phenomena, which expressed the far more complex and problematic collective unconscious, the psychological reality of archetypal images that is mixed in with individual psychology (Jung, 1946).

Behind Jung's disagreement with Freud over the nature of the transference lies a fundamental difference between them over the nature of unconscious processes. The unifying concept for the understanding of mental processes in the psychology that Freud created is the unconscious. Frequently muddled by colloquial use and by imprecise clinical thinking, even by Freud himself, the unconscious is central to Freud's insight into the inner world. In Freud's most developed model the unconscious is not a noun – a storage tank of repressed material – but an adjective describing the most general and important property of mental processes. In Freud's psychology, it is not simply that some mental processes are unconscious but that mental processes 'are in themselves unconscious' (Freud, 1915b).

Anecdotally, we all know that much of our mental processing occurs outside the consciousness. Solutions to problems 'come' to us, ideas 'occur' to us, we 'suddenly' remember to do something. Our acquisition of language is entirely outside the range of conscious awareness. Our feelings emerge unconsciously in the situations in which we find ourselves. Freud turned these commonplace observations into the centrepiece of his approach to human mental life. Consciousness becomes an internal perceptual apparatus by which we become aware of our internal unconscious processes (Solms, 1996). Such a relationship between unconscious and conscious mental processing is frequently encountered in the arts but it occurs no less frequently in scientific discovery.

Enrico Fermi, a versatile physicist known for many leading contributions to physics in the 1930s and 1940s, is most famous for his work with neutrons, in particular his discovery of the exceptionally high reactivity of slow neutrons. The precursor to the discovery involved absorbing a large amount of confusing and apparently contradictory experience. To sort it out Fermi had to allow his unconscious processes to speak to him.

One day, Fermi thought that a piece of lead, an absorber of neutrons, inserted in the neutron beam would be the thing to try next. But he found himself dithering. He had the lead carefully machined when any old piece would have done. He found other excuses for not putting the lead in place. Finally he could postpone the experiment no longer. But as he began to proceed he suddenly stopped and said to himself (Schwartz, 1992): 'No, I do not want this piece of lead here. What I want is a piece of paraffin.' Paraffin does not absorb neutrons; it slows them down. As Fermi later described his process: 'It was just like that, with no advance warning, no conscious prior reasoning. I immediately took some odd piece of paraffin and placed it where the lead was to have been' (p. 181).

Fermi's experience, one of many such stories in the history of scientific discovery, is easily understood in terms of Freud's model of the unconscious processes of the mind. Fermi had absorbed innumerable, subtle clues, sensory experiences that were being processed unconsciously in his mind. The final step in the process was to allow the integrated experience to come to consciousness. He did this by being attentive to himself – his dithering, his feeling bothered, his delays – until the solution 'came' to him. He did not want a neutron absorber. He wanted a neutron moderator.

Freud's model places consciousness as a highly organized internal perceptual process that permits us to become aware of the integrative action of unconscious mental processes on external perceptual signals. In this way Freud's model of mental processes as being unconscious becomes a direct linking step between the neural processing of external signals and their integration (unconscious) into psychological phenomena.

Jung, on the other hand, saw the unconscious not as an adjective but as a noun. The unconscious in Jung's psychology was not simply a repository for repressed material but a repository for (unconscious) memories of the entire human race.

It is possible to come to an understanding of Jung's views from what Jung called Freud's materialist perspective. The power of myth and symbol to evoke deep, mysterious feelings in us makes it clear that Jung's psychology must be addressing a significant aspect of human psychology. A collective psychology could be transmitted from generation to generation in early infant learning. If the first question asked of the parents of a new-born child is: 'Is it a boy or a girl?', this must be only the visible tip of a series of unconscious signals that will be transmitted to the new-born about his or her gender and its relationship to the culture in which he or she has just been born. One then has a way to picture a similar mechanism for the transmission of the archetypal contents of the collective unconscious. Through gesture, stance, tone of voice and the acquisition of language itself, all of which are transmitted unconsciously and absorbed unconsciously by the developing human infant (all mental processes are unconscious), the infant absorbs cultural meanings which can be powerfully evoked later in development by myth and symbol and be expressed unconsciously in dreams or in the transference to a receptive analyst. This would be one way a so-called materialist or personalist psychoanalyst could attempt to understand Jung's view.

But Jung would feel that such an interpretation misses the very dimension of spirituality that he sought to identify as a central part of human psychology. In his defence of the element of chance – the throwing of three coins – involved in consulting the *I Ching* as a probe of the unconscious, Jung rejected any attempt to explain the chance element further (Jung, 1949): 'The heavy-handed pedagogic approach that attempts to fit irrational phenomena into a preconceived rational pattern is anathema to me' (p. xxix). Jung insisted on the importance of religious and spiritual experience in its own right. He saw spiritual experience, including the irrationality of chance occurrence, as an essential, irreducible element of human psychology, a dimension that had to be accepted as a fact, on its own terms.

Jung was the first of many to claim psychoanalysis for purposes other than those Freud had in mind. Jung wanted to position psychoanalysis as an extension of philosophy. This book could be said to be trying to position psychoanalysis as an extension of the Western scientific tradition as a way of understanding the human inner world. To an extent the three sensibilities are complementary – the scientific emphasizes understanding, the religious, transcendence and the philosophical, value, among other things. But the three disciplines are so very different that it has been difficult to achieve a mutual understanding of their similarities and differences, particularly on the question of clinical efficacy.

The importance to Jung of collectively shared unconscious processes had clinical consequences. First, Jung was rather more relaxed about the importance of the one-to-one transference in the analytic relationship than was Freud. As he put it (Jung, 1946): 'I personally am always glad when there is only a mild transference or when it is practically unnoticeable' (p. 9). For Jung, the personalized transference in the sense of the patient's feelings about the therapist could be strongly, weakly or not present at all and he argued that not only was it not required for treatment but that it was impossible to require it – such feelings would either appear or not according to the structure of the patient's unconscious. For Jung the vicissitudes of the (personalized) transference did not determine the success of the treatment.

On another level, however, while he remained relaxed about the transference – the patient's feelings with the therapist – he was absolutely insistent on the centrality of the countertransference – the therapist's ability to feel *with* the patient, and, in particular, on the absolute necessity for the doctor to be open to the suffering of the patient and to the overwhelming feelings arising from the patient's unconscious processes (Jung, 1946).

A genuine participation, going right beyond professional routine, is absolutely imperative, unless of course the doctor prefers to jeopardize the whole proceeding by evading his own problems, which are becoming more and more insistent. The doctor must go to the limits of his subjective possibilities, otherwise the patient will be unable to follow suit. (p. 35)

In his insistence that the therapist remain open to the patient's suffering in such a way that he or she actually absorbs the suffering, Jung anticipated many of the developments in classical psychoanalysis that were still to come: the recognition of the importance of the countertransference as a clinical tool, the importance of attunement and the difficulty in managing the inevitable entanglements that attunement would produce. But Jung's concept of the collective unconscious and its expression in the transference, that is to say, Jung's social psychology, is still not treated within classical psychoanalysis with the seriousness that it deserves.

The systematic exploration of the subjective feelings in the analytic relationship expressed in the transference has raised and continues to raise questions for modern Western epistemology. Foremost among these is the question of suggestion. The Trilby patient submits to the suggestions of the Svengali therapist with the result that nothing the patient says can be trusted. As Friedländer wrote in 1911 in his review of the psychoanalytic treatment of hysteria:

But I do not maintain that all cases are under the influence of auto-suggestion when they come for the psychoanalytic treatment. What I maintain is that they either know or suspect the method which will be used upon them, or that after a short time they are suggestively influenced by questions. It cannot be said that they are not questioned. When they relate their dreams they are asked if nothing else occurs to them; their falterings and hesitations are interpreted as resistances that must be overcome. The examiner in question must find something in accordance with his scientific convictions; he seeks – and he finds. (p. 316)

Friedländer's description is in fact accurate. Questions put by analysts are selective – falterings and hesitations can be interpreted or not, the analyst may indeed have feelings of being confirmed by an analysand's response. But the question is not whether such things happen in the analytic hour. They do. It is how they are handled that is crucial to the therapy and its subsequent theorization.

For Freud, suggestion was a special example of the transference reaction of patient to physician. Citing hypnotism as the best-known model of suggestion, Freud argued that the suggestibility of the subject was not due to a mystical power of the hypnotist but to a (transference) reaction involving love or fear of an authority figure, from the patient to the hypnotist. The hypnotist exploits the transference to add something to the patient's unconscious process – a command to do something. In psychoanalysis, however, the opposite happens. The psychoanalyst exploits the transference reaction of the patient to take away something from the unconscious processes – the resistance and the forgotten memories. The hypnotist leaves the transference intact; the psychoanalyst analyses the transference so that it eventually dissolves, leaving the patient free from the unconscious repetition of past experience, including the love or fear of an authority figure.

In 1917, Freud elaborated his ideas about the contaminating role of suggestion at greater length in his lectures on the general theory of neurosis given at the University of Vienna:

You know what we are going to discuss today. When I admitted that the influence of psychoanalytic therapy is essentially founded on transference, i.e. upon suggestion, you asked me why we do not make use of direct suggestion, and you linked this up with a doubt whether, in view of the fact that suggestion plays such a large part, we can still vouch for the objectivity of our psychological discoveries. (p. 456)

The answer for Freud lay in the analysis of the transference.

In every other suggestive treatment the transference is carefully preserved and left intact; in analysis it is itself the object of the treatment and is continually being dissected in all its various forms. At the conclusion of the analysis, the transference itself must be dissolved; if success then supervenes and is maintained it is not founded on suggestion, but on the overcoming of inner resistances effected by the help of suggestion, on the inner change achieved within the patient. (p. 461)

For Friedländer, trained in the traditions of nineteenth-century science and medicine, the mere presence of suggestion was enough to disqualify explorations of the inner world as being unavoidably contaminated. The fact that suggestion could be discussed, explored and itself treated could not be entertained because of the received wisdom about the correct practice of science and medicine.

But if suggestion was an example of how the patient's report could not be trusted, there was and continues to be a problem with trusting the analyst's report too. In Freud's report, the central feature was his assertion that he felt compelled to ask the woman to stop bringing flowers. How do we know, apart from his word, that Freud had this feeling of obligation? In fact, how did *he* even know that he felt obliged? Perhaps he felt something else entirely. Why should we believe his report about his feelings, let alone believe what he says about what went on between him and the woman? In short, why should we believe *anything* Freud says? From the very beginnings of psychoanalysis questions have been raised about the reliability, the scientific reproducibility and the objectivity of this kind of subjective report.

However, Freud's story of the rejected flowers has a certain authentic feel to it. The receptive reader senses that Freud is not only telling the truth but is also telling us something about ourselves and the painful parental rejections we may have experienced as children. In this report, evocatively titled, 'Two Lies Told by Children' (Freud, 1913b), Freud is story-telling in the manner of a fine novelist, and many of us will feel without a doubt that he is telling the truth.

To those who regard the world of human feeling as inherently unreliable, who distrust the novel and poetry as a source of human knowledge, the claims of psychoanalysis will always be unsatisfactory.

To such people the contribution of psychoanalysis to our understanding of the world of human mood and feeling can never be more than another form of fiction – if not exactly 'made up' then merely subjective and a quite unreliable rendering of human experience in contrast to the presumably solid objective report traditionally associated with the development of knowledge in the natural sciences.

The question of the existence of transference re-enactments and the method of reporting them focuses attention on the strange new epistemological questions raised by psychoanalysis: can we in any circumstances reliably know the world of human mood and feeling? Asked this way, the answer seems obvious. Of course we can. We do it every day in our relationships with each other. But if it is so obvious then why is the reliability of this knowledge so hotly denied?

And we return in a more focused way to Western mistrust of the world of human subjectivity. Statements such as 'Don't be emotional', 'But that's only my subjective opinion' or 'I think I am being completely objective when I say . . .' tell us just how much nineteenth-century concepts of rationality continue to dominate our discourse. Whether the denigration of the inner world of human feeling will continue to influence public and private discourse in Western societies, is a question involving the resolution of historical trends that extend beyond the scope of psychoanalysis. But on the level of an open exploration of the world of human emotions, psychoanalysis is the only discipline that takes our feelings seriously – as experiences to be trusted and understood.

The problems of psychoanalysis are not failures of reproducibility or the presumed confounding role of suggestion. It is in the very nature of the analytic encounter and all human encounters, for there to be non-reproducibility and suggestion. The question, again, for psychoanalysis to answer is, have we learned anything useful, reliable and interesting from what has gone on in the analytic hour?

Certainly the systematic exploration of transference re-enactments in the analytic hour is sufficient to secure its place as a valuable addition to our knowledge disciplines. But, to jump ahead of the story, there is also a major theoretical contribution that psychoanalysis has to make about our understanding of ourselves as human beings.

Great general statements – laws of nature – about human psychology have proved difficult to find. There is a reason for this. General laws are possible only when the behaviour is the same for all times and places. The chemical elements owe their differeng properties in large part to the fact that every electron in the universe is *exactly* the same as every other. But when the history of the universe reaches the point where life makes its appearance the new forms of matter can no longer be understood in terms of general laws. Organisms are not *exactly* like each other. The universal cell structure of living matter might be one generality of biology. But as opposed to physics, with its great general laws of matter in motion, knowledge of the phenomena of biology is simple, concrete, and specific.

In psychology there is even less generality than there is in biology. The long maturation time of the human infant outside the womb means that more than any other species the human is a product of its interaction with its unique social environment as in its acquisition of language. And although the human race has biological capacities in common, the specific realization of these capacities is an outcome of the history of each individual in its unique developmental setting. We know that we are all different.

Nevertheless psychoanalysis does have one single general law to offer. As formulated by the Scottish psychoanalyst Ronald Fairbairn in 1946, it is that human beings are fundamentally, in their very nature, relationship-seeking. The history of psychoanalysis has been a struggle between Fairbairn's proposition and Freud's hypothesis, derived from the framework of nineteenth-century physiology, that the human being is fundamentally pleasure-seeking. The struggle between what the US psychoanalyst Stephen Mitchell has called a relational/conflict psychology and a drive/conflict psychology is a dispute over the fundamental principles of what constitutes a human being. The challenge of modern psychoanalysis is the discovery, through accumulated clinical experience, that we have a biological need for human relationships, a need that if not met in a good enough way can lead to profound and even irreversible damage, both psychological and physiological. And so psychoanalysis, in the course of its development in the twentieth century, challenges one of the most entrenched myths of Western societies, the myth of the Man Alone, a challenge that could not fail to arouse deep opposition both within and outside psychoanalysis.

7

Expanding the Frontier:
Psychoanalysis
in the United States I

In Europe, the high-cultural appeal of psychoanalysis took it far beyond narrow medical circles. In Britain, France, Germany and Austria many of the most distinguished early practitioners were lay analysts drawn to psychoanalysis from the disciplines of literature, philosophy, law, pedagogy and natural science because of their interest in what was being discovered about the human psyche in the analytic hour.

The situation in the United States was quite the reverse. Here psychoanalysis developed almost exclusively as an extension of medical practice by doctors trained in psychiatry and neurology. Medical training was to become a prerequisite for psychoanalytic training and psychoanalysis was to become a leading branch of psychiatric practice. But within this narrowed professional scope, the frontier spirit prevailed. Psychoanalysis was adapted by a grouping of creative practitioners to treat cases of the most profound mental distress – the psychoses – in large institutional settings in the face of opposition from the Old World that it could not be done.

In 1890, the State of New York passed the State Care Act, ordering the removal of the indigent mentally ill from poor-houses to state hospitals where treatment rather than custodial care was to be offered. In addition, the Act established the New York State Pathological Institute, the first institution for psychiatric research in the US. The Institute opened in 1895, moved to Ward's Island in New York City, changed its name in 1924 to the New York State Psychiatric Institute, in association with the Department of Psychiatry of the College of Physicians and Surgeons of Columbia University, and moved again to new buildings at its present location in Washington Heights at 722

West 168th Street in 1929. The 1890 Act marked the beginning of the modern administrative phase of US psychiatry.

In 1893, the Association of Medical Superintendents of American Institutions for the Insane, eventually to become the American Psychiatric Association, invited Weir Mitchell, famous for his rest cure for mental distress, to deliver its fiftieth anniversary address. Mitchell's brief was to criticize existing practices in psychiatry 'boldly and with no regard for persons' (White, 1909). Mitchell's rest cure consisted of a programme of strengthening of the body until such time as the physician could exert an influence on the patient's emotional state. A milk diet, building slowly to more substantial food, absolute bed rest, to the extent that the patient was only slowly allowed to sit up for a few minutes each day, faradism of large muscles (stimulation of the muscles through electromagnetic induction of nerve firings), massage, passive and then active exercise, led to the beginnings of a psychological therapy for the complete range of nosological categories including phobias, obsessional neurosis, anxiety neurosis, schizophrenia and manic depressive psychosis. As Beverley Tucker, a family friend and colleague of Mitchell recalled (Tucker, 1936): 'His patients told him everything as he dug into their psychogenic experiences and he patiently explained to them and suggested away their problems' (p. 345). Mitchell delivered his expected critique of the standard medical approach to mental distress. Sixteen years later, William Alanson White (1909), referring to the effect of Mitchell's address, wrote: 'This criticism went home and it hurt because of the truth it contained – the study of insanity must be primarily a study of the mind' (p. 7).

The reforming factions of US psychiatry and psychology received the new dynamic psychiatry developing in Europe with interest. In 1893–4, William James, the leading psychologist in the US, lectured on Freud's and Breuer's new conceptions of hysteria at Harvard. In 1895, Bronislow Onuf, a Russian-born neurologist working in the New York State hospital system, produced an abstract of Freud's paper, 'The Neuropsychoses of Defence'. The following year, *Studies on Hysteria* was favourably reviewed in an unsigned article in the *Journal of the American Medical Association*, while in 1898 Havelock Ellis's rave review of *Studies* in the St Louis journal, *Alienist and*

Neurologist, clearly showed the appeal of an analysis that moved beyond classification to the identification of the actual causes of hysteria. In 1900, August Hoch (1868–1919) began to practise psychodynamic therapy at McLean Hospital in Waverly, Massachusetts. Morton Prince, who received his doctorate in 1889 in psychology from Harvard with a thesis on mental dissociation and multiple personality under the supervision of William James, organized the first study group devoted to psychoanalysis, which was regularly attended by the leading lights of the Boston psychological and neurological communities including William James (Coriat, 1945). A year later, in 1906, Prince founded the *Journal of Abnormal Psychology*, which was to become the leading journal for the presentation of psychoanalytic developments until *The Psychoanalytic Review* was established in 1913 by William Alanson White (1870–1937) in Washington DC and Smith Ely Jelliffe (1866–1945) in New York.

In 1905 White and Jelliffe had published their translation of *The Psychic Treatment of Nervous Disorders* by the Swiss psychologist Paul DuBois, the first book-length treatment of the new psychology available in English. They wrote in their preface: 'That psychic disorders require psychic treatment, that many distressing and dangerous nervous disorders are purely or primarily psychic, these are the theses for which the book contends' (p. vi).[1] Three years later, the Boston psychiatrist Richard C. Cabot commented on the significance of the translation of DuBois (Cabot, 1908): 'It was not until the translation of DuBois' epoch making book that the American medical public became aware that there was such a thing as a scientific mind cure' (p. 2).

Prior to the establishment of the first professional groups, the US pioneers made extended visits to the leading European centres – to Zurich, Vienna, Paris, Berlin – and to the hospital of Emil Kraepelin in Munich which, as White (1936) recalled, 'became the Mecca of psychiatrists the world over' (p. 21). Jelliffe and White went to Europe twelve times altogether in the years 1905 to 1914. In 1906, Frederick Peterson, professor of clinical psychiatry at the College of Physicians and Surgeons of Columbia University, went to Zurich to work with Jung on the physiological correlates of Jung's word association tests. On his return to the States in February, Peterson sent Abraham Brill, his former student, to Jung and Bleuler at the Burghölzli. In the winter of 1909, August Hoch went to work with Jung for three months. In September 1911 James J. Putnam, Professor of Neurology at Harvard, travelled to the Third Psychoanalytic Congress in Weimar by way of Zurich, where he met Jung and also had six hours of psychoanalysis with Freud who was visiting Jung on his way back from a holiday in Bolzano (McGuire, 1974).

The traffic was not just one-way. In 1906, Putnam invited Pierre Janet to Harvard to give a series of fifteen lectures on the new dynamic psychology and in 1908 Ernest Jones, then working in Toronto, was invited by Morton Prince to present Freud's ideas to members of the Boston study group. Freud, accompanied by Jung and Ferenczi, made his famous trip to the US in September 1909 to speak at the twentieth anniversary of Clark University in Worcester, Massachusetts, at the invitation of the president of the university, psychologist G. Stanley Hall who, from his own travels in Europe, knew where interesting new work was being done (Hall, 1881, 1912).

The Worcester trip has an extensive literature. The correspondence between Jones and Freud of 18 May 1909, 1 June 1909 and 6 June 1909 details some of the political considerations that went into the planning of the trip, including Jones's suggestion that Freud should concentrate on psychoanalytic theory rather than specific case studies and that he should speak in English. The letters to Ferenczi of 5 May 1909, 25 July 1909 and 9 August 1909 are full of the concerns that accompany the planning of any major trip and illustrate Freud's well-documented travel anxieties. Freud's son Martin (1957) wrote an evocative memoir of the family summer in the resort town of Ammerwald on the Austrian–Bavarian border just before his father left for America. Meanwhile, G. Stanley Hall's autobiography (1923) and his biographer Dorothy Ross (1972) tell the story from the American point of view – Hall's *coup* in getting Freud to the US to speak at the upstart and relatively unknown Clark University. When Jones remonstrated to Freud that perhaps Clark University was not the best place for him to be first introduced to US audiences, Freud replied: 'I am going to where I have been invited.' Freud's co-speakers at Worcester were Jung on the word association tests, Adolf Meyer on his theory of the causes of schizophrenia, and the experimental psychologist Edward Bradford Titchener (1867-1927) on abnormal mental states. The August 1997 issue of *Vanity Fair* contains an amusing history of the summer 'camps' of the Eastern seaboard elite in the Adirondacks, along with some stunning photographs of the strange New World environment in which Freud found himself.

The famous US anarchist and feminist Emma Goldman was present at the Worcester lectures. In 1895–6 she had attended Freud's lectures on hysteria when she was studying for diplomas in nursing and midwifery at the General Hospital in Vienna and her life had been transformed by his discussion of sexuality (Goldman, 1931): 'For the first time I grasped the full significance of sex repression and its effect on human thought and action' (p. 173). At Clark University she was similarly moved:

I was deeply impressed by the lucidity of his mind and the simplicity of his delivery. Among the array of professors, looking stiff and important in their university caps and gowns, Sigmund Freud, in ordinary attire, unassuming, almost shrinking, stood out like a giant among pygmies. He had aged somewhat since I had heard him in Vienna in 1896. He had been reviled then as a Jew and irresponsible innovator; now he was a world figure; but neither obloquy nor fame had influence on the great man. (pp. 455–6)

The Worcester trip resulted in Freud's most popular book, *Five Lectures on Psychoanalysis*. It also marked the beginning of Jung's turning away from Freud: aboard ship Freud refused to discuss his dreams openly with Jung and Ferenczi for fear, as Jung recalled, that it would undermine his authority with his younger colleagues. To welcome their visitors to their exclusive summer home in the Adirondacks, the Putnam family hung the German flag, not realizing that Jung was Swiss, Freud was Austrian and Ferenczi was Hungarian.

The following spring, on 2 May 1910, at the 36th annual meeting of the American Neurological Association at the Willard Hotel in Washington DC, the American Psychopathological Association was founded with Morton Prince as president and Edouard Claparède, August Forel, Sigmund Freud, Pierre Janet and Carl Jung elected as honorary members. That September, Jones proposed to Putnam the founding of an American Psychoanalytic Association, but he was pre-empted by Brill who established a New York Psychoanalytic Society in February 1911 with himself as president, Bronislow Onuf as vice president and Horace Frink as secretary. The New York Society restricted its membership to 'physicians actively engaged in psychoanalysis' (BrillP).[2]

On 9 May 1911, at the Stafford Hotel on Baltimore's Vernon Square, nine East Coast psychiatrists founded the American Psychoanalytic Association with James J. Putnam as president and Jones as secretary.[3] In 1914, G. Lane Taneyhill at Johns Hopkins University Medical School in Baltimore offered the first optional course in psychoanalysis, and psychiatrists interested in psychoanalysis asked the visiting Paul Federn for the first training analysis in the US. Also in 1914, under the leadership of William Alanson White, the Washington Psychoanalytic Society was formed, meeting bi-weekly and, in direct opposition to New York, admitted lay members, a decision that prefigured the splits in US psychoanalysis that were to surface in the 1940s.

By virtue of his personal and professional prestige, it was the Harvard professor of neurology, James J. Putnam, who was instrumental in securing a hearing for psychoanalysis in the US medical establishment. Earlier in his career, Putnam, an upper-class progressive, had done research on lead poisoning from water pipes and on arsenic poisoning from wallpapers. In 1879 he had campaigned for the admission of women to the new four-year medical degree at Harvard Medical School.[4]

After initial reservations, Putnam was won over to psychoanalysis as a result of his participation in Prince's study group and after receiving Freud personally at his home in the Adirondacks after Freud's lectures at Clark University. Putnam fully accepted the clinical importance of childhood sexual experiences (Hale, 1971): '. . . the fierce yet often needless conflict between natural instincts and artificial social organization striving blindly and often cruelly for mastery' (p. 21). He made the first major professional presentation of the new psychoanalytic methods in the United States on 3 May 1910, presenting accounts of his work with twelve people (Putnam, 1910). One case was a forty-one-year-old woman who doubted whether her name was really her own and feared she was going insane.

After her father's death when she was very young, she was raised by her mother with the strict middle-class values of puritan New England. In her sessions with Putnam over the period of a year, she realized that she had been an imaginative child given to day-dreams which had been filled with sexual desires. She felt she couldn't ask her mother about her thoughts and feelings and felt humiliated about her curiosity about sex. She recalled, with great guilt, playing getting married with a boy playmate with a ceremony of joint urination to symbolize their marriage. She had masturbated for a while and had had sexual fantasies. As a young woman she had reproached herself for unladylike sexual thoughts and was frightened of her feelings, which seemed so in contradiction to the values her mother had tried to instil in her. Putnam summarized his picture of her situation (Putnam, 1910):

I have indicated only a portion of the facts that slowly came into the light of the patient's conscious memory, but enough to show that here was a tangle, made up of natural desires gone astray, needless self-reproaches, fears of discovery, fears of insanity, the assumed condemnation [of masturbation] by science and the Scriptures, the assumed abandonment of her maternal standards.

In the midst of this network struggled the patient, like a fly in a spider's web, feeling her life a contradiction, her mind diseased and so unworthy of her trust, and yet unable to see and face the causes of her distress. What wonder, that, as a result she reasoned herself to be incapable of reason. (p. 665)

The hour-and-a-half discussion following his paper stopped short of outright attack only because of Putnam's reputation (Putnam, 1910). 'We owe a debt to a man like Dr Putnam for the manner in which he has approached and attempted to develop this subject. However . . .' (p. 633). Dr Edward B. Angell of Rochester, New York, said that parasitic ideas needed ruthless treatment and should not be indulged by the physician. In his practice he had had a patient with a doubting mania and whenever such thoughts came to her he had made her sit up and say out loud: 'What a damn fool I am!' Two such treatments apparently relieved 'the whole train of morbid ideation' (p. 631).

Dr George Lincoln Walton, a consultant neurologist at the Massachusetts General Hospital, responded in a similar vein. In 1906 Walton had been invited to speak to students at the Boston Normal School of Gymnastics about worry, obsession and hypochondria, and had expanded his lecture into a best-selling self-help book called *Why Worry?*, which went through twenty-one printings from 1908 to 1932 (Walton, 1908). Walton said: 'Between getting up and doing something and analysing a dream it seems to me that an ounce of Muldoon is worth a pound of Freud' (p. 631). Putnam replied in rebuttal that in light of Walton's own book 'it would seem to be almost a cynicism to say to a psychopathic invalid "Why worry?" without ever putting the further question, "Why *do* you worry?"' (p. 638).

On 25 June 1910 Putnam wrote to William James about the success of his presentation (Hale, 1971): 'My "ovation" to which you refer was of course a Freudian victory alone, if victory it was. I do think that as much interest was manifest as one could fairly look for.' Ernest Jones, who had attended the conference to support Putnam, was quite pleased. He wrote to Freud immediately from the hotel: 'The feeling of the meeting was certainly more fair-minded than might have been expected and as many of the men said after "The Freudians won hands down." Outside the meetings, your work has been all the week the centre of interest and I am bombarded with questions. Many men are strongly in favour and are trying hard to learn it' (4 May 1910).

But psychoanalysis was not easy to learn. Freud's strength as an analyst of human emotions lay not only in his effective use of theory to help master the difficult feelings that appeared in the consulting room, but also in his unique quality of critical sympathy with which he was able to absorb even the most appalling stories of childhood distress. Physicians accustomed to dealing with organic nervous disorders associated with epilepsy, syphilis, burst blood vessels in the brain or multiple sclerosis, by close questioning about symptoms, found it difficult to get results with the method of sustained, unstructured listening and interpretation that psychoanalysis required. Nearly 100 years later Paul and Bluck (1997) described the emotional difficulties they experienced as psychiatric trainees in making the transition from the brief, focused interviews they had conducted as physicians and the hour-long unstructured listening they had to contend with in psychotherapy. In 1910, the Boston neurologist Philip Coombes Knapp replied to Putnam that he had tried Freud's method, finding it not only time-consuming but potentially dangerous (Putnam, 1910): 'Certainly in the cases due to a conscious experience if we sit down and harrow up the patient's feelings again in regard to that emotion we may reproduce the nervous disorder' (p. 635).

The difficulties associated with 'harrowing up' the patient's feelings lie in the fact that emotional disturbances arise not from emotional experiences *per se* but from the failures in the way they were processed. When feelings are made unacceptable they become part of an unresolved conflict that lies at the root of emotional disturbance. Physicians who themselves felt that sexual feelings in children were dirty and inappropriate would, if they attempted psychoanalysis, run the risk of repeating the original childhood experience where, as in Putnam's case study, the damage was caused by the mother stigmatizing her daughter's feelings rather than helping her to understand and accept them. In psychoanalysis, in place of repression – 'I mustn't feel this way' – there must be a conscious recognition and acceptance of feelings leading to their satisfactory expression in non-destructive ways. In the language of the times, repression was to be replaced by conscious sublimation. Physicians who, by virtue of temperament, training or conviction, found themselves unable to respond openly to their patients' emotional lives, backed away from emotional engagement with their patients' lived experience of life and, in spite of the appeal of a dynamic theory of symptoms, rejected psychoanalysis as being unworkable.[5]

Those attracted to Freud's work were drawn by his demonstration that symptoms had causes that could be understood. In 1913, in their two-volume handbook on the modern treatment of nervous and mental disease, White and Jelliffe wrote:

[Previous treatments] have been too narrowly concerned with details albeit important ones, such as disorders of gait, of power, of sensation and of related phenomena, to the neglect of the larger human problem of the individual, the man, the biological unit and his social relations. Practically all such works have stopped short at the point where they should have begun. They have told us in large measure how to patch up broken machinery, but rarely have they ever suggested or given directions for avoiding the wrecks. (p. v)

Brill (1942) recalled his dissatisfaction with the psychiatry of the 1900s as a 'barren more or less descriptive science with a poor background, a hopeless prognosis and a haphazard therapy' (p. 540).

What first appealed to me in psychoanalysis was not just its *modus operandi* which naturally keeps the physician interested and on the alert, but the logical system and the dynamism that underlies the whole therapy. Every symptom is definitely determined by something within the patient's own experience. Unlike other therapies which strove to remove this or that particular symptom without any regard for its basic cause, psychoanalysis considers the symptom as a surface indication of a disturbance in the total personality. (p. 542)

In the 14th edition of his *Outlines of Psychiatry* (1935) White wrote:

The most important single thing stressed by Freud and his followers has been the deterministic attitude towards psychological facts. No matter what the idea or feeling it must have an adequate explanation in psychological terms. No matter how apparently foolish it may be, an adequate study of all the conditions surrounding it will serve to explain it. No longer is it possible to rest content with calling a given idea a delusion or describing the products of delirium as incoherent. Such words only label the phenomena, they do not serve to throw any light upon them, they offer nothing by way of explanation. It was by approaching the neuroses with the absolute conviction that they had meaning and that the meaning could be discovered that explanation took the place of labelling, and the further the search was carried the more understandable the symptoms became. (p. 14)

The need was there. Physicians had become the port of call for help with emotional problems. Morton Prince recalled his slow realization that most of the people who rang his bell were not physically ill but suffered what were called at the time functional disorders (Taylor, 1928):

I remember well, how after graduation and I had hung up my 'shingle' and entered upon general practice, I expected that it would be patients with organic diseases, diseases of the heart, lungs and kidneys, typhoids and other infectious fevers etc that would ring my doorbell or send their calls in urgently.

It was only gradually that it dawned upon me that these were but a small part of the ills for which a physician's services are needed; and I found that it was the functional disturbances of a major and minor character that to an equal extent, at least with organic disease, incapacitated poor humanity from 'carrying on' and which I was called to rectify. (p. 97)

Patients, too, were attracted to psychoanalysis for the same reasons as physicians: existing treatments could at best relieve symptoms without effecting their permanent remission. As one woman wrote to Jelliffe (1916):

Dear Sir – The fact that you are one of the translators of — has led me to address this letter to you.

My husband suffered a complete nervous collapse in July 1909. He was pronounced a victim of neurasthenia by local physicians which opinion was later confirmed at the Hospital for the Insane. The patient took medicine for two years. Rest and change of scene have greatly improved but have failed to cure. He is possessed by worry, indecision, nervousness etc. I desire to find a physician who uses psychoanalysis in the treatment of nerves. Our local physicians seem either afraid or ignorant of that method and I have failed utterly in gaining any help in looking up the proper person to consult.

Will you recommend someone that uses this treatment? Our need is very great and that is my only excuse for asking this favour from a stranger.

In the background, behind the activities of White, Jelliffe, Brill and Prince, was Adolf Meyer, the director, from 1902–10, of the New York Pathological Institute. Born in Switzerland in 1866 and trained under August Forel, Meyer had emigrated to the United States in 1892 at the age of twenty-six, and held two posts at psychiatric hospitals, one as a pathologist at the Illinois Eastern Hospital for the Insane in Kankakee, Illinois, and the second as clinical director of the Worcester Hospital for the Insane in Massachusetts. Meyer, like other members of his generation, appreciated the accomplishment of Emil Kraepelin in eliminating the diagnosis of terminal dementia, effectively a death sentence for the mentally ill.

Kraepelin had introduced a scale of severity – acute, chronic and sub-acute – and new typologies – mania, melancholia and terminal or primary dementia – all of which brought a measure of disciplined thinking to the confusing array of symptoms confronting physicians in mental hospital settings. 'Kraepelin's creation of dementia praecox [is] the greatest advance in psychiatry in recent times,' wrote Meyer in 1906. Kraepelin's distinction between mania and dementia, which in today's terms would be equivalent to manic depression and schizophrenia, still defines the two major categories of severe mental distress.

Dedicated to a psychiatry that sought causes rather than simply treatments, Meyer created in the Pathological Institute on Ward's Island, New York City, the first institutional base for US psychiatrists interested in the new dynamic psychiatry emerging in Europe. Charles Macfie Campbell, Clarence Oberndorf, Abraham Brill and Trigant Burrow were among the well-known American psychiatrists who worked with Meyer on Ward's Island. In 1910, Meyer moved to the newly endowed Phipps Psychiatric Clinic at Johns Hopkins Medical School. His place as director of the Pathological Institute was taken by August Hoch who had become Professor of Psychiatry at Cornell University Medical College in Manhattan. It was due to Meyer's influence that Peterson and then Brill, Freud's first English translator, travelled to Europe in 1907.

Abraham Brill, who became the leading orthodox Freudian in the US, was born in Kanczuga in Galicia and migrated alone and penniless to the United States at the age of fourteen. In the tradition of the Great American Success Story, Brill worked his way through college and medical school, in his case by giving language and mandolin lessons, receiving his medical degree from Columbia in 1903. In 1907, sent by Peterson, Brill visited Jung and Bleuler in Zurich where he met Jones for the first time. The two of them then travelled on to meet Freud in Vienna. At this meeting, Freud granted Brill the English translation rights to all his works. As the first translator of Freud into English, and as a committed defender of Freud's ideas, Brill earned Freud's unquestioning loyalty. As Jones recalled, when he tried to tell Freud that Brill's translations were ruining the elegance of his prose style, Freud replied (Jones, 1959): 'Better to have a good friend than a good translator' (pp. 231–2).[6]

Brill was instrumental in winning Jelliffe over to a psychoanalytic point of view. In 1943, Jelliffe wrote to Brill (JelP):

I had been reading Freud but you made it vital and real for me. It was a 'forge' into which things could be plunged and you hammered it into shape. This you helped me to do and your help was generous and unstinted. Your genuine and intrinsic honesty, as well as good sense, made me cleave to you as a brother I never really had and supplemented my contacts with White that had been so invaluable. I had something to give to him also thanks to you, and White further simplified these for general use. It really was always Jelliffe, White *and* Brill, from that time onward.

Aside from Brill, Freud was not enamoured of the Americans nor of Jones, the Celt from Wales. In 1908, he wrote to Jung:

Jones and Brill have been to see me twice. I have arranged with Brill for the translation of a selection. He also called on Breuer and had a very odd reception. Jones is undoubtedly a very interesting, worthy man but he gives me a feeling of, I was almost going to say racial strangeness. He is a fanatic and doesn't eat enough. 'Let me have men about me that are fat' says Caesar etc. He almost reminds me of a lean and hungry Cassius. He denies all heredity; to his mind even I am a reactionary. How with your moderation were you able to get on with him? (3 May 1908)

Two months later Jung responded with his own impressions of Jones:

Jones is an enigma to me. He is so incomprehensible that it's quite uncanny. Is there more to him than meets the eye, or nothing at all? At any rate he is far from simple; an intellectual liar (no moral judgement intended!) hammered by the vicissitudes of fate and circumstance into too many facets. But the result? Too much adulation on the one hand, too much opportunism on the other? (12 July 1908)

In the meantime, Jones and Freud exchanged remarks about the failings of their colleagues in America. About Prince and his new journal Freud wrote: 'Now you will have found out what he is, the most arrogant ass you can imagine' (2 March 1911). Three years later, Freud wrote: 'Your friend, Morton Prince I still consider to be a plain ass' (22 February 1914). Jones, who usually kept his own counsel on the matter of personalities, wrote back: 'You are quite right about

Morton Prince. He is an amusing and agreeable companion, but is utterly stupid' (22 April 1914). About Meyer, Jones wrote: 'Adolf Meyer I like less and less. He bores me, which is the most unpardonable crime in civilized society' (4 May 1910). Freud agreed, writing: 'You are quite right about A. Meyer, he is unreliable and tries to turn things to his personal profit' (22 May 1910). About Putnam, Jones wrote: 'Putnam is incorrigible. He is a woman not a man' (22 Feb 1914), with Freud, who always had a soft spot for Putnam, replying: 'Perhaps you are too hard on him. He is over 60 and a doubter by constitution, he is brave for all this' (25 February 1914). Jelliffe came in for criticism, in connection with a translation for Jelliffe and White's *Psychoanalytic Review*: 'Jelliffe [was] a liar as always,' Freud wrote (25 December 1914).[7]

The Americans for their part refused to be drawn on the issues that were dividing European psychoanalysis. On 4 November 1913, in response to a request by Freud to intervene in American affairs on behalf of the movement, Jones wrote from his new base in London: 'In general the Americans find it very hard to enter into our conflicts. They regard them as merely personal, and rather to be deplored, and do not consider the scientific differences good ground for separating.'

After the war, White wrote to Jelliffe, who was making the rounds of the European centres: 'I am glad you have decided to call on Freud. Go and see Jones too. Let us take the attitude that if anyone wants to fight they can do the fighting. We haven't got the time nor the disposition' (16 June 1921). In September, on hearing Jelliffe's account of his visit to Vienna, he wrote: 'I am overjoyed at your opportunity to see all the Vienna group, to get into personal touch with them and to remove a lot of false ideas about our methods. I think it would be very helpful if we could all work in peace and harmony. I find myself quite out of conceit with the tendency which exists there, especially as near as I can understand, for everyone feels so antagonistic to everyone else' (22 September 1921).[8]

The medical institutions of the US, in which psychoanalysis found its niche, also served to inhibit its development. The physician's vision of the human organism revolved around the complex interactions between organ, tissue, cell and molecule. For the physician emerging from modern medical training with detailed visual images of the structure and functions of the parts of the human body, the whole human being was inevitably the sum of its organic parts. When confronted with the mysterious mental fragmentation of schizo-phrenia, it was inevitable that there would be physicians who would feel that this was an abnormality of the workings of the body. The insulin shock, cardiazol shock, amphetamine shock, electroshock therapies of the 1930s arose out of a frustrated medico-mechanistic sensibility. And even though the efficacy of such treatments was acknowledged to be limited for the confusing array of mental symp-toms for which something had to be done, there was nothing better on offer. The US psychiatrist Otto Will recalled psychiatric treatments that included injecting 15cc of serum from the blood of horses into the spinal columns of psychotic patients to create a fever that might kill possible organisms responsible (Thompson and Thompson, 1998). The British psychiatrist Tom Mayne recalled how the various shock treatments improved staff morale when they first came in (MetP): 'It began with giving fits chemically to people and the now famous insulin treatment. This raised the morale of staff enormously. I don't know how much good it did to the patients directly but because it improved the morale of the staff, the whole place changed and became optimistic and with a staff of high morale, patients were benefited' (p. 252).

In the US, the medicalization of psychoanalysis became contro-versial over the issue of the admission of the non-medically trained to psychoanalytic training programmes when in 1914 Washington said yes and New York said no. But behind this disagreement between Washington and New York lay a deeper divergence of perspective.

In New York, Abraham Brill, following theoretical guidelines adopted in Vienna, accepted only one out of eleven referrals as being suitable for psychoanalysis in the first twelve years of his practice, rejecting applicants on the basis of age and his assessment of their 'mental endowment' and 'character' (Brill, 1942). In classical psycho-analysis, schizophrenia could not be treated because of withdrawal from the outside world, an over-absorption with the self (excessive libido absorbed by the ego) and an apparent apathy, making the formation of the transference difficult if not impossible. As Freud (1914) wrote: '[Schizophrenic patients] display two fundamental characteristics, megalomania and diversion of interest from the external world – from people and things. In consequence of the latter change, they become inaccessible to the influence of psychoanalysis and cannot be cured by our efforts' (p. 66). Brill later modified his views, regretting that he had referred so many early patients to institutions, and found methods of establishing rapport deemed not strictly analytic but which seemed to be effective (Brill, 1929).

In Washington, William Alanson White rejected Viennese leadership and remained committed to a psychoanalytic understanding of the severe distress he was seeing in hospitalized patients, a completely different group from the socially successful people that Brill was admitting to psychoanalysis. White insisted that psychosis could be treated dynamically. In 1919, at the first meeting of the American Psychoanalytic Association after the war, Clarence Oberndorf (1949) recalled that White rose and declared: 'The time has come to free American psychiatry from the domination of the Pope in Vienna' (p. 159). White was on the geographical periphery of the professional centres of New York and Boston in the southern city of Washington DC. There he had the institutional support and relative freedom to create the base that was to lead to the development of interpersonal psychoanalysis – the distinctive US contribution to the development of psychoanalysis.

In October 1903, White had been appointed Medical Superintendent of the Government Hospital of the Insane in Washington, a post he held until his death in 1937. A high-level political appointment made by executive order of President Theodore Roosevelt, White's mandate was to modernize the treatment of the mentally ill, to replace prejudice and ignorance with scientific knowledge.

Roosevelt's appointment of White in 1903 contrasts with the eugenic legislation adopted by the State of Indiana in 1907 and the State of California in 1909, which permitted compulsory sterilization of patients admitted to state mental hospitals for the conditions of familial feeble-mindedness, schizophrenia or manic depression. Between 1907 and 1940, 18,552 mentally ill people in state institutions were surgically sterilized, over half of this number in California, with thirty states enacting their own versions of compulsory sterilization (Grob, 1985). A 1934 investigation of the practice of sterilization by a committee of the American Neurological Association, funded by a grant from the Carnegie Foundation, recommended that the practice should be voluntary rather than compulsory. In Germany, the Nazi government was able to justify its own sterilization programme by reference to US laws in general and to the California experience in particular. By March 1938, an estimated 250,000 sterilization operations had been carried out in Nazi Germany compared to a total number in all categories of 11,484 in California and 25,403 in the US as a whole. A contemporary US observer supported the policy (Smyth, 1938): 'Investigators agree that the policy there [in Germany] is being enforced in a scientific spirit without racial or political implications and with a minimum of difficulty' (p. 1234).

In 1903 White, aged thirty-three and with ten years of psychiatric experience in the New York State Hospital system at Binghampton, brought a disciplined scientific humanism to his work as a psychiatrist. As he recalled in his autobiography (1938), he had entered psychiatry with a trust in science 'to search with an abiding faith in the understandability of psychological happenings' (p. 77). In 1925, for a festschrift for Morton Prince, he wrote (White, 1925a): 'Through the long years that the so-called "insane" have remained outside our ken, it has been sufficient to dismiss their comments, ways of thinking and conduct as simply "crazy", which implied that they were altogether alien to us and nothing more be said' (p. 32). White's often quoted guiding statement about people in extreme mental difficulty was (White, 1937): '. . . these patients are very much like the rest of us, in fact very much more *like* the rest of us than they are *different* from us' (p. 58).

White developed a line of work parallel to that of Eugen Bleuler (1857–1939) in Switzerland. Bleuler, like White, was interested in understanding the apparently incomprehensible utterances of many of his institutionalized patients. He lived with his patients in the Rheinau Hospital for the Insane continuously for twelve years and was directly involved in all therapeutic interventions. With this innovative approach, Bleuler anticipated the progressive programmes of community care instituted by White and others in the US in the 1920s. Bleuler believed that intensive care for patients with acute conditions was essential if the patients were not to deteriorate under hospitalization. His concept of schizophrenia as a fragmentation of the psyche, in which normal associations no longer occurred, took the place of

Kraepelin's less descriptive category of dementia praecox (Bleuler, 1911).

White taught his staff to respect and protect those entrusted to their care. His guideline to staff faced with difficult questions of management and care of people in extreme distress was: 'Which course is best for the patient?' In 1928, he authorized the dismissal of two attendants for striking a patient, refusing to permit them to resign. In response to an official government enquiry from E. C. Pinney, First Assistant Secretary of the US Department of the Interior, questioning both White's action and the reliability of the testimony of patients, White replied:

If it were necessary, in order to dismiss a brutal attendant for the abuse of patients, to have witnesses of sound mind, a situation would be created which would make it physically impossible in the majority of cases to effect such a dismissal and would place a not inconsiderable number of patients in the Hospital who are helpless because of their mental condition at the mercy of such employees. It is the duty of every attendant to protect the patients in the Hospital whether they be under his immediate charge or not, and in the particular instance under discussion there were two attendants present and still the patient was not protected.[9]

In 1903, at the Government Hospital for the Insane, White found a backward, unkempt hospital of 100 buildings spread over 855 acres, with 2300 patients, a quarter of whom slept on straw beds on the floor, and a demoralized staff 'beset with a swarm of grafters, chiselers, and misguided politicians' (Sullivan, 1937). He immediately forbade the use of restraint with bolted chairs, leather wristlets, hand muffs, wire helmets, room lock-ups and straitjackets as methods of control of patients whose behaviour provoked fear and panic among staff. Although the idea of non-restraint had first been introduced at the Lincoln Asylum in England in 1837 and had been developed in England by John S. Conolly (1856) into a general philosophy and theory of hospital management, in the US, non-restraint remained a minority view of a few radicals. As White (1938) recalled: 'Everybody protested that they could not get along without restraint' (p. 96).

White instituted modern methods of working by insisting that thought was required to heal the mentally disturbed rather than force to subdue them. In 1911, in an official letter clarifying his position on restraint, he noted that of 2921 patients in the hospital in the month of February, there were only seven incidents requiring the use of restraint to prevent the patients from injuring themselves. At the same time he affirmed his basic principle that mental illness was not to be punished but was meant to be understood (Grob, 1985): 'I believe that a tremendous amount of suffering is still the lot of the insane person because he is misunderstood' (p. 72).

The tensions between treatment and control encountered by White in 1903 still remain unresolved in psychiatric practice to a large extent, as can be seen in the ongoing debates today over the use of electro-convulsive shock therapy (ECT) and the use of drugs as chemical straitjackets (Scull, 1993). In the 1970s the organized views of patients against forced drug and ECT treatments could be heard from the Mental Patients Liberation Project in Boston, an initiative that developed in the 1990s into Support Coalition, an alliance of thirty local patient groups in the US, Canada, Europe and New Zealand; the UK mental health organization Mind; the UK organiz-ation of mental health workers, Psychotherapists and Counsellors for Social Responsibility; and the Psychology Politics Resistance network of psychologists and non-psychologists concerned with patient rights (Brown, 1973; Oakes, 1997).

At his own hospital White personally interviewed every patient admitted. He introduced evening staff meetings to discuss current clinical and research issues which were open to all doctors in the Washington area. In 1909, he initiated the publication of a bulletin to make the evening talks available to the wider Washington com-munity. In 1913 he began programmes of occupational therapy and continued an interest in industrial safety with a study of the effects of fatigue on work-related medical conditions. In 1916, White had the name of the hospital changed from the Government Hospital for the Insane to St Elizabeths Hospital on the grounds that the word Insane in the original name stigmatized the sufferers of mental illness.

Guiding his practice was his straightforward use and development of psychoanalysis. At the 70th annual meeting of the American Psych-iatric Association in Baltimore in 1914, in response to an attack on dream analysis, psychic causation and the sexual aetiology of neurosis, White said (D'Amore, 1976): 'I have no doubt that many hypotheses will be laughed at in years to come as being at fault, perhaps some of them ridiculous, but what we want is their correction at this point; we want more light; we want more truth; it does not do any good to call them absurd and let the matter go at that' (p. 71).

White was an exemplar of the progressive tradition of the professional middle class as it was developing in the US in the last quarter of the nineteenth century. In pre-war segregated Washington, a city of the South, he opened the doors of St Elizabeths to African-American students at Howard University against protests by the administrations of white-only medical schools whose students refused to train with African-American colleagues. In 1905, he appointed Dr Mary O'Malley (1867–1939), with whom he had worked at Binghampton, as the first woman physician on the hospital staff. He was utterly opposed to the use of sterilization and in 1916, when the Secretary of the Lunacy Commission of the State of Maryland wrote to ask him if he would speak about the procedure at a conference on mental defectives, White replied: 'I do not believe that there is the slightest particle of justification for the mutilating operations that are being advocated broadcast over the country at this time, and should I happen to talk in Baltimore at your meeting I should unhesitatingly denounce the sterilization propaganda.' And in 1936 White responded to a query from C. M. Hincks, General Director of the National Committee for Mental Hygiene, about the efficacy of insulin shock therapy: 'I have the suspicion that some of the schizophrenic patients get well with insulin shock treatment and other similar methods that are exceedingly painful and disagreeable in order to get out of the sanitarium where they use such methods or at least escape their repetition. What do you think of that?'[10]

After one of White's many appearances before Congressional Committees as a leading defender of modern methods of treatment of mental illness, the *New York Herald Tribune* described him in the following terms:

Dr W. A. White, leader of the most advanced thought in the care of the insane, president and director in learned societies, author of many fundamental articles and treatises and books, an authority quoted by many others, leader of his profession, devotedly admired by his co-equals and looked up to as the 'master' by youngsters growing up in the science of saving sick souls, philosopher and friendly guide to every human being who crosses his path – Dr William A. White is the witness. (1 May 1927)

And, in one of the few positive remarks Ernest Jones was to make about Freud's rivals, he wrote (Jones, 1959): '. . . he had two valuable gifts: one of inspiring and encouraging his staff at Washington in a remarkable degree, the other a capacity for fluent and lucid exposition that brought him a wide audience among all classes in the United States' (p. 233).

Part of White's influence was due to his publishing activities with Smith Ely Jelliffe on the *Psychoanalytic Review*, begun in 1913, and the *Nervous and Mental Disease* monograph series, started in 1907. Jelliffe had already purchased the leading psychiatric journal, *The Journal of Nervous and Mental Disease*, in 1902. The Jelliffe–White partnership lasted for forty years, their close personal and professional relationship augmented by annual month-long visits to Jelliffe's summer cottage on Lake George in upstate New York, where the two men would psychoanalyse each other, talking all day on walks around the lake and in the surrounding countryside. In a correspondence with Harry Stack Sullivan after White's death in 1937, Jelliffe wrote (JelP):

He was my foremost teacher. He was pre-eminent but it was not for me to say so without apparently attacking Meyer whose academic prestige has been so extolled. He was the greater man even if he did not have the background of Meyer nor was he equipped with the intellectual tools so amply, but he did put psychiatry on the map even if he did not put partly castrated pupils in professional chairs, most of them excellent persons but none so far great 'liberators' as you so aptly put it. (1 June 1937)

The two men had first met when Jelliffe took a summer appointment at Binghampton in 1896. Both were New Yorkers, Jelliffe from secure circumstances born in a brownstone on West 38th Street in Manhattan, White from a relatively poor middle-class neighbourhood in Brooklyn. Jelliffe was older than White by four years. After graduating from

Columbia with his medical degree in 1889, Jelliffe spent a year in Europe, paid for with $1000 from his cousin Smith Ely, the reforming mayor of New York. White, on graduating from the Long Island College Hospital Medical School in 1891, got a job as house and ambulance surgeon at the Eastern District Hospital of Brooklyn, where he tended the often horrific cases associated with inner-city urban life (White, 1938): '[I saw] people burned to a crisp, smashed, crushed, broken by machinery and by being run over, suicides, murders' (p. 41). Then, prior to his appointment as fourth assistant physician at the state hospital in Binghampton, he worked under similarly difficult conditions at the Alms House, Work House and Penitentiary Hospitals on the East River. Meanwhile, after returning from Europe, Jelliffe proceeded to establish a private practice in Brooklyn, and married Helena Dewey Leeming in 1893 at the age of twenty-seven, moving his practice to 231 W 71st Street on Manhattan's West Side. White came late to marriage, marrying, at the age of forty-eight, Lola Purman Thurston, the widow of John Mellen Thurston, former Republican Senator from Nebraska

Both Jelliffe's and White's national reputations were enhanced by their participation in two of the most famous trials in the US. In 1906, the society architect and notorious womanizer Stanford White was shot dead by the Detroit millionaire Harry K. Thaw while he was dining in Madison Square Garden at the Roof Top restaurant, designed by White himself. At his second trial in 1908, Thaw was acquitted by reason of insanity on the basis of testimony given by Jelliffe. In 1924, William Alanson White testified for seven straight hours at the even more famous trial of Nathan Loeb and Richard Leopold, who had endeavoured to commit a 'perfect crime' by murdering thirteen-year-old Bobby Franks. The defence conducted by the legendary Clarence Darrow featured White as his star witness and succeeded in saving the defendants from the electric chair.[11]

The fundamental problem confronting the early US analysts, the problem that divided Washington and New York, was how to move beyond the mechanistic medical sensibility of seeing the human organism, in Adolf Meyer's words, as a 'mechanical-reflex machine' to an understanding of how the human organism integrates the sum of its parts 'to constitute itself as a subject' (Meyer, 1922). In agreement with

Meyer, White, instead of looking inward at the arrangement of body parts as the origin of the human subject, looked outward at the network of interpersonal relationships as the source of human individuality and selfhood. In an exchange of views with Meyer, White wrote (JelP):

You know my concept of the individual, or at least you know that I do not think there is any such thing as an individual in the ordinary sense, that the individual as we ordinarily think of him is a pure abstraction, the individual merely merges into his environment and is part and parcel of it. (5 November 1919)

White's view of human individuality as being fundamentally social was radically different from Freud's concept of the human being as a biological organism whose instinctual conflicts needed to be tamed as part of the process of entering the social environment. Freud saw the untamed human group as a potential threat to the civilized individual. White saw the human group as fundamental, as necessary for the very existence of the individual.

In 1921, Freud put forward the fundamental questions he believed needed to be asked about groups: What is a group? How does the group exert its influence on an individual? What is the nature of the psychological influence that the group exerts on the individual? (Yalom, 1974). But for White these problems did not exist. As he explained to Meyer:

I believe in other words that when we think of a group of units as being associated we are much too much inclined to think that their association is the mathematical sum of what each of them individually represents, but I believe this to be a very gross error. Society is composed of individuals, the smallest society conceivable would be composed of two individuals, but there is another element that enters that is of great importance and that is the relationship between the two individuals, and that relationship is a higher state than either one of the individuals alone and contains possibilities which are not resident in either one.

White, the optimistic American in a period of the emergence of America as the dominant global capitalist power, saw no limit to the possibilities of human progress. Socially secure in a gentile identity as a doctor, with the high social status the United States conferred on its medical profession, White, who in his professional development remained available and open and alive to the experience of patients, saw himself as intrinsically connected to the rest of humanity in an indissoluble matrix.

As a gentile he was not subjected to the notorious anti-Semitism of the US medical profession, a profession that did not relax its restrictions against admission of Jews to medical training until the mid-1960s, when progressive political currents in the US successfully created equal opportunities for women and members of the ethnic minorities (Barinaga, 1997). Julius Axelrod, a Nobel-prizewinning biochemist, recalled the anti-Semitic restrictions that prevented him, in 1933, from attending medical school (Axelrod, 1996): 'When I graduated from City College, I applied to several medical schools but couldn't get into any. At that time there were quotas for Jewish students; many of them were very bright and there were too many Jewish students applying for the limited number of places. I wasn't in the top echelon. My grades were good but they weren't extraordinarily good' (p. 30).

White, while not consciously anti-Semitic, thought in terms of race, phrasing Jung's concept of the collective unconscious as 'a racial inheritance' (White, 1924). His ideas included many of the prejudices of the 1920s about the so-called Jewish race. In 1924 he consulted Otto Rank for six analytic sessions, apparently about marital problems. 'I was prepared to fall for him hard' he wrote to Jelliffe (7 August 1924). But White was unhappy about being billed for the week that he could not come to New York, writing:

Of course he has something that I want and I have got to pay him for it I suppose – whatever he asks, but it does seem such a shortsighted policy. A man's success in this world seems to me to depend more on his friends than on himself and when you take every possible occasion to alienate the friendship of everybody that seeks you out I wonder what the answer can be. Is his [Rank's] ability great enough to stand it? Perhaps it is. On the other hand I should think he would have more feeling for the regard in which race is held. These are just the things which spoil our whole reaction towards their race after we have gotten it in pretty good shape, and so that is that.

Freud, on the other hand, the pessimistic European, a Jew living in a threatening anti-Semitic culture, felt quite the opposite – his personal achievements were in spite of, not because of, his connectivity to the social world. White felt that the human being *was* the group. Freud, on the other hand, believed that the 'group mind' imposed a lower level of civilization on the individual. Using the powerful image of the primal horde, Freud evoked the dangers to civilized values presumed to be, not the result of historically formed social arrangements, but universals, inherent in all human social groupings. As Adler might have put it, Freud's experience of life was such that he had little social feeling.

White understood the fundamental radical implications of psycho-analysis for psychiatry. And in the tradition of American radicalism he had the confidence to take from Europe what was needed in the US without being awed by European personalities, traditions and accomplishments. Throughout a distinguished career, he defended and advanced the principles of psychoanalysis without needing to either attack or defend Freud himself but simply acknowledging Freud as the creator of psychoanalysis. In his presidential address to the 81st meeting of the American Psychiatric Association in May 1925, White (1925b) criticized the views of psychiatrists who located mental illness as a psychological disturbance caused by an infectious agent, rather than being able to accept the psychoanalytic view that developmental events experienced subjectively over a number of years were the most likely aetiological agents.

Since the advent of psychoanalysis we, for the first time, have our vision directed to where the real trouble has taken place, and our interest centred upon the actual mechanism that is producing the symptoms. We understand that the deflection of our vision to the body or to the infectious organism are but examples of that mechanism of projection with which we have become so familiar, and it was because of the emotional necessity for seeing causes elsewhere than in ourselves that we, for so many centuries, have been unable to face the facts of our own mental life. (p. 9)

Citing Janet, Bernheim, Liébault and Kraepelin for bringing in a new era of dynamic psychiatry, White reserved special praise for Freud:

'. . . for this order of things we have one man to thank more than anyone else in all the world and that is Professor Freud and his method of psychoanalysis' (p. 8).

White's leadership of one of the most important mental health institutions in the US, and his insistence that psychoanalytic ways to understand and treat extreme mental states would yield results, offered a viable alternative to the Freudian orthodoxy practised in New York and Boston.

8

New Theory, New Splits:
Psychoanalysis
in the United States II

Under the leadership of William Alanson White, the facility at St Elizabeths, originally designed for 3000 beds, became so oversubscribed that in 1926 a report by a special commission appointed by Hubert Work, Secretary of the Department of the Interior, called for two new hospital buildings, expanding the unit by 1500 beds (Kline et al., 1926). White, with his programme to educate Washington area physicians about modern approaches to mental health, and with his vigilance that those admitted were not to be treated as objects of medical curiosity but as human beings in difficulty, had made St Elizabeths the obvious place to refer people in psychological trouble. New psychoanalytic theory coming out of Washington was based on the clinical approach begun by White.

Among White's staff was Nolan Don Carpenter Lewis (1889–1979), pathologist at St Elizabeths from 1919 to 1922 and director of clinical psychiatry there from 1923 to 1936. In 1936, Lewis became director of the New York Psychiatric Institute until his retirement in 1953. He was also a leading consultant on Nazi psychology at the Nuremberg war crimes trials in 1945–6. Throughout his period at St Elizabeths, Lewis kept clinical case notes of his patients (LewP). His cases illustrate the range of presenting problems of patients admitted to St Elizabeths. They show clearly what White meant when he said that mental patients were very much more like the rest of us than they are different from us, that they were people in great pain and that immediately upon admission they were entitled to protection and humane treatment rather than being treated as 'other', with a corresponding licence to experiment on them.

*

A married woman of twenty-six with two children came for treatment for a cycle of manic episodes. She was the only, much-indulged child of wealthy parents, had had a normal childhood but always seemed to be 'oversexed'. She had been on the *Titanic* when it sank, had saved two children and had suffered considerable shock. Despite this, she was convinced the experience had nothing to do with her present condition. She had had exceptionally difficult labours when giving birth to each of her two children. After the birth of her first child she developed a severe depression with inertia, fatigue, headaches and morbid pessimism. Nothing seemed worth the effort. She then experienced a period of elevated mood in which she had many visitors, wrote many letters, spent a lot of money, and told 'smutty jokes'. She had experienced six of these cycles before coming for treatment during a depressed phase.

A thirty-two-year-old Navy physician had suffered several cycles of depression and excitement before being referred and admitted to St Elizabeths. In spite of his apparently successful education and career as a physician he was self-deprecating, and felt timid and anxious. During his excited periods he was very preoccupied with women, and dated many of them, but was unable to feel any love. He felt he let people trample over him. Believing that his teeth were responsible for his depressions he had had them removed. He then felt deformed and embarrassed by his false teeth to the extent that he believed that he would never be able to love or kiss a woman.

A twenty-nine-year-old lawyer from Washington DC came for analysis, suffering from anxiety. He was anxious trying cases. In the past he would have been able to control his anxiety, but now he occasionally lost the thread of his argument. During very severe anxiety attacks he drank heavily to seek relief and went for long walks, often from one o'clock to four in the morning. He experienced pressure and nervousness throughout his body, broke out into cold sweats and had palpitations. Although he had a relationship with a woman he saw regularly, he had never had sexual relations. He had been plagued with sexual thoughts ever since he was a boy, which filled him with shame.

*

A forty-five-year-old man, with inherited wealth from his father's successful chain of hotels, had been under medical observation before being referred for psychoanalysis. Fourteen years previously, he had had a small sore on his genitals for which he took three Wassermann tests. Two of the tests were negative but one gave a weak positive result. Although assured by the specialist that the positive was a false positive, the man was so frightened he had himself tested for syphilis 'in all the cities of the United States'. His physician finally obtained all the Wassermann tests and destroyed them. The man was both disturbed and excited by his physician's action. The result, however, was that he began to form a system of phobias related to the theme of contamination: a great fear of blood, a fear of wounding himself, a fear of cleaning his teeth in case he made his gums bleed and constant hand-washing with a special blue antiseptic soap. He sent his clothes to the cleaners frequently and threw out large numbers of shirts, socks and underwear. Although very sexually active in the past, over the past three years he had developed fears about touching or kissing his current girlfriend whom he now introduced as his sister. In other sexual encounters, he checked carefully beforehand to see if the women had pimples or blemishes of any kind. He slept poorly and had suicidal thoughts.

Such cases of individual mental distress continue to separate mental health workers along a continuum between the poles of those who seek organic origins for mental pain of this kind and those who seek their origins in the cumulative failures of interpersonal relationships.

At St Elizabeths, the exploration of the organic correlates of mental disturbance were a central part of White's treatment of the whole person. Nolan Lewis investigated the mind–body mechanisms that were involved in causing high leucocyte counts, increased adrenalin output and the production of fevers associated with emotional states. And approaching this from the reverse angle, Lewis was also interested in mental states that were caused by genuine organic disturbances in the brain. He did *post mortem* studies on St Elizabeths' patients, establishing behavioural and experiential patterns associated with injuries or lesions in specific areas of the brain – the pre-frontal lobes, the corpus callosum, the frontal lobes and the anterior fossa.

In spite of the attention paid to the physiology of mental distress, the approach at St Elizabeths with its insistence on the importance of psychoanalysis and the impossibility of reducing mental distress to purely physiological causes, brought it into conflict with mainstream American psychiatry and neurology. In 1930, Lewis put the St Elizabeths case to the annual meeting of the Society of Neurological Surgeons in Washington DC (Lewis, 1931):

While I have always placed great hopes on neuropathological developments and have many emotional investments there at present, I am unable to conceive that even the finest methods yet to be devised will ever be able to determine the content of a hallucination or a delusion, or that any examination of the cortex will reveal the presence or absence there of those most important events in the early childhood of life – those relationships with the parents, educational mistakes, psychic traumatas and emotional attachments, all of which constitute a part of the personality and in fact determine a goodly portion of the so-called constitution. (p. 34)

The St Elizabeths' argument was not entirely against the tide. In the 1920s and 1930s there was widespread revulsion against the brutalities of standard psychiatric treatments. But, although the abuses of psychiatric treatment have been memorably represented for the present generation by Ken Kesey's fable of repressive tolerance, *One Flew over the Cuckoo's Nest* and in the film adaptation directed by Milos Forman (1976), starring Jack Nicholson and Louise Fletcher, the real gothic horror of treatment in mental hospitals, which White was concerned to prevent, is not well known.

In the 1920s, at the Trenton State Hospital in New Jersey, Henry A. Cotton, a former student of Adolf Meyer, was, as superintendent, given a free hand to practise his own unique focal infection theory of mental distress (Scull, 1984). Primary among the organs held responsible for mental illness were the teeth, the tonsils and the colon. In 1919–20 Cotton had 4000 teeth extracted from the inmates under his care, and a further 6000 teeth in 1920–1. A visitor to the hospital commented on the 'sadness' he felt at seeing so many toothless patients, none of whom had been given the promised dentures. Cotton also carried out colectomies, the surgical removal of part of the colon, on the patients in his care.

When added to the now-discredited treatments of insulin shock therapy, camphor-induced convulsions, histamine shock and trans-orbital and pre-frontal lobotomies, along with the current practices of electro-convulsive shock therapy and regimens of drug-induced chemical straitjackets, most observers at a distance will feel that drugs and psychiatry are the last resort, tantamount at best to throwing in the towel and at worst to torture as an expression of ignorance and hatred, or in the words of one experienced worker with psychotic patients, 'a desperate manic defense of frustrated therapeutic omni-potence' (Weigert, 1939).

On a different medical front, orthodox Freudians in the US were building up their practices, trying to gain respectability for psycho-analysis within the US medical profession and looking to Vienna and Berlin for training and theory. In September 1921, four leading members of the New York Psychoanalytic Society – Leonard Blumgart, Albert Polon, Abram Kardiner and Clarence Oberndorf – were in analysis with Freud, following the example set by Adolf Stern, Monroe Meyer and Horace Frink two years earlier. On 12 May 1927, Clarence Oberndorf spoke of the problem of the lack of originality in American psychoanalysis in an address to the American Psychoanalytic Associ-ation (Oberndorf, 1949):

It must be conceded regretfully that American investigations which have altered or essentially supplemented the vast amount of research of European analysts in regard to the theory of the neuroses or to the functioning of the unconscious, or to the sciences of religion and politics, to the interpretation of aesthetics and the psychology of the artist are relatively meagre. (p. 161)

The issue of lay analysis was central to Freudians in the United States in their concern to be accepted by the US medical profession. In 1921 Brill wrote to Jelliffe: 'I have always objected to laymen practising psychoanalysis on patients and the more I see of it the more strength-ened I am in my conviction.' Brill's position in his American context

of wanting acceptance by a conservative anti-Semitic medical establishment ran against that of Freud who was strongly in favour of lay
analysts. The issue was hotly debated by the International Psychoanalytic Association in a famous meeting in 1927 (anon., 1927).

Brill and Oberndorf, supported by Jelliffe, led a New York delegation that argued that US conditions were such that psychoanalysis
would never be accepted unless its practice was restricted to the
medically qualified. Franz Alexander, a Hungarian analyst based in
Chicago, opposed the New Yorkers, arguing that psychoanalysis
needed medicine far less than medicine needed psychoanalysis: 'It is
not worthwhile to get rid of the lay analyst simply in order that
psychoanalysis may be admitted to full recognition by academic medicine' (anon., 1927, p. 229). The New York delegation met further
opposition from the Hungarians, led by Sándor Ferenczi, who argued
that a psychoanalysis dealing with the unconscious was a speciality
of its own with little or no substantive relationship to the anatomy
and physiology learned in medical training:

... we are of the opinion that psycho-analytical therapy is a special method
of healing which cannot be included in university curricula under present
conditions of medical training. The centre of gravity of medical studies lies
in anatomy and physiology, that of psychoanalysis in psychological subjects;
a qualified physician is therefore scarcely better fitted for psychoanalysis
than an educated layman. (p. 281)

Freud was unable to persuade the New Yorkers that the spirit of
psychoanalysis was not medical. On 6 July 1927 he wrote to Jones about
his disagreement with New York: 'Originally I wanted to have a more
detailed discussion with the New Yorkers, who betray just as low a level
in this question as in other matters, but I gave it up as fruitless.'

The Brill wing of US psychoanalysis continued to reject the non-
medically qualified for training, ensuring that the class, gender and
ethnic restrictions of US medical education would also apply to
psychoanalysis, narrowing its social base and restricting its intellectual
perspective until the late 1980s when a law suit, arguing restraint of
trade against the American Psychoanalytic Association, bolstered the
efforts of those inside the American Association to gain passage of

a bye-law amendment admitting the non-medically qualified to its training (Chiarandini, 1994).

In contrast to Brill, White sought consolidation of psychoanalysis in America by broadening its appeal and widening its training. In so doing he created the space for the generation that was to become known as the Washington or interpersonal school of psychoanalysis. By 1926, St Elizabeths was the leading institution for research into the treatment of psychoses by psychoanalytic methods, for research into the prevention of mental disease, for its professional and popular publication programme, for its specialized training for physicians, nurses and social workers, and for its use of non-medically trained professionals – psychologists, nurses and psychiatric social workers – for primary patient care in the hospital, particularly in preventing the deterioration associated with the infamous back wards of mental hospitals (Woolley and Hall, 1925).

At the level of theory, it fell to Harry Stack Sullivan to achieve the most influential theoretical expression of the practice of the Washington school of psychoanalysis. His interpersonal psychoanalysis was the distinctive American contribution to the development of psycho-analytic theory. Sullivan graduated from medical school in 1917 at the age of twenty-five. After working as an army psychiatrist and as a public health psychiatrist, he joined White at St Elizabeths as a Veterans Bureau Liaison Officer. In 1923 he took a job at the Sheppard and Enoch Pratt Hospital in Towson, Maryland, where from 1925 to 1930 he was director of clinical research.

At the Sheppard Sullivan accumulated the clinical experience that was to inform his theoretical writing. His first published paper, *Schizophrenia: Its Conservative and Malignant Features*, written a year after his appointment to the Sheppard, shows the respect for human motivation and purpose he observed in White's work at St Elizabeths (Sullivan, 1924):

In attacking and understanding the problem of understanding and treatment of schizophrenia, the element of motivation seems logically fundamental to all others. As Dr William A. White has said, 'We must understand what the patient is trying to do. If the element of purpose and means is eliminated, there results sterile brain physiology [and] psychologization . . . (p. 78)

Sullivan believed that the distinguishing feature of the human being was in the specific organization of the human brain to allow the development through language of a cerebrally integrated organism or self. As such, the problems of psychopathology became problems in communication. 'From this view point, it will be seen that any problem in psychopathology is a problem in symbol functioning, a matter of seeking to understand and interpret eccentric symbol performances' (Sullivan, 1925, p. 72). Central to Sullivan's approach to the psychotherapy of schizophrenia was his insistence that there was no such thing as 'word salad', that all communications from the severely disturbed were meaningful. 'The incomprehensible is to be regarded as fragments of intent which come to light after the patient has ceased his efforts at and abandoned his hopes of communicating with the environment' (p. 72).

Sullivan's approach to extreme mental states is appealing. One feels that sufferers of these states of mind would be in good hands with such a clinician. But there is the question of clinical efficacy, a question that deeply concerned Sullivan himself. Sullivan tape-recorded over 350 sessions with his most disturbed patients at the Sheppard. Both his successes and failures became the clinical evidence – presented at length as verbatim reports of exchanges – with which he argued his views. His cases illustrated the difficulties that caused classical psychoanalysts to feel that such individuals were unreachable by the methods of the talking cure.

A young man of eighteen was admitted to Sullivan's care in the midst of a paranoid breakdown. After a previous period of several months of seclusion in his room at his parents' home, he had attended a party where he felt confused and observed himself laughing frequently for no reason. Some days later he panicked, and began to walk through the streets, believing that he was being chased by the cars on the road, that only every third house was lit and that he was about to be crucified or otherwise killed.

Sullivan found that the young man retained memories leading to his present state, including episodes of sexual abuse at the hands of his elder brother, shameful early homosexual experiences and shameful present desires for cunnilingus. Sullivan was able to reconstruct with the young man the sequence of his thoughts on his night of terror before his admission to hospital. He had begun with suicidal thoughts at home, leading him to walk the streets, his suicidal feelings subsequently displaced on to people in passing cars who he felt wanted to kill him, and then to fears of violating his religious beliefs, for which he was to be ceremonially killed, every third house being lit as part of the ceremony.

After some months of therapy, the young man was able to talk about his fantasies and fears and to resolve them to the extent that his desires no longer made him feel suicidal. Sullivan concluded: 'He is now in training for an occupation for which he has capacity. He is not "normal" but his cravings no longer disorder his thinking and behaviour. Schizophrenic phenomena, projections, compensatory and decidedly pathological sublimatory activities are no longer in evidence' (p. 37).

More extreme cases were less amenable to treatment. Mr O., a thirty-six-year-old assistant superintendent at a public utility, married with three children, became increasingly irritable at work. On 12 July 1924, O. had held a meeting with his district superintendent at a hotel where O. alleged that his Catholic superiors were conspiring to fire him. Two days later, he returned home from work early at 3 p.m. and was later found standing rigidly at his desk in his room. A doctor was called and administered morphine to bring his pulse rate down. He went to bed and woke the next morning insisting he was all right, had a cup of coffee and, before anyone could stop him, took off at great speed in the family car. The road was blocked by a 5-ton truck and he crashed the car, utterly demolishing it. Miraculously, he was uninjured. He was then handcuffed and taken to jail where he was silent and refused to eat. He was admitted to the Sheppard the next day still refusing to talk.

For a period after his admission to the hospital, O. remained mute. He refused food and had to be force fed. He freely urinated and defecated in his clothes. A month after admission, he stalked the night nurse and attempted to choke him from behind. After a hard struggle he was put to bed, but he leapt up and struck his head against the window-guard, breaking its heavy screen. He was then restrained in a 'rest' jacket.

Three weeks later, after only written communications with staff,

Mr O. began to speak and on 3 September he saw Sullivan for the first time. He told Sullivan that he had been well treated except for a beating he had received one night. Sullivan asked him about the beating and was told that he had vaguely seen the silhouette of a figure in the doorway and that it had come to him that he must put the man outside the room. He tried to do this, only fully waking up when he was thrown to the floor. It then came to him that he would be killed or seriously injured if he did not escape and he attempted to jump through the window. When Sullivan told him that in fact he had attempted to choke the night nurse, he denied any memory of this and showed no emotion, making only polite expressions of regret. He remained similarly unable to communicate with Sullivan and the rest of the staff for the four months he was at the Sheppard.

On 20 November he was transferred to a state hospital where he remained similarly isolated, engaging in private rituals. His wife had him released on 15 March 1925, 270 days after the onset of the acute condition. At home his wife felt that he had improved, but the neighbours were increasingly distressed by his behaviour which included standing alone in one spot in the street for long periods, apparently oblivious to everyone, and they were able to have him returned to the state hospital, where in Sullivan's description he was 'mean, uncooperative and seemingly about to repeat his stupor reaction'.

The feature of this case that Sullivan wished to emphasize was the internal rationality and sensibleness of the man's actions, as expressed in a 'truly remarkable' written record. In his four months at the Sheppard, Mr O. produced a mass of unsent letters, written documents, songs and drawings, including 390 pages of a correspondence to and from 'Sara', a woman he had loved at the age of eighteen. These documents showed that Mr O.'s actions, as in the assault on the night nurse, were comprehensible within a framework of peculiar thought processes and that, far from being non-existent, there were definite, highly elaborated thought processes involved in such schizophrenic episodes.

Sullivan understood the failure of the therapy to be due to his inability to find a way into the peculiarities of Mr O.'s thought processes in order to establish consistent human contact with him.

While granting the therapeutic failure, Sullivan was concerned to make plain the understandable thought processes experienced by schizophrenics, and to bring them back from a frightening shadow land into the human family (Sullivan, 1924):

Schizophrenic thinking shows in its symbols and processes nothing exterior to the gamut of ordinary thinking, including therein that of reverie and dreams. Even its extraordinary symbol situations have parallels in the extravaganzas of dreams. Neither is its occurrence explicable on the basis of any novel cognitive processes. It is as a whole a peculiarly inadequate adaptation of the cognitive processes to the necessities of adult life. (p. 92)

At the Sheppard, Sullivan designed and operated a special ward, based on the clinical principle that patients needed immediate, constant, skilled human attention from the very first moment of admission if a decline into a deteriorated and unreachable mental state was to be avoided. Limited to six patients, the ward had sitting rooms and a bath and was shut off from the rest of the floor. There were six attendants, four on a twelve-hour day shift and two on a twelve-hour night shift. The attendants were specially selected and trained by Sullivan for their ability to relate to altered states of consciousness. At least two were in analysis themselves. Interviews with the last living attendants from this ward have shown that Sullivan also recruited gay attendants to counteract the homophobia gay patients would otherwise have encountered. Sullivan opened his own house, near the hospital grounds, to his staff and it became the location of effective staff conferences for attendants who were normally excluded from professional case conferences in the hospital proper.

But in the spring of 1930, less than two years after the special ward had been opened, Sullivan resigned from the Sheppard. Part of the problem was financial. He had not been given the salary he thought appropriate, nor had he been given enough money for research. And part of the problem was that he had expected to be given the responsibility of administering the entire seventy-five-bed ward for receiving new patients, a responsibility he felt, with reason, that he alone could execute properly in the best interests of the patient. The Superintendent of the Sheppard, Ross McClure Chapman, decided that Sullivan's impatience with the training and performance of existing staff made this unworkable. Chapman wrote to Edward A. Robinson, chair of the Board of Trustees, on 3 April 1930, explaining Sullivan's resignation (Forbush, 1971): 'One thing that hurt him was my regretfully having to cancel plans for his taking over the administration of the Reception Building. That was quite out of the question on account of the impossibility of his co-operating with the administrative department' (p. 108).

Sullivan resettled in New York but was unhappy there. 'It is so very difficult for me to get started here,' he wrote to Jelliffe in October 1931 (JelP). In the same year Sándor Ferenczi made the first open challenge in Europe to the exclusion of psychosis from psychoanalysis. Analysing a failed case, Ferenczi (1931) argued that the problem was not one of failed selection for analysis but a failure of psychoanalytic technique. In 1932, in Britain, Melanie Klein insisted that psychotic disorders were routinely found in disturbed children and psychoanalysis must develop adequate techniques to deal with them (Klein, 1932). In the psychoanalytic treatment of psychosis, Europe was now fifteen years behind the US and was held back even further until the 1950s by the marginalization of Ferenczi and by the divisive dispute between Anna Freud and Melanie Klein over the principles of child analysis.

Back in New York, Sullivan eventually found his feet and within six years had established the William Alanson White Foundation, the Washington School of Psychiatry and a new journal, *Psychiatry*, devoted to the exploration of relational and social perspectives in human development. Chestnut Lodge, founded in 1910 in Rockland, Maryland, under the leadership of Dexter Bullard, became the leading centre for the treatment of schizophrenia using Sullivan's principles, and Sullivan himself gave 246 lecture-discussions for staff at the Lodge. The bestselling autobiographical novel (1964), *I Never Promised You a Rose Garden* by Hannah Green (Joanne Greenberg) describes the inspired treatment she received with Frieda Fromm-Reichmann at Chestnut Lodge for her schizophrenic breakdown.

The extension of psychoanalysis to the treatment of extreme mental states pioneered by White and consolidated theoretically by Sullivan as interpersonal psychoanalysis, still left great difficulties with practical treatment. Harold Searles worked at Chestnut Lodge for fifteen years.

Searle's account and theorization of the feeling states experienced by the psychoanalytic therapist during the treatment of schizophrenia has been a constantly consulted resource for two generations of clinicians. Among the complex messiness of the difficulties that the clinician must negotiate – not always successfully – are feelings of hatred that must be endured between patient and therapist, where an unconsciously expressed sadism inevitably informs the attitude of 'the dedicated physician' (Searles, 1967).

The therapist's functioning in the spirit of dedication, which is the norm among physicians in other branches of medicine, represents here, in the practice of psychotherapy and psychoanalysis, an unconscious defense against his seeing clearly many critical aspects of both patient and himself. (p. 74)

The work is exceptionally difficult. Searles describes the sense of failure he felt when he left Chestnut Lodge after fifteen years (Stanton and Searles, 1992): 'I realized after I had left there that I had not been able to keep the negative mother transference on their part sufficiently in perspective and I had come to accept that I was in fact a totally ineffectual mother to them, that my own sense of self-worth had become swallowed up in this collective mother transference to me' (p. 325).

It can be all too easy to imagine that the work with extreme states carried on at leading institutions such as the Sheppard and Enoch Pratt Hospital and Chestnut Lodge is routinely successful. A memoir by Ann-Louise Silver (1997), director of education at Chestnut Lodge, cautions against facile optimism.

Chestnut Lodge has become a beacon. Seen only dimly at a distance, it becomes to the idealizing viewer something different from both how it is and how it was. Our work has always been messy, filled with improvisation and complex tensions and with the uniqueness of each patient's and each therapist's personality and style. Therapists' questions increase as treatment progresses. Spectacular results were and are rare. We mark progress by modifications, not transformations. Therapists use their interpersonal skills, trying whatever seems promising, then bringing their work to the review of their colleagues. (p. 245)

Silver describes the transition of her own Sullivanian work over a twenty-year period at the Lodge to evolve into what she calls 'an assertive "psycho-biosocial" strategy of treatment' for schizophrenia under the pressures of managed-care approaches to mental distress dominant in the US since the 1980s. She describes her nine years of work with J., a forty-four-year-old woman who had suffered from schizophrenic breakdowns since she had been a teenager. The Lodge was her eleventh institution and her fiftieth hospitalization.

In addition to psychotherapy with Silver, J. took a daily cocktail of eight drugs – atenolol, divalproex, clomipramine, clozapine, fluoxetine (Prozac), lerothyroxine, lorazepam, and thiothixine – to moderate her depression, anxiety, her obsessive behaviour and the effects of the drugs themselves. Mainly acting on the neurotransmitters serotonin and dopamine, these pharmacological agents are now considered by staff at Chestnut Lodge to be necessary to help make patients psychologically available for psychotherapy.

J.'s behaviour included an aggressive repetitive demand for help with elementary aspects of daily life. She would stand at a busy nurses' station and demand someone tell her the time.

'What time is it?'
'Tell me again. What time is it?'
'Are you sure?'
'Let me repeat it just one more time. You said it was fifteen minutes after, that is past, that is a quarter after or what was it? Fifteen minutes after?'
'Don't interrupt! Now I have to start all over again. I told you not to interrupt.'
'Now could you tell me what time it is?'

Silver describes features of their relationship, the important moments and the flexibility of approach to boundaries that characterized Sullivan's interpersonal perspective. Silver's insistence that J. should not shout at her would be considered a reasonable boundary in conventional thinking, but she told J. the reason was that it reminded her of her own mother – a questionable personal disclosure in classical technique. Similarly, Silver went on regular outings with J. and sang with her in sessions.

Silver notes that, in conventional terms, the treatment could be considered a failure in that J. was not living on her own, did not and never had had a job, and had not had an 'intimate sexual relationship'. Nevertheless Silver reports that J. 'has changed profoundly. We often feel comfortable, trusting, open, and spontaneous with each other. That comfort must inevitably influence and reflect all of J.'s interpersonal dealings whether with actual people in her life or with the people in her mind' (Silver, 1997).

The underlying Sullivanian principle informing Silver's work with J. is to create an environment where the patient has an opportunity to regain contact with the external world that had previously been given up because of unbearable anxiety. Sullivan had identified continuous anxiety caused by care-givers as the aetiologic agent leading to what he called 'not-me' experiences as the ultimate cause of schizophrenic breaks (Sullivan, 1953):

The not-me is literally the organization of experience with significant people that has been subjected to such intense anxiety, and anxiety so suddenly precipitated that it was impossible for the then rudimentary person to make any sense of, to develop any true grasp on the particular circumstances which dictated the experience of this intense anxiety. (p. 314)

Within this theoretical framework, the therapeutic goal is to create safety in the therapeutic relationship: 'Nothing matters except that the analyst permit the patient to feel comfortable and secure enough to give up his defensive narcissistic isolation and to use the physician for resuming contact with the world' (p. 245).

Sullivan, as an only surviving child in a poor isolated farm in upstate New York, knew the importance of human attachment and the consequences of doing without it. But his capacity for relating to people experiencing extreme states of isolating distress cannot be attributed so simply to family history. What is characteristic of Sullivan, as of many pioneers, is his sureness of insight. He knew in his bones that classical psychoanalysis was incomplete. Occupying and developing the space created by White, Sullivan had the confidence to accumulate the clinical experience that confirmed the centrality of failed human relationships in the aetiology of mental illness. Instead of working from the inside of the one-person psyche, as the classically trained analysts were having to do, Sullivan knew from the very beginning that the central feature of human development was not the mastery of drives but the adequacy of the interpersonal relationships through which the human infant becomes a human being.

In the 1920s and 1930s psychoanalysis in the United States developed in parallel strands centred in Washington and New York. William Alanson White in Washington applied the philosophy and techniques of psychoanalysis to the treatment of psychosis in the institutional setting of St Elizabeths. Abraham Brill in New York sought to legitimate psychoanalysis as a medical speciality in a clinical setting of private medical practice. Both were successful. But tensions were building within and between the two strands that were to lead to spectacular splits in US psychoanalysis, beginning in the 1940s and lasting until the 1990s.

The pioneers had established that the analytic hour was a powerful tool for investigating and treating human mental states and conditions. It had a number of theoretical advances to its credit – not all human motives are conscious, symptoms and dreams have real meanings, repressed sexuality is the cause of much psychological pain and mystery, and childhood sexuality is a part of human development. But when the brutal treatment of symptoms by 'mad doctors' became discredited and psychoanalysis became the psychiatric treatment of choice, psychoanalysis then had to start answering sincere questions about its strengths and limitations.

Why did psychoanalytic treatment take so long? Why did it require such a lengthy training? What was the relationship of psychoanalysis to established medicine and science? What were the sources of psychoanalytic understanding and theory? How were they arrived at? Classical psychoanalysis in the US was unable to answer these questions with honest and frank assessments, a legacy of timidity, over-reliance on Vienna, and the intellectual and social limitations of US medical education.

In 1953, Franz Alexander, a past president of the American Psychoanalytic Association and director of the Chicago Institute of Psychoanalysis, was alive to the danger of defensive attitudes among psychoanalysts as psychoanalysis emerged from its relative isolation to become the treatment of choice in American psychiatry.

Whenever such a transition from leading an opposition to participating in government, from heroic fight to responsible teaching and practice, takes place in a short period of time, there is danger that the pioneers will not be flexible enough for the required emotional reorientation; that they may remain – as we psychoanalysts say – fixated to an attitude which has become outmoded. The result is a tendency to misinterpret the attitude of others, a Don Quixote fight against windmills. Every question is misunderstood as a sign of hostility based on resistance. Valid criticism provokes instead of reconsideration and re-examination, violent counterattacks. Smug complacency can only partly cover up the inner insecurity which accompanies the new position of responsibility. Instead of progressive improvement of knowledge and practice, the tendency to rest on the laurels of the past appears in the form of dogmatism. Repetition of the common historical pattern of a once progressive movement changing into stagnant doctrinairism is imminent. (Alexander, 1953, pp. 17–18)

In 1955, David Levy, in a speech celebrating the tenth anniversary of the founding of the Columbia University Clinic for Psychoanalytic Training and Research, described the inflexible dogmatism that characterized psychoanalytic training in the US in the 1930s and 1940s (Person, 1990):

Our story begins with a protest against authoritarianism in science, a protest against the pollution of the atmosphere of free inquiry with the smog of doctrine, of dogmatism, of personal vituperation. It was an atmosphere in which students soon learned to ask the 'right' questions, which meant the questions that betrayed no evidence of 'resistance' to psychoanalytic doctrine. The 'wrong' question would too often elicit a blast from the instructor that the student had not been properly analysed, that he still was evincing hostility and rivalry towards the father, that his approach to the problem was still adolescent etc. In this manner the classroom was a replica of the discussion that took place in the meetings of psychoanalytic societies. (p. 10)

But these institutional countercurrents themselves had a tendency towards orthodoxy. As Person (1990) noted: 'Like revolutionaries everywhere, the founders of the Columbia Clinic had a defensive zeal that sometimes brooked no differences of opinion' (p. 10). The result in the US of these defensive postures was a stunted intellectual development, a squandering of the advances of the early years and the inevitable splits that defensive postures provoke.

In Washington, the Washington–Baltimore Society divided in 1947 in a polarized atmosphere caused by theoretical disagreements between Sullivan and the orthodox Freudian views of Jenny Waelder-Hall, who had arrived in Washington in 1943. There were similar splits in Chicago over the innovations introduced by Franz Alexander, with his ideas of corrective emotional experience and short-term analysis, opposed by a more orthodox grouping associated with the name of Lionel Blitzsten, who had been Alexander's analysand in Berlin in the 1920s. In Detroit, a division developed between the Viennese analysts Editha and Richard Sterba and a group associated with Morton Barnett. A group of psychoanalysts in Los Angeles formed the Society for Psychoanalytic Medicine of Southern California in 1950, having split off from the Los Angeles Psychoanalytic Society which had been formed only four years earlier. A further break was initiated by twelve members from both Californian societies because of the refusal of the American Psychoanalytic Association to authorize the training of a specific group of non-medically qualified candidates, leading to the formation of the Institute of Contemporary Psychoanalysis in 1991 (Bergman, 1991).

In New York, where classical psychoanalysis was strongest, the splits were even more intense. Sullivan and Clara Thompson, who had both moved to New York from Washington, along with the European refugees Erich Fromm and Karen Horney and New Yorker William V. Silverberg, formed the Zodiac group in opposition to the prevailing dominant orthodoxy in New York. In 1939, trainees requested case seminars from differing points of view, particularly from Sullivan and Horney, on treatment of severe disturbance. Although supported by Clara Thompson and David Levy, the New York Institute refused this request. Trainees then queried the use of censorship and intimidation for departures from classical theory and practice. The Education Committee of the Institute, chaired by Sandor

Rado, attempted to deal with this issue but could only draw the conclusion that the tension was the work of troublemakers (Jeffrey, 1992):

Your Committee is coming reluctantly to the conclusion that the 'serious condition which exists among the students' and the 'something rotten is going on' referred to by Dr Thompson is due to the fact that the minds of certain students are being poisoned by hostile and irresponsible members of the Society. (p. 21)

Rado's refusal to take seriously the charge of censorship and intimidation was sufficiently outrageous for Lawrence Kubie, president of the Institute, to conclude that he was temperamentally unsuited to chair the Education Committee and had him removed in December 1940. But at a famous meeting on 29 April 1941, Karen Horney was disqualified from being a teacher and a training analyst by a vote of 24 to 7 with an extraordinary 29 abstentions. Horney and four colleagues, in a prepared gesture, then walked out of the meeting and, on the sidewalk outside, sang the African-American freedom song 'Let My People Go'. Fourteen trainees resigned along with them, forming a new organization, the Association for the Advancement of Psychoanalysis, and a new training institute, the American Institute of Psychoanalysis, with Horney as dean and Sullivan and Fromm as honorary members. Two years later this group itself divided over the issue of lay analysis, with Erich Fromm being denied the right to be a training analyst in order to safeguard the new institute's association with New York Medical College. This time twelve members resigned, including Clara Thompson and Sullivan, to form a New York branch of the Washington School of Psychiatry, which in 1946 became the present William Alanson White Institute.

In the meantime, Rado had been quietly negotiating, since September 1939, with Adolf Meyer to create a new psychoanalytic centre in a university setting (Tomlinson, 1996). Following his dismissal as education director, Rado, along with David Levy, Abram Kardiner and George Daniels, began to organize a separate group within the New York Psychoanalytic Institute. Meeting for the first time on 12 June 1942 at Levy's home, the group was eventually able to overcome serious obstacles to create, in 1946, a new psychoanalytic institute at Columbia University. The Columbia Clinic for Psychoanalytic Training and Research was formed with the active support of Frieda Fromm-Reichmann and Franz Alexander in the American Psychoanalytic Association and the sponsorship of Nolan Lewis, who had become chair of the Department of Psychiatry at the College of Physicians and Surgeons of Columbia University, in addition to his duties as Director of the Psychiatric Institute.

In the aftermath of the splits of the 1940s, Sullivan's interpersonal psychoanalysis continued to be developed by Erich Fromm, Clara Thompson, Janet Rioch Bard and Ralph Crowley at the William Alanson White Institute in New York (Stern et al., 1995). Classical drive theory was to remain dominant in conventional American psychoanalysis for another generation but with the introduction of an important theoretical innovation called ego psychology, associated with the names of Heinz Hartmann, Ernst Kris, Rudolf Loewenstein and David Rapaport.

The different structures of the inner world are interesting to different individuals according to their own dynamic development and personal history – in relationship to the demands of the times. In the early splits, Freud was drawn to the exploration of unconscious processes while Adler was drawn to the exploration of obstacles to the human capacity for autonomous action. As we have seen, Freud freely acknowledged the validity of Adler's interests but then, badly stung by Adler's resignation, derided the role of conscious human agency as mere overtones in the 'mighty primordial melody of the instincts' (Freud, 1914). A decade later, in a change of metaphor, Freud characterized the ego as the rider on the horse of wild directionless drives, located in the mental structure called the id (Freud, 1923b).

In spite of Freud's personal preferences there were bound to be individuals within classical psychoanalysis who were drawn to so-called ego considerations, just as Adler had been. Conscious human agency is not only interesting but essential to an understanding of human action. In 1936 Anna Freud published her *Ego and the Mechanisms of Defence*, which attributed to the ego considerable flexibility (autonomy) in its choice of defence mechanisms. In 1937, just before the final exit of psychoanalysis from Nazi-controlled Europe, Heinz

Hartmann proposed an extension of psychoanalytic theory by granting the ego its own energy and its own autonomous aims, separate from its combative relationship to the drives (Hartmann, 1958). Using Freud's metaphor, the ego was now off rather than on the horse.

Hartmann was Freud's last training patient (Blanck and Blanck, 1974; Greenberg and Mitchell, 1983; Hale, 1995). He had the kind of elite background that appealed to Freud. An ancestor on Hartmann's father's side had been the sixteenth-century astronomer Adolf Gans, a colleague of Johann Kepler. Hartmann's maternal grandfather was Rudolf Chrobak, a collaborator with Breuer in 1867 on research into the origins of fever, and later professor of gynaecology and obstetrics at the University of Vienna. Ludo Hartmann, his father, was a famous professor of history at the University of Vienna and, after the First World War, Austrian ambassador to Germany. Hartmann himself had been educated privately until he attended the University of Vienna where he took a medical degree, also studying academic psychology and sociology. He was able to attract funds from the Rockefeller Foundation to support the publication of his first book in 1927, *Fundamentals of Psychoanalysis*. Hartmann was ambitious for psychoanalysis. From his background in psychology and sociology he recognized that psychoanalysis could never be a complete theory of human psychology unless it included an explanation for how human rational behaviour could arise out of a drive psychology. Concerned with the part of human behaviour where 'not every adaptation is a conflict' (p. 8), Hartmann was interested to understand more fully the conflict-free aspects of the ways individuals adapted to their environments as in, for example, the process of learning to walk upright.

Robert Holt, a former student of David Rapaport, summarized the attractions of ego psychology for his generation of students (Hale, 1995):

[Ego psychology] presented psychoanalysis as a reasonable, intelligible discipline, by no means exclusively focused on intrapsychic conflict and unconscious infantile wishes, but with much concern for a person's real setting, especially his social, cultural, and historical milieu, the groups and traditions that shaped his identity, and the *mise-en-scène* of interpersonal relations in which his life was played out. (p. 238)

Hostile appraisals of ego psychology as a socially conformist, socially uncritical psychology, simply adapted to the status quo, were to an extent unjustified. Hartmann anticipated this criticism of his views (Hartmann, 1958):

It may not be superfluous to mention again that by adaptation we do not mean only passive submission to the goals of society but also active collaboration on them and attempts to change them. (p. 32)

But this caveat proved to be ineffective in practice. It was no accident that in 1950s' McCarthyite America ego psychology became the dominant psychoanalytic theory in mainstream US psychoanalysis, combining as it did an unchanged drive psychology along with a vision of mental health consisting of a satisfactory/unconflictual relationship with society at large. In the 1950s, in the US, twenty-five psychoanalysts, about half of those asked, took part in the Appeals of Communism Project funded by the Carnegie Corporation. The participating analysts provided case studies of thirty-five Communist Party patients, giving not only psychological profiles of their analysands but also information on 'time and occasion of admission to the party' and on their 'nature of participation' (Musto, 1996). By giving this information, the participating analysts effectively became political informers in violation of the basic principles of psychoanalytic confidentiality. Social conformity was the version of adaptation that ego psychoanalysts as a group in the US were seen to be transmitting to their patients, inspiring a search for alternatives.

For a number of analysts who came to maturity in the 1960s in the US, ego psychology was a stop-gap measure, a bridge between drive theory and the relational theories of human psychology represented by the Washington School. Merton Gill (1994) has written a personal account of his forty years of experience of the twists and turns of US classical psychoanalysis in a transition from a one-person drive psychology to the two-and-more-person relational psychologies. The politically conscious generation of the 1960s and 1970s was to choose

Sullivanian interpersonal theory and the British school of so-called object relations over classical drive theory as the psychoanalysis that offered the best chance of understanding social experience in the light of human unconscious processes.

9

Child Psychoanalysis:
Beginnings of
a New Paradigm

Thomas Kuhn, the historian of science and former physicist, achieved a genuine advance in our understanding of science with his idea of the paradigm shift, the radical change of theory that characterizes the history of natural science. For the first time, members of the public became aware that science did not advance in steady increments by generations of workers working harmoniously together. Instead, there were intense periods of conflict where, under the pressure of accumulated experience, previous assumptions were challenged, thrown up in the air and discarded in favour of entirely new ideas which could be in total contradiction to previous beliefs.

The concept of the paradigm shift has now become a handy metaphor to describe a fundamental change of belief systems. What Kuhn did not describe, however, was the messy, painful reality of the process of the paradigm shift – the polemics, the tortured arguments, the blind alleys, the confusions, the hatreds, the mental breakdowns, the suicides, the sheer inertia ('You never understand a new theory. You just get used to it.' R. Feynman) that have accompanied significant reorientations in frameworks of understanding. The paradigm shift in psychoanalysis, begun in the 1920s and still not completed in the late 1990s, is a case in point. In the case of psychoanalysis, the paradigm shift began to emerge with the psychoanalysis of children associated with the name of Melanie Klein.

By all accounts Melanie Klein was a difficult woman. Described as having no friends, just enemies and disciples, she was exasperating and inspiring by turns, a personality to rival that of Freud in the history of psychoanalysis. As Phyllis Grosskurth, her biographer, remarked (1986): 'Few professional women have been subjected to as much distilled malice and rumour accepted as fact as Klein endured both during her lifetime and since her death' (p. x). The sympathetic Grosskurth biography – 'I hope that I have in some measure presented a more balanced evaluation' – repays a close reading, giving ammunition to both admirers and detractors. But the obituaries and tributes to Klein after her death in 1960 give a more immediate impression of her strengths and weaknesses as they were experienced by her colleagues.

On her scientific style:

I do not think you could really influence her. When she felt misunderstood, she felt bewildered, it was so plain to her and she turned away either in anger or loneliness. (Eva Rosenfeld, KleinP)

She could not believe that something so clear to a person as ordinary as herself was not equally clear to everyone else and this led her at times to think that opposition to her views was based on perversity when in fact doubts were quite genuine. (Mrs R. W. Dixon, KleinP)

Melanie Klein had the character and courage, fortitude and generosity to match her gifts. Her compassion and understanding of human nature were combined with ruthlessness when she felt that scientific integrity was tampered with. (W. Bion, E. Rosenfeld and H. Segal, 1961)

Her unyielding defence [of her work] may sometimes be mistaken for concern about her own position in the history of science. (R. E. Money-Kyrle, KleinP)

On her achievement:

So I went to hear and then to see Melanie Klein, and I found an analyst who had a great deal to say about the anxieties that belong to infancy and I settled down to working with the benefit of her help. I took her a case written up in great detail, and she had the goodness to read it right through . . . I went on to try to learn some of the immense amount that I found she already knew. (D. W. Winnicott, 1962)

Though I have never been able to accept her views in toto I have never doubted the importance of her pioneering work. (Marjorie Brierley, 1960)

On her limitations:

Klein claimed to have paid full attention to the environmental factor but it is my opinion that she was temperamentally incapable of this. (D. W. Winnicott, 1962)

[Her isolation] was exacerbated by her lack of any formal scientific training, which made her incapable of subordinating her own private way of thinking to the discipline of scientific discourse. All this . . . has put emotional obstacles in the way of objective sifting and appraisal of the work of one of the most intuitive and creative minds that have been dedicated to psychoanalysis. (Charles Rycroft, 1961)

Melanie Klein was born in 1882, the fourth child of Moriz Reizes and Libussa Deutsch. Her father was a doctor in the small town of Deutschkreutz in the province of Burgenland in eastern Austria near the Hungarian border. The family moved to Vienna just before Melanie was born. There, Moriz Reizes, as a Jew from the provinces, was unable to establish a practice and opened up a dental surgery instead, working as a part-time doctor in the evenings. The Reizes household prided itself on its interest in culture – Moriz spoke ten languages – very much in reaction against the ways of the ghetto. Klein grew up with a horror of the Yiddish language and was revolted by the long caftans worn by her father's sister and husband when they visited the Reizes household on a trip from Galicia.

According to Phyllis Grosskurth, Klein grew up as 'a beautiful Jewish princess'. She married Arthur Klein, a second cousin on her mother's side, when she was twenty-one years old, after a two-year engagement. Her three children – Melitta, Hans and Erich – were born in 1904, 1907 and 1914. The marriage was unhappy and the couple separated for the last time in 1924. In 1914, at the age of thirty-two, a restless and ambitious Klein read Freud's article *On Dreams* and was converted to psychoanalysis. She began psychoanalysis with Sándor Ferenczi, probably the same year.

Melanie Klein came into psychoanalysis at a time when Freud and Ferenczi were beginning to feel that there was much to be learned from the analysis of children. Following the work of Hermine Hug-Helmuth who, beginning in 1913, had explored the interplay between educational and psychoanalytic issues in child development, Freud encouraged his daughter Anna to qualify as a psychoanalyst in order to build on her prior work as a teacher of children. At the same time, in Budapest, Ferenczi was encouraging his analysand Melanie Klein to develop what he saw as her intuitive skills with children by entering the field of child psychoanalysis. On 29 June 1919, Ferenczi wrote to Freud: 'A Frau Dr Klein (not a physician) who recently made some very good observations on children, after she had several years of instruction with me, is supposed to help [in the Society for Child Research].'

With Ferenczi's support, Klein began analysing her own children. Such practices were common enough in the first generation of psychoanalysis. In addition to Freud's analysis of his daughter, Anna, Carl Jung analysed his daughter Agathli, Karl Abraham analysed his daughter Hilda, and Ernst Kris analysed both his children. Anna Freud's first patients were her nephews. The networks of analysts, analysands and their children form what has justly been called a spaghetti junction of kinship and analysis (Falzeder, 1994). No one knew they were playing with fire. As Grosskurth (1986) comments in her discussion of Klein's analysis of her own children: 'One wonders if Melanie Klein ever experienced misgivings about the wisdom of what she was doing . . . In the dark hours of the night it might have occurred to her that in the case of her children she could have actually caused irreparable damage either to their psyches or to their relationship with her' (p. 99). In fact Klein did earn the hatred of her daughter Melitta, who became a psychoanalyst herself. It is difficult to see how the instrumental nature of Klein's relationship with her daughter was not a factor in Melitta's subsequent hatred of her mother.

Melanie Klein prided herself on being exquisitely sensitive to the internal emotional experiences of children. In her unpublished autobiography, written in the 1950s, she wrote (Grosskurth, 1986): 'During this analysis with Ferenczi, he drew my attention to my great gift for understanding children and my interest in them, and he very much encouraged my idea of devoting myself to analysis, particularly child analysis' (p. 74). In 1960, in her obituary, Hanna Segal related her observation of Klein's capacity to attune to children in an incident where she saw Klein scoop up a pre-verbal toddler, seat him on her lap and say to him 'Now tell me a story'. Klein then observed the toddler in minute detail in 'a kind of rapt attention' (KleinP). Although one can feel some discomfort at the possibility that this child might have found the experience of being placed under an emotional micro-scope by a rather formidable adult quite disagreeable, Segal describes here a quality of attunement that characterizes Klein's approach to child psychoanalysis – the desire to hear a story from inside the child's emotional life.

And what stories she heard! Klein's account of infancy is a maelstrom of threats and deprivation, of destruction, of fears of retaliation, of an ever-present malevolence, of terrible anxiety, of terror. By 1933 Klein could summarize her sense of the internal world of the small child in relation to its parents as a tale of gothic horror (Klein, 1933):

We get to look upon the child's fear of being devoured, or cut up, or torn to pieces, or its terror of being surrounded and pursued by menacing figures as a regular component of its mental life; and we know that the man-eating wolf, the fire-spewing dragon, and all the evil monsters out of myths and fairy stories flourish and exert their unconscious influence in the phantasy of each individual child, and it feels persecuted and threatened by these evil shapes. (p. 249)

In 1936, Joan Riviere presented her own vision of early infant aggression fantasies in vivid Kleinian terms:

Loose motions, flatus, and urine are all felt to be burning, corroding and poisoning agents. Not only excretory but all other physical functions are pressed into service of [aggressive] phantasy. Limbs shall trample, kick and hit; lips, fingers and hands shall suck, twist, pinch; teeth shall bite, gnaw, mangle and cut; mouths shall devour, swallow and 'kill' (annihilate); eyes kill by a look, pierce and penetrate; breath and mouth hurt by noise, as the child's sensitive ears have so experienced. (p. 286)

By 1946, Klein's presentation was more formal but the emotional impact of the language was just as great:

From the beginning the destructive impulse is turned against the object and is first expressed in phantasized oral-sadistic attacks on the mother's breast which soon develop into onslaughts on her body by all sadistic means. The persecutory fears arising from the infant's oral-sadistic impulses to rob the mother of all its good contents, and from the anal-sadistic impulses to put his excrements into her (including the desire to enter her body to control her from within) are of great importance for the development of paranoia and schizophrenia. (p. 2)

A generation later, trainees at the Institute of Psycho-Analysis in London were introduced to Klein with a similar account by Hanna Segal, a leading exponent of Klein's vision (Segal, 1973):

The child turns to his mother's body all his libidinal desires but, because of frustration, envy and hatred also his destructiveness. These desires also involve objects phantasized inside mother's body, and in relation to them the infant also has greedy libidinal desires and phantasies of scooping them out and devouring them or, because of his hatred and envy, aggressive phantasies of biting, tearing and destroying – as in Erna's phantasy of making 'eye salad' of the contents of her mother's body.

Soon, to the oral sadism is added urethral sadism, with phantasies of drowning, cutting and burning, and anal sadism which in the early anal phase is of a predominantly explosive kind and in the later anal phase becomes more secret and poisonous. These attacks on the mother's body lead to phantasies of its being a terrifying place full of destroyed and vengeful objects, amongst which father's penis acquires a particular importance. (p. 5)

Where does such a powerful, terrible vision of the infant's inner world come from? Where, in fact, do any of our ideas about the world come from? In our knowledge disciplines, we have been content with the ideology of genius – Einstein, Newton, Darwin – to account for the process by which successful ideas have occurred to the great figures of science. And we have little sense of the detailed processes by which these ideas came to be accepted by their colleagues, even in the famous episodes informing Kuhn's introduction of the paradigm shift.

And yet, if we accept that theory is a tool, designed and used to meet specific needs, we can see that the creation of successful understandings must occur in well-defined social and historical circumstances. Our needs for understanding change under the influence of new experience, or because a new generation grows up that is dissatisfied with the weaknesses of the understanding of its elders, or because new social groupings with differing life experience enter a field, bringing with them needs for a different shape to theory. The neat nineteenth-century story that facts determine a theory is inadequate to account either for the actual processes by which human understanding is created by human imagination or for the processes by which that understanding emerges from the needs and sensibilities of the time. As the logo above the Wellcome Museum for the History of Science in London says: 'Facts are to science as words are to literature.'

The process by which facts are put together in order to become theory takes effort. The creation of theory is just as influenced by its specific location in time and place as is the creation of literature. In 1918, Oswald Spengler's bestselling *Decline of the West*, addressed middle-class fears accompanying Germany's defeat, revolutions in Germany, Hungary and Russia and the still poorly understood effects of the post-war restructuring of the Western world's political and economic map, with the emergence of the multinational corporation as the dominant social institution of a new world order. In Austria, *The Last Days of Mankind*, a play by the famous satirist Karl Krause, contributed an Austrian version of events. In psychoanalysis Freud's *Reflections on War and Death* offered a Freudian analysis of the existential fears of the period.

The psychoanalysts of Europe were responding to the same events as was everyone else. Theory in psychoanalysis, in its own way, had to cope with turmoil, uncertainty and death. Melanie Klein's vision of the terrors of the child's inner world was as situated in the uncertainties and brutalities of the aftermath of the First World War as was the literature, the movies and the architecture.

On 16 October 1918, a month before the armistice ending the First World War, Kaiser Karl I announced the creation of a new federal state ending the 800-year-old Austro-Hungarian monarchy. On the same day, Freud wrote Ferenczi: 'I congratulate you on your political independence as a Hungarian. I would like it if your people would only understand how to make something out of it and to guard themselves against chauvinism.'

Hungary was in political turmoil. In January and again in June there had been general strikes. Intense political manoeuvring in October led to the formation of a new government. On 31 October, the streets of Budapest were filled with people waving white chrysanthemums. Ferenczi feared both the anti-Semitism unleashed in the political upheaval – there was looting of Jewish houses in the provinces – and the prospect of a world working-class revolution. On 7 November 1918 he wrote to Freud:

Your prophecy about our imminent proletarianization has come true – but the magnates and the capitalists are hovering in the same danger. If Bolshevism gets its way in Germany, then the collapse of the entire civilization of the world is unavoidable – France, England, America and Japan will also get their turn, and an epoch of brutalization and infantilization will confront the world. We are living – nebbish – in a great time!

Freud's diary records the intense progression of political events (Gay, 1988): 30 October – 'Revolution Vienna & Budapest'; 2 November – 'Oli back. Republic in Bulgaria?'; 6 November – 'Revolution in Kiel.'; 8 November – 'Republic in Bavaria!! Traffic with Germany interrupted'; 9 November – 'Republic in Berlin. Wilhelm abdicates.'; 12 November – 'Republic and connection with Germany'; 16 November – 'Republic in Hungary' (p. 376).

The Republic of Hungary of 16 November 1918 was declared with Count Mihaly Karolyi of the Independence Party as state president. The next day, Freud wrote to Ferenczi, giving his analysis of the political situation. Germany was not going to be Bolshevik and would develop 'sensibly'. But in Austria there was little to work with: 'The Habsburgs have left behind nothing but a pile of crap.' More importantly, the Social Democratic leader, Victor Adler, Freud's old adversary from his youth, had died unexpectedly on 11 November. 'Limitations and deprivation are worse than ever. We lost the best man, perhaps the only one who might have been up to the task, through death; nothing can be done with the Christian Socialists and the German Nationalists.'

Social Democratic reconstruction of Hungary with a predominantly Jewish business and professional middle class, opposed by an impoverished gentry and a reactionary semi-feudal nobility and clerical estate, faced a difficult task in dealing with food and clothing shortages, eliminating privation and in modernizing the country. One third of the Hungarian people had been kept illiterate by the Magyar nobility.

Ferenczi, in spite of himself, was drawn to the Social Democratic reforms. On 24 November 1918 he wrote to Freud:

They have simply annexed the streetcar companies and handed them over to the capital city as property, they have also requisitioned for home bound soldiers many articles of clothing from everyone who has more than three suits, winter coats, more than seven shirts etc. – Up to now I have always stood aloof from politics, never participated in the election of members of Parliament. But these days the usefulness of the workers' organization that has saved Budapest's culture has made such an impression on me that I joined the newly founded Social Democratic Physicians' Union.

As part of the 'advance of all progressive tendencies' brought about by the Social Democratic government, Ferenczi reported to Freud that 1000 students had petitioned the University of Budapest to be allowed to study psychoanalysis. Ferenczi, while cynical about the sincerity of the government's positive attitude towards psychoanalysis, was nevertheless ecstatic. He wrote to Freud: 'The home of psychoanalysis is indeed Budapest and not Vienna; you should move here!' The sociologist, Oscar Jászi (1924), then Minister of Nationalities in the Social Democratic government, wrote two years later: 'During the revolutions . . . Freudianism was the idol of Communist youth.'

By the end of the year, Ferenczi's mood was more cautious. On 26 December 1918 he wrote to Freud: 'Another year gone by – and what a year! Certainly a free – but dirt poor Hungary has arisen out of the proud – but feudal – Hungary in the few months since we last saw each other. It is very doubtful how things will stand with respect to science in *such* a Hungary. I think that in a very short time a clerical-reactionary tide will come and also harm the young Hungarian psychoanalysis.' On 1 January 1919 Freud replied: 'Is the Golden Age already here? Will these pains bring birth?'

The political situation was ominous. Amidst the shortages, Romanian, Czech and Slav troops occupied the newly drawn borders to the east, the north and the south of the country. Hungary lost two thirds of its territory and two thirds of its inhabitants. Karolyi resigned as prime minister on 1 December and on 1 January Dénes Berinkey formed a new government. Tension increased between the right and a left increasingly represented by the Communist Party under the leadership of Béla Kun. On 6 January Ferenczi wrote to Freud:

Everything is pressing toward a showdown between the extreme parties: the Communists on the one hand, the reactionaries on the other. The parties of the centre (also the Social Democratic, which is now in power) may not hold. The reactionaries will probably be promoted by the French.

On 20 March 1919, under pressure from the French who had occupied part of southern Hungary and who spoke for the victorious *entente*, demanding that Hungary shrink its eastern, northern and southern borders, the government resigned. The next day, on 21 March 1919, a Revolutionary Governing Council under Béla Kun took power and declared a Council [Soviet] Government of Hungary. Four days later, on 25 March, Ferenczi described the stresses of the revolutionary situation to Freud.

Concerning the psychological effects of the events here – which on the surface have taken place very peacefully – I can only say they were and are overwhelming. The upsets of war and of the first revolution can't be compared to them. The transfer of such significant deeply rooted libidinal cathexes, in the way in which one requires it, places uncommon demands on the adaptive capability of the hitherto propertied class, to which I was beginning to belong, and as a child of well-to-do parents, actually did belong.

On the same day, on his first post-war trip to a Europe of closed borders, an ill and mourning Ernest Jones – his wife Morfydd Owen had died the previous summer – wrote to Freud from Zurich about the Hungarian events and the corresponding situation in England. 'You may imagine how concerned we are about affairs in Hungary, but one can hardly write about political matters which alter from day to day. About England my opinion is on the whole optimistic. I don't think it will come to civil war there, and if it doesn't then the old order will be on the whole maintained – naturally with much better conditions for the working classes.'

In England, the events Jones alluded to were the great strikes on the Clyde in February 1915, the strike of 200,000 Welsh miners in July 1915 and the strike of 250,000 engineering workers in May 1917, precursors of the June 1917 national convention of trade union leaders held in Leeds which passed resolutions calling for the establishment of workers' and soldiers' councils throughout Britain. The shop stewards' movement actively supported the Russian revolution and those British troops who had mutinied after being ordered to Archangel as part of the White invasion of Russia. In a secret memorandum the British Prime Minister David Lloyd George wrote (Milton, 1978):

The whole of Europe is filled with the spirit of revolution. There is a deep sense not only of discontent, but of anger and revolt amongst the workmen against pre-war conditions. The whole existing order in its political, social and economic aspects, is questioned by the masses of the population from one end of Europe to another. (p. 16)

In Hungary, the revolutionary government was too inexperienced to recognize the dangers that it faced. Years later the anti-Communist writer Arthur Koestler (1952) recalled that his family had survived on state-supported vanilla ice cream: '[It was] typical of the happy go lucky, diletanttish and even surrealist way in which the Commune was run. [It was] all rather endearing – at least when compared to the lunacy and savagery which was to descend on Europe in the years to come' (p. 67).

The revolutionary Hungarian government was unable to make an effective alliance with members of the middle class who, like Ferenczi, were frightened by what they saw as the red terror of expropriations and a taking over of the bourgeois institutions. In Ferenczi's case, his industrial stocks were declared invalid and withdrawals of his bank deposits were strictly controlled. His basic salary with the newly formed Workers Health Service was intact but his private patients could no longer afford to pay him. Housing was socialized and all rent payments, including those to Ferenczi's wife who owned property, were halted. Ferenczi's apartment was requisitioned. Trials were declared null and void, and justice was to be administered by the workers' state. The law faculty of the university was disbanded. The army was reconstituted to include only workers. The situation felt alarming and out of control.

On 1 April 1919, Freud wrote to Ferenczi describing his feelings about the corresponding revolutionary process that was taking place in Austria: 'The overly great tension, the insight into helplessness, inability to know what to do, and lack of understanding about everything that is happening makes one apathetic in the end and casts one back into one's own discomfort, which is motivated by little worries and disruptions in diet and health.'

Meanwhile, in mid-April, Ferenczi was appointed full public professor for psychoanalysis and director of a new psychoanalytic clinic to be established at the university – in part due to the efforts of the young Hungarian psychoanalyst, Sandor Rado, who was playing an active part in political affairs. In keeping with the proletarianization of the professions Ferenczi also had to report as a physician to the revolutionary army. He wrote to Freud: 'Ça va bien – said the man from the height of the second floor' (29 April 1919).

On 10 June 1919 Ferenczi sensed the onrushing approach of the pavement: 'Yesterday was a black day for me: the publication of Hungary's new (planned) borders.' Six weeks later, on 1 August 1919, the revolutionary government of Hungary was overthrown by the violent clerical-landowning-peasant fascist party led by Admiral Miklos Horthy, supported by an invasion by the Romanian army. The Hungarian Commune had lasted 133 days. As after the Paris Commune forty years earlier, terrible reprisals were carried out as punishment for working-class hubris in attempting to take power.

In Paris, 25,000 communards had been murdered by invading government troops. As an American eyewitness reported (Edwards, 1973): 'Much must be pardoned to soldiers heated with battle, and taught to believe every prisoner they take an incarnate devil. But making all allowances, there is no excuse for the wholesale butcheries committed by the troops' (p. 164). In Hungary, on 3 and 4 August, the Romanian army occupied Budapest. Miklos Horthy and his 'Christian Course' took over the country from his base in the town of Szeged on the Yugoslav border, and began reprisals against Communists, Socialists and Jews. Over 5000 people were summarily killed, many in 'sadistic secret torture chambers' (Rhodes, 1986) and others in mass executions by roving bands of White terrorists. On 28 August 1919 Ferenczi wrote to Freud from occupied Budapest:

After the unbearable 'Red terror' which lay heavy on one's spirit like a nightmare, we now have the White one. For a short time it seemed as if they would succeed in moderating the parties towards a just compromise, but in the end the ruthless clerical-anti-Semitic spirit seems to have eked out a victory. If everything does not deceive, we Hungarian Jews are now facing a period of brutal persecution of Jews . . . not a soul is permitted to show himself on the streets at 9:30, otherwise one is taken prisoner by the Romanian guards. The police jails are full of anonymously reported 'Bolshevists' who are being mistreated there. The blackest reaction prevails at the university. All Jewish assistants were fired, the Jewish students were thrown out and beaten. From these few data you may get a picture of the situation that prevails here!

Among the atrocities hinted at by Ferenczi were the mass murders and tortures committed at Siófolz in August and September 1919 and in the Orgóvony wood in November 1919 by the Paul Prónay gang. Adalbert Somogyi, editor of *Nepszava*, the Social Democratic news-paper, exposed the atrocity at Orgóvony. On 20 February 1920, in reprisal, Paul Prónay, with two accomplices, captured Somogyi, put out his eyes and drowned him in the Danube (Jászi, 1924).

Oscar Jászi, having been forced out of office by the Red revolution the previous March, observed the qualitative difference between the calculated vindictive murders and tortures perpetrated by the White terror compared to the clumsy cruelties of the Red:

This raging of the White Terror makes one of the darkest pages of Hungarian history. A whole literature has been devoted to it. In excuse of its horrors, the statement is often heard that the White Terror really only continued the method of the Red. I have no desire whatever to palliate the brutalities and atrocities of the proletarian dictatorship; its harshness is not to be denied, even if its terrorists operated more with insults and threats than with actual deeds. But the tremendous difference between the Red and White terror is beyond all question. During the counterrevolution the decreased spread of the Terror was compensated by increased brutality and by an entirely different psychological and moral quality. The terrorist actions of the Reds usually revealed the primitive cruelty of coarse and ignorant men; the Whites worked out a cold, refined system of vengeance and reprisal, which they applied with the cruelty of scoundrels masquerading as gentlemen. The worst atrocities of the Red Terror were usually the acts of depraved and semi-bestial proletarians: those of the Whites were the deliberate actions of elegant officers. (p. 160)

The Hungarian Jewish middle class – the businessmen, artists, writers, musicians, physicians and mathematicians – were forced into exile. Among them were the psychoanalysts including Sandor Rado, Geza Roheim, Franz Alexander and the then unknown Melanie Klein, aged thirty-eight, with her three children, Melitta, Hans and Erich.

In the flat, affectless way that the experience of emigration is so frequently described, Klein, in her unpublished autobiography written forty years later, wrote (Grosskurth, 1986):

When the short lived but very stringent Communist regime started in 1919 at the end of the war, we left Budapest and I went to live for a year in Slovakia with my parents-in-law with whom I had always been on very good terms, especially my mother-in-law, and my husband found a position in Sweden. Having been by birth an Austrian subject, I had now become a Czecho-Slovakian subject. My husband having settled in Sweden, soon managed to become a Swedish subject, since he was not keen on being a Czecho-Slovakian. In this way I became a Swedish subject, which, at a later date, was very useful to me. (p. 83)

As with many other Hungarian intellectuals, Klein moved to Berlin, flourishing amidst Germany's revolutionary turmoil as a centre of cultural activity. Professionally, the attraction was the Berlin Psychoanalytic Society and the new Berlin Polyclinic, which opened on 16 February 1920, led by Karl Abraham and funded by the independently wealthy psychoanalyst Max Eitingon. Klein went into analysis with Karl Abraham. On 3 February 1921, a month after her arrival, she gave her first paper on child analysis to the Berlin Society.

The paper, 'The Child's Resistance to Enlightenment', was not exactly a report of a child analysis but an account of a child's responses to being told the facts of life. As Klein said: 'These observations with their only occasional interpretations could not be described as a treatment; I would rather describe it as a case of "upbringing with analytic features"' (Klein, 1921, p. 44). She had not yet begun to examine the deep interiority that was to become the signature of her work but she introduced another dominant theme, the desirability of preventive child analysis. 'I am of the opinion that no upbringing should be without analytic help, because analysis affords such valuable, and from the point of view of prophylaxis, as yet incalculable assistance' (p. 45).

The Berlin Klein entered was still in the midst of its own revolutionary events. In January 1920, forty-two Socialist demonstrators were killed, and 105 wounded by machine-gun fire, in a protest outside the Reichstag against a bill that would have prevented working-class representatives from gaining access to the accounts of their companies (Maier, 1975). Two months later, at 5 a.m. on 13 March, Pan-German reactionaries with white swastikas painted on their helmets, headed by a former government bureaucrat, Wolfgang Kapp, in command of General von Luettwitz's notorious Erhardt Brigade, along with other displaced Freikorps gunmen, occupied Berlin. Kapp declared himself Reichs Chancellor and von Luettwitz Defence Minister. The German high command and right-wing politicians, who had had advance warning of the *coup*, watched from the sidelines. The Social Democratic government fled, going first south to Dresden and then on 15 March further south to Stuttgart, where it called a successful general strike, supported even by mandarins in the civil service. Twelve million workers went on strike. A Red Army of 100,000 armed workers was formed in the Ruhr. On 17 March 1920 the *coup* collapsed; Kapp escaped to Sweden and Luettwitz resigned (Schrader and Schebera, 1990).

During the 1920s, the political, scientific and artistic certainties of nineteenth-century bourgeois Europe had come apart at the seams. Freud was sixty-four years old in 1920 and he was not in a good mood. He had written to Ferenczi: '. . . my ability to adapt is on strike, I don't have power against the world. I remain a disgruntled person, by whom one should avoid being infected, as long as one feels young and strong' (1 January 1919). But the psychoanalysis he had created was an ongoing discipline defined through its literature, its practice and its presenting problems, a discipline that was shared, even if experienced differently, by its participants. In the case of Melanie Klein, eager at the age of thirty-eight to make her name in the field, child psychoanalysis was suggested to her by her male analysts, Ferenczi in Budapest and Abraham in Berlin, as the sure way to make a contribution to current concerns about the early, pre-Oedipal, development of mental life. To this work in understanding the inner world of the human infant she brought her own sensibility, a capacity to achieve a distanced attunement with a child's inner experience, a sensitivity to terror and victimization, coupled, as it proved, to an active rejection of the realities of the external world – an external world that was too hot to handle.

The fundamental theoretical problem posed by child analysis was to understand the origin of childhood anxieties. Klein pioneered the technique of play analysis – the use of a set of small toys as a substitute for the technique of free association. Through observation of the play, the depths of a child's inner world could be reached by making immediate interpretations about the child's earliest feelings and unconscious fantasies, many of which have made an important contribution to our understanding of early separation anxiety. In Klein's treatment (1923) of a seven-year-old patient, Fritz, she describes her analysis of his anxiety about going to school in the morning in the following terms:

He once told me that he would quite like going to school if only it were not for the road. He now phantasized that, in order to avoid the road, he laid a ladder across from the window of his room to that of his school mistress, then he and his mother could go together, by climbing from rung to rung. Then he told me about a rope, also stretched from window to window, along which he and sister were drawn to the school. (p. 95)

Klein comments that the fantasy about getting to school by avoiding the road was 'part of a very long and abundantly determined phantasy which yielded material for various theories of procreation and birth'. The child also described his fantasies of inventing a machine which could throw a rope to different parts of town to enable him to get to places without using the road. Klein saw this as a symbolic expression of the child's vision of procreation. 'This phantasy again revealed his idea of being procreated by his father, amalgamated by ideas of coitus on his own part' (p. 95).

The reader may not be surprised to learn that 'Fritz' was Klein's youngest son Erich, aged six, whose anxieties were connected to the fact that in the Berlin of 1921 he was being tormented and hit by neighbourhood boys for being Jewish. As Grosskurth (1986) says: 'Was she so bewitched that she could not see the forest for the trees?' (p. 96).

The tension in Klein's work consisted of an apparent exclusion of external experience in favour of what appeared to be internal explanations of childhood anxieties. Klein's formulations had an appeal in that it seemed she had gone to the very deepest levels of the child's personality. The question that had to be resolved was whether Klein had really seen deeper, indeed to levels so deep that they were untouched by parental relationships, let alone the political situation. In Erich's case he may well have been made deeply anxious by his actual journeys to school but in Klein's formulation he would have had earlier experiences, internal experiences, that were far more fundamental in shaping his psychological processes. The question in Klein's early work, that took an entire generation to clarify, was whether the location of childhood anxieties, including their most extreme forms such as annihilation anxiety, was to be found on the human genome or found as a hitherto unappreciated consequence of the failure of human relationships.

Pursuing a different track from Klein in the development of child analysis was Anna Freud, Sigmund Freud's daughter. Anna Freud sought to extend psychoanalysis outwards to deal directly with contemporary events. In 1918, at the age of twenty-three, from a background in teaching, she had entered analysis with her father as preparation for a career in psychoanalysis. She had her first two analytic patients by 1923 and became part of the famous Kinderseminar in Vienna, the group of analysts that included Wilhelm Reich, Otto Fenichel, Siegfried Bernfeld and August Aichhorn, all of whom brought socialist concerns to the applications of psychoanalysis. Reich attempted to bring psychoanalysis and sexual liberation to the youth of the revolutionary labour movement in Germany and Austria, while Fenichel was concerned with psychoanalytic contributions to the psychology of class antagonisms and social alienation in capitalism. Aichhorn pioneered the psychotherapy of juvenile delinquency, relating its dynamics not to neurosis as in classical psychoanalysis, nor to the theory of hereditary degeneracy, popular in mainstream psychiatry, but to the realities of social deprivation. And Bernfeld initiated the application of psychoanalysis to the problems of homeless and orphaned children in his Baumgarten Children's Home which opened on 15 October 1919.

Anna Freud's version of child analysis was based on her experience of alternative education, work with homeless children, her observations of children in foster homes and a knowledge of the Viennese school, day care and welfare systems, acquired in collaboration with Bernfeld and Aichhorn. On 13 January 1924, she wrote to Lou Andreas-Salomé about the education she was receiving from Aichhorn about the social realities in Red Vienna: 'He drags me to all the most remote regions of the city and shows me institutions and welfare arrangements and we meet the people involved in them. And it is really very interesting, a special and very impressive world.' In 1927, their efforts were recognized by the Social Democratic government of Vienna by an offer of municipal land for the Vienna Psychoanalytic Society's headquarters (Young-Bruehl, 1988).

Anna Freud approached the problems of children far more circumspectly than Melanie Klein. She felt that a child's dependence on the still-developing relationship with its parents precluded the possibility of a transference (substitute) relationship developing with the therapist. Instead, the child needed support and education, a non-analytic preparation for dealing with its problems. Anna Freud kept in close touch with the parents and compiled the exceptionally detailed life histories of each child that were the hallmark of her later work at the

Hampstead Clinic in London. With the publication of her book, *Introduction to the Technique of Child Analysis* in 1927, written in part as a critique of Klein's approach, the issues became polarized. Swords crossed at the 1927 Symposium on Child Psychoanalysis at Innsbruck, Freud and Jones exchanged heated letters on the merits of Anna Freud v. Melanie Klein, with full-scale hostilities exploding in the bitter so-called Controversial Discussions held in wartime London from 1941 and 1945.

Klein found little support in Berlin for theoretical views that went so much against those of Freud's daughter and of Freud himself. But her approach found a resonance in British psychoanalysis, in the confident, apolitical, Bohemian world of gentile Bloomsbury, whose members included Leonard and Virginia Woolf, and James and Alix Strachey – the English language translators of Freud's complete works.

In 1924, at the age of thirty-two, Alix Strachey went to Berlin, on the advice of Freud, to begin analysis with Karl Abraham for her melancholia. Born in Nutley, New Jersey, of artistic parents, she was taken to London as an infant and was educated at Bedales, the Slade School of Art, and Newnham College, Cambridge. She married James Strachey in 1920. Her letters to James written during her year in Berlin describe her discovery of Melanie Klein and the successful moves she made that resulted in Klein's emigration to England in 1926 (Meisel and Kendrick, 1985).

In addition to her analysis with Abraham, Alix Strachey attended meetings at the Berlin Polyclinic and tried to establish herself socially. On 11 December 1924 she wrote to James describing her pleasure at being able to visit the home of the wealthy Max Eitingon, where 'it was heavenly' to see books, elegant furniture, thick carpets '& 2 or 3 almost passable pictures'. Two days later she heard Melanie Klein speak for the first time at the regular Saturday night meetings at the Polyclinic. Klein presented two of her cases, designed to show that immediate interpretations of the aggressive and sexual implications of children's play could be the only way to establish contact with a distressed child. Alix Strachey was enthralled. To her, Klein had presented a more pure and psychoanalytically correct view of child analysis than that of Siegfried Bernfeld and August Aichhorn in Vienna, who Alix considered to be 'hopeless pedagogues', or that of Anna Freud who, in the light of what Klein was presenting about the difficulties of childhood, Alix considered to be an 'open or secret sentimentalist'.

Alix Strachey was also intrigued to hear the idea that a child's fear of its parents was entirely an internal fear. Children projected their inner fears outwards so that they simply appeared to be coming from outside when in reality these fears had innate primal origins:

Two more women backed Melanie. One was [Karen] Horney and the other a Frau [Josine] Mueller who said something rather interesting, which was that children often *projected* their already-formed Ueber-Ichs [self-punishing guilty conscience] back onto their parents, & so feared them in a quite exaggerated way, & often thought them tyrannous and cruel when in reality they were as mild as milk. (13 December 1924)

Strachey felt that Klein saw children as they really were, was hard-nosed about them and thus was able to help them. From London, James Strachey was similarly impressed. By return post he asked Alix to prepare a summary of Klein's talk for a reading at the next meeting of the British Psycho-Analytical Society on 7 January.

Excited by the interest shown by the Stracheys, Klein began a campaign to come to England '. . . she's very keen to know the state of affairs in England as to child analysis & has asked me about it' (18 December 1924). Meanwhile, the London meeting, attended by forty people, went well. Klein's paper, fourth on the agenda, was well received and produced reservations only about the possible role of suggestion in Klein's relationship to the children she treated. Most important was Jones's reaction which James described to Alix: 'Jones, of course, is an absolutely heart-and-soul whole-hoggin pro-Melanie' (8 January 1925).

Back in Berlin, Klein was pleased to get the typed, edited English summary of her talk. She proposed that she and Alix talk about England. Alix found Klein difficult. But she found her ideas about children fascinating: '. . . she says it's amazingly different what one finds in the little brats, from what one expects' (12 January 1925). Klein proposed that she should give a series of lectures in London, urging Alix to get James to float the idea to Jones. Alix was enthusiastic – it would be a *coup* if London got Klein's first series of lectures before Berlin did (Alix to James, 12 January 1925). James wrote back that their proposal had been received with 'unanimous rapture' (26 January 1925). In preparation, Alix began to give Klein English lessons, writing to James: 'I *do* think it important to back her point of view' (25 January 1925).

The lectures were arranged for the beginning of July 1925. As the date approached James Strachey began to grow anxious that Klein would disgrace not only herself but the Stracheys as well, as they were by now so closely identified with her (7 May 1925). He told Alix that she must write Klein's lectures for her. On 12 May Alix communicated her own concerns with a description of Klein's performance at the Saturday night meeting in the Polyclinic where, in a lecture by Abraham, Klein veered off the subject of hysterical bleeding in adults into a disorganized irrelevant account of her childhood cases of hysterical colds and tonsillitis: 'It was *intolerable* to sit & listen to her. The effect of the muddle was increased by the fact that she forgets to put in full stops – or any stops, except for breaths – in her speeches.'

Alix grew increasingly dismayed. Klein was slow in getting her lectures typed, leaving little time for practising her delivery. Unknown to Alix she was in the middle of an intense love affair that had begun that spring and lasted until late July, with Chezkel Zvi Kloetzel, a travel journalist for the *Berliner Tageblatt*. On 16 June, Klein dumped her unfinished last lecture on Alix with the remark: 'I've added a paragraph but I was in such a hurry I hadn't time to put it in a suitable place. Would you please do this for me?' Exasperated, Alix wrote to James: 'Touching isn't it? But she's a damn lazy bitch' (17 June 1925).

In London, Klein's lectures were delivered successfully at 50 Golden Square, in the heart of bohemian Soho, in the drawing room of Virginia Woolf's brother, Dr Adrian Stephen and his wife Dr Karin Stephen, both of whom were training to be psychoanalysts. On 7 July, after receiving two letters from Klein from London, Kloetzel wrote back (Grosskurth, 1986): '. . . it appears that this success has surpassed our expectations; and I am very happy about it' (p. 143). On 17 July, Jones, knowing very well Freud's reservations about Klein, gave him an exceptionally positive review of her lectures: 'She made an extraordinarily deep impression on all of us and won the deepest praise both by her personality and her work.'

Over the following year Klein, with the additional assistance of Joan Riviere, manoeuvred to obtain an invitation from Jones to relocate to England. The campaign succeeded. Part of the arrangement was that she was to analyse both Jones's children and his second wife, the Austrian Katherine Jokl Jones, for her parenting anxieties. Klein arrived in London in September 1926 and began her analysis of Jones's children – Mervyn on 15 September, Gwenith on 27 September – and of Katherine Jones on 4 October. She gave her first paper at the London Society on 17 November 1926. Forty years later, in 1965, Edward Glover, Alix Strachey's analyst following the death of Abraham, and also the analyst of Klein's daughter Melitta, recalled that after the arrival of Klein, 'the Society felt fairly cock-a-hoop about developing new ideas . . .' (Grosskurth, 1986, p. 154). Klein's arrival catalysed the emergence of a distinctly British school of psychoanalysis.

Alix Strachey had responded strongly to the self-punishments that Klein reported taking place in children's early development as well as to the violent imagery in children's thoughts about their parents. In her report to James about Klein's 1925 presentation in Berlin, she described the development of conscience in the child as coming in 'with full violence', while Klein's case study of a six-year-old girl who had fantasies of 'being given horrible food to eat, being shut up in a cellar, being held up to scorn and even killed by her mother' was fascinating because the violent world depicted was interpreted to be pure fantasy: 'a child [can come] to attribute quite unmerited cruelty to its father or mother' (Meisel and Kendrick, 1985, p. 328).

In 1927, at the Innsbruck symposium, Klein and her Bloomsbury supporters argued polemically that Anna Freud's educational approach to children – that the child's confidence needed to be won before any great interpretations could be attempted – not only was unnecessary but was incompatible with psychoanalysis (Klein, 1927): 'Analysis is not in itself a gentle method: it cannot spare the patient *any suffering* and this applies equally to children' (p. 344). And Joan Riviere (1927), in an often-quoted statement, passionately rejected the relevance of reality in the conduct of a deep psychoanalysis: '. . . even analysts still hesitate to probe these depths. But analysis has no concern with anything else: it is not concerned with the real world, nor with the child's or the adult's adaptation to the real world, nor with sickness or health, nor virtue or vice. It is concerned simply and solely with the imaginings of the childish mind, the phantasized pleasures and the dreaded retributions' (p. 377).

Freud was appalled – not just by the attack on his daughter's work – but by the fact that Kleinian analysis appeared to have taken leave of its senses. He wrote to Jones on 23 September 1927: 'In this symposium, such an otherwise clever person as Riviere lets herself get carried away by theoretical assumptions which run counter to everything we know and believe and which indicate a new path to the derealization of analysis.'

Jones, in the meantime, had been playing his own game. To Freud, he had written that he had tried to make Riviere less extreme. But Riviere had herself written to Freud saying that Jones had pressured her into taking an extreme position and had told her how pleased he was with her presentation. On 27 November 1927, Freud described these events to Eitingon (Young-Bruehl, 1988):

I don't believe that Jones is consciously ill-intentioned; but he is a disagreeable person, who wants to display himself in ruling, angering and agitating, and for this his Welsh dishonesty ('the liar from Wales') serves him well. Riviere claims that he chased her into her position, congratulated her on the telephone for her theoretical propositions, and then betrayed her when he told me he had tried unsuccessfully to tone her down. (p. 171)

But the coach had already left the station. British psychoanalysis was in the process of transforming itself from being a dependent satellite of Vienna and Berlin into an independent centre, a historical development that was to transform classical psychoanalysis from its dependence on the metaphors of nineteenth-century physics into the independent psychology that Freud originally dreamed of creating.

10

Breakthrough
in Britain

The contribution of Melanie Klein to the consolidation of experience into theory that we call a breakthrough contains two principal themes. As many writers have emphasized, it was she who insisted on the importance of the parent–infant relationship straight from birth for the development of the human psyche. And it was she who first attempted to describe the forms that childhood anxieties took as so-called objects in the child's inner world (Hinshelwood, 1997).

But the theoretical resources were not available in inter-war Europe to explore the origin of childhood anxieties. So Klein used the nearest tools to hand. She postulated an instinctual psychology based on Freud's so-called death instinct to account for the terrible fears and anxieties she reported seeing in her young patients. It took thirty years to disentangle Klein's theory of childhood anxiety from her observation of its existence. The theoretical work of Ronald Fairbairn in Scotland, the clinical work of Donald Winnicott and Michael and Enid Balint in London, and the ethological perspective of John Bowlby in London, helped to explain the profound anxiety – even annihilation anxiety – that traumatic separation from, or attacks upon, the parent–child bond can cause.

In 1927, Fairbairn was thirty-eight, Winnicott was thirty-one and Bowlby was only twenty. All three were to make their contributions from the margins of British psychoanalysis. Fairbairn, geographically isolated in Scotland, engaged in mature dialogue with Melanie Klein's ideas but was distanced from the dispute between Klein and Anna Freud that was to divide psychoanalysis in London. Winnicott and Bowlby were just beginning their careers. Both of them needed to complete their analyses – Winnicott after ten years with James Strachey and another five with Joan Riviere, Bowlby after ten years with Joan Riviere – before being able to absorb what was new in Klein's work and develop it in their own way.

Freud's postulation of the death instinct was a solution – created in the aftermath of war and the violence of post-war revolutionary Vienna – to an important clinical problem. Freud had begun with a vision of human motivation as being fundamentally pleasure-seeking (reduction of tension). In *Beyond the Pleasure Principle* (1920) he wanted to understand patients who found themselves compulsively repeating painful, rather than pleasurable experiences: the benefactor who repeatedly experienced bitter ingratitude from those he had helped; a man's love affairs that always took the same course with the same unhappy outcome; the man whose friendships consistently ended in betrayal (perhaps Freud himself). The element of choice – of protégés, lovers, or friends – meant that this kind of repetition could be understood as an unconscious attempt to overcome feelings of helplessness associated with previous emotional injury. Repetition offered the individual the chance to master previously overwhelming emotional experiences, as in the recurrent dreams of war traumas suffered by returning soldiers from the First World War. Such repetitions could be more or less consistent with the pleasure principle in that an ultimate resolution would be tension-reducing.

But Freud argued further that there were unexplored depths in the compulsion to repeat. Citing so-called passive experiences, not involving choice – the woman who three times married men who became gravely ill and had to be cared for before they died – Freud argued that the repetitive nature of these passive experiences seemed to indicate the operation of deeper forces than could be accounted for by the pleasure principle (Freud, 1920): 'If we take into account observations such as these, based upon behaviour in the transference and upon the life histories of men and women, we shall find the courage to assume that there really does exist in the mind a compulsion to repeat which over-rides the pleasure principle' (p. 293). The principle that was meant to account for the overriding of the pleasure principle was the death instinct.

To most analysts, the argument was not persuasive. On 20 August 1920, Jones wrote to Freud that he had mixed feelings about the work.

Of the two main ideas, he had no doubts about the importance of the repetition compulsion, but he was not at all sure he understood the necessity of postulating the existence of a death instinct: 'The second idea, that this [repetition] is independent of the Pleasure Principle, I have only so far imperfectly digested.'

Freud was attempting to come to grips with the effects of aggression on the human psyche. But, in his approach to the problem of aggression, Freud was betrayed in part by his past involvement in neuroscience. At the age of sixty-four, living in a post-war Vienna torn by violent class conflict and the traumatic experience of mechanized war, he was tired, cranky and feeling impotent to affect events. Instead of leaning forward in his chair and actively seeking the psychological origins of repetitive self-destructive tendencies, he leaned back among his books and memories and returned to the sensibility of his scientific youth, a sensibility informed by classical physics. The death instinct was a line of thought that, in 1920, he acknowledged as being 'speculation, often far fetched speculation' (Freud, 1920, p. 295).

The biologists of Freud's youth had struggled with reconciling the phenomenon of the complexity of living matter with the second law of thermodynamics, that physical systems always move in the direction of increasing randomness. Expressed dramatically in the popular science of *fin de siècle* Europe as the inevitable heat-death of the universe where all matter and energy would be uniformly distributed throughout space, it seemed that biology needed to account for the development of living organisms towards increasing organization – an apparent contradiction to the second law of thermodynamics.

One attempt to resolve this apparent contradiction was by Ewald Hering, Breuer's collaborator on the action of the vagus nerve, who had, in 1882, offered Freud a job in Prague. Hering postulated the existence of two opposing tendencies in all living matter – one to assemble material and grow, the other to disassemble, disperse and die. Using Hering's idea as evidence of the possible existence of a life and a death instinct, Freud attempted to theorize that living matter had from its earliest evolution incorporated in it an urge, an instinct, a drive, a tendency, to return to the quiescent, uniform state characteristic of inorganic matter.

But Hering's idea was a false lead. In modern molecular biology there is no contradiction. The biochemical reactions of life *all* obey the second law of thermodynamics. The final state of every biochemical reaction is always more probable (less complex) than the initial state. In the modern, detailed understanding of fundamental life processes, symbolized perhaps by the well-understood replication of bacterial viruses, there is no violation of the laws of physics and no need for the hypothesis of life or death instincts (Hayes, 1970).

Melanie Klein was feeling her way into the child's inner world where she sensed there was far more structure than had previously been acknowledged. Needing, as a woman and also a classless outsider, to legitimate her intuitions, she became more Freudian than Freud. Klein's embrace of the metaphor of the death instinct as one corner-stone of her theory was an intuitive attempt to make sense of the violence she was seeing in the child's inner world. But it was also an attempt to seize the theoretical high ground as the developer of Freud's latest thinking. As the rivalry between her and Anna Freud intensified in the late 1930s after the Freud family had escaped from Nazi-occupied Vienna to London, Klein wrote to Ernest Jones: 'It is tragic that his daughter, who thinks that she must defend him against me does not realize that I am serving him better than she' (KleinP, D33).

In the late 1930s, in London, questions about the structure of the child's inner world, instead of being able to be faced squarely, became deflected into a bitter succession struggle between Melanie Klein and Anna Freud. Kate Friedlander, an ardent supporter of Anna Freud, dismissed Klein during the Controversial Discussions for her bad biology, saying (King and Steiner, 1991): 'Mrs Klein's theories of phantasies . . . are in complete contradiction to the anatomical and physiological knowledge of the development of the brain during the first year of life' (p. 408). But Friedlander, tied as she was to a classical Freudian theory of instincts, was unable to look behind the metaphorical expression of Klein's understanding to see its psychologi-cal importance. It took the action of determined third parties under the organizational leadership of Sylvia Payne, and the intellectual leadership of Marjorie Brierley, to create the space for the new theory begun by Klein to develop.

Formal discussions to resolve the Anna Freud–Melanie Klein ten-sions in the British Psycho-Analytical Society began in 1941. There were two agendas: discussion of the theoretical differences dividing the Society and the need to democratize decision-making within the Society. The meetings in the first year were fraught with, among other things, Klein's daughter Melitta Schmideberg bitterly attacking her mother from the floor. The tensions were no less behind the scenes. On 31 May 1942, Melanie Klein wrote a letter to Sylvia Payne, accusing Edward Glover of being out to get her from the beginning: 'I am quite sure – and have very good grounds to think so – that he has for many years planned gradually either to crush my work and myself completely or to discredit my work to such a degree that he can get me out of the Society. From the moment the Viennese came, they were welcome allies to him in this cause' (BrP, CKB/F01/17). All members recognized that the temperature had to be lowered. At the meeting of 10 June 1942, Marjorie Brierley, with the support of Sylvia Payne, Ella Sharpe and Barbara Low, introduced a resolution prohibiting charges, counter-charges or personal attacks in further discussions.

The intense politicking for control of the organization continued outside the formal meetings. Here Sylvia Payne exercised the diplomatic skills that prevented the Society from splitting. Recognizing that much of what Klein had to contribute was essential to the development of the field, Payne knew she needed to convince Klein that Anna Freud must not be driven out of the Society. In a letter of 26 November 1942 she told Klein that she must moderate the way she presented her views because if Anna Freud were to leave suddenly, she would, in Payne's estimation of the situation, have Jones's support. Jones would inform all the many absent members of the Society that Anna had been driven out by Klein, and, with no first-hand experience of the situation, they would then vote with Jones, giving Anna and Jones a majority. There was then the danger that the majority could declare Klein's views not-psychoanalysis, thus effectively driving her out. 'I am convinced that you should not actively attack the Viennese at this moment, but do as you said and seek common ground' (KleinP, E2).

In the meantime, Marjorie Brierley was making every effort to educate Klein and her supporters on how to conduct an intellectual dispute in a principled fashion. On 21 May 1942 she wrote privately to Klein:

It does seem to me a simple fact that up to now your own attitude and that of your adherents about your work has been felt to be a difficulty in the way of getting to grips with the work itself. This statement does not impugn either your work or yourself and is definitely not made with hostile intent. The intent is to make clear what I believe to be a very real source of difficulty and a disadvantage all around. My own relations with you and your friends have always been amicable and I hope they remain so, but this has not prevented my feeling profoundly uneasy about this matter of attitude to work, and this uneasiness has not been confined to me. Various labels have been attached to this subtle something in attitude from time to time. They might be summed up in the phrase 'insufficiently scientific'.

Klein, in daily contact with her supporters during this intense period wrote to both Susan Isaacs and Joan Riviere about 'Dr B.'s' letter. On 29 May 1942, Riviere wrote a plaintive letter to Brierley (BrP): '. . . your criticism of us is still so indefinite . . . The principal difficulty about your point of view is that you do not *define* precisely what is wrong with our "attitude to the work". In what way is it "unscientific"? . . . until we can understand exactly what our offence is, and precisely *because* you do not formulate it explicitly we are left with no alternative but to regard your position towards us as unjustified and unfair and in fact quite subjective.'

Brierley, still trying to do her best to help the Society grow up, explained herself further to Klein on 5 June 1942 (BrP):

I will only say now that I believe it to be an 'objective' fact that your attitude has been a source of fairly widespread uneasiness, and that it has sometimes hampered people in arriving at a just appreciation of your work. I used the term 'insufficiently scientific' as the most general term I could find to cover all the various experiences I have heard used about it by different people at different times. I called it a 'subtle something' because it is intangible. To my mind it is far more a matter of mental attitude and emotional atmosphere than of words and deeds.

She, then, with some effect, tried to get Klein and her followers to separate their observations of the apparently universal importance of childhood aggression from the metaphors with which Klein was attempting to understand it. 'The main root of my own misgivings has always been the direct first hand impression that neither Mrs Klein nor her closest adherents are sufficiently realistic about her work' (King and Steiner, 1991, p. 625).

Sylvia Payne tried to support Klein's recognition of the importance of the mother and the significance of aggression in early infant experience while casting doubt on the necessity for the death instinct to account for what she was seeing. 'Personally, I cannot see that her findings require the theory of a death instinct' (King and Steiner, 1991, p. 746). After remarks attempting to remind the membership that the death instinct in Freud's hands was a passive movement towards an inanimate state and not the active self-destructive impulses attributed to it in Klein's theory, she concluded:

I think that if we examine clinical facts we shall find more direct evidence that aggression manifested actively is either a defensive reaction or in combination with the libido is manifested as a perversion than it is a sign of the existence of an active death instinct. If this is true it does not seem to me to lessen the value of Mrs Klein's researches on the importance of aggressive fantasies, and the part they play in influencing psychical [mental] development. (King and Steiner, 1991)

In the summary of comments following Payne's remarks, the minute-taker (not identified) records Klein as being prepared to reconsider her position. 'Mrs Klein said that: Her conclusions did not stand or fall on the concept of the death instinct' (p. 747).

Here was a possible turning point. But as so frequently happens in human affairs, the participants were not equal to the occasion. Instead of a pause that such an acknowledgement would seem to deserve, the discussion continued with a tragi-comic dispute about sleep, with Joan Riviere suggesting that sleep was a state of death and Bowlby and Payne retorting that sleep made possible a renewal of life (King and Steiner, 1991, p. 749).

As the discussions drew to a close in mid-1944 the theoretical differences between Klein and her sympathizers in the middle group became more pronounced as did the impossibility of resolving them. On 1 March 1944, in a discussion of Klein's account of childhood depression, Brierley said that Klein did not distinguish carefully enough between the outer and inner worlds, between the relationship as it actually existed between parent and infant and the infant's subjective experience of the relationship (King and Steiner, 1991, p. 816).

On 3 May 1944, Klein responded to Brierley with the same combination of insight and inflexibility that characterized her career in Britain. On the question of infantile depression, she reaffirmed that the central issue was separation and loss – themes which Bowlby was to develop independently (King and Steiner, 1991):

In my view the emotional experiences of losing the loved object and regaining it are an essential part of early mental life. The first loss is the separation from the mother at birth but it is in relation to the mother's breast, to losing it (and the mother) again and again that depressive feelings develop through the suckling period. (pp. 833–4)

In Klein's hands, separation and loss were a manifestation of innate, devouring, cannibalistic impulses, whose expression frightened the infant so that it believed it would lose the love object. Expressed with the certitude that had so alienated potential sympathizers, she said: 'The fact that cannibalistic impulses exist in every infant whether or not he is stressed in his feeding situation is established beyond doubt' (p. 836). And finally, Klein insisted, in opposition to Winnicott, that there was no possibility of the existence of a non-aggressive phase, because an acceptance of this observation was 'ultimately to deny the painful fact that ambivalence and aggression are inherited'. It is no wonder that in his tribute to Klein after her death, Winnicott said that he thought Klein was temperamentally incapable of relating her observations to real-life experience.

The final result was an agreement to disagree. In 1945, Sylvia Payne initiated talks with Anna Freud resulting in a compromise to establish parallel training schemes. Candidates in training analysis with Kleinian or Anna Freudian analysts would choose their second supervisor from the non-Kleinian members of the A group, subsequently referred to as the Middle Group or Independents. The British Psycho-Analytical Society effectively divided into three groups: Kleinians, Anna Freudians and Independents. In contrast to the developments in US psychoanalysis, a formal split had been avoided. But feelings remained high.

John Bowlby began to explore the fundamental issue of attachment and loss. Interested from the beginning of his career in the problem of separation, Bowlby built on the wartime work of Anna Freud and Dorothy Burlingham, who had studied the effects of separation on children who had been evacuated from wartime London, and of René Spitz's work on the effects of separation on children in orphanages. By the late 1950s he had accumulated a body of observational and theoretical work to indicate the fundamental importance for human development of attachment from birth – with its loss being experienced by the child as mourning. Instead of his efforts being welcomed, he was ostracized by most of British psychoanalysis.

Anna Freud and René Spitz disagreed with Bowlby theoretically, arguing that infants do not mourn. The Kleinians disagreed with the observations themselves. In 1952, Bowlby and James Robertson, in a joint presentation to the British Psycho-Analytical Society, showed their film *A Two Year Old Goes to Hospital*, an account of the grief experienced by a child separated from its parents because of a ten-day stay in hospital. The film was instrumental in the successful campaign headed by May Walker of the National Association for Welfare of Children in Hospital to relax UK hospital restrictions on parental visits to hospitalized children and has been a standard teaching tool in medicine and psychotherapy for four decades. Wilfred Bion, a leading Kleinian analyst, was in the audience and raised the objection that the child's grief was not caused by the separation but by unconscious fantasies connected to the fact that the mother was in the early stages of pregnancy. Even though Bowlby and his co-workers had controls showing that small children whose mothers were not pregnant exhibited similar signs of grief, his arguments did not begin to be taken seriously by the British Psycho-Analytical Society until the 1980s (Bowlby, Figlio and Young, 1986).

Bowlby's patrician background and his early training in the natural sciences gave him the confidence to resist an orthodoxy he could not support. Bowlby's father, Major-General Sir Anthony Bowlby, Royal Surgeon to King Edward VII and King George V, was awarded a baronetcy in 1920 when he became President of the Royal College of

Surgeons. He married May Mostyn, granddaughter of Lord Mostyn of Mostyn, North Wales. Bowlby was the fourth child of six. In 1914, at the age of seven, he and his older brother Tony, aged eight, were sent away to boarding school. Bowlby later said: 'I wouldn't send a dog away to boarding school at age seven.' He went to Cambridge in 1925, then at the height of its fame in natural science as the home of the Cavendish Laboratory.

At Cambridge, Bowlby won prizes and emerged with a first-class degree in pre-clinical sciences and psychology. Before going on to medical school, he worked at a progressive school, an off-shoot of A. S. Neill's Summerhill. After qualifying in medicine at University College London in 1933, he trained at the Maudsley in adult psychiatry and in 1936 was appointed to the London Child Guidance Clinic. While in medical school he entered psychoanalysis with Joan Riviere. He qualified as a psychoanalyst in 1937 and in the same year chose Melanie Klein as his supervisor for further training as a child psycho-analyst.

Bowlby was resistant to psychoanalytic orthodoxies from the begin-ning. The clinical and social psychologist, Eric Trist, who also was in analysis with Joan Riviere at the same time, recalled (King, 1993): 'By a strange coincidence, we had the same analyst. John's disagree-ments with her are well known. I was far too awed to challenge her candidly which did my analysis no good' (p. 825). As Bowlby himself recalled his subsequent supervision with Melanie Klein (BowlbP): 'I refused to be dominated' (A1/13). Although he had been attracted to Klein's work with children as early as 1932, in the event he was put off by Klein's insistence that only the inner world of his three-year-old patient mattered. As Pearl King recalled in her obituary of Bowlby (King, 1993): 'What upset Bowlby was that Melanie Klein seemed to refuse even to discuss the effect the mother's illness and behaviour might have had on his child patient' (p. 824). It took ten more years for Bowlby to realize how incompatible his views were with those of his Kleinian analyst and Kleinian supervisor. In 1984, he described his thinking, as he recalled it, in a letter to Phyllis Grosskurth (BowlbP):

At that time I had not realized that my interest in real-life experiences and situations was so alien to the Kleinian outlook; on the contrary I believed my ideas were compatible with theirs. Looking back on the years 1935–39, I think I was reluctant to recognize the divergence. That became crystal clear to me only after the war, especially as I became increasingly shocked by their intransigent attitudes. (A5/7)

We know from the last twenty years of infant observation studies that newborn infants are not amorphous, inchoate beings. Newborn motor responses are co-ordinated in response to threats of smothering or in guarding themselves against approaching objects. They show discriminating responses to both the presence and absence of affection and tenderness. They withdraw and defend themselves against abrupt, insensitive handling, a fact well known to experienced neonatal nurses. Under close observation the faces of infants register clearly identifiable states of curiosity, frustration, excitement, pleasant relaxation or of being perplexed (Trevarthen, 1993). Detailed slow-motion studies of videotaped feeding and holding sessions between mother and infant demonstrate that from birth there is intense structure to the mother–infant interaction and a recognition by the infant of 'the other' immediately after birth (Stern, 1985).

In Ronald Fairbairn's formulation of this structured interaction, feeding became not just instinctual gratification of hunger, but, far more importantly, a channel for relationship. Klein, with her intuitive, if unsympathetic, attunement to children's emotional states, sensed that this must be the case – the infant, from birth, is dealing with the vicissitudes of relationships. As Anna Freud was to acknowledge years later (Coles, 1992):

I think it is fair to say that Mrs Klein and those who have called themselves Kleinians, have always been more willing to do analysis with children [than we were]. I think we have to be rather careful about this – *hesitant*, I'd say, to engage with a child psychoanalytically, and *clear, very clear*, in our minds as to why, exactly why, we are doing so, if we decide to do so. Children quite normally and commonly go in and out of difficulties, and they also gradually build up for themselves ways of dealing with those difficulties. I have always felt that it is wrong to enter a child's life unless there is a good reason, a reason that gives us warrant. Perhaps you could say I was more cautious than Mrs Klein – and we disagreed on that basis. But you know much of that is old history. We did work together at times: she and I discussed our views, and agreed to disagree. Perhaps I am now putting the best light on what was not such a good moment. She had enormous energy, and she was – how should I say it? – more imaginative than I was willing to be in my daily analytic work with children, more imaginative, maybe, about what takes place in the minds of young children. (p. 123)

What was trying to emerge in the 'not such a good moment' referred to by Anna Freud, was the recognition that the human being is born with a drive towards relationship, a drive, according to Bowlby, towards attachment. Or, in the subsequent formulation of Ronald Fairbairn, the developing human being turns to pleasure-seeking in the form of bodily gratification only as a result of the deterioration of its human relationships. Or, in the words of Donald Winnicott: 'There is no such thing as an infant, there is only a mothering pair.'

In Washington DC, William Alanson White and Harry Stack Sullivan had realized that the fundamental human anxiety was separation anxiety. As White wrote in 1937:

When for any reason this feeling of belonging is interfered with or destroyed, when the individual is separated as it were from those whom he loves or upon whom he is dependent or to whom he looks for guidance, then there develops the separation anxiety which is at the bottom of neuroses and psychoses and in its more virulent form results in hate and anger and an aggressive attitude toward the source of suffering. (p. 459)

But in classical, mainstream psychoanalysis in Vienna and Berlin, where the reality of childhood sexual abuse had been seriously questioned, where disputes had been dealt with by secession, and where the violence of the First World War had taken on new, unprecedented civil forms, the grave clinical consequences caused by real, not imagined, separations were difficult to recognize. Melanie Klein had to emigrate to London, where a far more secure scientific culture that insisted on disciplined rules of evidence and argument created the space for an advance on her theories and those of Anna Freud.

Anna Freud was the woman whom it was easy to love. Melanie

Klein was the woman whom it was easy to hate. As John Bowlby recalled in his recollections of Anna Freud: 'Our meetings were always most friendly and one was struck of course by her warmth, charm, vitality and lucidity. The characteristics which impressed me especially however were her modesty and respect for others, characteristics which were sometimes in marked contrast to those of other colleagues' (BowlbP, A.616).

The 'other colleagues' referred to by Bowlby included Melanie Klein, who, friend and foe alike agreed was, at best, difficult. The task of separating the personality from the theory was achieved by a more mature approach to psychoanalysis than had been possible in the first generation, and took the form of a struggle to shift attention away from personalities towards the facts of the case. For Bowlby, however, who liked and respected Anna Freud, affection and respect were not enough: 'I never felt that Anna Freud understood the nature of the scientific method, namely that the progress of science turns on comparing the explanatory powers of alternative theories in the light of an increasing array of empirical evidence.' While for Winnicott, who grew to dislike intensely the rigidities of Melanie Klein's theory and practice, dislike was not enough to prevent him from acknowledging her central role in guiding his attempts to make sense of the experience of early childhood (Winnicott, 1962): 'Melanie Klein had a way of making inner psychic reality very real' (p. 173).

Marjorie Brierley, the most insightful of Klein's critics, had no intellectual respect for Anna Freud. Years later she told Phyllis Grosskurth (1986): 'She's never written anything (apart from child reports) that questioned her father's findings in any essential way. She developed some of his findings, but never questioned their validity. The whole experience of the public debates was very unsettling for Anna so soon after Freud's death and her settling in England. She was horrified to hear any criticism of Freud, but of course poor dear she had to get used to it' (p. 300). As for Klein and her fatal preoccupation with aggression and self-destruction – the so-called negative transference – Brierley was equally scathing: 'She liked it to stay there because she had this liking for control over people' (p. 300).

Brierley wanted decisions to be made on the issues, not on the personalities. As she put it at the Controversial Discussions meeting of 18 February 1942 in her summation of the issues that divided Melanie Klein and Anna Freud: 'One way of stating the problem before us is to ask the question: Is a theory of mental development in terms of infant object relationships compatible with theory in terms of instinct vicissitudes?' (King and Steiner, 1991). In Bowlby's hands, the answer was yes, instincts and object relations are compatible but only if one expanded the concept of instinct to include an instinct for attachment. In the eyes of his psychoanalytic colleagues, Bowlby was a renegade, forsaking exploration of the inner world in favour of external factors that shed no light on inner dynamics.

Bowlby's contribution was to show that early separations and losses were pathogenic and needed to be attended to with as much care as daily bodily needs. In 1940 he wrote (Holmes, 1993): 'If it became a tradition that small children were never subjected to complete or prolonged separation from their parents in the same way that regular sleep and orange juice have become nursery traditions, I believe that many cases of neurotic character development would be avoided' (p. 21).

Bowlby's depth of insight into the pain and distress associated with separation enabled him to create an intellectual framework that he hoped would be taken up by those within psychoanalysis who were more attuned than he to the inner world of experience, to show how traumatic separations were incorporated into the child's inner world. His life's work is consolidated in his trilogy *Attachment and Loss:* volume 1, *Attachment*; volume 2, *Separation: Anxiety and Anger*; volume 3, *Loss: Sadness and Depression* (Bowlby, 1969, 1973, 1980). By 1986 these books had been translated into six languages, had sold about 250,000 copies in English editions, and were selling at around 5000 copies per year – unusually high figures for a serious specialist account of psychiatric issues.

When Melanie Klein encountered the anxious, self-punishing internal world of children it was difficult to accept that such states could have their origin in apparently benign parents. The profound effect of threats of abandonment as a means of discipline – 'If you don't stop that I am going to leave this house' – were poorly understood. In addition, actual physical cruelty to and torture of children, skilfully disguised by severely disturbed parents, was not yet documented

(Daniels, 1997; Southall et al., 1997). Instead, the fear, aggression and anxiety displayed by a child could be more easily located, not externally but internally, where it resonated strongly with the traditions of the Western Christian world of original sin in the form of deep feelings of personal responsibility.

What then was the mechanism that lay behind the formation of a severe self-punishing conscience? Freud developed the first preliminary insight into the important phenomenon of self-punishment in his analysis of Joan Riviere. Riviere was the analyst most committed to the self-contained integrity of the inner world. She was introduced to the Bloomsbury meetings about the new psychoanalytic psychology through her uncle A. W. Verrall, professor of classics at Cambridge. At a memorial after her death in 1962, James Strachey recalled her at these early meetings as 'a tall, strikingly handsome distinguished looking woman'.

In 1910, a year after her father's death, Riviere suffered a nervous breakdown and spent time in a sanatorium. She was twenty-seven years old, married to a barrister, Evelyn Riviere. The couple had a child aged two. Coming from an established upper-middle-class background in Sussex, Riviere had always been closest to her father and had looked down on her mother – an efficient and strict household manager, intolerant of sloppiness and things 'done stupidly' – as being a mere housewife (Hughes, 1991).

Riviere later began a five-year analysis with Ernest Jones in 1916, interrupted by a year in which she had tuberculosis. According to her biographer Athol Hughes (1991), who inspected the entire Jones–Riviere correspondence, Jones broke all the professional boundaries short of having a sexual relationship with her. He was lax with appointments, giving her no regular appointment times. He confided to Riviere his problems in both his marriages and he lent her his summer cottage in Elsted on a regular basis. She was, in addition, actively involved with Jones in the translation of German psychoanalytic articles, further damaging their therapeutic relationship. At the beginning of 1922, Jones sent her to Freud in the hope that Freud could patch things up: '. . . it is the worst failure I have ever had' (22 January 1922).

Riviere suffered from free-floating anxiety and a lack of self-confidence. In meetings at the London Psychoanalytic Society she was too anxious to speak. She had many lovers but found herself to be sexually unresponsive. Jones complained to Freud that his generosity in lending her his cottage 'led to a declaration of love and to the broken hearted cry that she had never been rejected before'. After that incident, Jones complained to Freud that Riviere 'devoted herself to torturing me without any intermission and with considerable success and ingenuity, being a fiendish sadist'. Jones, the Welsh radical, also found her elitism difficult to take: 'Incidentally, she has a strong complex about being a well-born lady (county family) and despises all the rest of us especially the women' (22 January 1922).

On 5 February 1922, Freud wrote back to Jones: '. . . on Mrs Riviere, whom I expect on the 25th of Febr; you may imagine how little charmed I was by the prospects opened in your letter. I will spare myself any further remarks on the subject as you seem to have suffered sufficiently for your mistake. But let us hope that all these adventures belong to the past.'

Much later, Riviere reported that Freud had begun her analysis with enthusiasm, saying (Riviere, 1939): 'Well I know something about you already, you had a father and a mother.' One may admire Freud's skill in being willing to break his own rule of analytic abstinence to put Riviere at her ease. He was there to hear her story. He was not going to use any prior knowledge he might have had from Jones in his work with her. On 23 March 1922 Freud wrote to Jones that her analysis was proceeding well. 'Mrs Riviere does not appear to me half as black as you had painted her.' Freud was relieved that Jones had not slept with her. 'I am very glad you had no sexual relations with her as your hints made me suspect.'

Feeling anxious and exposed, Jones badgered Freud about her analysis. Was Freud taking her side against him? Did Freud understand that he in fact was not unkind to her? Did Freud understand how truly difficult she was? On 22 May 1922 Jones wrote to Freud that in London: 'People are most curious to see if her disdainful way of treating other people like dirt beneath her feet will undergo any modification.' On 26 May, in response to Freud's request that Riviere be put in complete charge of translations, Jones wrote: 'I should not be able to work under her orders because of the impossible tone in which she gives them.'

Freud had had enough. On 4 June 1922 he gave Jones some solid cuffs around the ears. The first was to remind him that it was Jones himself who was responsible for the difficulties in the case.

A secondary analysis like this is no easy or pleasant task. Special duties were imposed on me which I am to discharge with the least possible damage to the parties concerned.

The second was to remind Jones what it meant to be an analyst.

Now in this situation given you must be prepared to my taking her side, defending her interest and even turning against you in favour of her analysis. It means simply doing my duty as an analyst . . . There was no chance of making her see the abnormality of her reactions unless she had got the acknowledgement of your errors where you had committed them.

The third was to criticize Jones about his fear of powerful women.

And in fact I cannot praise the way you handled her. You reminded me yourself of your relations with another powerful woman and made me remember that in that case too much was due to the faults of your own demeanour.

And finally, and most importantly, he pointed out that Jones had simply failed to analyse Riviere's difficulties.

When Mrs R. brought up her unpleasant reactions you seem to have treated her as a bad character in life but you never got behind her surface to master her wickedness.

What became apparent to Freud, but had completely escaped Jones, was how wicked Riviere was with herself. Not only was she 'harsh, unpleasant and critical' with Freud, just as she had been with Jones, she was also impossible to herself. She was as intolerant of her successes as she was of her failures. Far from being an elitist she was a democrat – she treated everyone miserably, including herself: '. . . she projects her self-criticism to other people, turns her pangs of conscience into sadistic behaviour, tries to make other people unhappy because she feels so herself'.

Where did this severe conflict between her real self and her idea of an ideal self originate? Freud did not know. 'Our theory has not yet mastered the mechanism of these cases. It seems likely that the formation of a high and severe ideal took place in her at a very early age, but this ideal became superseded, "repressed" with the onset of sexual maturity and ever since has worked in the dark' (4 June 1922). Freud turned these musings into his 1923 book, *The Ego and the Id*, an attempt to understand the origins of severe conscience in terms of a new mental structure, the superego, which in cases like Riviere's declared war on the ego and became punishing and destructive instead of simply civilizing (Freud, 1923b).

Riviere, like Klein, was acutely attuned to the most painful aspects of inner life. In 1936 she firmly took Klein's side on the question of childhood depression (Hughes, 1991): 'The content of the depressive position (as Melanie Klein has shown) is the situation in which all one's loved ones *within* are dead and destroyed, all goodness dispersed, lost in fragments, wasted and scattered to the winds; nothing is left *within* but utter desolation' (p. xiii). The pain evoked by these powerful words represents real internal states of feeling. And it is Riviere's achievement to have found the words to express these states. The question that proved more difficult to answer was the identification of the processes leading to such devastating inner emptiness.

Riviere's sensitivity may well have been formed by her parental relationships – a harsh and unyielding housebound mother, an idealized accomplished absent father. Such influences can form the style of a psychotherapist. Marjorie Brierley tried to understand Riviere's position on endogenous sources of pain by relating it to her adaptation to a difficult childhood through the mechanism of introjection (Brierley, 1939):

People who make considerable use of introjection in maintaining their personal adaptation to life on the whole probably feel more at home with concepts relating to 'internalized objects'. For that very reason they may accept hypotheses concerning them too readily and too uncritically. They are naturally disposed to feel that the world within really matters more than the world without. (p. 242)

But as Freud had repeatedly to point out to his followers, it is inexcusable to treat arguments in psychoanalysis as expressions of personality faults. During the disputes about child psychoanalysis at the 1927 Symposium on Child Psychotherapy, he wrote to Jones in response to Jones's argument that Anna Freud was insufficiently analysed:

When two analysts have differing opinions on some point, one may be fully justified in ever so many cases in assuming that the mistaken view of one of them stems from his having been insufficiently analysed and he therefore allows himself to be influenced by his complexes to the detriment of science. But in practical polemics such an argument is not permissible, for it is at the disposal of each party, and does not reveal on whose side the error lies. We are generally agreed to renounce arguments of this sort and in the case of differences of opinion, to leave the resolutions to advancements in empirical knowledge. (31 May 1927)

And that autumn he had written in a similar vein to Joan Riviere explaining that he was not angry with her about her theoretical disagreement with Anna but with her and Jones's use of the insufficiently analysed argument (Hughes, 1992): 'I only became angry when Jones, in a private letter and publicly in the symposium ascribed Anna's views to the fact that she was insufficiently analysed. This is plain indecent, it should not have been allowed to occur' (9 October 1927).

The usually clear-thinking Brierley had reduced the Kleinian argument to the pathology of its makers. What was needed was to locate the source of such serious internalized distress in the external world. This source, the fundamental importance of human interpersonal relationships, was to be identified in concise, theoretical form in the work of the Scottish psychoanalyst Ronald Fairbairn.

Although Ronald Fairbairn had been ill through much of 1960, and was to suffer ill health until his death in 1964 at the age of seventy-five, he nevertheless made a point of travelling 400 miles from Edinburgh to London to attend the funeral of Melanie Klein at Golders Green cemetery. Fairbairn repeatedly told colleagues how much Klein's work had meant to him and, according to his biographer J. D. Sutherland (1989), it was very much in Fairbairn's character to want to acknowledge her work with this public gesture.

The feeling was not mutual. Klein had shown little respect for Fairbairn's development of her ideas. As she had been arguing throughout the Controversial Discussions, she accused Fairbairn both of not following Freud and of not paying sufficient attention to hate and aggression (Klein, 1946): 'This conclusion is in line not only with his rejecting Freud's concept of primary instincts but also his underrating the role which aggression and hatred play from the beginning of life' (p. 179).

In a major paper published in 1941, Fairbairn had turned Klein's ideas on their head. For Fairbairn the problem of human development was not a problem of hate but a problem of love: '. . . the great problem of the schizoid individual is how to love without destroying by love, whereas the great problem of the depressive individual is how to love without destroying by hate' (p. 49). Fairbairn's achievement was to show how failures in the outer world could produce the structures Klein was seeing in the inner world. These failures were, following Bowlby, failures of love and attachment, the theme Heinz Kohut was to explore in the US thirty years later.

Melanie Klein was acutely sensitive to feelings of hate and aggression. She felt them to be around her everywhere, operating, like gravity, from the deepest levels of the psyche. She created a gothic tale of human development that evoked the power and the mystery that these feelings held for her. It was inevitable that she should clash with Anna Freud, because Anna Freud did not privilege hate and aggression in the same way. In 1946, the Red Cross notified Anna Freud about the fate of her four aunts, her father's sisters Marie, Dolfi, Rosa and Pauline. Left behind as old women in Vienna with sufficient means to sustain them, they had been rounded up by the Nazis and put to death in the concentration camps – Marie in Theresienstadt, Rosa in Auschwitz, Dolfi and Pauline in Treblinka. When asked later by a psychoanalytic colleague how she could explain why four old women could be murdered in this way, she replied (Young-Bruehl, 1988): 'The Nazis wanted their apartments' (p. 280).

But Anna Freud – practical, down-to-earth, socially engaged – was, like many of the analysts of the second generation who succeeded in escaping from the Nazis, too tied to the instinctual theories of her father to be won over to the developments generated by the British School. Her generation had participated in the development of psychoanalysis when it was not only a novel way to understand the human personality but also a way to understand oneself, to achieve an often enviable balance and clarity about one's own life. This generation lived a psychoanalysis that was not merely a tool but a discipline that claimed the heart.

Fairbairn, a graduate in Mental Philosophy from the University of Edinburgh, had been attracted to psychoanalysis because he wanted to understand more deeply the problems of anxiety and guilt (Guntrip, 1961). Conservative in politics – he had been sworn in as a Special Constable (Motor Section Duty) on 8 May 1926 to help break the British General Strike (Birtles, 1998) – and deeply rooted in Scottish intellectual traditions, Fairbairn approached psychoanalysis, not as a way of life, as it was for other psychoanalysts of his generation, but as a tool to further his understanding.

In 1929, he attended the International Congress of Psycho-Analysis held in Oxford. In trenchant notes taken at the time, he observed the intense interest psychoanalysis held for analysts themselves to become 'a completely analysed person'. Fairbairn recognized that there was something 'morally impressive' about this dedication. But he also noted the influence of Nietzsche on the psychoanalytic movement in that a 'completely analysed person' is not a normal human being but a superman. Fairbairn also noted the similarity between the training analysis and an initiation rite and between a perfect analysis and the religious ideal of salvation, where 'the completely analysed person' has achieved the equivalent of redemption (Fairbairn, 1929).

Fairbairn aligned himself with the Middle Group in the Controversial Discussions but he was so isolated from London tensions that when Marjorie Brierley wrote to him in March 1942 to find out whose side he was on, he wrote back saying that he had had no idea there was so much politicking going on in the organization (Birtles and Scharff, 1994):

. . . I might have expressed my views rather differently if I had realized the extent to which the Society is now riven into 'political' camps each with a different scientific legend upon its banner. It was only after I had written the paper that Dr Glover initiated me into some of the mysteries of the Society's internal politics and so disturbed my innocence; and only since the era of the Extraordinary Meetings was ushered in that the scales have finally fallen from my eyes and the present sordid scene has presented itself in all its nakedness to my somewhat bewildered gaze.

As for his views about Klein, Fairbairn acknowledged his debt to her while maintaining that, in his view, he had advanced beyond her (Birtles and Scharff, 1994):

The point of view which I have developed is admittedly of Kleinian lineage, although privately I regard it as a definite advance beyond the Kleinian standpoint. I understand from Dr Glover, however, that the Kleinian group disclaim any paternity – or should I say 'maternity'? I feel therefore somewhat of an orphan. Perhaps I have been disinherited as too independent-minded a child, whilst at the same time suffering from the disadvantage of my lineage in the eyes of those who look askance at it. At the same time, the last thing I contemplated when I wrote the last paper was that I should be caught up in the maelstrom of any political struggles within the Society. That of course was just the inevitable and I think pardonable, ignorance of a country bumpkin innocent of the wiles of the great Metropolis. (p. 444)

Like Sullivan in the US, Fairbairn came to feel sure that the psychology of the personality was bound up with tensions and conflicts in human relationships rather than tensions and conflicts arising from instincts and their gratification. Fairbairn's experience showed that biological interpretations of patients' conflicts quickly ran dry. Life was brought back into the analytic relationship only when he began to explore with his patients how they had internalized the disappointing, painful and unsatisfying aspects of their interpersonal lives. In his famous paper of 1946, where he argued the proposition that the human individual is not pleasure-seeking but is, instead, so-called object- or relationship-seeking, he introduced his argument with the often-quoted statement:

The clinical material on which this proposition is based may be summarized in the protesting cry of a patient to this effect – 'You're always talking about my wanting this or that desire satisfied; but what I really want is a father. (p. 137)

But Fairbairn did more than propose a radical rethink of Freud's fundamental hypothesis that the human organism sought tension reduction through the gratification of instinctual desires. Instead of simply proposing an alternative object-relations theory to the dominant theory of instinctual motivation, Fairbairn worked through how the two approaches could be related. In doing this, he distanced himself from what he saw as the excesses of Klein and her supporters. As he wrote to Marjorie Brierley:

I agree with you in some measure at least about the desirability of correlating the new with the old. This is, in my opinion, a task which the Klein group have never faced. What they have done, so far as I see it, is to adopt new ideas while retaining old views so far as these suited them without considering how far the two sets of views are compatible. The result has been a considerable amount of confused thought, even amounting at times (e.g. in some of Melanie Klein's sentences) to complete nonsense. (Birtles and Scharff, 1994, p. 445)

Fairbairn's theory was the fully psychological theory of the human personality that Freud had been searching for at the turn of the century. Fairbairn's theory of the personality left biology behind in its view of the human personality as a property of the whole human organism that is formed in human relationships.

Fairbairn's scientific style consisted of a long, intense and consistent engagement with the object of study – the person – over many years. His understandings slowly emerge and, instead of leaping at them, he holds them until he is sure he understands how it relates to what has gone before. For Fairbairn it was not enough to posit that the human being was fundamentally relationship-seeking, he had to understand how it was that Freud saw the human being as being fundamentally pleasure-seeking. Fairbairn's approach demonstrated a sensitivity, not just to his own need for understanding, but a sensitivity to the requirements of the problem. This kind of ego-less engagement with a problem at hand is characteristic of the classics of the scientific literature.

In Fairbairn's psychology, we are all fundamentally relationship-seeking. The human being is born with a 'self' and from birth the infant actively seeks and enters into human relationships consistent with its level of ongoing physical and psychological development. The breast is not just a source of nutrition but is also, more fundamentally for human psychology, a channel for relationship. Aggression is the result of lived experience, a response to the deprivation produced by habitual frustration and disappointment. The most basic childhood anxiety is separation anxiety.

Within this framework, Freud's concept of the human being as pleasure-seeking becomes a special case. Pleasure-seeking represents deterioration of relationships. Physical pleasure, the release of the tension of unmet relational needs, simply to reduce tension *per se*, represents a deterioration of relationships – as in compulsive sexuality, the seeking of sexual pleasure for its own sake, where every encounter no matter how casual can be felt to contain possibilities for sexual gratification, but where the other person involved is unimportant.

Unsatisfying relationships have complex psychological consequences involving the human capacity to internalize experience. In the case of ordinary human conscience, the parental voice is internalized, eventually to become no longer a voice but a distinct part of ourselves. In the case of repetitive dissatisfaction, neglect, violence or the threat of violence, the developing infant internalizes not a parental voice but the entire unsatisfactory part of the parental relationship. This psychological process is analogous to the formation of conscience. Its purpose is to defend us against the helplessness of deprivation by allowing us to manipulate the experience internally.

In Fairbairn's development of Klein's concept of object relations, when relationships cannot be put right, we create inside ourselves a deeply felt hope that the relationship can be better. We are tantalized, excited, by what we still feel to be the possibilities for satisfaction in the bad relationship. At the same time we internalize our dissatisfaction as rejection. But these are not simply feelings of hope and rejection. We experience a rejected part of ourselves, and we also experience a tantalized, excited part of ourselves. These are felt to be structures, objects, literally parts of ourselves that are not integrated with our central sense of self. These internalized structures are repressed – we 'forget' where they came from but they exert forces on us that we manage using certain characteristic techniques.

In the late 1990s, in the Anglophone middle classes, the most familiar technique is the situation where we project the exciting hopeful aspect of the bad relationship outwards and retain the rejecting part internally. The abusive father is idealized as a wonderfully strong man, the abused son is sure that he is indeed weak and contemptible. In agoraphobia, the exciting and rejecting objects can both be projected outwards – home is safe and good, the street is bad and dangerous. In paranoia, the rejecting part is projected outwards and the exciting part is retained – 'I am fine. People don't like me' – while the tension of retaining both exciting and rejecting 'objects' internally is managed by obsessive and compulsive behaviour. In all cases a Fairbairnian therapy aims to heal the original schizoid split.

Habitual unmet relational needs can produce in us an exaggerated sense of proper conduct – a so-called ego ideal. We must make ourselves better persons so that our parents will stop disappointing us and will meet our needs. This then would be the Fairbairnian analysis of Joan Riviere's vicious self-punishing – 'nothing is good enough, especially me' – ego ideal and the obvious pain that it causes.

In Fairbairn's developmental scheme, the challenge to the developing infant and its parents is to manage the split experience of rejection and excitement caused by failures in relationship, as the child moves from a state of infantile dependence through a long transition to a final state of mature dependence. What is significant in this scheme is Fairbairn's emphasis on mature dependence, not mature *in*dependence. The concept of adult independence that most of us hold as an ego ideal is a damaging part of the ethos of Western civilization, dating from the early modern period, of the Man Alone. The ideal of the Man Alone is an ideal that finds it too painful to acknowledge that people matter to each other (de Zulueta, 1993).[1]

By the end of the 1950s a fully psychological theory of the human personality had been achieved in Britain on the margins of the psychoanalytic establishment. The origin of Sullivan's 'difficulties in living' were now located in difficulties in meeting an infant's needs. Aggression and hate were a response to frustration. Childhood sexuality as an endogenous drive in conflict with the organized mores of civilization was replaced by the broader concept of a need for attachment which could also be read as a need for love. Habitual failures of parental love, the failure to meet the growing child on its own terms, required the child to invent techniques to manage the ensuing pain. These techniques, described as 'internal objects', produced complex structures in the personality analogous to conscience, deep-seated translations of aspects of the failed relationships that enabled the growing child to control and manage failure of parental provision.

At this time, the new relational/attachment paradigm, known as British object relations, was in competition with Freud's and Klein's old instinctual paradigm, where the origin of mental pain lay in parental failure to manage adequately the conflict between the infant's instinctual drives and the requirements of social reality. What happened was that instead of the hand-to-hand combat intimated by Thomas Kuhn, the new paradigm surrounded the old from the outside. Central to this development was the work of Donald Winnicott, whose public broadcasts helped teach a generation of British parents to become aware of the emotional needs of their children, and whose technical writings educated a new generation of psychotherapists into the realities of the therapeutic relationship.

Winnicott was the poet of psychoanalysis. His words became part of the language of both specialist and popular discourse. His phrase – primary maternal preoccupation – became shorthand for describing how a parent comes to attune to an infant, while the 'ordinary devoted mother' helped relieve some of the anxiety of parenting. The phrase, 'good-enough mothering' further took the pressure off parents: parenting did not and could not be perfect, it just had to be good enough. Parental responsibility to facilitate normal maturational processes was encapsulated in the phrase 'facilitating environment' and, perhaps most widely familiar, 'true self and false self' communicated at a deep level the pain experienced by the child in its response to parental requests that it be compliant rather than authentic. The parent said by Winnicott to 'substitute her own gesture for the child's', described how the parent creates the compliant false self, a result of the mismatch between a child's emotional needs for authentic relationship and the lack of parental satisfaction.

Uniquely among psychoanalysts of the second and third generations, Winnicott achieved a wide popular audience with his books and broadcasting. From 1939 to 1962 he delivered approximately fifty BBC broadcasts on topics that included the contribution of fathers, the only child, the importance of visiting children in hospital, the dynamics of adoption, and the psychology of step-parents. He gave six public lectures, which were published in the pamphlet *Getting to Know Your Baby*. Nine further broadcasts appeared as *The Ordinary Devoted Mother and Her Baby* (Kahr, 1996).

Winnicott had trouble with the psychoanalytic establishment in London. He was told repeatedly by Klein and Riviere that whatever he had to contribute had already been done and that his ideas, far from being new, simply represented his inability to properly understand Klein's theories. Klein, who had had her son Erich treated by Winnicott, referred to him late in her life as 'that awful man'. Trainees at the Tavistock Clinic, after its training became dominated by a Kleinian sensibility, were taught to avoid Winnicott (Kahr, 1996).

On 3 February 1956, after a particularly confusing seminar given by Klein on her new thoughts about envy and gratitude, Winnicott wrote to Riviere, his former analyst, a conciliatory but angry letter about Klein's lack of understanding about the real importance of the mother (Newman, 1995):

My trouble when I start to speak to Melanie about her statement of early infancy is that I feel as if I were talking about colour to the colour-blind. She simply says that she has not forgotten the mother and the part the mother plays at the very beginning. (p. 181)

With his experience of paediatrics, Winnicott had been drawn to Klein in the 1930s because he knew from his own observation that important things were happening much earlier in a child's development than Freud's dating of the start of the Oedipus complex. Similarly, he was pulling away from Klein in the 1950s because he also knew that the relationship between mother and infant was far more complex than Klein was willing to admit. Just as, following Middlemore (1941), he had been emphasizing that there was no such thing as a baby, there was only a mothering pair, he now took serious issue with Riviere about Klein's concept of the 'good breast' as existing outside the lived experience of the infant–mother relationship. In Fairbairn's terms he saw the breast as a channel for relationship (Newman, 1995):

The 'good breast' is not a thing. It is a name given to a technique. It is the name given to the presentation of the breast (or bottle) to the infant, a most delicate affair and one which can only be done well enough at the beginning if the mother is in a most curious state of sensitivity which I for the time being call the State of Primary Maternal Preoccupation. Unless she can identify very closely with the infant at the beginning she cannot 'have a good breast' because just having the thing means nothing whatever to the infant. (p. 182)

Winnicott was pained by Klein's rejection of him: 'It is a matter of great grief to me that I cannot get Melanie to take up the point or to see that there is a point to be discussed' (p. 182). But he was too dedicated to psychotherapy to accept anything less than what he could observe with his own eyes.

There was a certain simplicity about Winnicott. But this simplicity, informed by his long experience in paediatrics and the depth of his sympathy and understanding of childhood experience, made for the creation of Winnicott's poetic contributions to psychoanalysis. He saw straight through to the most fundamental psychological processes and instead of seeking to frame an understanding of them, as did Fairbairn, he found the words to give them expression. And it is in the process of finding words that Winnicott is unsurpassed. The false self is more than a name, it is a way to represent the complex process by which the child adapts to a mismatch between its real needs and how its parents are able to respond.

In the 1920s and 1930s every psychoanalyst read their Freud. In the 1960s and 1970s every psychoanalytic psychotherapist read Winnicott. The paradigm shift, as consolidated in the work of Fairbairn, Bowlby and Winnicott, took hold on the outside of the psychoanalytic establishments in the US and in Britain. By the 1950s, classical psychoanalysis had become a medieval city, a network of tiny streets twisting around within the confines of the city walls. This medieval city housed secret, family networks of guilds, the inhabitants connected in inflexible, sometimes hostile, relationships. But beyond the city walls, were ten-lane superhighways, whizzing cars, towering office blocks, astonishing shopping malls. This is where Winnicott was read, where the new psychoanalytic paradigm took hold. The medieval psychoanalytic town was surrounded by the countryside, making the methods of the old town a matter of historical interest. As Anna Freud lamented in 1974 (Young-Bruehl, 1988): 'Psychoanalysis is above all a drive psychology. But for some reason people do not want to have that.' In the 1960s and 1970s, a generation of newcomers to psychoanalysis did not want a drive psychology. Who were these newcomers? And what experience did they bring to psychoanalysis that led them to avoid the drive in favour of the relational paradigm put in place by the British School of Object Relations?

11

Transmuting Collision:
Psychoanalysis, Feminism
and the Sixties

For the last 150 years, the dominant family arrangement in the West has been the bourgeois family, currently the stereotypical middle-class nuclear family, the family with an average of 2.4 children, the father as breadwinner, the mother as homemaker. In this social arrangement, fathers, deprived of daily contact with their growing children of more than a few minutes each day, have been deskilled in their parenting role, leaving mothers to do the work of tending to the emotional and physical needs of the children as well as those of their husbands. At the symbolic level, it is no accident that in the 1993 film *Mrs Doubtfire*, directed by Chris Columbus, Robin Williams, playing a divorced father, needed to impersonate a woman in order to have contact with his children (Burgess and Ruxton, 1996).

Freud believed strongly in the sexual division of labour of the traditional bourgeois family. In his often-quoted exchange with Martha Bernays about the emancipation of women he wrote:

I remember a main argument in the pamphlet I translated was that the married woman can earn as much as the husband. I dare say we agree that housekeeping and the care and education of children claim the whole person and practically rule out any profession; even if simplified conditions relieve the woman of housekeeping, dusting, cleaning, cooking etc. (15 November 1883)

With men isolated from their families and deskilled in their capacities to respond to the emotional needs of others, the work of making relationships work became the work of women. Girls were raised to be aware of and attend to the emotional needs of others at the expense of their own. Boys were taught the skills of hand–eye coordination and competitiveness at the expense of an articulate awareness of human feeling. And in a male-dominated society the work of women became invisible.[1]

The second wave of feminism of the 1960s and 1970s refused to accept the invisibility of women's work. United across class and national boundaries by the invention of the consciousness-raising group, women began to challenge every social institution of the West, not simply demanding equal opportunities but calling for changed attitudes towards the way institutions should work. Politically active women, realizing that they knew far more than men about meeting human emotional needs, rejected male-dominated meetings and political agendas with the slogan 'The personal is political'. In the countries of Western Europe and North America, not only was the era of women's invisibility over, but the work that women had been doing behind the scenes was also brought into view, not least by the time-honoured technique of withholding it in family, social and work situations.

As with the science of the seventeenth century, which represented the theorization of experience of the outer world, achieved by men in their roles as craftsmen and builders, psychoanalysis in the twentieth century represented the theorization of experience of the inner world gained by women in human relationships in their role as the provider of emotional needs in Western families. Such an institution could not fail to attract the critical attention of women of the 1960s and 1970s. Feeling that the consciousness-raising group had been unable to address fully the problem of women's internalized sense of inferiority, women turned to psychoanalysis for help in providing a way to understand the unconscious processes involved. Psychoanalysis, challenged by a collision with a large grouping of politically conscious women, found itself growing both institutionally and intellectually in new directions.

Historically, women have been among the most important contributors to the development of psychoanalysis. From Hermine Hug-Hellmuth to Anna Freud and Melanie Klein, women were seen by male analysts as being uniquely capable of connecting to the world of children. But women as theorists in their own right, with a specifically

female point of view, have often been treated with hostility or condescension, as in the often-voiced opinion of male analysts of the 1930s:
'She's a good clinician.' Helene Deutsch, recognized for her accurate
description of the lived experience of women, worked exclusively
within the theoretical model of classical psychoanalysis. Karen
Horney, in 1922 the first woman to address the Congress of the
International Psycho-Analytical Association on the subject of women
and the construct of femininity, was marginalized within psychoanalysis because of her rejection of the patriarchal biases that dominated
theory in the field.

Between 1922 and 1935, Horney, anticipating feminist concerns of
the 1960s and 1970s, wrote fourteen papers on the subject of the
psychology of women. She voiced the opinion that the theory of
penis envy, so central to a psychoanalytic understanding of female
development, was not only a misplaced metaphor for female envy of
male power, but taken literally as a universal female experience was
actually quite incomprehensible as a theory (Horney, 1923):

... we have assumed as an axiomatic fact that females feel at a disadvantage
because of their genital organs – without this being regarded as constituting
a problem in itself – possibly because to masculine narcissism this has seemed
too self-evident to need explanation. Nevertheless, the conclusion so far
drawn from the investigations – amounting as it does to an assertion that
one half of the human race is discontented with the sex assigned to it and
can overcome this discontent only in favourable circumstances – is decidedly
unsatisfying, not only to feminine narcissism but also to biological science.
(p. 38)

Three years later, Horney proposed that the psychoanalytic view
of women was the same view that little boys had about little girls.
Little boys assume everyone has a penis; little boys then realize that
girls do not have a penis; little boys assume that the girl has had her
penis taken away from her and that the same punishment could befall
them. The boy fears the girl's envy of what she has lost. Because of
male power such views can come to be the unconsciously assimilated
views women have about themselves (Horney, 1926):

An additional and very important factor in the situation is that women have adapted themselves to the wishes of men and felt as if their adaptation were their true nature. That is, they see or saw themselves in the way that their men's wishes demanded of them; unconsciously they yielded to the suggestion of masculine thought.

If we are clear about the extent to which all our being, thinking and doing conform to these masculine standards, we can see how difficult it is for the individual man and also for the individual woman really to shake off this mode of thought. (p. 57)

Horney, in her determination to redefine the role of women within psychoanalytic theory, was ahead of her time. In the 1970s, Nancy Chodorow, interested in exploring connections between current feminist concerns and the experience of female psychoanalysts of the 1930s, interviewed surviving analysts about their experiences as women in psychoanalysis. She found that in her sample none of the women had had the same concerns as Horney. European women analysts had expected to have careers, were in a more favourable position with their careers than the overwhelming majority of their mothers, or even other women of their generation, and had not felt to any significant degree that it was a disadvantage to be a woman. In this sense they shared Horney's critique of penis envy. As one of Chodorow's unnamed interviewees stated (Chodorow, 1989): 'We strongly have the feeling that it's nonsense to think that every woman thinks she has a terrible lot and then finally makes the best of it, the way Freud really presents it' (p. 204). But women analysts of the 1930s were far more concerned with economic issues than they were with the issues of concern to women of the 1970s in the US and Western Europe. As another of Chodorow's interviewees put it: 'Why should a woman who works not have the same payment and the same status as the man? But otherwise, it is very good to be a woman. And a mother' (p. 212).

When feminists of the 1970s turned to psychoanalysis they were interested in whether it could be useful in the practical project of personal and social change by shedding light on the developmental process by which gender identity was acquired, on the way sex role stereotyping was internalized, what made it so hard to shift, and the way physiological difference got converted into deep psychological structures.[2]

What they found was the tool of the analytic hour, the transference–countertransference paradigm and a few theorists – Klein, Winnicott, Fairbairn, Bowlby, Ferenczi's former student Michael Balint in the UK, Karen Horney, Clara Thompson, Harry Stack Sullivan, Erich Fromm in the US, and Jacques Lacan in France – whose theories of human development seemed the most promising for a feminist project of the exploration of the inner and outer world of the psychology of gender difference. What they brought to psychoanalysis was energy, determination and a well-developed understanding of women's role and lived experience in the societies of the US and Western Europe.

These gender-conscious psychotherapists were uniquely enabled to hear and to understand what women had to say about their inner lives. For feminists of the 1970s, the outstanding feature of their own, their mothers' and their grandmothers' socialization into their traditional roles as girls, women, wives and mothers, was the repudiation of their own needs in favour of attending to the needs of others. Raised by their mothers' cautionary voices, women had been taught that their role would be as the midwives to the realization of wishes of others. Such a training in the societies of the West produced women with deep conflicts over the legitimacy of needs, and produced men whose needs were to be attended to without their even knowing they had them. These gender-coded roles were integral to sustaining the Western myth of male independence and female dependence – the man alone stands tall, the woman sheltering at his side.

In taking to the streets with other members of the generation of 1968, women, no longer content to accept the teachings of their mothers, withdrew their labour, making it painfully obvious to men how much they had depended on women to achieve satisfactory emotional and social contact. Women were no longer content to 'draw men out', to get men to talk about themselves. They were no longer satisfied with being the facilitators of social situations; they began to reject flirtation – sex as social grease – in their relations to men and sought each other's company in preference to the one-sided conversations that had characterized social contact between the sexes. Women began to question the primacy of men, not simply as the ones who had the inside track to the best jobs but to whom the most desirable, indeed the most necessary, relationships would be made. And from its previous hegemonic position in the culture as the biologically natural order of things, heterosexuality itself began to be questioned. In the immortal words of New York civil rights attorney Florence Kennedy: 'A woman needs a man like a fish needs a bicycle' (Luepnitz, 1988).

In making visible what had previously been invisible – that it took work to make relationships and that women had been doing this essential work – feminists provided living evidence for Fairbairn's understanding of human development formulated thirty years previously: the human being moves from a stage of infantile dependence through a transition phase to a stage of mature dependence, that is to say, a stage of continuing adult need for relationship.

The centrality of the mother–daughter relationship hinted at by Klein became the centrepiece of a new psychology of women, replacing the dominant classical psychoanalytic concept of women as failed men. In hundreds of transference interactions, gender-conscious psychoanalytic psychotherapists found women repudiating their own needs, seeking to attend to the therapist's needs, fearing the space of the analytic hour, fearing that previously unmet intense longings for attachment and relationship would either overwhelm the therapist, leading to rejection and isolation, or engulf the therapist, leading to merger and loss of identity. The central feature of women's psychology in late twentieth-century Europe and United States was not a mythical female dependency with women having difficulties in separation but, as is so frequently the case on closer inspection, the opposite – having difficulties in attachment. And, in a painful internal world of insatiable needs, it was not surprising that, for women, feelings of physical hunger – physical need – would be problematic. In the 1960s and 1970s 50 per cent of women in the United States had some form of eating problem. Compulsive eating was a feminist issue, with bulimia and anorexia not far behind.

In the developing analysis of the mother–daughter relationship in the female-parent child-rearing arrangements of the West, the fate of boy children could also be seen to have difficult dynamics. From day one the mother knows the sex of her child and is conscious of the social roles that its gender requires it to play. In addition, the confined social role of women generates feelings in the mother about the child of either sex. In the case of boys, the male social role can generate unconscious hostility towards her son in an isolated mother with, in Adler's terms, a withdrawal of her tenderness; or an over-involved mother seeking to share male privilege through over-identification with a boy child; or it can generate the vicissitudes of Freud's Oedipal triangle with its sexualization of the boy–mother–father relationship. In many parenting arrangements the boy-child raised by the single mother/absent father is led to repudiate the mother in the process of separation, leaving him essentially parentless. He then has no transitional period of secure relationships from which to create mature attachments based on mutually acknowledged needs for adult relationship.

With women rejecting traditional roles and behaviour, men were forced to examine the implications for themselves of their gender roles. Put as a series of questions to women for the purpose of highlighting the male experience, the extent to which men had been invisibly absorbing rigid gender stereotypes was made transparent:[3]

o What would it be like if women, in the name of their womanhood, had to go out and kill other women?

o What would it be like if from infancy you were taught that it was unwomanly to weep or show your grief?

o What would it be like if you could not touch or get close to other women? What would it be like if the only intimacy society approved of were sexual, if it were unwomanly to be affectionate or tender?

o What would it be like if you were taught that your functions were to assume all responsibility, make all decisions, never be wrong, and to work to provide for all your family's requirements, incidentally supplying occasional seed for reproduction?

By the 1990s traditional gendered roles for women and men had been scattered to the winds. Where they resettle depends on the outcomes of the ongoing day-to-day conflicts that accompany significant social change.

A major implication of the feminist analysis of the mother–daughter relationship for psychoanalysis was that the mother's or other parenting figure's subjectivity must be acknowledged. For it is through parents' unconscious communications that we absorb much of our sense of possibility and limitation, the childhood introjections that can last a lifetime. And so one arrives at a position where the so-called objects of a child's developmental history, must become subjects if we are to understand the dynamics of human psychological development. Parenting figures could no longer be seen as merely objects for a child but, to complicate psychoanalytic theory, were subjects in their own right as well.

The relational approach of the interpersonalists in the United States, and the breakthrough of British object relations in beginning to specify how relational failures get represented as objects in the inner world of the developing child, were expanded and developed by gender-conscious clinicians and theorists who had entered the field. The conjunction of a strand of thinking within psychoanalysis and the influx of new experience and a new agenda from outside psychoanalysis made for new theoretical approaches to the understanding of events taking place in the analytic hour.

Freud's psychoanalysis was based on a so-called one-person psychology. The analyst was to reflect without judgement what was considered to be the analysand's material as expressed in the transference relationship. In Winnicott's approach, there was in addition the acknowledgement of a real relationship between therapist and analysand, with the therapist aiming to acknowledge mistakes and misattunements as they actually happened in the consulting room. This was a two-person psychology, as in Winnicott's statement 'There is no such thing as a baby there is only a mothering pair.' Feminists took Winnicott's point and insisted that there was also the mother's subjectivity so that there then was no such thing as a mothering pair, there was only the mothering pair in the social arrangements of the time, a many-person psychology as reflected into the mother–child relationship through the socially formed subjectivity of the mother. Now it will be the intersubjective field, the relational space between analyst and analysand, where the subjectivities of both are expressed, that will be the subject of the analysis.

Once one reformulates events taking place in the analytic hour as mutually created, the concept of the therapist as expert must change. In its place, instead of being seen as an expert, possessing a specific body of knowledge about the structure of the human psyche, the analyst now assumes the role of an experienced guide to unknown inner worlds, undertaking a journey there jointly with the analysand. The analyst cannot know the inner world of the analysand beforehand. This knowledge must be created together by examining what happens between them in the intersubjective field.

While many feminists interested in what psychoanalysis had to offer were drawn to Anglophone psychoanalysis, others were put off by the patriarchal biases all too evident in theory and practice in Britain and the US that accepted as natural the parenting-by-mother arrangements of the previous 150 years. Across the channel from Britain, the revolutionary events of May 1968 had left as a legacy a new psychoanalytic culture in France, associated with the name of Jacques Lacan (Turkle, 1978).

In France, the number of students in higher education rose from 100,000 at the end of the Second World War to over 200,000 by 1960 and to 651,000 by 1970. The great majority of these students were the first in their families to go to university. They brought a critical stance towards established authority which exploded in France in the events of May 1968. Protests against overcrowding and other indignities at the new University of Nanterre on the outskirts of Paris spread to the Latin Quarter. On 3 May, there was violence between police and students and the building of the first barricades. Three days later, more barricades went up, the police used tear gas and truncheons, the students charged the police, cars were set alight. The population was opposed to the students. But the government decision to occupy the streets and colleges of the Latin Quarter with thousands of armed, helmeted police, culminating in two nights of extreme violence on 11 and 12 May, provoked on the morning of 13 May a call by the unions for a general strike, and in the afternoon a mass demonstration of 800,000 supporting the students against the repressive measures of the government. Over the next two weeks, workers followed the example of the students and occupied the factories. By 24 May 1968, 9 million people were on strike. The country was being run from the occupied institutions: physicists and technicians on strike at the Centre for Nuclear Studies at Saclay, outside Paris, made and delivered radio-isotopes to Parisian hospitals which needed them, using 30,000 litres of petrol supplied by strikers at Finac in Nanterre (Pesquet, 1968).

In 1968, Lacan was sixty-seven years old, a major public figure in France as the psychoanalyst who had made his interpretation of Freud interesting to a French intellectual culture formed between the poles of Marxism and Catholicism. In 1953 he had begun his public lectures on psychoanalysis that were to run for twenty-seven years. Also in 1953, the splits in French psychoanalysis had begun, similar in their intensity to those in the United States (Roudinesco, 1990). Ten years later, the International Psycho-Analytical Association had issued a report banning Lacan from training prospective analysts and banning trainees from attending his seminar. Lacan had formed his own group, the Ecole Freudienne de Paris in 1964 and declared his support for the students in May 1968, a contributing factor to the attraction the young political left felt for his ideas about the construction of human subjectivity.

As a young psychiatrist in the 1930s, Lacan was strongly attracted to surrealism, meeting Salvador Dali in 1931 and writing two articles for *minotaure*, the surrealist journal, in 1933. He had an early interest in psychotic states and his scientific style could be said to have been dominated by a need to explore disintegration and the inverse processes by which the human subject is constructed. His repudiation of prevailing social structures led him to produce a unique personal vocabulary of psychoanalysis, with borrowings from linguistics, algebra and topology.

Lacan's use of terms from mathematics has been attacked with justified indignation by the mathematical physicists Alan Sokal and Jean Bricmont (1998). Lacan's vocabulary is informed by private rather than shared meanings so that his writing is invariably opaque, a result of an impossible goal to create a language uncontaminated by prevailing social arrangements. His attempt has inevitably been experienced as psychotic and does simulate psychosis in its repudiation of normal discourse.

With its rhetorical appeal to linguistic, algebraic and topological structures, Lacan's system has had a strong appeal for those who have felt challenged to learn his language and engage with his text. Those with a background in literary criticism have particularly responded to the Lacanian challenge. Tired of picking apart yet another defenceless nineteenth-century novel, they found that Lacan's texts offered ample scope for their formidable interpretive skills. And here again is another example in psychoanalysis of the divide between Western literary culture and Western scientific culture. In the literary tradition, the words do their work on the reader. In the scientific tradition the reader does the work on the words. The polarity is between response and assimilation.

Readers with a background in literary criticism have been willing to let Lacan's words work on them. Others, frustrated by the opacity of his rhetoric, have been repelled, seeing Lacan's writing variously as a defensive measure to cover his lack of understanding or against criticism from hostile institutions, or as an elitist measure designed to create a self-contained clique of adepts. As one reviewer of a Lacanian primer has observed (Kupersmidt, 1998): 'As Fink well knows, the whole Lacanian enterprise is sometimes seen as designed to confer an exclusive distinction on the initiated and to confound the psychoanalytically naive . . .' (p. 65). But what is in Lacan constitutes a serious challenge to modern Western concepts of the human individual, including the equating of subjectivity with consciousness and the assumption of a biological origin of the subjectivity of men and women, including their sexualities. This was the challenge that drew the attention of Anglophone psychoanalytic psychotherapists and feminist theories to Lacan.

Lacan, in his early interest in the non-continuous juxtaposition of mental states represented by surrealism, came to emphasize unconscious processes as the centre of his interest in the human internal world. The central point was Lacan's rejection of human subjectivity or human essence as being present at birth. The human subject – 'thou art *that*' – was constructed/structured through the relational experience of the infant in its passage from neonate to human child. Such a vision then included female subjectivity as socially constructed. Biology was no longer destiny.

Lacan's contribution to psychoanalysis has been difficult to place with accuracy because it is in its essence philosophical. Lacan points to an area of concern rather than adding to our understanding of it. His famous aphorism, that the unconscious is structured like a language, suggests a category, a way of thinking about human psychology. If the unconscious, through which human subjectivity is formed in the transition from neonate to human child, is structured like a language, then subjectivity is not biological because there is no language at birth. And because we become human through unconscious symbolic processes expressed through language, there can be no autonomous ego at all. Human subjectivity, like the language we speak, is not biologically determined. With his own unique militancy, Lacan argued repeatedly over a twenty-year period that those who attempted to locate human subjectivity in pre-natal biology were looking in the wrong place.

Although precedents for the framing of an understanding of the human subject as a social phenomenon are long-standing in the sociology of Marx and in the structural anthropology of Lévi-Strauss, such views continue to challenge one of the great ordering principles of Western life. As the philosopher Richard Lichtman (1982) has been at pains to explore: 'The belief that individual self-realization can be achieved outside of society is one of the deepest principles of bourgeois ideology' (p. 219).

Ideas about the unconscious, about the body, about sexuality, about intelligence, that locate our essence as acquired are difficult to entertain. We really do believe that our individuality, our very essence, is located outside society and inside ourselves. Such a dominant ordering idea is not to be given up without a fight. How could the unconscious be structured like a language? What could this mean?

The capacity for language is a property of our species as a whole. We speak the language we speak, including an accent, by an accident of birthplace. The language we speak emerges in the passage of neonate to human infant. If, with Lacan, unconscious processes are a linguistic phenomenon, then variations in our individual unconscious processes are like variations in language. The source of the variation is not to be located on the genome, but in the passage of neonate to human infant. We acquire our unconscious. We acquire our subjectivity. We acquire our mother tongue.

The dominant idea of our epoch, that our subjectivity exists outside society is what the Jungians call a numinous idea. We believe it whether we want to or not.[4] The force of these ruling ideas, expressed not only in language but in gesture, stance, intonation and the quality of relating that form the human subject, led Lacan to insist that ego autonomy was an illusion, that the real autonomy lay with the so-called Symbolic order by which ruling ideas are transmitted and absorbed.

Of all the theoretical writings in psychoanalysis, those of Lacan address the problem of the formation of the human subject most uncompromisingly. With reason, Anglophone feminists were attracted to Lacan. Similarly, Lacan became a powerful individual intellectual force in France, particularly because, in the revolutionary climate of 1968, his public could sense that fundamental issues lay at the root of his concerns. But when students shouted that structures do not take to the streets, Lacan replied that the students would simply replace their old masters by new ones unless they interrogated their unconscious motivations more critically (Lacan, 1991). It was a new version of Adler's approach to revolution – change the person and the system will change. Lacan had reproduced the central tenet of bourgeois ideology he sought to undermine – that human individuality can be liberated from the processes that form it – instead of advancing our understanding of the human being both making and being made by the world in a complex intersubjective network without which there may be a hairless ape, but there is no human being. Isolated attempts to free the individual from social bonds lead to disintegration and madness, not to freedom.

Lacan, like Freud and Jung before him, knew more than he understood. He tried hard to understand the processes involved in the formation of the human subject. But he was too isolated and, unlike Wilfred Bion, he never acknowledged the difficulties in using the tools of linguistics and mathematics to understand human subjectivity and unconscious processes. As in other attempts to formalize psychoanalysis, there was a fetishization of mathematics at work – the form was mistaken for substance. The problems at hand were felt to be too formidable and the theoretical resources too limited to sustain the continuous engagement necessary to make progress. Relief was then sought in distant disciplines thought to embody the qualities of precision and success felt to be lacking closer to home.[5]

Nevertheless, Lacan succeeded in creating a possible framework for understanding the formation of the human subject with his idea that the unconscious is structured like a language. But in his appeal to algebra and topology as a way to understand such a structure, he mystified rather than clarified the way forward. An algebra is not simply a system of notation. Lacan's mathematical efforts were more sophisticated than Bion's but also, because of Lacan's theatricality, less honest. Bion was able to write (1962): 'Unfortunately obscurities also exist because of my inability to make them clearer' (p. ii). Lacan was unable to issue such a caveat.

Lacan's work was spontaneous, self-centred and deliberately controversial. As one of the earliest intersubjectivists, he saw that the transference could not accurately be viewed as a one-way street entirely belonging to the patient, but must involve the subjectivity of the analyst as well. But Lacan went his own way, not addressing the exponentially growing Anglophone literature on countertransference in favour of a stance that placed him outside developments within the field. It remains to be seen whether the outreach efforts of Lacanian-oriented psychotherapists (Evans, 1996) will be reciprocated and will succeed in breaking the isolation that the Lacanians have accepted as the price for living with the work of Lacan over the last twenty years.

Lacanian developments in the psychology of human subjectivity in the Europe of the 1960s and 1970s had their parallel in the United States in the divergent strand of mainstream psychoanalytic thinking called self-psychology associated with the name of Heinz Kohut. The concept of the self had long been undertheorized within psychoanalysis and was often confused with the ego, which is only a part of the whole person. The self is the whole human subject, as in 'I am not myself today.' Its complexities can be seen in our capacities to observe ourselves where, as Rycroft (1991) has put it: '[The self] is not only an experiencing subject, but also its own object.' The self in Anglophone psychoanalysis was the missing subject that Lacan made the centrepiece of his system in France. Kohut attempted, with some success, to create a relational psychoanalysis of subjectivity by reformulating classical drive theory. His efforts were accompanied by the usual cries of 'not psychoanalysis' from colleagues at the centre of mainstream US psychoanalysis.

Heinz Kohut was born in Vienna in 1913. His father co-owned a paper business but typically for middle-class Jews was a Social Democrat with strong interests in culture, especially music. He was an accomplished pianist. Kohut was classically educated at the local Döblinger Gymnasium in the 19th district of north Vienna, taking his Matura in 1932. Kohut's father died in 1937, a year before the *Anschluss* and a year before Kohut completed his medical degree at the University of Vienna. Kohut managed to escape from Vienna in February 1939 to England. In March 1940, both he and his mother managed to resettle in Chicago where his mother opened a successful shop and Kohut did a residency in neurology, moving on to become an instructor in neurology and psychiatry. In 1945, Kohut became a US citizen. He had lost almost his entire family to the Nazis. In 1946, in a briefing letter to August Aichhorn, his former analyst in Vienna, he wrote: 'Unfortunately, almost all my relatives died in various concentration camps: a brother of my mother's and his small daughter, a brother of my father's along with his wife and son, a sister of my father's, another sister together with her husband etc., etc. An aunt, an "Aryan", still lives in Vienna' (2 June 1946).

Originally, self-psychology, the psychology of a fragile self, prone to fragmentation and disintegration of the kind experienced by Jung in his childhood, was complementary to drive psychology. But once one has admitted the significance of early developmental processes, drive theory can become questionable. In the drive/conflict model, if early drive conflicts have not been adequately handled, the conflict comes to be repressed into the instinctual structure of the id, where it becomes impulsive and out of control, leading to neurotic symptomatology. Kohut was concerned to understand why the original drive conflict was not properly managed.

Kohut located this failure in early relational deficit. Using this formulation there was now no need for the concept of drive as the causal agent in psychopathology. All difficulties in development could be traced to relational failure, causing subsequent disorders of the self. Kohut wrote to Robert Stolorow, a leading developer of Kohut's model: 'I now say that all forms of psychopathology, including the Oedipal conflict neuroses, are ultimately disorders of the self' (16 February 1981).

The central elements of Kohut's system included his rejection of the drive – 'a vague and insipid biological concept' – together with an emphasis on adult need for continuous attachment – in place of an ideal of a presumably self-sufficient adult, and recognition of the Oedipal phase of development as a positive happy phase, with Oedipal *conflict* arising only as a failure of relationships in the family (Kohut, 1977).

Kohut's shift from Freud's structural model of relationships between ego, id and superego to a developmental theory of the self met with a hostile reception from colleagues. In another painful episode of intellectual indiscipline, as Kohut came to emphasize deficit rather than conflict as the causal, aetiological agent of psychic distress, his contribution was inevitably rejected as not-psychoanalysis by his classically trained colleagues – among them Anna Freud. In June 1978, following the publication of *The Restoration of the Self*, he was voted off the governing body of the Chicago Institute of Psychoanalysis. Three years later he wrote to a colleague that 'former friends no longer greet me', that colleagues known to be interested in self-psychology were being prevented from becoming training analysts, and that papers of his friends and colleagues were being accepted for forums and journals only if they did not quote his work (7 March 1981).

In concert with the mood of the times, Kohut's assertion of the primacy of the human subject brought him national publicity, with articles about him in *People Magazine* (16 February 1979), the *New York Times Sunday Magazine* (9 November 1980) and *Time Magazine* (1 December 1980).[6] This did not strengthen his position within classical psychoanalysis. Had Kohut had a more radical temperament there could have been another split in US psychoanalysis. But he was deeply attached to the institution of classical psychoanalysis and, even though he had able collaborators, he rejected proposals to leave. As he wrote to a colleague: 'I am, despite my new views, which, according to some analysts, constitute a kind of heresy, a dedicated psycho-analyst, and I am convinced that my work lies in the mainstream of this vital science' (27 April 1978).

Certain elements of Kohut's revision of classical psychoanalysis, particularly his recognition of adulthood as a stage of mature depen-dence, had been introduced by Ronald Fairbairn in Scotland thirty years previously. But Kohut located the internal consequences of relational failure centrally in the formation of the self rather than in the formation of internal object relationships. Kohut's vision took human subjectivity, the self, as the basic unit of psychology. And what was genuinely new in Kohut's contribution to our understanding of human psychology was his insistence that the most extreme human anxiety was caused by feelings of a crumbling self, a broken self, a fragmenting self – not a separation anxiety, but, more painfully and more frighteningly, an annihilation anxiety (Mitchell, 1997).

For Anna Freud, an eloquent and humane exponent of drive psy-chology, the deepest anxiety observed in children was the fear of being 'unprotected against the pressures of their drives' (A. Freud, 1966). For Sullivan, separation anxiety, the threatened loss of relationship, was the most serious. In the US, Kohut attempted to bridge the incompatibility of the two models by his interpretation of drive psychology as a special case of relational failure. In parallel with the work of Jacques Lacan in France, Kohut, coming from within the psychoanalytic establishment of the United States, problematized the process of the formation of the human self, the whole human subject.

The appearance of women on the world stage in the 1960s and 1970s pulled psychoanalysis decisively away from a one-person psychology based on conflicts originating in biologically based drives and into a social psychology. For contemporary Latin American feminist psychoanalysts, the historical moment, while contiguous with North American and European experience, was far more demanding. Human suffering in Argentina, Uruguay and Chile in the dirty wars of the 1970s and 1980s required an expansion of psychoanalysis to include treatment for the multiple effects of state terror on the human psyche.

In 1981, Nancy Hollander, the US Latin American scholar and psychoanalyst, travelled to Spain to interview women who had been forced into exile in Madrid (Hollander, 1997):

One woman told of her having to abandon her children to relatives as she frantically scrambled to elude the military forces stalking her from house to house; another revealed how, as she walked along the wide avenues of Buenos Aires, she was kidnapped by hooded men leaping out at her from one of the infamous unmarked Ford Falcons used by the right-wing death squads, only to be left for dead on a remote country road after being tortured and raped in one of the government's clandestine concentration camps; another spoke of having been sought by military forces who, bursting into her home without a warrant and finding only her younger brother, kidnapped him instead, torturing and killing him for no reason in particular; yet another told of being forced to watch while prison guards tortured her elderly parents in order to secure information she did not have; and one reported how, when her pregnant daughter suddenly vanished, clearly a victim of a military or death-squad action, her endless searches for her daughter and grandchild had yielded nothing but a gaping hole in her heart; many told of having narrowly escaped similar fates before they were forced to flee into the uncertainty and dislocation of exile. The stories went on like this for hours. (p. 6)

The hundreds of hours of interviews Hollander collected show the need for a psychoanalytic treatment informed by the realities of a period where analysands could be dragged from the consulting rooms by invading police and where in place of formal arrests and prosecutions, torture and disappearances became the dominant technique of political repression. The task of therapy in this context was to help patients with the difficulties of finding a language to express their experiences of terror and unprecedented loss, what the Uruguayan psychoanalyst, Laura Achard de Marie called the loss of the 'common object', the country and its ideals that are held in common (Langer, 1981):

[In] a country in social crisis, faced with periods of national upheaval, we believe that the fate of the common object, as well as the treating of external events both on the transferential plane and in relation to internal objects, must be taken up in the session – sometimes as a point of urgency. (p. 168)

The loss of the common object was the consequence of the psychological events that Rosa Levine had observed in the Bavarian disaster sixty years earlier, of the loss of critical perspective in revolutionary moments. The Chilean psychologist and psychoanalyst, Elizabeth Lira, identified similar mechanisms at work in Chile in the overestimation of the strength of the progressive forces by the movement for social change (Hollander, 1997):

From my perspective they projected their own unshakeable commitment to support Chilean democracy by any means necessary onto the hundreds of thousands who came to the spirited demonstrations they organized. They mistakenly assumed that the progressive forces would stand fast if the country moved into an armed confrontation. They were blinded to the difference for most people between taking part in a demonstration for a day and putting their lives on the line in the face of an increasingly violent enemy. (p. 89)

Lira described the difference in treatment that a survivor received at the hands of an analyst who shared the goals of the Allende project with one who did not (Hollander, 1997): 'It was difficult for an analyst who did not feel that the Allende government had constituted an extraordinary social project to comprehend how its loss could represent a profound catastrophe. Such sentiments in a torture victim would simply be devalued by a therapist who didn't understand this' (p. 137).

In Argentina, when the military junta seized the state apparatus on 24 March 1976, the generals began the systematic murder of sections of the civilian population. General Iberico Manuel Saint-Jean, governor of the Province of Buenos Aires, said (Hollander, 1997): 'First we are going to kill all of the subversives, then their collaborators, then their sympathizers, then the indifferent, and finally the timid' (p. 79). The men who ruled Argentina by state terror were driven by the same fear and outrage that characterized the White Terror in Europe in the 1920s. And they shared the same outlook on culture (Hollander, 1997): 'Argentina has three main enemies: Karl Marx because he tried to destroy the Christian concept of society; Sigmund Freud because he tried to destroy the Christian concept of the family; and Albert Einstein because he tried to destroy the Christian concept of time and space' (p. 93).

One practice of the military regime was that an estimated 400 babies of murdered parents were offered to otherwise childless couples, who remained either ignorant or covertly silent about the origins of the children they received. The treatment of these children posed unique difficulties for the psychotherapists involved. The therapists distinguished two sequential traumas suffered by these children, who had entered treatment after having been located by their families of origin. The first was the original destructive trauma of being stolen and subsequently raised in a climate of lies by adoptive parents who had often been directly involved or deeply implicated in the murder of their biological parents. And the second trauma was the necessity to integrate the facts of their history in order to reconstruct a life based on the truth about their origins. The psychological difficulties of the two-fold framing included dealing with grief that their true parents had been tortured and murdered, often with the direct involvement or awareness of their adoptive parents, along with survivor guilt that they had survived their biological parents and with guilt that by loving their adoptive parents they had betrayed their true parents.

A major figure in the treatment and theorization of the psychological sequelae to state terror was the Austrian-Argentinian psychoanalyst, Marie Langer. One of six co-founders of the Argentina Psychoanalytic Association in 1942, Langer was instrumental in bringing Melanie Klein's work, with its emphasis on the reproductive capacities of women, to the attention of Latin American psychoanalysts. Langer recalled his feelings on encountering Klein's work (Hollander, 1997):

When I reread Freud in the early years in Buenos Aires, I was put off by his phallocentric views on women. It seemed to me that he knew nothing of the female experience. I was asked to help translate into Spanish the work of Melanie Klein, whose seminal thinking began the tradition within psychoanalysis known as British object relations. I was very excited because I felt that Klein returned to us women our femininity. Unlike Freud, who viewed the woman as a castrated male and female unconscious conflict as a reflection of her envy of men, Klein showed how woman's unconscious conflict is rooted in her anxieties related to her reproductive capacities. (p. 57)

Marie Langer was born in Vienna in 1910, the second of two daughters of wealthy Jewish parents. From an early age she was repelled by the idle life of her mother – the only visible choices for a woman seemed to be love or frivolity – and was attracted to the stories of Vera Zasulich and Vera Figner, the nineteenth-century Russian revolutionary women. As Langer recalled (1981): 'Yes obviously, joining the revolution was once the appropriate way to escape the fate outlined for women' (p. 35).

Langer grew up in the Social Democratic Red Vienna of the 1920s. She was sent to a private primary school for girls where in her final year she organized a school 'parliament' in solidarity with the democratic ideals of the new republic. She waged a pitched battle with her mother to be allowed to attend a secondary school that would prepare her to enter university, her mother finally permitting her to attend the famous Schwarzwald Schule in Vienna run by Frau Doktor Eugenie Schwarzwald.

Then in her forties, Schwarzwald had received her doctorate at the University of Zurich, the first university in Europe to admit women. In Vienna she started and ran the Schwarzwald Realgymnasia for young women as well as a chain of holiday homes for old people. Langer remembered her as 'a liberated woman, with short grey hair, married to a bank manager. She used to bring her lovers to school and hired some excellent, politically committed Marxist scholars' (Langer, 1981, p. 48). One of these teachers was Aline Klatschko Furtmüller, wife of Carl Furtmüller and organizer of the Furtmüller Sunday evenings attended by the politically minded psychoanalysts in pre-war Vienna. In the 1920s Furtmüller was a Social Democratic city councillor in addition to her post at the Schwarzwald Schule.

Furtmüller was a decisive influence in Langer's development. Once Langer cut school to meet her teenage lover at the local ice rink. When asked the reason for her absence she told her teacher that she had had her period. The teacher referred her to Furtmüller. As Langer recalled, Furtmüller told her (Langer, 1981): 'This time you can go.

But remember, if you want to have the respect men have, if you want to study and work just like men do, then don't ever again complain of this kind of malaise'. Langer was deeply affected. 'I think it is strange that, of all the thousands of things that are said to you in school or during your life, there should be one that affects you as much as this affected me' (p. 49). When in her last year of gymnasium Langer was forced by her mother to get married, Aline Furtmüller made it possible for her to finish secondary school as a married woman.

In 1932, at the age of twenty-two, Langer joined the Austrian Communist Party. As she later recalled (Langer, 1981):

When I was asked why I chose the Communist Party and not the Socialist Party – which at that time meant culture, politics, human relations, the Schwarzwald Schule, feminism, the unions, so many things – I could answer that I joined because the Communist Party promised revolution . . . Not even the majority of the Social Democrat leaders seriously wanted change. They opted for the status quo even though they promised socialism in the future. They would reach it when, thanks to their achievements and struggle, they could demonstrate through democratic elections that more than half the Austrian people were with them. It was a tragic mistake, as the military coups in Chile and Bolivia show today. (p. 66)

In January 1933 the Nazis came to power in Germany. Freud's books were publicly burned that August. The Institute for Social Research in Frankfurt was closed for 'tendencies hostile to the State'. Storm troopers sacked the interior. The Frankfurt psychoanalysts emigrated immediately. With the new support of the elected Nazi state, the propaganda campaign against Jews was intensified. A Nazi magazine on health issues introduced a series of articles on the role of the Jew in medicine with an editorial (Brecht et al., 1985):

Under this heading we will publish on a regular basis some impressive material on the destructive and criminal activity of the Jew in medicine. He used it clandestinely as an instrument to make Germans ill, to kill them, to prevent sick persons from being cured, to stop all natural care, and as a doctor, to vent his Asiatic sensuality on fair-skinned women and children.

We are setting up an archive in this field, and we ask our readers to report to us their relevant observations, so that we can not only put a stop to the activities of the last Jewish doctors, but in particular root out from German medicine the spirit and work of the Jews. (p. 101)

The first article was on the psychoanalysis of 'the Jew Sigmund Freud'.

Psychoanalysis is an impressive example of the fact that nothing good for us Germans can ever come from a Jew, even when he produces scientific achievements. Even if he gave us 5% that was novel and apparently good, 95% of his doctrine is destructive and annihilating *for us*. His own fellow-Jews and other races may derive advantage from Jewish ideas, we Germans and all peoples with Nordic blood always find it turns out badly for us if we eat anything out of the Jew's hand. (p. 101)

In August in Berlin, Ernst Simmel was arrested and kept incommunicado. Edith Jacobson joined the newly formed Social Democratic underground resistance group New Directions, returning from the safety of Scandinavia to work in the resistance. She was arrested by the Gestapo two years later and charged with high treason. Ernest Jones began to organize an international campaign on her behalf but was warned by telegram by Felix Boehm, the new gentile president of the German Psychoanalytic Society, that such action would threaten the future of psychoanalysis under National Socialism. Jones travelled to Berlin in late November 1935 to investigate the situation for himself. On his return he wrote to Anna Freud that Jacobson had been lucky to be kept in custody by the judicial system instead of by the Gestapo. Jacobson was sentenced to two years for planning treason. She escaped in 1938 to New York by way of Prague when she was released to have an operation.

In February 1934, the fascist government in Austria occupied Socialist Party offices in Linz in an effort to disarm the Socialist Schutzbund. The Socialist Central Committee decided by a margin of one vote to call a general strike. At medical school, Marie Langer witnessed the invasion of the school by fascists in a scene that was reproduced with great accuracy by the Hollywood director Fred Zinnemann, himself a refugee from Austria, in his 1977 film *Julia*, starring Jane Fonda,

Jason Robards and Vanessa Redgrave. After four days of fighting, the government shelled the Karl Marx Hof, the centre of working-class militancy in Vienna and then hanged several prisoners, one of whom was Aline Furtmüller's nephew. Langer found herself in her sister Gucki's apartment where she was engulfed by 'uniformed fascists dancing, enjoying themselves and drinking toasts to the victory' (Langer, 1981, p. 72). Politics moved underground in Austria following the suppression of the Socialist Party after the defeat of the 1934 general strike (Gardiner, 1983).

Marie Langer qualified as a doctor in 1935 and approached Heinz Hartmann for analysis. Finding that she couldn't afford his fees, she went to Richard Sterba. In 1936, after an interview with Anna Freud, she was accepted for training. Events intervened: in July 1936, Spanish fascists under army chief of staff General Francisco Franco invaded Spain from Morocco. The British Labour Party organized a medical team to Spain and, lacking surgeons, they approached the Austrian Social Democrats. Langer's husband, Max, wanted to go. Marie Langer decided to go with him as his anaesthetist. Her mother commented (Langer, 1981): 'This is what happens when a woman is educated' (p. 82).

In Spain, Langer served in front-line hospitals in the battle of Jarama and behind the lines where she and Max tried to develop prostheses for those who had lost limbs as a result of osteomyelitis. At the end of 1937 they travelled to Paris where they were to receive money for a factory to make prostheses. They were told to go to Nice for a rest. Langer was in her seventh month of pregnancy. A baby girl was born prematurely. There were no incubators. The baby died slowly after three days. Langer recalled (1981): 'In Nice, I went through the worst time of my life. The money didn't arrive, the baby had died, so many comrades as well, and not only Spain but all of Europe was falling apart' (p. 90).

At dawn on 12 March 1938, Nazi troops marched into Austria. A day later, on 13 March, the Board of the Vienna Psycho-Analytic Association decided that 'everyone who could, should flee the country and move the seat of the Association to wherever Freud settles' (Brecht et al., 1985, p. 142). Anna Freud was interrogated twice by the Gestapo, Martin Freud was arrested and released, the Freud household was subjected to repeated searches. Freud's assets were confiscated so that the Nazi-imposed obstacle of an emigration tax could not be paid. Princess Marie Bonaparte paid it and Freud left Vienna on 4 June 1938, arriving in London by way of Paris.

The Langers immediately made arrangements to leave Europe. President Lazaro Cardenas had declared Mexico open to political and racial refugees. But the Mexican consulate in Prague was unco-operative with the issuing of a visa. The Langers managed to get on a boat to Uruguay. After their arrival in Montevideo, they moved to Buenos Aires where, in 1939, Langer was able to begin her career as a psychoanalyst.

In 1984, Langer's provisional ten-point guidelines, created together with colleagues of the Internationalist Mental Health Team in the service of social reconstruction in Nicaragua, outlined their experience of using psychoanalytic principles in the treatment of the psychological effects of state terror (Langer, 1989):

1. You have to learn how to listen and how to ask questions. You also have to learn the importance of catharsis.
2. The unconscious does exist. Dreams, delusions, everything has a meaning.
3. Our attitudes and acts, and also our ideologies, are in part over-determined by unconscious motives.
4. We are always in conflict and we are afraid of change in the same way that we are afraid of the unknown.
5. We are always ambivalent. There is no love without hatred: even a mother, tired and overstretched, can hate her baby.
6. The history and infantile sexuality of our patients are important because they repeat as adults what they lived as children.
7. We repeat also our infantile loves and hates. When these are projected onto the therapist we speak of transference.
8. What the therapist feels about his/her patient, consciously or unconsciously, we call countertransference. No one is neutral. Doing psychotherapy is a political task.
9. In complementary lines we are the result of constitutional factors

and of early and late experiences. The combination of these and of ideological factors conditions our resistance or fragility in the face of traumatic situations.

10. We are all wonderful but also crazy, heroes but also cowards (important in learning to master fear). We are loving but also perverse. It is important to diminish guilt feelings because they generally do not help, but paralyse the person.

Throughout her career, Marie Langer was concerned about the connections between the personal and the political. For herself, she felt that she had been guided by her teacher, Aline Furtmüller, who had spoken seriously to her in the Red Vienna of the 1920s: 'There are people who say you shouldn't get involved with politics, that politics is dirty. None the less, if you don't actively participate in politics they'll make politics with you all the same' (p. 69). Late in life, Langer sought to understand non-neurotic militancy as an expression of the human need for transcendence, a form of the sublimation that in psychoanalysis has always been a signpost of mental health.

Now that I am an old woman, I understand [the need for transcendence] more as the need to survive individual death. Freud, in *Civilisation and Its Discontents*, tells us that there are few remedies for saving ourselves from this malaise and mentions sex, science, drugs, art and faith. Curiously enough, he does not mention politics. Politics is precisely that for me: what to do about your transcendence faced with the certainty of death, without a hereafter . . . At one point it is your turn to die, but if you have lived on the side of history then you will die with the feeling that you will remain part of it, that you will exist beyond your personal life and that you will have contributed to the future, to however small a degree. (Hollander, 1997, p. 192)

The entry of women as active historical agents has transformed psychoanalysis. Women have incorporated their actually lived experience into psychoanalytic theory, replacing women as a category of male fantasy with women as subjects having not only an independent voice that could defend and articulate the experience of women, but also having knowledge that was previously excluded from the psychoanalytic dialogue. Latin American subjectivities, informed by the experience of state terror, have created yet another literature within psychoanalysis that had previously been excluded. And there now remain the subjectivities of other marginalized groups to be included within the compass of psychoanalysis.

I2

Futures

As I neared completion of this history of psychoanalysis a colleague asked me what my experience of writing the book had been. I was surprised to hear myself say: 'I have been continuously shocked to find how much I was leaving out.'

The history of psychoanalysis is seriously overgrown. Like pruning an unruly, overgrown fruit tree of its distracting spurs and branches, the shape – or at least a shape – of psychoanalysis becomes clear and its fruiting, in principle, improved with a clear-out of most of the branching growth. Other writers, of course, would shape the same material differently.

The story I have told is one of promising beginnings – a contribution of the first rank by an ambitious, poverty-fearing neuroscientist turned neurologist in Vienna – followed by a stagnation caused by inexperience in the face of powerful social events, followed by a recovery of the discipline and an openness that may permit the field to consolidate its advances in preparation for renewed development.

I have been concerned to present the major developments in psychoanalysis that have been pushed out of view for half a century by an overgrowth of Freud studies: the interpersonalist approach of Harry Stack Sullivan in the US; the British object relations school, originating with the contributions of Melanie Klein but developed as an alternative to Freud by Ronald Fairbairn, John Bowlby and Donald Winnicott; and thirdly, the contributions from feminism, beginning with Karen Horney and most significantly developed by the gender-conscious clinicians and theorists of the last twenty years. Other counter-views to the classical Freudian model, including the work of Kohut, Langer and Lacan, have contributed to the confluence of these three main counter-strands to produce a new psychoanalysis.

Specialists will have noted the relative absence of the US ego psychologists, a development I have never found to be very interesting because in comparison to the US interpersonalists it accepted Freud's views on the role of instincts. I was surprised to find that the important contributions of Donald Winnicott in the UK, whose writing educated an entire generation of psychoanalytic psychotherapists, played a relatively minor role in this account of the main lines of development of psychoanalysis. The importance of Alfred Adler, long over-shadowed by the dominance of Freud, appears early in the story but not later as I have felt that the main themes of Adler's contribution have been either absorbed indirectly or developed independently by workers in the US and Britain. French psychoanalysis, a story told at great length and, to a specialist, in very satisfying detail, by Elisabeth Roudinesco, does not in itself justify repeating. Jacques Lacan is more interesting for his construction of the central problem of psychoanalysis as the problem of human subjectivity rather than for his theorizing in its own right. Also missing is a discussion of the roots of psycho-analysis and the discovery of the unconscious as related by Henri Ellenberger twenty-five years ago.

Most problematic, in terms of omissions, is the work of Carl Jung. Although Jung's original split with Freud was a turning point in the history of psychoanalysis, a proper integration of the subsequent growth and development of Jungian theory in the twentieth century into the history of psychoanalysis demands a treatment of its own. Like all theory, Jung's idea of a collective psychology, operating at a very deep level in the human psyche, appeals strongly to certain sensibilities. We have a lot to learn from Jung's insights into how we are formed collectively, both in our collective unconscious and our collective conscious, but the way that Jung has theorized his under-standing is too confusing, too rooted in Western religious traditions for me as a third-generation atheist, to grasp. I hope that Jungian colleagues will take this apology not as an attack but as an invitation. The Jungian development of psychoanalysis is a separate trunk grow-ing off the same root system and as such has developed similar branches emphasizing the therapy relationship, the importance of real world

experience, extensive use of the countertransference and a close attention to gender issues. The connections are there and they deserve to
be explored at length.

This shaping of the history of psychoanalysis, then, has followed
the initial development of psychoanalysis as a promising branch of
nineteenth-century neuroscience, the subsequent stagnation of classical Freudian theory as evidenced by splits in the original movement,
the slow development of three alternative directions – US interpersonalists, British object relations theorists and feminist psychoanalysts,
psychotherapists and theorists. The joining of these different paths
has now formed the beginnings of a new theory of human subjectivity.
What does the future hold?

In 1975, Jim Yorke, an applied mathematician at the University
of Maryland, was completing a write-up of some new results on
instabilities in classical mechanics then undergoing a renewal of interest after decades of neglect. Looking for an arresting way to present
the work that would lift it out of the dry linguistic confines of formal
mathematics, he hit on the title 'Period 3 Implies Chaos'. Remarkably,
Jim Yorke's metaphor became Chaos Theory – a popular metaphor
for the unpredictability of the future.

Chaos theory is not a theory of determination but a theory of
contingency. Not a theory of 'If this, then that' but a theory of 'If
this, maybe that', a theory of uncertain outcomes depending on the
existence of intermediate conditions whose effect on the course of
events cannot be predicted but must be observed. Chaos theory tells us
that there are many paths to the future. Which one will be taken is
contingent on conditions encountered along the way. But whereas in
chaotic weather systems, where the dynamics of the air–ocean interaction is outside of immediate human control, in the dynamics of human
interaction we have, in principle, the means to affect situations that
could lead to hurricanes instead of to quickly dissipating squalls.

Three tensions dominate psychoanalysis as it enters the twenty-first
century. Within the discipline itself there is the tension caused by
conflicting points of view, a tension expressing the continued confusion
about the place of science in the psychoanalytic project. Within the
profession of mental health there exists a tension between psycho-

analysis and psychiatry. And thirdly, characteristic of societies of the West as a whole, is the still-widespread tension between the importance of emotional life for human well-being and its denial and repudiation in public life.

Within psychoanalysis, the polarization of views between instinctual and relational conflict as the source of human psychological distress has been to an extent resolved, with every school of psychoanalysis adopting its own version of a relational paradigm. But the appreciation and integration of difference into psychoanalytic theory and practice still remains difficult.

A part of the difficulty lies in the historical roots of psychoanalysis in the middle-class communities of Europe and the United States. Psychoanalysis has had a tendency to restrict its horizons rather than widening them to include in theory and practice the differing experiences of groups lying outside the dominant middle-class cultures of Western Europe and United States.

In 1918, as the First World War was coming to a close, Freud recognized that the future of psychoanalysis lay in its development away from its upper-middle-class origins in Imperial Vienna to members of other social classes. Speaking from a prepared text at the Fifth International Psycho-Analytical Congress in Budapest on 29 September, he said (Freud, 1919):

[It] is possible to foresee that at some time or other the conscience of society will awake and remind it that the poor man should have as much right to assistance for his mind as he now has to the life-saving help offered by surgery; and that the neuroses threaten public health no less than tuberculosis, and can be left as little as the latter to the impotent care of individual members of the community. When this happens, institutions or out-patient clinics will be started to which analytically trained physicians will be appointed, so that men who would otherwise give way to drink, women who have nearly succumbed under the burden of privations, children for whom there is no choice but running wild or neurosis, may be made capable, by analysis, of resistance and of efficient work. Such treatments will be free. (p. 167)

There is now a small body of literature on the practice of psychoanalysis in different national and class settings.[1] But difference still poses problems for psychoanalysis, which has always had difficulty in sustaining an engagement with alternative views in the interest of advancing the field as a whole. Part of Fairbairn's achievement was to do just this. The conflict between Freud's view of the human being as fundamentally pleasure-seeking (tension reduction) and Fairbairn's view, as it developed in his clinical experience, of the human individual as fundamentally relationship-seeking, did not lead Fairbairn to start his own school. Instead, he actively sought to bring the two points of view into contact to see if he could understand how they were related to each other. As we have seen, his result was to understand pleasure-seeking as a real effect but as an effect due to the degradation of relationship – the individual seeks the reduction of tension through physical means when the satisfaction of human relationships no longer seems possible.

Another obstacle to achieving a capacity to hold the tensions between conflicting points of view lies in part in the nature of clinical training. Clinical work is applied work, with a priority on developing effective treatment procedures and not on developing understanding of how the procedures work. Clinicians need to go into their consulting rooms with an emphasis on what they know, not on what wants further understanding. But as we move further away in time from Freud, Klein, Sullivan, Winnicott and Lacan, what is needed now is a Fairbairnian effort to bring differences into contact with each other with a view to establishing the relationship between them.

Is there a conflict between drive and relational points of view? Perhaps not if one posits a drive towards relationship as seems to be indicated by infant attachment studies. Is there a need for the death instinct in Melanie Klein's theory of object relationships? Perhaps not if one posits that broken attachments are far more destructive than we have previously understood. What are the significant differences, if any, between Kohut's self-psychology, Sullivan's interpersonal theory and Bowlby's attachment theory? And most difficult of all, how is the discussion to be structured? What might some useful rules be so that one might decide which, if any, of these competing understandings might be better than another?

Psychoanalysis, the science of the human inner world, needs to carry forward from its origins in nineteenth-century neuroscience the discipline – no more and no less – of the scientific enterprise of which it is a part: to accept that the goal is to understand, that understanding is created by hard work and plenty of it and that the deepest understandings are created as a result of sustained engagement with the issues of concern, not just by a few innovators but by all of those in the field. Psychoanalysis offers the possibility of treatment for inner conflicts that prevent the realization of the human goals of love, work and justice. And such treatments will be free. To what extent difficulties with difference within the field will hinder psychoanalysis from making its needed contribution to the development of the human race is one of the contingencies along the path to the future.

A second contingency lies in the playing out of the tensions between psychoanalysis and psychiatry. At the same time that psychoanalysis was expanding at its periphery in response to the 1960s and its encounter with feminism, at the centre of its practice in US medical schools the discipline had been steadily losing ground to a new biological psychiatry. Questions from medical students about the strengths and limitations of psychoanalysis, instead of being handled with the thoughtfulness they deserved, had been interpreted as expressions of resistance. Donald Klein, a pioneer researcher in psychopharmacology, recalled how his teenage interest in psychoanalysis had been negated by his exposure to psychiatry in medical school in the 1950s (Klein, 1996):

The psychiatry courses were terrible. Terrible. We had one guy who would read to us from a book. And finally we delegated some people to go and talk to him and say 'we all know how to read'. And he said 'this was our resistance against understanding the real truth'. So that was terrible . . . So I got involved with basic science. It was a lot of fun. We built our own chromatography apparatus. But I maintained my interest in psychoanalysis. (p. 343)

Klein's interest in psychoanalysis was to decline to the vanishing point.

I kept telling my analyst that I was interested in doing something more systematic and interesting in the way of human experimentation which he told me was my sadism . . . I lasted in analysis for a couple more years. I told my first analyst that we were not getting anywhere and he agreed very happily so they gave me another analyst who was a complete idiot. I lasted about five months with him. (p. 347)

Abraham Brill's vision of psychoanalysis as a medical speciality had been brilliantly achieved in the United States. By the 1960s, it was not possible to become chair of a department of psychiatry in US medical schools unless one was a psychoanalyst. Twenty years later, it was not possible to become the chair of a department of psychiatry in US medical schools if one were a psychoanalyst. The price paid for the inability to contain and make use of the differences in views within psychoanalysis was the loss of two generations of medical students.

By the 1990s, aided by the magical aura of molecular biology, biological psychiatry had become the paradigm of choice in psychiatric medicine. A new generation of the medically trained had moved in to insist, with considerable support from funding agencies, that the cause of human mental pain, especially in its most extreme forms, lay in the material structures of the brain.

The loss of the medical school base of psychoanalysis was in many ways to be welcomed. Psychoanalysis never should have become a medical speciality. But in the polarized atmosphere that has accompanied the medical disenchantment with psychoanalysis, what has been lost yet again are opportunities to advance our understanding of the interrelationships between the somatic and the psychological. In a recent account by a well-known historian of psychiatry, the psychoanalytic exploration of the human inner world was found to be an unfortunate deviation – a Jewish deviation no less – from the straight, true path of modern molecular psychopharmacology (Shorter, 1997). A basic step in redressing the polarization of mind versus body in the aetiology and treatment of mental illness is to be clear that biological psychiatry has its strengths and limitations just as psychoanalysis does.

We know that repeated psychological trauma can do real somatic damage which, if left untreated, militates against the effectiveness of psychotherapy. Kay Redfield Jameson (1997) describes how important lithium treatment was for her manic depression. Lithium enabled her to gain relief from her manic symptoms so that psychotherapy could begin to work for her. But there is not even a speculative understanding of how lithium carbonate, discovered by accident by John Cade in Australia in 1948 in a search for drugs that would calm patients down, produced the effects on her that it did. Even the most enthusiastic of the new psychopharmacologists acknowledge that the drugs, like aspirin, ameliorate the damage without curing it. We do not understand how the new psychoactive drugs work beyond the knowledge that they block or enhance the action of specific neurotransmitters, presumably by competitively occupying neurotransmitter binding sites.

These blunt instruments can easily come to re-medicalize human mental pain in a scenario where the human being, while being more than a molecular biologist's body-bag of reactants, enzymes and metabolites, simply suffers from a biochemical deficiency just like sufferers of insulin deficiency. Without an understanding of how psychological damage can cause physical damage, there has been plenty of room to argue that it is hypothetical lesions of the nervous system or, in more contemporary versions, overstimulation or inhibition of neural pathways associated with the action of specific neurotransmitters, that is the *cause*, not the consequence, of mental distress.

The work of many dedicated researchers to locate the biochemical and physiological correlates of severe mental disturbance is potentially invaluable. There is every possibility that the repeated trauma of unbearable childhood anxiety at the hands of care-givers, identified by Sullivan as the aetiological agent in development of schizophrenia and manic depression (bipolar mood disorder in the language of the 1990s), can cause irreversible physiological damage for which the only effective therapy may be biochemical.

Practically, however, progress in understanding is painfully slow. Even in the relatively simple case of sodium thiopental, a barbiturate used as an anaesthetic, where there is a simple and direct correlation between the electrical activity of the brain (EEG) and the course of action of the drug, the precise connections between the drug and the electrophysiology remains completely unknown (Schwartz et al., 1971). These difficulties are not always respected by researchers who, in their eagerness to get results, do not do justice to the complexities of the problem.

In the 1960s, there was a fad for studying biochemicals secreted in the urine (metabolites) to see if there were important differences between patients diagnosed as schizophrenic compared to controls. One study in the laboratory of Nobel Prizewinner Julius Axelrod, now known as the cautionary tale of the Pink Spots, consistently found two pink spots in the chromatograms of patients diagnosed as schizophrenic compared to controls. Axelrod had too much respect for the complexities of biology to trust such a simple result (Axelrod, 1996): 'It was too good to be true' (p. 48). His group looked carefully at the diets of their subjects and found that their control group happened all to be Mennonites who did not drink coffee. The pink spots in the chromatograms of the schizophrenic patients were due to an irrelevant metabolite of coffee.

To some extent, such cautionary tales from the history of psychopharmacology have been heard. To some extent they have not. In particular, we need to bear in mind the risks associated with drug treatment. Many of the drug treatment protocols tested in the wards of mental hospitals have resulted in the deaths of the patients (Angst, 1996).

A further factor is the central role of the necessarily market-oriented pharmaceutical companies in the research and development of psychotropic drugs. The first worldwide meeting on chlorpromazine in Paris in 1955 was supported by the pharmaceutical firm Specia of the Rhone-Poulenc Group. Chlorpromazine had been synthesized at the Specia laboratories as part of a programme of making antihistamines, some of which had been used in psychiatry as sedatives. Trials with chlorpromazine showed that it had the unusual property of sedating the person without inducing sleep. Patients retained consciousness but were oblivious to their surroundings. More powerful drugs followed, now measured in chlorpromazine equivalents, along with the knowledge that chlorpromazine blocked the post-synaptic dopamine receptor, preventing the re-uptake of dopamine into the neurone and leaving the dopamine free to continue to act on other receptors in the synaptic cleft. The use of chlorpromazine and its equivalents since the 1950s has arguably permitted the reduction of psychiatric beds by up to 75 per cent. But in the forty years since the introduction of chlorpromazine, the pharmaceutical companies have engaged in the 'me too' research well known to critics of the industry by simply marketing different drugs that all exploit the same mechanism of re-uptake inhibition – of which fluoxetine (Prozac) is the most famous. As Leslie Iversen (1997), one of the leading figures in the field of psychopharmacology points out, over 100 different drugs have been marketed for the treatment of schizophrenia, every one of them acting in the same way as chlorpromazine.

The conflict between biological psychiatry and psychotherapy raises again the deep problem of the interrelationships of the different levels of organization of matter. As the evolutionary biologist Ernst Mayr has written in a critique of the reductionist programme of molecular biology (Schwartz, 1992):

We know that an inventory of all the molecules of the liver is not sufficient to reconstruct a description of the function of the entire liver. Without a knowledge of the mitochondria and other cellular organelles and structures (membranes), without understanding the blood circulation and the structure of the capillaries, without knowing what the normal input and output of the liver is, and without a knowledge of many other aspects of the liver and the body as a whole, it would be utterly futile to try to arrive at a correct picture of liver function. (pp. 133–4)

In psychiatry similar questions need to be raised about the programme of understanding mental distress simply, as in diabetes, as a lack of a specific neurochemical or a malfunction of a specific neural structure. An important study of manic depression by Wayne C. Drevets and an interdisciplinary group of six colleagues (1997) at the Washington University School of Medicine in St. Louis, using the modern technique of magnetic field imaging, found significant differences in electrical activity between sufferers of depression and normal controls in the subgenual prefrontal cortex, a small localized region in the front of the brain. Ancillary studies of experimental animals indicated that this region could be involved in the processing of emotions. Drevets and his colleagues found that of 38 patients suffering from manic depression or depression, the left side of the subgenual prefrontal cortex was greatly reduced in size by approximately 45 per cent ± 5 per cent compared to the same region in 21 controls. A review by a co-worker in the field praised the study as a most important contribution (Damasio, 1997):

Drevets et al. have found consistent functional and structural anomalies in one component of a system whose large-scale function is to organize emotional responses to complex personal and social situations. In other words, they have identified a key player in one of the several systems that underlie emotional processing – a valuable finding indeed. (p. 769)

What has been found is a defined region of the brain that seems to suffer significant reduction in size in a sample of sufferers of depression. Yet we do not have even the beginnings of an understanding of this effect or its significance. Can such a diminution account for the feelings and behaviour of people who are clinically depressed? And how are we to understand the origin of the diminution? Is it due to genetics, a lack of specific protein needed for the normal functioning of the suspect area? Is it due to a developmental lack, an abnormality of brain development of as yet unknown aetiology? Is it due to repeated traumatic emotional experiences of the making and breaking of significant attachments?

It is perfectly reasonable and possibly invaluable to follow such a lead to see what can be found out. Drevets himself feels that recent, as yet unpublished post-mortem work on this area of the brain indicates that in manic depression there may be a pronounced lack of a particular species of cell in the subgenual prefrontal cortex, a finding that if sustained would further localize the abnormality. Such a finding would have the potential of indicating a possible drug-related therapy if the biochemical role of the hypothetical missing cells could be identified. But we would still not know anything about how the experience of clinical depression relates to the malfunction in this component of the brain system.

Investigations of the diminution of certain cells in the subgenual prefrontal cortex hold out the possibility of a therapy that could perhaps restore the missing cells, a treatment that could well prove effective or even perhaps lifesaving in the case of manic depression. No clinician would refuse or deny that there can be great value in drugs to ameliorate states of mind that can cause deep anguish, feelings of depersonalization, the giddy rushes of manic energy, the terror of feeling one's self dissolving away. But the great weakness of biological psychiatry is that in the absence of a deeper understanding of mind–

body connections, such pharmacological agents will always have a certain hit or miss quality to them. We are now seeing what is colloquially called Prozac poop-out, the decreasing effectiveness of the long-term use of fluoxetine to ameliorate feelings of depression. The question in the biological approach to mental ill-health is whether the agents employed can be used wisely instead of simply widely, with a full awareness of their limitations. The dream of a magic bullet is a nineteenth-century Romantic illusion from the great days of the isolation of bacterial agents of disease. To cure at the stroke of a magic prescribing pen is a lovely dream. But everything we have learned about complexity tells us that the world is not that simple.

The third contingency along the path towards the future lies in how successfully we can create social arrangements that are based on the satisfaction of fundamental human relational needs. In the nineteenth century, natural science eliminated our omnipotent fantasies about our relationship with nature, replacing them with a more mature, intimate and real relationship, based on understanding rather than fantasy. It is no accident that the celebrated classics of the great Romantic epoch of Western science are statements of limitation – energy cannot be created or destroyed, perpetual motion machines are impossible, nothing can go faster than the speed of light.

And so too does psychoanalysis have the potential to replace our fantasies about human relationships with more mature understanding of human relational needs as revealed under the microscope of the analytic hour. And if, in a culture that makes a fetish of independence with its myth of the Man Alone, we have inner conflicts about the validity and satisfaction of our relational needs it is psychoanalysis that affords the space for the exploration and resolution of this inner conflict. What psychoanalysis has to teach us is that human relationships are central to our development and growth, that distortions in the fulfilment of fundamental human relational needs have lasting negative consequences for human happiness – that there is no such thing as the Man Alone. The analytic hour is an indispensable tool for the treatment and resolution of painful, immobilizing inner conflicts. Just as the insights of natural science were central to the creation of a material well-being associated with the Industrial

Revolution, the insights of psychoanalysis are crucial to the creation of emotional well-being and to a humanity that can embrace difference and find common solutions to the difficulties created by modern life.

Notes

1   Boundaries

1. The original article appeared on 18 November 1993. The responses and counter-responses appeared on 3 February 1994, 12 May 1994, and 11 August 1994. In an obvious attempt to boost circulation by importing controversy, the debate crossed the Atlantic to appear in London in the *Independent* on 25 January 1994, 1 February 1994 and 8 February 1994. The pompous verbosity of these exchanges with their focus on Freud's integrity did little to clarify present thinking about the very real problems we face in attempting to understand and treat mental pain.

2. Michael Oppenheimer (1998), 'Global warming and the stability of the West Antarctic Ice Sheet', *Nature*, v. 398, pp. 325–32; *Observer*, 25 January 1998, p. 25; *Guardian*, 13 May 1998, p. 9; *Guardian*, 15 May 1998, special section on Third World debt; *Guardian G2*, 22 July 1998; Adam Jukes (1993), *Why Men Hate Women*, London: Free Association Books; *Today Programme*, BBC Radio 4, 19 December 1998.

2   Freud

1. 'The Fabric of the Universe' appeared as a *Times* leader on 11 November 1919.

2. Sketches of Victor, Emma and Friedrich Adler are given by Maitron and Haupt (1971). The standard work on Adler *père et fils* is Braunthal (1965). For Adler's relationship with Einstein, see Clark (1971). Clark and Braunthal base their accounts on the Adler archive held in the University of Vienna.

3. Freud's physics teacher Josef Stefan (1835–93) is known for the Stefan–Boltzmann law on the energy radiated from a heated body. Freud's older friend, teacher and collaborator Josef Breuer identified the Breuer–Hering

reflex in breathing, the discovery that the action of the vagus nerve simultaneously limits inhalation and excites exhalation. Freud's first teacher of microscopy, Carl Toldt (1840–1920) is known for Toldt's Law, delineating the distinctive features of human facial bones. Freud's teacher of anatomy and dissection was Professor Carl Langer (1819–87) whose *Textbook of Systematic and Topographic Anatomy* went through twelve editions. Freud's teacher of chemistry was Professor Franz Schneider (1812–97), a leading physiological chemist who made his name with the development of the first tests for mercury and arsenic poisoning. Freud was taught botany and plant physiology by Eduard Fenzl (1808–79), an expert in plants of the polar regions. Fenzl's textbook *Elements of Scientific Botany*, 3 vols, went through three editions until 1913.

4. For a discussion of the failure of the Social Democratic movement to respond adequately to anti-Semitism in Germany and Austria see Berkley (1988). For a discussion of the specifically Viennese brand of anti-Semitism informing Billroth's remarks, see Klein (1985).

5. Josef Stefan's biographer, Albert von Obermayer (1893), professor of physics at the Technical Military Academy of Vienna described his skill in these terms:

Stefan possessed in great measure the ability to treat scientific subjects in a way that made them easy to understand. This skill of his was particularly noticeable in those lectures in which, with superb and incomparable clarity, he explained the most involved problems. He carefully adapted all the mathematical developments to the level of comprehension his audience was capable of, having arranged them in such a way that the arguments could be easily understood. (pp. 67–8)

6. Other examples of Freud's critical observant attitude are in his letters of 6 March 1874 to Fluss, 22 October 1874 to Silberstein, 6 August 1878 to Knoepfmacher '([I] am preparing myself for my proper profession – mutilating animals or tormenting human beings').

7. Freud's letters to Martha of 6 October 1883, 7 January 1884, 18 January 1884, 28 January 1884, 7 February 1884, 29 March 1884, 19 April 1884, and 3 August 1884 express Freud's continuous anxiety about publication.

8. Sherrington (1906), Brazier (1959) and Clark and Jacyna (1987) are standard references for the history of neurophysiology in the nineteenth century.

9. In letters to Martha of 29 June 1884, 17 May 1885, 18 January 1886, 20 January 1886 and 2 February 1886, Freud describes his use of the drug. As late as 1895, Freud was writing to his friend Wilhelm Fliess that he needed cocaine to help him deal with health problems (12 June 1895). Peter Swales

(1986) and E. M. Thornton (1983) have argued that Freud became a cocaine addict with consequent deleterious effects on his clinical and scientific judgements.

10. The literature on the syndrome of hysteria is overwhelming. Freud's review article (1888) is still valuable for an early medical, pre-psychoanalytic view. Medical views of the syndrome are relatively unchanged in the century since Freud (Berkow, 1992; Macpherson, 1992). Micale (1990, 1995) is perhaps definitive on the historiography of hysteria. Feminist interest in hysteria as an expression of women's social experience as written on the body has been well treated by Showalter (1985). A recent review from a Lacanian perspective is Bronfen (1998).

4 First Theories

1. The papers were 'The Neuropsychoses of Defence' (Freud, 1894); 'Obsessions and Phobias' (Freud, 1895a); 'On the Grounds for Detaching a Particular Syndrome from Neurasthenia under the Description "Anxiety Neurosis"' (Freud, 1895b); 'A Reply to Criticisms of My Paper on Anxiety Neurosis' (Freud, 1895c); 'Heredity and the Aetiology of the Neurosis' (Freud, 1896a); 'Further Remarks on the Neuro-Psychoses of Defence' (1896b). The talk was titled, 'The Aetiology of Hysteria' (1896c).

2. The vignettes are in Freud (1896c), pp. 206 and 215; Freud (1896a), p. 152; Freud (1896b), p. 180; Freud to Fleiss, 6 December 1896 and 11 January 1897.

3. Letters to Fliess of 8 March, 13 March, 20 March, 28 March, 11 April, 20 April, 26 April and 27 April 1895. Additional details are in Freud (1937), p. 222 and Masson (1984), pp. 252–3.

4. There can be no question of exaggeration due to mistranslation here. The German transcription of Freud's handwriting of the letters of 11 January and 24 January 1897 is in Masson and Schröter (1986). Masson's English translation (1985) is perfectly accurate.

5. On Belgium see the *Guardian*, 21 October 1996, p. 3; *London Review of Books*, 14 November 1996, p. 25; *Guardian*, 16 December 1996, p. 5. On Northern Ireland see Chris Moore (1996), *The Kincora Scandal: Political Cover-up and Intrigue in Northern Ireland*, London: Marine; *London Review of Books*, 4 July 1996, p. 12; *Observer*, 13 October 1996, p. 11. On North Wales, Leicestershire, Staffordshire and Merseyside, see the *Guardian*, 6 June 1996, p. 17, 12 June 1996, G2, pp. 1–3; *Guardian*, 15 October 1997, p. 1, G2, p. 1. On the Catholic Church see the *Guardian*, 4 October 1996, p. 4. With the publication in the UK of the Utting Report on child abuse in

boarding schools, boys' homes, foster care and prisons, the *Guardian* editorial of 20 November 1996 read: 'Ending a legacy of abuse. Vulnerable children need a national strategy now' (p. 20).
6. Freud's statements can be found in the order in which they are quoted, in Freud (1905a), pp. 57, 220, 234; Freud (1926), p. 107; Freud (1931), p. 242; Freud (1939), p. 75; Freud (1940), p. 187, and Freud (1931), p. 232.

5   First Splits

1. Freud's comments can be found in the *Minutes* v. 1, pp. 396, 404, 368; v. 2, p. 258; v. 3, p. 84.
2. The Industrial Census of 3 June 1902 showed that of the 105,750 businesses in Vienna nearly 90 per cent employed fewer than five persons with a total employment of one third of the workforce (Barea, 1966).
3. A transcription of the original typescript made by Ernst Falzeder was made available to me by the Sigmund Freud Copyrights. I acknowledge Ernst Falzeder's work in making this transcript from the original holograph and I thank Tom Roberts of the Sigmund Freud Copyrights for posting me a xerox copy of it.
4. The Kreuzlingen gesture refers to Jung's protest at a secret visit Freud made to Ludwig Binswanger when Binswanger was diagnosed with cancer, at which time Freud did not call upon Jung.

6   The Transference

1. In the technical literature the emotional response of analyst to analysand is itself the subject of specialist discussion. The totality of the therapist's emotional responses to client is now most frequently called the counter-transference and includes a number of quite different emotional processes, including projective identification which can be described as feelings that the therapist has that the client is unable to have for himself; complementary counter-transference, feelings that the therapist has that significant figures have had in response to the client in the past; and concordant countertransference, feelings that the therapist has that are a reflection of what the client himself is feeling.

7 Expanding the Frontier: Psychoanalysis in the United States I

1. The translation was actually done by Jellife's wife, Helen Dewey Leeming.
2. The core New York group consisted of Clarence B. Oberndorf, Brill, Morris Karpas and Horace Frink.
3. The nine founding members were Trigant Burrow, Ralph C. Hamill, August Hoch, Ernest Jones, John Thomson MacCurdy, Adolf Meyer, J. J. Putnam, G. Lane Taneyhill and G. Alexander Young.
4. Putnam held liberal opinions throughout his life. In 1911, at the age of sixty-five, he wrote to his daughter Molly from the Psychoanalytic Congress in Weimar about aristocratic Europe (Hale, 1971): 'The most important movements in history have been and will be the (unpicturesque) *people's movements* and the history of the King-fellars is of little significance as seen against the background of the history of *the people* and as bearing on the people's life. *Institutions* and the evidences of the *struggles of the people*: those are what we really want to see – whether at Versailles or at Chartres' (p. xiv).
5. The difficulties potentially receptive physicians found with psychoanalysis were not always handled with the greatest tact and understanding by the 'with us or against us' sensibility of many of the early converts. The Boston neurologist Samuel Hamilton, who was in Washington that May for the formation of the American Psychopathological Association, later commented on the arrogance of early advocates of psychoanalysis (Hamilton, 1945):

Perhaps some of the analytic followers were a little verbose, a little inclined to take up full time at a medical meeting and more than a little inclined to think that no other type of psychotherapy was worth much and that no other type of explanation of the motivation of conduct was worth even thinking about. It is but natural that a new movement should attract some who are impatient, inconsiderate and long-winded as well as many of more concise and useful diction. (pp. 31–2)

6. Brill translated the *Three Essays on the Theory of Sexuality* in 1910, *Interpretation of Dreams* in 1913 and *The Psychopathology of Everyday Life* in 1914, translations which have now been discarded in favour of Joan Riviere's *Collected Works* and Strachey's *Standard Edition*. Strachey, in turn, did not entirely solve the difficult problem of rendering Freud's solution, in German, to the problem of creating a vivid language to describe human subjective experience, producing a rather scientistic, rigid Freud in English.

Strachey explains his choices, particularly the controversial rendering of *Trieb* (drive) as 'instinct' in the introduction to the *Standard Edition*. Waelder (1960) gives a thoughtful critical discussion of Strachey's choice while Kiell (1988) gives a useful overview of the arguments about what has been lost in the translations from Freud's German. Freud was notoriously lax in the granting of translation rights. In the 1930s there were three separate English language translations of *Inhibition, Symptom and Anxiety* in circulation (Meisel and Kendrick, 1985).

7. That Jones found Adolf Meyer boring did not prevent him from trying for a job with Meyer at Johns Hopkins at the Phipps Clinic in 1910–11. Meyer, although quite positive about Jones's abilities, seemed to be put off by his bohemianism and his affair with Loe Kahn, who was Jewish. Meyer wrote to his brother after the 1911 Baltimore conference, where the American Psychoanalytic Association was formed (Leys, 1981): '. . . Mrs Jones and Ernest Jones, the best Freudian, expert scholar and earlier assistant to Horsley, came from Toronto and caused a minor storm here; too much Bernard Shaw and lack of restraint; she in addition is a Dutch Jewess, very emancipated and also in bad health and has to rely on morphines; I had often thought about bringing him here to B. But this just can't be done though he is pressing for it' (19 May 1911).

8. Two years later, White was less sanguine about the possibility of amicable co-operation as tensions over English language translation rights of psycho-analytic articles increased between Jones and the White/Jelliffe partnership. White wrote to Jelliffe about the possibilities of joint publishing efforts:

I am constitutionally opposed to making alliances with my enemies, and Jones and the whole bunch of them are at least if not our active enemies so superciliously damned superior in their own estimation that any alliance we could make would run against us. (2 May 1923)

In 1926 when Max Eitingon was soliciting $25 from each member of the International for Freud's 75th birthday celebration, White wrote Jelliffe with reservations about making the donation:

Of course I have the deepest respect for Freud himself and would be glad to do this for him, but to think that it has to drizzle through the hands of a lot of high-binders and short horns is not pleasing. They all hate us over there, I presume because they think we have money. (3 February 1926)

9. The brutality of hospital attendants was a serious problem. In 1929, Harry

Stack Sullivan spoke at the annual meeting of the American Psychiatric Association about the criminal lack of trained attendants in mental hospitals.

What the hospital employee is permitted to do to patients often beggars any layman's fancy ... It seems that in some cases personnel drifts in; is sorted by a method as efficient as flinging it against a ceiling and seeing what sticks; subjected to wholly irrational and unpredictable interventions from above; maintained in a state of degradation calculated to produce an atmosphere of vicious dissatisfaction; and all too frequently housed in a fashion conducive to slow deterioration. No one is inspired to the pursuit of any valid goal other than 'getting by with it'. (Sullivan, 1929, p. 539)

10. Correspondence describing White's position on the issues of the day from 1910 to 1936 is in Grob (1985), pp. 72–4, 89–94, 108–28, 170–4, 270–1.

11. The two cases were made into Hollywood films – the Stanford White case in 1955 as *The Girl in the Red Velvet Swing*, directed by Richard Fleischer, starring Ray Milland and Joan Collins; the Leopold and Loeb case twice, in 1948 as *Rope*, directed by Alfred Hitchcock and starring Farley Granger and John Dall, and in 1959, as *Compulsion*, directed again by Fleischer and starring Orson Welles and Diana Varsi. Stanford White's great granddaughter, Suzannah Lessard (1997), a staff writer at the *New Yorker*, tapped a continued resonance that the case of Stanford White has in the US with an account of her bizarre family history including its history of sexual abuse against its daughters.

10 Breakthrough in Britain

1. To some extent, Sándor Ferenczi had anticipated Fairbairn's placing of conflicts around love as the key problem of human development. In the 1920s Ferenczi attempted to bring classical psychoanalysis to a deeper recognition of the importance of love, risking his own relationship with Freud, suffering expulsion from the inner ranks of senior analysts and having his contributions pathologized.

Ferenczi attempted a number of innovations in technique that could facilitate access to the pain associated with the mismatch between a child's needs and their unconscious prohibition by parental authority as a result of adults not being able to give permission for what they themselves had been denied (Balint, 1949).

In the UK, Ian and Jane Suttie, both based at the Tavistock Clinic in London, anticipated Fairbairn and Bowlby in their concern about frustrations in love as the primary pathogen in mental illness. Emphasizing the importance of early parental attachments, Ian Suttie expressed his point of view in a steady stream of papers over a period of thirteen years, culminating in the publication in 1935 of the consolidation of his views, shortly before his death, in his book *The Origins of Love and Hate*. This was subsequently acknowledged by Bowlby (1988) 'as a milestone' in the origin of object relations and in the focusing of attention on separation anxiety and the 'dread of loneliness'. Suttie's work remains of more than historical interest because his analysis of what he called a taboo on tenderness reflects current concerns with the psychological effects of the culture of violence in the West and its repression of human emotional life (de Zulueta, 1993).

11 Transmuting Collision: Psychoanalysis, Feminism and the Sixties

1. Times are changing. A 1993 European survey showed that nearly 90 per cent of both men and women surveyed believed that men should be 'very involved' with the raising of children from an early age (Eurobarometer, 1993). But the exact meaning of being 'very involved' remains unclear. For many, fathers are important simply because of their gender, as in the formula: 'families need fathers'. Or fathers are seen to be important in families because of their gendered role in the Oedipal triangle, or because they represent the world of work or because children become too attached to the mother if the father is absent. In this model of fatherhood, children's development is aided because of the aura of the father's masculinity in the family. Studies of actually involved fathers in the 1980s and 1990s indicate that basic parenting skills are largely gender-independent – men and woman do substantially the same things when they are relating to their children although they bring to their children differing unconscious communications and meanings because of their own different gender experience (Samuels, 1995; Burgess and Ruxton, 1996).

2. Phyllis Chesler (1972), *Women and Madness*. New York: Avon; Nancy Chodorow (1978), *The Reproduction of Mothering: Psychoanalysis and the Sociology of Gender*. Berkeley: University of California Press; Dorothy Dinnerstein (1976), *The Mermaid and the Minotaur*. New York: Harper & Row; Luise Eichenbaum and Susie Orbach (1983), *Understanding Women*. New York: Basic Books; Harmondsworth: Penguin; Jane Flax (1978), 'The Conflict Between Nurturance and Autonomy in Mother–Daughter Relationships and Within Feminism', in *Feminist Studies*, v. 4, pp. 171–89; Carol

Gilligan (1982), *In a Different Voice: Psychological Theory and Women's Development*. Cambridge, MA: Harvard University Press; Jean Baker Miller (1983), *Toward a New Psychology of Women*. Boston: Beacon Press; Juliet Mitchell (1974), *Psychoanalysis and Feminism*. New York: Pantheon; Susie Orbach (1978), *Fat is a Feminist Issue*. New York: Berkley Books; Jean Strouse (ed.) (1974), *Women & Analysis. Dialogues on Psychoanalytic Views of Femininity*, New York: Dell.

3. From an article by Charlie Kreiner in *Present Time* (no date). I am grateful to Margaret Green for bringing this work to my attention.

4. I am indebted to Andrew Samuels for introducing me to the important concept of the numinous idea.

5. What is lacking in the many attempts to mathematize the social sciences is the understanding that mathematical formalisms express relationships. Algebra – symbolic arithmetic – permits the human mind to conceptualize relationships between measurable quantities more easily, as in the school problem: 'Mary is 24 years old. Mary is twice as old is Ann was when Mary was as old as Ann is now. How old is Ann?' By letting Ann's age be expressed symbolically by the letter x the sentences in question can be re-expressed as $24 = 2(x - (24 - x))$. The advantage of such a formulation lies in the fact that the symbols can be manipulated by the rules of arithmetic (the ages are, after all, numbers) to give for Ann's age $x=18$ years old. But when Bion writes that a man's gait is a function (F) of his personality, which is composed of two factors, love and envy, or $F = L + E$ (Bion, 1962), such symbolization adds nothing. The rules of arithmetic do not apply to love, personality and envy because they are not measurable and the relationships between them cannot usefully be described with the plus sign of arithmetic. It is without meaning to transpose Bion's 'equation' by the rules of algebra to write, $L = F \times E$.

6. Kohut was caught up in the political events of the 1960s through the political actions of his son Tom, an anti-Vietnam war activist. Tom Kohut recalled 'violent' confrontations with his father over his political involvement, beginning with his participation in a hunger strike in sympathy with anti-US Navy recruiter protesters at Oberlin College. Kohut wrote to his son:

Please don't throw away your chances for a productive life and happy future on the basis of an impulse, or even on the basis of a presently held strong conviction. To be a militant on campus does entail risks which may be greater than you allow yourself to know. Those on the other side of the fence do not see good will and idealism in their opponents, but only rebellion and obstructionism. Many of them are as fully convinced of the righteousness of their cause as you are of yours. And if those in opposition use provocative methods, they feel justified in suppressing them ruthlessly. I believe you should think long and hard before committing yourself to extreme causes and especially to extreme means of furthering them. (17 November 1968)

12 Futures

1. Alexandre Etkind (1995), *Histoire de la psychanalyse en Russie*. Paris: Presses universitaires de France; Enzo Morpurgo (1992), 'Psychanalyse et classe ouvrière: l'expérience du "Consulto Popolare di Niguarda" dans la ville de Milan (1969–1974)' in *Revue Internationale d'Histoire de la Psychanalyse*. Number 5; R. Moses (1992), 'A short history of psychoanalysis in Palestine and Israel', in *Israeli Journal of Psychiatry and Related Sciences*, v. 29, pp. 229–38; Luis Rodriguez (1992), 'La psychanalyse à Cuba', in *Revue Internationale d'Histoire de la Psychanalyse*. Number 5, pp. 529–40; M. Sebek (1993), 'Psychoanalysis in Czechoslovakia', in *Psychoanalytic Review*, v. 80, pp. 433–9; Dora Shu-fan Dien (1983), 'Big Me and Little Me: A Chinese Perspective on the Self', in *Psychiatry*, v. 46, pp. 281–6.

Bibliography

At the Manuscripts Division of the United States Library of Congress:

AdlP	Alfred Adler papers
BrillP	Abraham Brill papers
BrnflP	Siegfried Bernfeld papers
FreudP	Sigmund Freud papers
JelP	Smith Ely Jelliffe papers
LewP	Nolan Don Carpenter Lewis papers

At the Wellcome Institute for the History of Medicine, London:

BowlbP	John Bowlby papers
FlkP	S. H. Foulkes papers
KleinP	Melanie Klein papers

At the Institute of Psychoanalysis, London:

BrP	Marjorie Brierley papers

At the University of Essex, Colchester:

Braut	Martha Bernays courting letters to Sigmund Freud (the Brautbriefe)
JJL	Letters from Jung to Jones

In private possession:

MetP	Interviews conducted in 1986 by Andy Metcalf with Margaret Williamson and Jock Sutherland
GillP	Copies of correspondence from Merton Gill to Stephen Mitchell, courtesy of Dr Stephen Mitchell

Unless otherwise noted, all correspondence cited in the text by date is contained in the following collections:

Freud and Martha Bernays (E. Freud, 1960)
Freud and Ferenczi 1908–1914 (Brabant, Falzeder and Giampieri-Deutsch, 1992)
Freud and Ferenczi 1914–1919 (Falzeder and Brabant, 1996)
Freud and Fliess (Masson, 1985)
Freud and Jones (Paskauskas, 1993)
Freud and Jung (McGuire, 1974)
Heinz Kohut (Cocks, 1994)
James and Alix Strachey (Meisel and Kendrick, 1985)
William Alanson White and Smith Ely Jelliffe (JelP)

All quotations from the minutes of the meetings of the Vienna Wednesday Psychological Society are either by date or by volume and page number (Nunberg and Federn, 1962, 1967, 1974, 1975).

References to Freud's collected works, unless otherwise noted, are from the *Standard Edition* [SE] *of the Complete Psychological Works of Sigmund Freud*, translated from the German under the general editorship of James Strachey in collaboration with Anna Freud, assisted by Alix Strachey and Alan Tyson, twenty-four volumes, London, The Hogarth Press (1955).

*

Ackerknecht, Erwin H. (1957), 'Josef Breuer über seinen Anteil an der Psychoanalyse', *Gesnerus*, v. 14, pp. 169–71.
Adler, Alfred (1902), 'The Penetration of Social Forces into Medicine', in Alfred Adler (1965), *Superiority and Social Interest. A Collection of Later Writings*, Heinz L. Ansbacher and Rowena R. Ansbacher (eds), London: Routledge & Kegan Paul.
Adler, Alfred (1965), *Superiority and Social Interest. A Collection of Later Writings*, Heinz L. Ansbacher and Rowena R. Ansbacher (eds), London: Routledge & Kegan Paul.
Albury, David and Schwartz, Joseph (1982), *Partial Progress. The Politics of Science and Technology*, London: Zed.
Alexander, Franz (1953), 'A Review of Two Decades', in Franz Alexander and Helen Ross, *20 Years of Psychoanalysis*. New York: Norton, pp. 13–27.
Alexander, Franz and Selesnick, Sheldon T. (1965), Freud–Bleuler Correspondence, *Archives of General Psychiatry*, v. 12, pp. 1–9.
Althusser, Louis (1993), *Writings on Psychoanalysis. Freud and Lacan*, Olivier Corpet and François Matheron (eds). Translated and with a preface by Jeffrey Mehlman. New York: Columbia University Press (1996).

Anderson, Philip W. (1972), 'More is Different', *Science*, v. 177, pp. 393–6.

Angst, Jules (1996), 'The myths of psychopharmacology', in David Healy, *The Psychopharmacologists*. London: Chapman & Hall, pp. 287–308.

anon. (1910), *Neurologisches Centralblatt* (Hamburg), v. 19, pp. 659–62.

anon. (1912), 'Clash in Academy of Medicine When Vienna Physician Was Honored', *New York Times*, 5 April.

anon. (1927), *International Journal of Psycho-Analysis*, v. 8.

anon. (1937). 'The William Alanson White Psychiatric Foundation', *American Journal of Psychiatry*, v. 93, pp. 1456–9.

anon. (1967), *Nobel Lectures Including Presentation Speeches and Laureate's Biographies. Physiology or Medicine 1901–1967*. Amsterdam: Elsevier.

Ansbacher, Heinz L. (1959), 'The Significance of the Socio-Economic Status of the Patients of Freud and of Adler', *American Journal of Psychotherapy*, v. 13, pp. 376–82.

Ansbacher, Heinz and Ansbacher, Rowena R. (eds) (1956), *The Individual Psychology of Alfred Adler*. New York: Harper & Row.

Appignanesi, Lisa and Forrester, John (1992), *Freud's Women*. London: Weidenfeld & Nicolson.

Aron, Lewis (1991), 'The Patient's Experience of the Analyst's Subjectivity', *Psychoanalytic Dialogues*, v. 1, pp. 29–51.

Ascherson, Neal (1998), 'In this rich earth', *The Observer*, 25 October, pp. 24–7.

Axelrod, Julius (1996), 'The discovery of amine uptake', in David Healy, *The Psychopharmacologists*. London: Chapman & Hall.

Balint, Michael (1949), 'Sandor Ferenczi' in Michael Balint (1956), *Problems of Human Pleasure and Behavior*, New York: Liveright, pp. 241-50.

Barea, Ilsa (1966), *Vienna: Legend and Reality*. London: Secker & Warburg.

Barinaga, Marcia (1997), 'Affirmative Action: Ban Has Mixed Impact on Texas, California Grad Schools', *Science*, v. 277, pp. 633–4.

Barker, Chris, Pistrang, Nancy and Elliot, Robert (1994), *Research Methods in Clinical and Counselling Psychology*, Chichester and New York: John Wiley & Sons.

Baynac, Jacques (1985), *Le roman de Tatiana*. Paris: Denoel.

Becker, Hortense Koller (1963), 'Carl Koller and Cocaine', *Psychoanalytic Quarterly*, v. 32, pp. 309–73.

Bem, Sacha and de Jong, Huib Looren (1997), *Theoretical Issues in Psychology. An Introduction*. London: Sage.

Benedikt, Moritz (1906), *Aus meinem Leben: Erinnerungen und Erorterungen*. Vienna: Carl Konegen.

Berger, John (1972), *Ways of Seeing*. Harmondsworth: Penguin.

Bergman, Robert L. (1991), 'New Training Group Formed in Los Angeles', *American Psychoanalyst*, v. 25, no. 2, pp. 25–6.

Berkley, George E. (1988), *Vienna and Its Jews. The Tragedy of Success 1880s–1890s*. Cambridge, MA: Abt Books.

Berkow, Robert (ed.) (1992), *The Merck Manual of Diagnosis and Therapy*, 16th edn, Rahway, NJ: Merck Research Laboratories.

Bernal, J. D. (1965), *Science in History*, 3rd edn, v. 2. Cambridge, MA: MIT Press.

Bernays, Anna Freud (1940), 'My Brother Sigmund Freud', *The American Mercury*, v. 51, pp. 335–42.

Bernfeld, Siegfried (1944), 'Freud's Earliest Theories and the School of Helmholtz', *Psychoanalytic Quarterly*, v. 13, pp. 341–62.

Bernfeld, Siegfried (1949), 'Freud's Scientific Beginnings', *American Imago*, v. 6, pp. 163–96.

Bernfeld, Siegfried (1951), 'Sigmund Freud, M.D., 1882–1885', *International Journal of Psycho-Analysis*, v. 32, pp. 204–17.

Bernfeld, Siegfried and Bernfeld, Suzanne Cassirer (1952), 'Freud's First Year in Practice, 1886–1887', *Bulletin of the Menninger Clinic*, v. 16, pp. 37–48.

Bettelheim, Bruno (1991), 'How I Learned about Psychoanalysis', in *Freud's Vienna and other Essays*. New York: Vintage, pp. 24–38.

Billroth, Christian Theodor (1876), *Über das Lehren und Lernen der Medizinischen Wissenschaften an den Universitäten der Deutschen Nation nebst Allegemeinen Bemerkungen über Universitäten. Eine Culturische Studie*. Vienna: Gerolds Sohn.

Bion, Wilfred R. (1962), *Learning from Experience*. London: Karnac Books.

Bion, W. R., Rosenfeld, H. and Segal, H. (1961), 'Melanie Klein', *International Journal of Psycho-Analysis*, v. 42, pp. 4–8.

Birtles, Ellinor Fairbairn and Scharf, David E. (eds) (1994), *From Instinct to Self. Selected Papers of W. R. D. Fairbairn. Vol. II Applications and Early Contributions*. London: Jason Aronson.

Birtles, Ellinor Fairbairn (1998), Letter of 18 February 1998.

Blanck, Gertrude and Blanck, Rubin (1974), *Ego Psychology: Theory and Practice*. New York: Columbia University Press.

Bleuler, Eugen (1911), *Dementia Praecox of the Group of Schizophrenias*. Translated by J. Zinkin. New York: International Universities Press.

Bloom, Sandra (1997), *Creating Sanctuary*. London: Routledge.

Boehlich, Walter (ed.) (1990), *The Letters of Sigmund Freud to Eduard Silberstein 1871–1881*. Translated by Arnold J. Pomerans. Cambridge, MA: The Belknap Press.

Boltzmann, Ludwig (1887), 'Gustav Robert Kirchoff', in Ludwig Boltzmann (1905), *Populäre Schriften*. Leipzig: Johann Ambrosiana Barth, pp. 51–75.

Born, Max (1971), *The Born–Einstein Letters*. London: Macmillan.

Bottome, Phyllis (1939), *Alfred Adler. Apostle of Freedom*. London: Faber & Faber.

Bowlby, John (1969), *Attachment and Loss. Volume 1, Attachment*. Harmondsworth: Penguin.

Bowlby, John (1973), *Attachment and Loss. Volume 2, Separation: Anxiety and Anger*. Harmondsworth: Penguin.

Bowlby, John (1980), *Attachment and Loss. Volume 3, Loss: Sadness and Depression*. Harmondsworth: Penguin.

Bowlby, John (1988), 'Foreword', in Ian Suttie, *The Origins of Love and Hate*. London: Free Association Books, pp. xv–xviii.

Bowlby, John, Figlio, Karl and Young, Robert M. (1986), 'An Interview with John Bowlby, *Free Associations*, v. 6, pp. 36–64.

Boyer, John W. (1995), *Culture and Political Crisis in Vienna. Christian Socialism in Power, 1897–1918*. London: University of Chicago Press.

Brabant, Eva, Falzeder, Ernst and Giampieri-Deutsch, Patrizia (eds) (1992), *The Correspondence of Sigmund Freud and Sandor Ferenczi. Volume 1, 1908–1914*. London: The Belknap Press.

Bracher, Mark (1994), 'On the Psychological and Social Functions of Language: Lacan's Theory of the Four Discourses', in Mark Bracher, Marshall W. Alcorn, Ronald J. Corthell and Françoise Massardier-Kenney (eds) (1994), *Lacanian Theory of Discourse: Subject, Structure and Society*. New York: New York University Press.

Braunthal, Julius (1965), *Zwei Generationen Arbeiterbewegung*. Vienna: Verlag der Wiener Volksbuchhandlung.

Braun-Vogelstein, Julie (1932), *Ein Menschleben. Heinrich Braun und Sein Schicksal*. Tübingen: Wunderlich.

Brazier, Mary A. B. (1959), 'The historical development of neurophysiology', in J. Field., H. Magoun and V. Hall (eds) (1959), *Handbook of Physiology*, Section 1: Neurophysiology, v. 1. Washington DC: American Physiological Society, pp. 1–58.

Brecht, Bertolt (1990) *Letters 1913–1956*. Translated by Ralph Mannheim and edited with commentary by John Willet. New York: Routledge.

Brecht, Karen, Friedrich, Volker, Hermanns, Ludger M., Kaminer, Isidor J., and Juelich, Dierk H. (eds) (1985), '*Here Life goes on in a most peculiar way . . .' Psychoanalysis before and after 1933*. London: Goethe-Institut; Hamburg: Kellner Verlag.

Breton, André (1949), 'Interview du Professeur Freud', in *Le Pas Perdu* 8th edn. Paris: Gallimard, pp. 117–18.

Breuer, Josef and Freud, Sigmund (1895), *Studies on Hysteria*, Pelican Freud Library, v. 3. Harmondsworth: Penguin (*SE*, v. 2).

Brierley, Marjorie (1939), 'A Prefatory Note on "Internalized Objects" and Depression', *International Journal of Psycho-Analysis*, v. 20, pp. 241–5.

Brierley, Marjorie (1960), Letter to Willi Hoffer, quoted in Grosskurth (1986), p. 461.

Brill, Abraham A. (1929), 'Schizophrenia and Psychotherapy', *American Journal of Psychiatry*, v. 86 (old series), pp. 519–38.

Brill, Abraham A. (1942), 'A Psychoanalyst Scans His Past', *Journal of Nervous and Mental Disease*, v. 95, pp. 537–49.

Bromberg, Philip M. (1996), 'Hysteria, Dissociation and Cure: Emmy von N Revisited', *Psychoanalytic Dialogues*, v. 6, pp. 55–72.

Bronfen, Elisabeth (1998), *The Knotted Subject. Hysteria and Its Discontents*. Princeton: Princeton University Press.

Brown, Paul (1996), *Global Warming: Can Civilisation Survive?* London: Blandford.

Brown, Phil (ed.) (1973), *Radical Psychology*. New York: Harper & Row.

Bruch, Hilde (1982), 'Frieda Fromm-Reichmann Discusses the Rose Garden Case', *Psychiatry*, v. 45, pp. 128–37.

Brun, Rudolf (1936), 'Sigmund Freuds Leistungen auf dem Gebiet der organischen Neurologie', *Schweizer Archiv für Neurologie und Psychiatrie*, v. 37, pp. 200–7.

Burgess, Adrienne (1997), *Fatherhood Re-claimed*. London: Random House.

Burgess, Adrienne and Ruxton, Sandy (1996), *Men and Their Children. Proposals for Public Policy*. London: Institute for Public Policy Research.

Burnham, John C. (1983), *Jelliffe: American Psychoanalyst and Physician and His Correspondence with Sigmund Freud and C. G. Jung*. Foreword by Arcangelo R. T. D'Amore. Correspondence edited by William McGuire. Chicago: University of Chicago Press.

Butler, Declan (1997), 'Eugenics scandal reveals silence of Swedish scientists', *Nature*, v. 389, p. 9.

Bynum, W. F. (1994), *Science and the Practice of Medicine in the Nineteenth Century*. Cambridge: Cambridge University Press.

Cabot, Richard C. (1908), 'The American Type of Psychotherapy. An Introduction', *Psychotherapy. A Course of Reading Combining Sound Psychology, Sound Medicine and Sound Religion*, v. 1, pp. 1–12.

Cardinal, Marie (1975), *The Words to Say It*. Translated by Pat Goodheart. London: The Women's Press.

Cassidy, David C. (1992), *Uncertainty. The Life and Science of Werner Heisenberg*. New York: W. H. Freeman.

Chandresekhar, S. (1987), *Truth and Beauty. Aesthetics and Motivations in Science*. Chicago: University of Chicago Press.

Chertok, L. (1961), 'On the Discovery of the Cathartic Method', *International Journal of Psycho-Analysis*, v. 42, pp. 284–7.

Chesler, Phyllis (1972), *Women and Madness*. New York: Avon.

Chiarandini, Irene Cairo (1994), 'An Interview with Arnold Richards', *American Psychoanalyst*, v. 28, no. 1, pp. 21–4.

Chodorow, Nancy (1978), *The Reproduction of Mothering: Psychoanalysis and the Sociology of Gender*. Berkeley: University of California Press.

Chodorow, Nancy (1989), *Feminism and Psychoanalytic Theory*. New Haven, CT: Yale University Press.

Cioffi, Frank (1988), ' "Exegetical Myth-Making" in Grünbaum's Indictment of Popper and Exoneration of Freud', in Peter Clark and Crispin Wright (eds), *Mind, Psychoanalysis and Science*. Oxford: Oxford University Press, pp. 61–87.

Claparède, Edouard (1926), Introduction in Sigmund Freud (1926), *Cinq Leçons sur la Psychoanalyse*. Traduction française, Yves LeLay, avec une note additonal sur la libido. Paris: Payot.

Clark, Edwin and Jacyna, L. S. (1987), *19th Century Origins of Neuroscientific Concepts*. Berkeley: University of California Press.

Clark, Ronald (1971), *Einstein: The Life and Times*. New York: Avon.

Clark, Ronald (1980), *Freud. The Man and the Cause*. London: Cape.

Claus, Carl (1884), *Elementary Textbook of Zoology*. Translated and edited by Adam Sedgwick. London: W. Swan Sonnenschein & Co.

Cocks, Geoffrey (1985), *Psychotherapy in the Third Reich. The Goering Institute*. Oxford: Oxford University Press.

Cocks, Geoffrey (ed.) (1994), *Curve of Life. Correspondence of Heinz Kohut 1923–1981*. Chicago and London: University of Chicago Press.

Coles, Robert (1992), *Anna Freud. The Dream of Psychoanalysis*. Reading, MA: Addison Wesley.

Conolly, John (1856), *The Treatment of the Insane Without Mechanical Restraint*. London: Smith & Elder.

Coriat, Isador H. (1945), 'Some Personal Reminiscences of Psychoanalysis in Boston', *Psychoanalytic Review*, v. 32, pp. 1-8.

Coward, Rosalind and Ellis, John (1977), *Language and Materialism. Developments in Semiology and the Theory of the Subject*. London: Routledge & Kegan Paul.

Craig, Gordon (1995), *The Politics of the Unpolitical. German Writers and the Problem of Power, 1770–1871.* London: Oxford University Press.

Cranefield, Paul (1966), 'Freud and the "School of Helmholtz"' *Gesnerus*, v. 23, pp. 35–9.

Crick, Francis (1994), *The Astonishing Hypothesis – The scientific search for the soul.* New York: Simon & Schuster.

Crombie, A. C. (1973), 'Descartes', in Charles Coulson Gillispie (ed.), *Dictionary of Scientific Biography.* New York: Scribners.

Damasio, Antonio R. (1997), 'Towards a neuropathology of emotion and mood. News and Views', *Nature*, v. 386, pp. 769–70.

D'Amore, Arcangelo, R. J. (ed.) (1976), *William Alanson White. The Washington Years, 1903–1937.* United States Department of Health, Education and Welfare, National Institute for Mental Health, Washington DC: Superintendent of Documents, US Government Printing Office.

Daniels, Alison (1997), 'Parents filmed torturing children', *Guardian*, 27 October, p. 11.

Davies, Jody Messler and Frawley, Mary Gail (1992), 'Dissociative Processes and Transference-Countertransference Paradigms in the Psychoanalytically Oriented Treatment of Adult Survivors of Childhood Sexual Abuse', *Psychoanalytic Dialogues*, v. 2, pp. 5–36.

Davies, Jody Messler and Frawley, Mary Gail (1994), *Treating the Adult Survivor of Childhood Sexual Abuse.* New York: Basic Books.

Delbrück, Max (1946), 'A Physicist Looks at Biology', in John Cairns, Gunther S. Stent and James D. Watson (eds) (1966), *Phage and the Origins of Molecular Biology.* Cold Spring Harbor, New York: Cold Spring Harbor Laboratory of Quantitative Biology, pp. 9–24.

deMause, Lloyd (1974), 'The Evolution of Childhood', in Lloyd deMause (ed.), *The History of Childhood. The Untold Story of Child Abuse.* London: Bellew (1991), pp. 1–75.

Dembe, Allard E. (1996), *Occupation and Disease. How Social Factors Affect the Conception of Work-Related Disease.* New Haven, CT: Yale University Press.

Devereux, George (1953), 'Why Oedipus Killed Laius', *International Journal of Psycho-Analysis*, v. 34, pp. 132–41.

Dinnerstein, Dorothy (1976), *The Mermaid and the Minotaur.* New York: Harper & Row.

Drevets, Wayne C., Price, Joseph L., Simpson, Joseph R. jr, Todd, Richard D., Reich, Theodore, Vannier, Michael and Raichie, Marcus E. (1997), 'Subgenual prefrontal cortex abnormalities in mood disorders', *Nature*, v. 386, pp. 524–7.

Dubois, Paul (1905), *The Psychic Treatment of Nervous Disorders,* 5th edn.

Translated and edited by Smith Ely Jelliffe and William Alanson White. New York: Funk & Wagnalls.

Easlea, Brian (1980), *Witch Hunting, Magic and the New Philosophy*. Brighton: Harvester Press.

Easlea, Brian (1983), *Fathering the Unthinkable. Masculinity, Scientists, and the Nuclear Arms Race*. London: Pluto Press.

Edwards, Stewart (ed.) (1973), *The Communards of Paris, 1871*. London: Thames & Hudson.

Eichenbaum, Luise and Orbach, Susie (1983), *Understanding Women*. New York: Basic Books, Harmondsworth: Penguin.

Eichenbaum, Luise and Orbach, Susie (1998), 'Visibility, Invisibility. Feminism's Contribution to Psychoanalysis', *At the Threshold of the Millennium*, International Psycho-Analytic Association International Conference. Lima, Peru, 13–24 April 1998.

Ellenberger, Henri F. (1966), 'The Pathogenic Secret and its Therapeutics', *Journal of the History of the Behavioral Sciences*, v. 2, pp. 29–42.

Ellenberger, Henri F. (1968), 'Freud's Lecture on Masculine Hysteria (15 October 1886): A Critical Study', in Mark S. Micale (ed.) (1993), *Beyond the Unconscious. Essays of Henri F. Ellenberger in the History of Psychiatry*. Princeton: Princeton University Press, pp. 119–36.

Ellenberger, Henri F. (1970), *The Discovery of the Unconscious. The History and Evolution of Dynamic Psychiatry*. New York: Basic Books.

Ellenberger, Henri F. (1973), 'Moritz Benedikt (1835–1920): An Insufficiently Appreciated Pioneer of Psychoanalysis', in Mark S. Micale (ed.) (1993), *Beyond the Unconscious. Essays of Henri F. Ellenberger in the History of Psychiatry*. Princeton: Princeton University Press, pp. 104–18.

Ellis, Havelock (1898), 'Hysteria in Relation to the Sexual Emotions', *The Alienist and Neurologist*, v. 19, pp. 599–615.

Eurobarometer (1993), *Europeans and Their Families*. Brussels: EEC.

Evans, Dylan (1996), *An Introductory Dictionary of Lacanian Psychoanalysis*. London: Routledge.

Exner, Sigmund (1877), 'Über Lumen-erweiternde Muskeln', *Sitzungberichte der Mathematisch-Naturwissenschaftlichen Classe der Kaiserlichen Akademie der Wissenschaften, Wien*, 3 Abteilung, Band 75, pp. 6–14.

Exner, Sigmund (1893), 'Biographische Skizze', in Otto Fleischl von Marxow (ed.), *Gesammelte Abhandlungen von Dr Ernst Fleischl von Marxow*. Leipzig: Johann Barth.

Fairbairn, W. Ronald D. (1929), 'Impressions of the 1929 International Congress of Psychoanalysis', in Ellinor Fairbairn Birtles and David E. Scharff (eds) (1994), *From Instinct to Self: Selected Papers of W. R. D.*

Fairbairn. Vol. II: Applications and Early Contributions. London: Jason
Aronson, pp. 454–61.

Fairbairn, W. Ronald D. (1935), 'The Sociological Significance of Commu-
nism in the Light of Psychoanalysis', in W. Ronald D. Fairbairn (1952),
Psychoanalytic Studies of the Personality. London: Routledge & Kegan
Paul, pp. 233–46.

Fairbairn, W. Ronald D. (1946), 'Object-Relationships and Dynamic Structure', in W. Ronald D. Fairbairn (1952), *Psychoanalytic Studies of the
Personality.* London: Routledge & Kegan Paul, pp. 137–51.

Falzeder, Ernst (1994), 'The Threads of Psychoanalytic Filiations or Psychoanalysis Taking Effect', *Cahiers Psychiatriques Genevois*, Special Issue,
pp. 169–94.

Falzeder, Ernst and Brabant, Eva (eds) (1996), with the collaboration of
Patrizia Giamperi-Deutsch, *The Correspondence of Sigmund Freud &
Sandor Ferenczi. Volume 2, 1914–1919.* Translated by Peter T. Hoffer.
Cambridge and London: The Belknap Press.

Federn, Ernst (1963), 'Was Adler a Disciple of Freud? A Freudian View',
Journal of Individual Psychology, v. 19, pp. 80–1.

Ferenczi, Sándor (1909), 'Introjection and Transference', in Sándor Ferenczi
(1952), *First Contributions to Psycho-Analysis.* London: The Hogarth
Press, pp. 35–93.

Ferenczi, Sándor (1920), 'The Further Development of an Active Therapy in
Psychoanalysis', in Sándor Ferenczi (1980), *Further Contributions to the
Theory and Technique of Psycho-Analysis.* New York: Brunner/Mazel,
pp. 198–217.

Ferenczi, Sándor (1926), Preface to Sándor Ferenczi (1980), *Further Contributions to the Theory and Technique of Psycho-Analysis.* New York:
Brunner/Mazel, pp. 7–9.

Ferenczi, Sándor (1931), 'Child Analysis in the Analysis of Adults', in Sándor
Ferenczi (1955), *Final Contributions to Psychoanalysis.* London: The
Hogarth Press.

Fido, Martin and Fido, Karen (1996), *The World's Worst Medical Mistakes.*
London: Seven Oaks.

Fielden, J. (1836), *The Curse of the Factory System*, 2nd edn with a new
introduction by J. J. Ward, 1969. London: Frank Cass & Co.

Flax, Jane (1978), 'The Conflict Between Nurturance and Autonomy in
Mother–Daughter Relationships and Within Feminism', *Feminist Studies*,
v. 4, pp. 171–89.

Flechsig, Paul (1884), 'Zur gyneakologischen Behandlung der Hysterie',
Neurologische Zentralblatt(Leipzig), v. 19/20, pp. 1–18. Quoted in William

G. Niederland (1968), 'Schreber and Flechsig: A Further Contribution to the "Kernel of Truth" in Schreber's Delusional System', *Journal of the American Psychoanalytic Association*, v. 16, pp. 740–8.

Fleck, Ludwig (1979), *Genesis and Development of a Scientific Fact*. Chicago: University of Chicago Press.

Fodor, Jerry (1995), 'West Coast Fuzzy. Why We Don't Know How Minds Work', *The Times Supplement*, 25 August 1995, pp. 5–6.

Forbush, Bliss (1971), *The Sheppard and Enoch Pratt Hospital 1853–1970. A History*. Philadelphia: Lippincott.

Forman, Paul (1972), 'Weimar Culture, Causality and Quantum Theory, 1918–1927. Adaptation by German Physicists and Mathematicians to a Hostile Intellectual Environment', *Historical Studies in the Physical Sciences*, v. 3, pp. 1–115.

Forrester, John (1990), *The Seductions of Psychoanalysis. Freud, Lacan, Derrida*. Cambridge: Cambridge University Press.

Fortune, Christopher (1993), 'Sándor Ferenczi's Analysis of "R.N.": A Critically Important Case in the History of Psychoanalysis', *British Journal of Psychotherapy*, v. 9, pp. 436–43.

Fortune, Christopher (1991), 'Psychoanalytic Champion of "Real-Life Experience": An Interview with John Bowlby', *Melanie Klein and Object Relations*, v. 9, pp. 70–86.

Freeman, Lucy (1972), *The Story of Anna O. The Woman Who Led Freud to Psychoanalysis*. Paperback edition, 1990. New York: Paragon House.

Freud, Anna (1927), *Introduction to the Technique of Child Analysis*, in Anna Freud (1964), *The Writings of Anna Freud*, v. 1, Madison, CT: International Universities Press.

Freud, Anna (1966), *Normality and Pathology in Childhood. International Psycho-Analytic Library No. 69*. London: The Hogarth Press.

Freud, Anna (1969), 'Dr Herman Nunberg: An Appreciation', *International Journal of Psycho-Analysis*, v. 50, pp. 135–8.

Freud, Ernst L. (ed.) (1960), *The Letters of Sigmund Freud 1873–1939*. Translated by Tania and James Stern. London: The Hogarth Press.

Freud, Ernst L. (1969), 'Some Early Unpublished Letters of Freud', *International Journal of Psycho-Analysis*, v. 50, pp. 419–27.

Freud, Ernst L., Freud, Lucie and Grubich-Simitis, Ilsa (eds) (1978), *Sigmund Freud. His Life in Pictures and Words*. Translated by Christine Trollope. London: André Deutsch.

Freud, Martin (1957), *Glory Reflected. Sigmund Freud, Man and Father*. London: Angus & Robertson.

Freud, Martin (1967), 'Who was Freud?' in Josef Fraenkel (ed.), *The Jews of*

Austria. Essays on Their Life, History and Destruction. London: Valentine, pp. 197–213.

Freud, Sigmund (1877), 'Über den Ursprung der hinteren Nervenwurzeln im Ruckenmark von Ammocoetes (Petromyzon Planeri)', *Sitzungberichte der Mathematisch-Naturwissenschaftlichen Classe der Kaiserlichen Akademie der Wissenschaften, Wien*, 3 Abteilung, Band 75, pp. 15–27.

Freud, Sigmund (1884), 'Die Struktur der Elementes des Nervensystems', *Jahrbuche für Psychiatrie und Neurologie*, v. 5, pp. 221–9.

Freud, Sigmund (1886a), 'Report on my Studies in Paris and Berlin: Carried out with the Assurance of a Travelling Bursary Granted from the University Jubilee Fund' (October 1885–end March 1886). *SE*, v. 1, pp. 5–15.

Freud, Sigmund (1886b), 'Observation of a Severe Case of Hemi-Anaesthesia in a Hysterical Male', *SE*, v. 1, pp. 25–31.

Freud, Sigmund (1888), 'Hysteria', *SE*, v. 1, pp. 41–57.

Freud, Sigmund (1891), *On Aphasia. A Critical Study*. New York: International Universities Press (1953).

Freud, Sigmund (1893a), 'Charcot', *SE*, v. 3, pp. 11–23.

Freud, Sigmund (1893b), 'On the physical mechanism of hysterical phenomena', *SE*, v. 3, pp. 27–39.

Freud, Sigmund (1893c), 'Some Points for a Comparative Study of Organic and Hysterical Motor Paralyses', *SE*, v. 1, pp. 157–66.

Freud, Sigmund (1893d), *Zur Kenntniss der cereballen Diplegien des Kinderalters*. Leipzig and Vienna: Deuticke.

Freud, Sigmund (1894), 'The Neuro-Psychoses of Defence', *SE*, v. 3, pp. 45–61.

Freud, Sigmund (1895a), 'Obsessions and Phobias', *SE*, v. 3, pp. 74–82.

Freud, Sigmund (1895b), 'On the Grounds for Detaching a Particular Syndrome from Neurasthenia under the Description "Anxiety Neurosis"', *SE*, v. 3, pp. 90–115.

Freud, Sigmund (1895c), 'A Reply to Criticisms of My Paper on Anxiety Neurosis', *SE*, v. 3, pp. 123–39.

Freud, Sigmund (1896a), 'Heredity and the Etiology of the Neurosis', *SE*, v. 3, pp. 143–56.

Freud, Sigmund (1896b), 'Further Remarks on the Neuro-Psychoses of Defence', *SE*, v. 3, pp. 162–85.

Freud, Sigmund (1896c), 'On the Etiology of Hysteria', *SE*, v. 3, pp. 191–221.

Freud, Sigmund (1897a), 'Abstracts of the Scientific Writings of Dr. Sigm. Freud 1877–1897', *SE*, v. 3, pp. 227–43.

Freud, Sigmund (1897b), *Infantile Cerebral Paralysis*. Miami: University of Miami Press (1968).

Freud, Sigmund (1900), *The Interpretation of Dreams*, 3rd (revised) English edn (1931). New York: Basic Books (*SE*, v. 4–5).

Freud, Sigmund (1904), Obituary of Professor S. Hammerschlag, *SE*, v. 9, pp. 255–6.

Freud, Sigmund (1905a), 'A Case of Hysteria', *SE*, v. 7, pp. 77–8.

Freud, Sigmund (1905b), 'On Psychotherapy', *SE*, v. 7, pp. 257–68.

Freud, Sigmund (1912a), 'The Dynamics of Transference', *SE*, v. 12, pp. 99–106.

Freud, Sigmund (1912b), 'Recommendations to Physicians Practising Psychoanalysis', *SE*, v. 12, pp. 111–20.

Freud, Sigmund (1913a), Preface to Bourke's *Scatologic Rites of All Nations*, *SE*, v. 12, pp. 335–7.

Freud, Sigmund (1913b), 'Two Lies Told by Children', *SE*, v. 12, pp. 306–7.

Freud, Sigmund (1914), 'On the History of the Psychoanalytic Movement', Pelican Freud Library, v. 15. Harmondsworth: Penguin, pp. 63–128 (*SE*, v. 14).

Freud, Sigmund (1915a), 'Observations on Transference Love', *SE*, v. 12, pp. 159–71.

Freud, Sigmund (1915b), 'The Unconscious', *SE*, v. 14, pp. 166–71.

Freud, Sigmund (1916), *A General Introduction to Psychoanalysis*. New York: Pocket Books (1953) (*SE*, v. 16).

Freud, Sigmund (1919), 'Lines of Advance in Psycho-Analytic Therapy', *SE*, v. 17, pp. 159–68.

Freud, Sigmund (1920), 'Beyond the Pleasure Principle', Pelican Freud Library, v. 11. London: Penguin Books, pp. 275–338 (*SE*, v. 18).

Freud, Sigmund (1923a), 'Psycho-Analysis', *SE*, v. 18, pp. 235–54.

Freud, Sigmund (1923b), 'The Ego and the Id', *SE*, v. 19, pp. 1–66.

Freud, Sigmund (1925), 'An Autobiographical Study', Pelican Freud Library. v. 15. London: Penguin Books, pp. 189–255 (*SE*, v. 20).

Freud, Sigmund (1926), 'The Question of Lay Analysis', *SE*, v. 20, pp. 183–258.

Freud, Sigmund (1931), 'Female Sexuality', Pelican Freud Library, v. 9. London: Penguin Books, pp. 371–92 (*SE*, v. 21).

Freud, Sigmund (1933), 'New Introductory Lectures on Psychoanalysis', Pelican Freud Library, v. 2. London: Penguin Books (*SE*, v. 22).

Freud, Sigmund (1937), 'Analysis Terminable and Interminable', *SE*, v. 23, pp. 216–53.

Freud, Sigmund (1939), 'Moses and Monotheism', *SE*, v. 23, pp. 7–137.

Freud, Sigmund (1940), 'An Outline of Psycho-Analysis', *SE*, v. 23, pp. 144–207.

Freud, Sigmund (1953), *A General Introduction to Psychoanalysis*. Translated by Joan Riviere. New York: Pocket Books.

Friedländer, Adolf, A. (1911), 'Hysteria and Modern Psychoanalysis', *Journal of Abnormal Psychology*, v. 5, pp. 297–319.

Furtmüller, Carl (1946), *A Biographical Essay* in Alfred Adler (1965), *Superiority and Social Interest. A Collection of Later Writings*. Heinz Ansbacher, and Rowena R. Ansbacher (eds). London: Routlege & Kegan Paul, pp. 330–93.

Gardiner, Muriel (1983), *Code Name 'Mary': Memoirs of an American Woman in the Austrian Underground*. New Haven: Yale University Press.

Gardner, Sheldon and Stevens, Gwendolyne (1992), *Red Vienna and the Golden Age of Psychology 1918–1938*. New York: Praeger.

Gay, Peter (1988), *Freud. A life for our time*. London: Dent.

Gelfand, Toby (1992), 'Sigmund-sur-Seine: Fathers and Brothers in Charcot's Paris', in Toby Gelfand and John Kerr (eds), *Freud and the History of Psychoanalysis*. Hillsdale, NJ: The Analytic Press, pp. 29–58.

Gilbert, Martin (1969), *Jewish History Atlas*. London: Macmillan.

Gilbert, Martin (1986), *The Holocaust. The Jewish Tragedy*. London: Fontana.

Gill, Merton M. (1994), *Psychoanalysis in Transition. A Personal View*. Hillside, NJ: The Analytic Press.

Gilligan, Carol (1982), *In a Different Voice: Psychological Theory and Women's Development*. Cambridge, MA: Harvard University Press.

Gilman, Sander L. (1986), *Jewish Self-Hatred: Anti-Semitism and the Hidden Language of the Jews*. Baltimore: Johns Hopkins.

Gilman, Sander L. (1993a), *The Case of Sigmund Freud. Medicine and Identity at the Fin de Siècle*. Baltimore: Johns Hopkins.

Gilman, Sander L. (1993b), 'The Image of the Hysteric', in Sander L. Gilman, Helen King, Roy Porter, G. S. Rousseau and Elaine Showalter, *Hysteria Beyond Freud*. Berkeley: University of California Press, pp. 345–452.

Goenner, Hubert (1993), 'The Reaction to Relativity Theory I: The Anti-Einstein Campaign in Germany in 1920', *Science in Context*, v. 6, pp. 107–33.

Goldman, Emma (1931), *Living My Life*, v. 1. New York: Knopf.

Goldstein, Rebecca (1983), *The Mind–Body Problem. A Novel*. New York: Dell.

Gorkin, Michael (1987), *The Uses of the Countertransference*. Northvale, NJ: Jason Aronson.

Gornick, Vivian (1983), *Women in Science. Portraits from a World in Transition*. New York: Simon & Schuster.

Gosling, F. G. (1987), *Before Freud. Neurasthenia and the American Medical Community, 1870–1910*. Urbana and Chicago: University of Illinois Press.

Graber, Gustav H. (1952), 'Der Sohn-Komplex der Vater', *Der Psychologue*, v. 4, pp. 250–8.

Greenberg, Jay R., and Mitchell, Stephen A. (1983), *Object Relations and Psychoanalytic Theory*. Cambridge, MA: Harvard University Press.

Greenberg, Valerie D. (1994), ' "A Piece of the Logical Thread . . .": Freud and Physics', in Sander L. Gilman, Jutta Birmele, Jay Geller and Valerie D. Greenberg (eds), *Reading Freud's Reading*. New York: New York University Press, pp. 232–51.

Greenson Ralph, R. (1967), *The Technique and Practice of Psychoanalysis*. London: The Hogarth Press.

Griffin, Susan (1978), *Women and Nature. The Roaring Inside Her*. London: The Women's Press.

Griffin, Susan (1992). *A Chorus of Stones. The Private Life of War*. London: The Women's Press.

Grob, Gerald N. (ed.) (1985), *The Inner World of American Psychiatry 1890–1940. Selected Correspondence*. New Brunswick, NJ: Rutgers University Press.

Grosskurth, Phyllis (1986), *Melanie Klein*. London: Hodder & Stoughton.

Grünbaum, A. (1983), *The Foundations of Psychoanalysis: A Philosophical Critique*. Berkeley, CA: University of California.

Grünbaum, A. (1993), *Validation in the Clinical Theory of Psychoanalysis: A Study in the Philosophy of Psychoanalysis*. Madison, CT: International Universities Press.

Guntrip, Harry (1961), *Personality Structure and Human Interaction. The Developing Synthesis of Psychodynamic Theory*. London: Karnac.

Gupta, K. (1983), *100 Short Cases for the MRCP*. London: Chapman & Hall.

Hale, Nathan G. Jr. (1971), *James Jackson Putnam and Psychoanalysis*. Cambridge, MA: Harvard University Press.

Hale, Nathan G. Jr. (1995), *The Rise and Crisis of Psychoanalysis in the United States. Freud and the Americans, 1917–1985*. New York and London: Oxford University Press.

Hall, Granville Stanley (1881), *Aspects of German Culture*. Boston, MA: J. R. Osgood & Co.

Hall, Granville Stanley (1912), *Founders of Modern Psychology*. New York: Appleton.

Hall, Granville Stanley (1923), 'The Life and Confessions of a Psychologist', in Edward Thorndike (ed.), *Biographical Memoirs*. New York: D. Appleton.

Hamilton, Samuel W. (1945), 'Notes on the History of the American Psychopathological Association, 1910–1931', *Journal of Nervous and Mental Disease*, v. 102, pp. 30–53.

Handlbauer, Bernhard (1990), *Die Adler–Freud Controverse*. Frankfurt: Fischer.

Haraway, Donna J. (1989), *Primate Visions: Gender, Race and Nature in the World of Modern Science*. London: Routledge.

Haraway, Donna (1992), 'Otherworldly Conversations; Terran Topics; Local Terms', *Science as Culture*, v. 3, pp. 64–98.

Harding, Sandra (1986), *The Science Question in Feminism*. Ithaca, NY: Cornell University Press.

Harris, Benjamin (1995), 'The Benjamin Rush Society and Marxist Psychiatry in the United States, 1944–1951', *History of Psychiatry*, v. 6, pp. 309–31.

Harris, Benjamin and Brock, Adrian (1991), 'Otto Fenichel and the Left Opposition in Psychoanalysis', *Journal of the History of the Behavioral Sciences*, v. 27, pp. 157–65.

Harris, Benjamin and Brock, Adrian (1992), 'Freudian Psychopolitics: The Rivalry of Wilhelm Reich and Otto Fenichel, 1930–1935', *Bulletin of the History of Medicine*, v. 66, pp. 578–612.

Hartmann, Heinz (1958), *Ego Psychology and the Problem of Adaptation*. Translated by David Rapaport. Madison, CT: International Universities Press.

Hayes, William (1970), *The Genetics of Bacteria and Their Viruses*, 2nd edn. New York: Wiley.

Heimann, Paula (1950), 'On Countertransference', *International Journal of Psycho-Analysis*, v. 31, pp. 81–4.

Heller, Judith Bernays (1956), 'Freud's Mother and Father', *Commentary*, v. 21, pp. 418–21.

Herman, Judith Lewis (1992), *Trauma and Recovery. The aftermath of violence – from domestic abuse to political terror*. New York: Basic Books.

Heyck, T. W. (1982), *The Transformation of Intellectual Life in Victorian England*, London: Croom Helm.

Hinshelwood, Robert D. (1994), *Clinical Klein*. London: Free Association Books.

Hinshelwood, Robert D. (1997), 'The Elusive Concept of "Internal Objects" (1934–1943)', *International Journal of Psycho-Analysis*. v. 78, pp. 877–97.

Hirsch, Irwin (1993), 'Countertransference Enactments and Some Issues Related to External Factors in the Analyst's Life', *Psychoanalytic Dialogues*, v. 3, pp. 343–67.

Hirschmüller, Albrecht (1989), *The Life and Work of Josef Breuer. Physiology and Psychoanalysis*. New York: New York University Press.

Hirschmüller, Albrecht (1994), 'The Genesis of the *Preliminary Communication* of Breuer and Freud', in André Haynal and Ernst Falzeder (eds) (1994), *100 Years of Psychoanalysis. Contributions to the History of Psychoanalysis*. Special Issue of the 'Cahiers Psychiatriques Genevois'. Distributed by Karnac Books, London and Médecine et Hygiène, Geneva.

Hitschmann, Eduard (1910), Preface to *Freud's Theories of the Neuroses*. 1917. Translated by Dr C. R. Payne, New York: Moffat Yard & Co.

Hobsbawm, E. J. (1964), 'The Fabians Reconsidered', in *Labouring Men: Studies in the History of Labour*. London: Weidenfeld & Nicolson, pp. 250–71.

Hobsbawm, E. J. (1987), *The Age of Empire, 1875–1914*. London: Weidenfeld & Nicolson.

Hoff, Hans and Seitelberger, Franz (1952), 'The History of the Neurological School of Vienna', *Journal of Nervous and Mental Disease*, v. 116, pp. 495–505.

Hollander, Nancy Caro (1997), *Love in a Time of Hate. Liberation Psychology in Latin America*. New Brunswick, NJ: Rutgers University Press.

Holmes, Jeremy (1993), *John Bowlby and Attachment Theory*. London: Routledge.

Horkheimer, Max (1948), 'Ernst Simmel and Freudian Philosophy', *International Journal of Psycho-Analysis*, v. 29, pp. 110–13.

Horn, Ferdinand (1876), *Offener Brief an Herrn Hofrath Dr. Theodor Billroth von Dr Ferdinand Horn*. Vienna: Alfred Hölder.

Horney, Karen (1923), 'On the Genesis of the Castration Complex in Women', in Karen Horney (1967), *Feminine Psychology*. New York: Norton, pp. 39–53.

Horney, Karen (1926), 'The Flight from Womanhood', in Karen Horney (1967), *Feminine Psychology*. New York: Norton, pp. 54–70.

Hubbard, Ruth (1990), *The Politics of Women's Biology*. London: Rutgers University Press.

Hughes, Athol (ed.) (1991), *The Inner World and Joan Riviere. Collected Papers 1920–1958*. London: Karnac Books.

Hughes, Athol (ed.) (1992), 'Letters from Sigmund Freud to Joan Riviere (1921–1939)', *The International Review of Psycho-Analysis*, v. 19, pp. 265–84.

Israels, Hans and Schatzman, Morton (1993), 'The seduction theory', *History of Psychiatry*, v. 4, pp. 23–59.

Iversen, Leslie (1997), Review of *The Psychopharmacologists*, *Science*, v. 275, pp. 1438–9.

Jacob, François (1988), *The Statue Within*. New York: Basic Books.

Jacoby, Russell (1975), *Social Amnesia. A Critique of Conformist Psychology from Adler to Jung.* Boston: Beacon Press.

Jacoby, Russell (1983), *The Repression of Psychoanalysis. Otto Fenichel and the Political Freudians.* New York: Basic Books.

Jameson, Kay Redfield (1997), *The Unquiet Mind.* London: Picador.

Jászi, Oscar (1924), *Revolution and Counterrevolution in Hungary.* Introduction by R. W. Seton. London: P. S. King & Son.

Jeffrey, William D. (1992), 'Psychoanalysis in New York: Splits, Schisms, and Separations. Report on the Oral History Workshop, "Psychoanalysis in New York, Part II: Institutes and Organisational Splits, 1931–1956", held 10 May 1990 at the Annual Meeting of the American Psychoanalytic Association', *American Psychoanalyst,* v. 26, no. 4, pp. 21–3.

Jelliffe, Smith Ely (1916), 'The Physician and Psychotherapy', *Medical Record,* 24 August 1919, pp. 1–8.

Jelliffe, Smith Ely (1937), 'Sigmund Freud as Neurologist. Some Notes on His Earlier Neurobiological and Clinical Neurological Studies', *Journal of Nervous and Mental Disease,* v. 85, pp. 696–711.

Jones, Ernest (1953), *Sigmund Freud: His Life and Work. Volume One: The Young Freud 1856–1900.* London: The Hogarth Press.

Jones, Ernest (1954), 'Freud's Early Travels', *International Journal of Psycho-Analysis,* v. 35, pp. 81–4.

Jones, Ernest (1955), *Sigmund Freud: His Life and Work. Volume Two: The Years of Maturity 1901–1919.* London: The Hogarth Press.

Jones, Ernest (1957), *Sigmund Freud: His Life and Work. Volume Three: The Last Phase 1919–1939.* London: The Hogarth Press.

Jones, Ernest (1959), *Free Associations: Memories of a Psychoanalyst.* London: The Hogarth Press.

Jordanova, Ludi (1989), *Sexual Visions: Images of Gender in Science and Medicine between the Eighteenth and Nineteenth Centuries.* Brighton: Harvester Press.

Jung, Carl Gustav (1929), 'Freud and Jung Contrasts', in *Collected Works,* v. 4, *Freud and Psychoanalysis,* Gerhard Adler, Michael Fordham and Herbert Read (eds). London: Bollingen, pp. 333–40.

Jung, Carl Gustav (1946), *The Psychology of the Transference.* Translated by R. F. C. Hull, 1954. Ark Edition, 1983. London: Routledge & Kegan Paul.

Jung, Carl Gustav (1949), Foreword to *The I Ching or Book of Changes.* The Richard Wilhelm Translation rendered into English by Cary F. Baynes. Bollingen Series XIX. Princeton: Princeton University Press (1950).

Jung, Carl Gustav (1961), *Memories, Dreams, Reflections.* Recorded and edited by Aniela Jaffe. London: Fontana.

Kahr, Brett (1991), 'The Sexual Molestation of Children: Historical Perspectives', *The Journal of Psychohistory*, v. 19, pp. 191–214.

Kahr, Brett (1996), *D. W. Winnicott. A Biographical Portrait*. London: Karnac Books.

Kapp, Yvonne (1976), *Eleanor Marx. The Crowded Years*. London: Virago.

Karpf, Anne (1996), *The War After*. London: Minerva.

Kausen, Rudolf (1972), 'Laius Complex and Mother–Child Symbiosis', *Journal of Individual Psychology*, v. 28, pp. 33–7.

Keller, Evelyn Fox (1985), *Reflections on Gender and Science*. New Haven, CT: Yale University Press.

Kerr, John (1994), *A Most Dangerous Method. The Story of Jung, Freud, and Sabina Spielrein*. London: Sinclair-Stevenson.

Kiell, Norman (1988), *Freud Without Hindsight: Reviews of His Work 1893–1939*. Madison, CT: International Universities Press.

King, Pearl (1993), 'John Bowlby', *International Journal of Psycho-Analysis*, v. 74, pp. 823–7.

King, Pearl and Steiner, Riccardo (eds) (1991), *The Freud–Klein Controversies 1941–1945*. London: Routledge.

Klein, Dennis B. (1985), *Jewish Origins of the Psychoanalytic Movement*. London: University of Chicago Press.

Klein, Donald (1996), 'Reaction patterns to psychotropic drugs and the discovery of panic disorder', in interviews by David Healy, *The Psychopharmacologists*. London: Chapman & Hall.

Klein, Melanie (1921), 'The Child's Resistance to Enlightenment', in Melanie Klein (1992), *Love, Guilt and Reparation and Other Works 1921–1945*. *The Writings of Melanie Klein. Volume 1*. London: Karnac Books (1995), pp. 25–53.

Klein, Melanie (1923), 'Early Analysis', in Melanie Klein (1992), *Love, Guilt and Reparation and Other Works 1921–1945*. *The Writings of Melanie Klein. Volume 1*. London: Karnac Books (1995), pp. 77–105.

Klein, Melanie (1927), 'Symposium on Child Analysis', *International Journal of Psycho-Analysis*, v. 8, pp. 339–70.

Klein, Melanie (1932), *The Psychoanalysis of Children*. London: The Hogarth Press.

Klein, Melanie (1933), 'The Early Development of Conscience in the Child', in Melanie Klein (1992), *Love, Guilt and Reparation and Other Works 1921–1945*. *The Writings of Melanie Klein. Volume 1*. London: Karnac Books (1995), pp. 248–57.

Klein, Melanie (1946), 'Notes on Some Schizoid Mechanisms', in *Envy, Gratitude and Other Works 1946–1963*. New York: Dell (1976), pp. 1–24.

Kline, George M., Mitchell, Harry W., Ruggles, Arthur H., Copp, Owen and Smith, Samuel E. (1926), 'Report of the Special Committee on St Elizabeth's Hospital', *Medical Record*, v. 87, pp. 2103–4.

Knoepfmacher, Hugo (1938), 'Sigmund Freud in High School', *American Imago*, v. 36, pp. 287–300.

Koestler, Arthur (1952), *Arrow in the Blue*. New York: Macmillan.

Kohut, Heinz (1977), *Restoration of the Self*. New York: International Universities Press.

Krull, Marianne (1979), *Freud and His Father*. Translated by Arnold J. Pomerans, 1986. New York: Norton.

Kupersmidt, Jane (1998), Review of *The Lacanian Subject, Psychoanalytic Books*, v. 9, pp. 61–6.

Kvarnes, Robert G. (1976), 'The Founding of the William Alanson White Psychiatric Foundation', in R. J. Arcangelo D'Amore (ed.) (1976), *William Alanson White. The Washington Years, 1903–1937*. United States Department of Health, Education and Welfare, National Institutes for Mental Health, Washington DC: Superintendent of Documents, US Government Printing Office, pp. 123–9.

Lacan, Jacques (1966), 'Responses to Students of Philosophy Concerning the Object of Psychoanalysis', in Joan Copjec (ed.) (1990), *Television*. New York: Norton, pp. 107–16.

Lacan, Jacques (1975), *Le Séminaire de Jacques Lacan. Livre XX. Encore 1972–1973*. Paris: Editions du Seuil.

Lacan, Jacques (1988), *The Seminar of Jacques Lacan. Book I. Freud's Papers on Technique 1953–1954*. Edited by Jacques-Alain Miller. Translated with notes by John Forrester. Cambridge: Cambridge University Press.

Lacan, Jacques (1991), *Le Séminaire de Jacques Lacan. Livre XVII. L'envers de la psychanalyse 1969–1970*. Paris: Editions du Seuil.

Lacan, Jacques (1994), *The Four Fundamental Concepts of Psychoanalysis*. Edited by Jacques-Alain Miller. Translated by Alan Sheridan. Introduction by David Macey. Harmondsworth: Penguin Books.

Langer, Marie (1981), *From Vienna to Nicaragua. Journey of a Psychoanalyst*. Translated by Margaret Hooks, 1989. London: Free Association Books.

Langer, Marie (1989), 'Psychoanalysis without the couch', *Free Associations*, no. 15, pp. 60–6.

Langer, Marie and Varchevker, Arturo (1989), 'Psychoanalysis and revolution in Latin America', *Free Associations*, no. 15, pp. 44–59.

Lasch, Christopher (1981), 'The Freudian Left and Cultural Revolution', *New Left Review*, no. 129, September–October, pp. 23–34.

Latour, Bruno and Woolgar, Steve (1986), *Laboratory Life. The Construction of Scientific Facts*, 2nd edn. Princeton: Princeton University Press.

Lee, Jonathon Scott (1990), *Jacques Lacan*. Amherst, MA: University of Massachusetts Press.

Lennon, Peter (1996), 'The evil sisters of mercy', *Guardian*, Part 2, 20 March, p. 4.

Lennon, Thomas M. (1993), *The Battle of the Gods and Giants. The Legacies of Descartes and Gassendi, 1655–1715*. Princeton: Princeton University Press.

Lesky, Erna (1976), *The Vienna Medical School of the 19th Century*. London, Baltimore: Johns Hopkins.

Lessard, Suzanne (1997), *The Architect of Desire: Beauty and Danger in the Stanford White Family*. London: Weidenfeld & Nicolson.

Leviné-Meyer, Rosa (1973), *Leviné. The Life of a Revolutionary*. Farnborough: Saxon House.

Lewis, Nolan D. C. (1931), 'Research in Psychiatry', *St Elizabeths Hospital Bulletin*, no. 7, US Department of the Interior, pp. 33–40.

Leys, Ruth (1981), 'Meyer's Dealings with Jones: A Chapter in the History of the American Response to Psychoanalysis', *Journal of the History of the Behavioral Sciences*, v. 17, pp. 445–65.

Lichtman, Richard (1982), *The Production of Desire. The Integration of Psychoanalysis into Marxist Theory*. New York: The Free Press.

Lidz, Ruth Wilmanns and Lidz, Theodore (1992), Letter to the Editor, *American Psychoanalyst*, v. 26, no. 2, p. 27.

Lomas, Peter (1987), *The Limits of Interpretation*. Harmondsworth: Penguin.

Löwenfeld, Leopold (1899), 'Die Freud'sche Theorie von der Sexualität in der Aetiologie der Neurosen', in *Sexualleben und Nervenleiden*. Wiesbaden: J. F. Bergmann, pp. 192–200.

Luepnitz, Deborah Anna (1988), *The Family Interpreted. Feminist Theory in Clinical Practice*. New York: Basic Books.

Macpherson, Gordon (1992) (ed.), *Black's Medical Dictionary*. 37th edn. London: A. & C. Black.

Maier, Charles S. (1975), *Recasting Bourgeois Europe*. Princeton: Princeton University Press.

Maitron, Jean and Haupt, Georges (eds) (1971), *Dictionnaire Biographique du Mouvement Ouvrier International*. Paris: Editions Ouvriers.

Mandel, Ernest (1969), Introduction to Leon Trotsky (1975), *The Struggle Against Fascism in Germany*. Harmondsworth: Penguin.

Marcuse, Herbert (1955), *Eros and Civilisation. A Philosophical Inquiry into Freud*. New York: Vintage.

Marx, Karl (1845), 'Concerning Feuerbach', in Karl Marx (1992), *Early*

Writings. Introduction by Lucio Colletti. Translated by Rodney Livingstone and Gregor Benton. Harmondsworth: Penguin Classics.

Masson, Jeffrey Moussaieff (1984), *The Assault on Truth. Freud and Child Sexual Abuse*. London: HarperCollins.

Masson, Jeffrey Moussaieff (trans. and ed.) (1985), *The Complete Letters of Sigmund Freud to Wilhelm Fliess, 1887–1904*. Cambridge, MA: The Belknap Press.

Masson, Jeffrey Moussaieff and Schröter, Gerhard (eds) (1986), *Sigmund Freud. Briefe An Wilhelm Fliess, 1887–1904*. Transcribed by Gerhard Fichtner. Frankfurt: S. Fischer Verlag.

McGuire, William (ed.) (1974), *The Freud/Jung Letters*. Translated by Ralph Mannheim and R. F. C. Hull. London: Routledge and The Hogarth Press.

McLean, Duncan (1998), 'Personal View', *Anna Freud Centre Newsletter*, no. 3, Summer 1998.

McLynn, Frank (1996), *Carl Gustav Jung*. New York: Bantam.

Meisel, Perry and Kendrick, Walter (eds) (1985), *Bloomsbury/Freud. The Letters of James and Alix Strachey*. New York: Norton.

Merchant, Carolyn (1980), *The Death of Nature. Women, Ecology and the Scientific Revolution*. San Francisco: Harper and Row.

Meyer, Adolf (1906), 'Fundamental Conceptions of Dementia Praecox', *British Medical Journal*, v. 2, pp. 757–60.

Meyer, Adolf (1922), 'Interrelations of the Domain of Neuropsychiatry', in Alfred Lief (ed.) (1948), *The Commonsense Psychiatry of Adolf Meyer. Fifty-Two Selected Papers*. New York: McGraw-Hill, pp. 565–75.

Meyer-Palmedo, Ingeborg and Fichtner, Gerhard (1989), *Freud-Bilbiographie mit Werkonkordanz*. Frankfurt am Main: S. Fischer Verlag.

Meyerson, Abraham, Ayer, James B., Putnam, Tracy J., Keeler, Clyde E., and Alexander, Leo (1936), *Eugenical Sterilisation*. New York: Macmillan.

Micale, Mark S. (1990), 'Hysteria and its historiography: the future perspective', *History of Psychiatry*, v. 1, pp. 33–124.

Micale, Mark S. (1995), *Approaching Hysteria. Disease and Its Interpretations*. Princeton: Princeton University Press.

Middlemore, Merell P. (1941), *The Nursing Couple*. London: Hamish Hamilton.

Millar, Stuart (1998), 'Blood and Black Gold', *Guardian*, G2. 6 July, pp. 1–3.

Miller, Arthur I. (1986), 'On Einstein's Invention of Special Relativity', in *Frontiers of Physics: 1900–1911. Selected Essays*. Boston: Birkhauser, pp. 191–216.

Miller, Jean Baker (1983), *Toward a New Psychology of Women*. Boston: Beacon Press.

Milton, Nan (1978), Introduction to John McLean, *In the Rapids of Revolution. Essays, Articles and Letters 1902–1923*. London: Allison & Busby, pp. 9–25.

Mitchell, Juliet (1974), *Psychoanalysis and Feminism*. New York: Pantheon.

Mitchell, Juliet and Rose, Jacqueline (eds) (1982), *Feminine Sexuality: Jacques Lacan and the école freudienne*. Translated by Jacqueline Rose. New York: W. W. Norton.

Mitchell, Peter Chalmers (1937), *My Fill of Days*. London: Faber & Faber.

Mitchell, Stephen A. (1988), *Relational Concepts in Psychoanalysis. An Integration*. Cambridge, MA: Harvard University Press.

Mitchell, Stephen A. (1997), *Influence and Autonomy in Psychoanalysis*. Hillside, NJ: The Analytic Press.

Mitscherlich, Alexander (1969), 'Introduction to Panel on Protest and Revolution', *International Journal of Psycho-Analysis*, v. 50, pp. 103–8.

Moll, Albert (1912), *The Sexual Life of the Child*. Translated by Eden Paul. London: George Allen.

Molnar, Michael (ed.) (1992), *The Diary of Sigmund Freud 1929–1939. A Chronicle of Events in the Last Decade*. London: The Hogarth Press.

Monush, Barry (ed.) (1994), *The International Motion Picture Almanac*, 65th edn. New York: Quigley.

Moore, Walter (1994), *A Life of Erwin Schrödinger*. Cambridge: Canto.

Morton, A. L. (1938), *A People's History of England*. London: Victor Gollancz.

Mühlleitner, Elke (1992), *Biographisches Lexikon der Psychoanalyse*. Tübingen: edition diskord.

Münsterer, Hans Otto (1963), *The Young Brecht*. English translation 1992. London: Libris.

Murchison, Carl (ed.) (1930), *A History of Psychology in Autobiography*, v. 1. Worcester, MA: Clark University Press, pp. 63–97.

Musto, D. F. (1996), 'The Pentagon and Psychological Research', *The Times Literary Supplement*, 12 January, p. 6.

Newcomb, Nora and Lerner, Jeffrey C. (1982), 'Britain Between the Wars: The Historical Context of Bowlby's Theory of Attachment', *Psychiatry*, v. 45, pp. 1–12.

Newman, Alexander (1995), *Non-Compliance in Winnicott's Words. A Companion to the Work of Donald Winnicott*. London: Free Association Books.

Noble, David F. (1992), *A Work Without Women. The Christian Clerical Culture of Western Science*. New York: Knopf.

Nunberg, Hermann and Federn, Ernst (eds) (1962), *Minutes of the Vienna Psychoanalytic Society*, v. 1: 1906–1908. New York: International Universities Press.

Nunberg, Hermann and Federn, Ernst (eds) (1967), *Minutes of the Vienna Psychoanalytic Society*, v. 2: 1908–1910. New York: International Universities Press.

Nunberg, Hermann and Federn, Ernst (eds) (1974), *Minutes of the Vienna Psychoanalytic Society*, v. 3: 1910–1911. New York: International Universities Press.

Nunberg, Hermann and Federn, Ernst (eds) (1975), *Minutes of the Vienna Psychoanalytic Society*, v. 4: 1911–1917. New York: International Universities Press.

Oakes, David (1997), 'Support Coalition and *Dendron*', *Psychology Politics Resistance Newsletter*, no. 4. Bolton Institute, Deane Road, Bolton UK BL3 5AB, pp. 5–9.

Obermayer, Albert von (1893), *Zur Erinnerung an Josef Stefan*. Vienna-Leipzig.

Oberndorf, Clarence P. (1949), 'Forty Years of Psycho-Analytic Psychiatry. The Paul Schilder Memorial Lecture', *International Journal of Psycho-Analysis*, v. 30, pp. 153–61.

Orbach, Susie (1978), *Fat is a Feminist Issue*. New York: Berkley Books.

Orbach, Susie and Eichenbaum, Luise (1995), 'From Objects to Subjects', *British Journal of Psychotherapy*, v. 12, pp. 89–97.

Pais, Abraham (1994), *Einstein Lived Here*. Oxford: Oxford University Press.

Paskauskas, R. Andrew (ed.) (1993), *The Complete Correspondence of Sigmund Freud and Ernest Jones 1908–1939*. London: The Belknap Press.

Paul, Moli and Bluck, Gill (1997), 'Entering the world of psychotherapy: General psychiatric trainees take their first steps', *British Journal of Psychotherapy*, v. 14, pp. 221–32.

Person, Ethel Spector (1990), 'The Columbia University Center for Psychoanalytic Training and Research', *American Psychoanalyst*, v. 24, no. 2, pp. 9–12.

Pesquet, Jacques (1968), *Soviets at Saclay?* Paris: Librarie François Maspero.

Pfeiffer, Ernst (ed.) (1972), *Sigmund Freud and Lou Andreas-Salomé Letters*. Translated by William and Elaine Robson-Scott. London: The Hogarth Press.

Phillips, John (1985), *It Happened in Our Lifetime. A Memoir in Words and Pictures*. London: Michael Joseph.

Pickering, Andrew (1984), *Constructing Quarks. A Sociological History of Particle Physics*. Chicago: University of Chicago Press.

Pines, Malcolm (1983), 'Change and Innovation, Decay and Renewal in Psychotherapy', *British Journal of Psychotherapy*, v. 4, pp. 76–85.

Poincaré, Henri (1913), *The Foundations of Science*. New York: The Science Press.

Porter, Roy (1987), *Mind-Forg'd Manacles. A History of Madness in England from the Restoration to the Regency*. Harmondsworth: Penguin.

Prater, Donald (1986), *A Ringing Glass. The Life of Rainer Maria Rilke*. Oxford: The Clarendon Press.

Pugh, Martin (1994), *State and Society: British political and social history, 1870–1992*. Dunton Green: Edward Arnold.

Puner, Helen Walker (1949), *Freud. His Life and His Mind*. London: Grey Walls.

Putnam, James J. (1910), 'Personal Experience with Freud's Psychoanalytic Method', *Journal of Nervous and Mental Disease*, v. 37, pp. 657–74. Discussion of Putnam's paper is published on pages 630–9.

Quinn, Susan (1988), *A Mind of Her Own. The Life of Karen Horney*. Reading, MA: Addison-Wesley.

Racker, Heinrich (1968), *Transference and Countertransference*. Madison CT: International Universities Press.

Rangell, Leo (1991), 'A Conversation with Leo Rangell', *American Psychoanalyst*. v. 27, no. 2, pp. 15–18.

Ree, Jonathon (1974), *Descartes*. London: Allen Lane.

Reeves, Nigel (1990), 'Kleist's Bedlam: abnormal psychology and psychiatry in the works of Heinrich von Kleist', in Andrew Cunningham and Nicholas Jardine (eds) (1990), *Romanticism and the Sciences*. Cambridge: Cambridge University Press, pp. 280–94.

Reidel-Schrewe, Ursula (1994), 'Freud's Début in the Sciences', in Sander L. Gilman, Jutta Birmele, Jay Geller and Valerie D. Greenberg (eds), *Reading Freud's Reading*. New York: New York University Press, pp. 1–22.

Reil, Johannes (1803), *Rhapsodien über die Anwendung der psychichen Curmethode auf Geisteszerruettungen*. Halle, Germany.

Rhodes, Richard (1986), *The Making of the Atomic Bomb*. London: Penguin.

Ritvo, Lucille B. (1972), 'Carl Claus as Freud's Professor of the New Darwinian Biology', *International Journal of Psycho-Analysis*, v. 53, pp. 277–83.

Riviere, Joan (1927), 'Symposium on Child Analysis', *International Journal of Psycho-Analysis*, v. 8, pp. 370–7.

Riviere, Joan (1939), 'On the Genesis of Psychic Conflict in Earliest Infancy', in Athol Hughes (ed.) (1991), *Joan Riviere. The Inner World and Joan Riviere. Collected Papers 1920–1958*. London: Karnac Books, pp. 272–300.

Roazen, Paul and Swerdloff, Bluma (1995), *Heresy. Sandor Rado and the Psychoanalytic Movement*. London: Jason Aronson.

Ross, Dorothy (1972), *Granville Stanley Hall. The Psychologist as Prophet.* Chicago: University of Chicago Press.

Ross, John Munder (1982), 'Oedipus Revisited. Laius and the "Laius Complex"', *Psychoanalytic Study of the Child*, v. 37, pp. 169–200.

Roudinesco, Elisabeth (1990), *Jacques Lacan & Co. A History of Psychoanalysis in France 1925–1985.* Translated by Jeffrey Mehlman. London: Free Association Books.

Ryan, Michael (1996), *Secret Life. An Autobiography.* London: Bloomsbury.

Rycroft, Charles (1961), 'Melanie Klein', in Charles Rycroft (1985), *Psychoanalysis and Beyond.* London: The Hogarth Press, pp. 128–31.

Rycroft, Charles (1991), 'On Selfhood and self-awareness', in *Viewpoints.* London: The Hogarth Press, pp. 147–62.

Samuels, Andrew (1993), *The Political Psyche.* London: Routledge.

Samuels, Andrew (1995), 'The Good-Enough Father of Whatever Sex', *Feminism & Psychology*, v. 5, pp. 511–30.

Samuels, Rafael and Thompson, Paul (1990), *The Myths We Live By.* London: Routledge.

Scharff, David E. and Birtles, Ellinor Fairbairn (eds) (1994), *From Instinct to Self. Selected Papers of W. R. D. Fairbairn. Vol. I, Clinical and Theoretical Papers.* London: Jason Aronson.

Schebera, Jürgen (1995), *Kurt Weill. An illustrated life.* New Haven: Yale University Press.

Schiebinger, Londa (1993), *Nature's Body: Gender and the Making of Modern Science.* Boston: Beacon Press.

Schneiderman, Stuart (1983), *Jacques Lacan: The Death of an Intellectual Hero.* Cambridge, MA: Harvard University Press.

Schrader, Bärbel and Schebera, Jürgen (1990), *The 'Golden Twenties': Art and Literature in the Weimar Republic.* London: Yale University Press.

Schusdek, Alexander (1966), 'Freud's "Seduction Theory": A Reconstruction', *Journal of the History of the Behavioral Sciences*, v. 2, pp. 159–68.

Schwalbe, Gustav (1879), 'The Oculomotor Ganglion: A Contribution to the Comparative Anatomy of Cranial Nerves', *Jenaische Zeitschrift für Naturwissenschaft*, v. 13, pp. 172–268.

Schwartz, Joseph (1992), *The Creative Moment: How Science Made Itself Alien to Western Culture.* New York: HarperCollins; London: Cape.

Schwartz, Joseph (1996), 'Physics, Philosophy, Psychoanalysis and Ideology. On Engaging with Adolf Grünbaum', *Psychoanalytic Dialogues*, v. 6, pp. 503–13.

Schwartz, J., Feldstein, S., Fink, M., Shapiro, D. M. and Itil, T. M. (1971),

'Evidence for a Characteristic EEG Response to Thiopental', *Electro-encephalography and Clinical Neurology*, v. 31, pp. 149–53.

Scull, Andrew (1984), 'Desperate Remedies: a Gothic tale of madness and modern medicine', *Psychological Medicine*, v. 17, pp. 561–77.

Scull, Andrew (1993), *The Most Solitary Affliction. Madness and Society in Britain 1700–1900*. New Haven, CT: Yale University Press.

Searles, Harold (1967), 'The "Dedicated Physician" in the Field of Psychotherapy and Psychoanalysis', in Harold Searles (1979), *Countertransference and Related Subjects. Selected Papers*. Madison, CT: International Universities Press, pp. 71–88.

Segal, Hanna (1973), *Introduction to the Work of Melanie Klein*. London: The Hogarth Press.

Shapin, Steven (1994), *A Social History of Truth. Civility and Science in 17th Century England*. Chicago: University of Chicago Press.

Shapin, Steven (1996), *The Scientific Revolution*. Chicago: University of Chicago Press.

Sherrington, Charles Scott (1906), *Integrative Action of the Nervous System*. New York: Scribners.

Shorter, Edward (1992), 'The Two Medical Worlds of Sigmund Freud', in Toby Gelfand and John Kerr (eds) (1992), *Freud and the History of Psychoanalysis*. Hillsdale, NJ: The Analytic Press, pp. 59–78.

Shorter, Edward (1997), *A History of Psychiatry. From the Era of the Asylum to the Age of Prozac*. New York: John Wiley & Sons.

Showalter, Elaine (1985), *The Female Malady. Women, Madness and English Culture, 1830–1890*. London: Virago.

Showalter, Elaine (1993), 'Hysteria, Feminism and Gender', in Sander L. Gilman et al., *Hysteria Beyond Freud*. Berkeley: University of California Press, pp. 286–344.

Siemens, Werner von (1893), *Inventor and Entrepreneur. Recollections of Werner von Siemens*. Translated by W. C. Coupland. London: Asher & Co.

Silver, Ann-Louise S. (1997), 'Chestnut Lodge, Then and Now. Work with a Patient with Schizophrenia and Obsessive Compulsive Disorder', *Contemporary Psychoanalysis*, v. 33, pp. 227–50.

Sinason, Valerie (ed.) (1994), *Treating the Survivors of Satanist Abuse*. London: Routledge.

Smith, David (1991), *Hidden Conversations. An Introduction to Communicative Psychoanalysis*. London: Routledge.

Smyth, Margaret H. (1938), 'Psychiatric History in California', *American Journal of Psychiatry*, v. 94, pp. 1221–42.

Sokal, Alan and Bricmont, Jean (1998), *Intellectual Impostures*. London: Profile Press.

Solms, Mark (1995), 'Is the brain more real than the mind?' *Psychoanalytic Psychotherapy*, v. 9, pp. 107–20.

Solms, Mark (1996), 'Was sind Affekte?', *Psyche*, v. 50, pp. 485–522.

Solms, Mark and Saling, Michael (1990), *A Moment of Transition. Two Neuroscientific Articles by Sigmund Freud*. London: Karnac Books.

Somkin, Fred (1973), 'Lubbock', in Charles Coulson Gillispie (ed.), *Dictionary of Scientific Biography*, New York: Scribners.

Southall, David P., Plunkett, Michael C. B., Banks, Martin W., Falkov, Adrian F. and Samuels, Martin P. (1997), 'Covert Video Recordings of Life Threatening Child Abuse: Lessons for Child Protection', *Pediatrics*, v. 100, pp. 735–60.

Stanton, Martin and Searles, Harold (1992), 'Harold Searles talks to Martin Stanton', *Free Associations*, v. 3, pp. 323–9.

Starr, Moses Allen (1913), *Organic and Functional Nervous Diseases. A Text-Book of Neurology*, 4th ed. London: Baillière, Tindall and Cox.

Steiner, George (1997), 'Review of *Hitler's Wien*', *Times Literary Supplement*, 31 January 1997.

Stekel, Wilhelm (1950), *The Autobiography of Wilhelm Stekel: The Life Story of a Pioneer Psychoanalyst*. New York: Liveright Publishing Company.

Stent, Gunther S. (1972), 'Prematurity and Uniqueness in Scientific Discovery', *Scientific American*, v. 227, December, pp. 84–93.

Stepansky, Paul E. (1976), 'The Empiricist as Rebel: Jung, Freud, and the Burdens of Discipleship', *Journal of the History of the Behavioral Sciences*, v. 12, pp. 216–39.

Stepansky, Paul E. (1983), *In Freud's Shadow. Adler in Context*. Hillsdale, NJ: The Analytic Press.

Sterba, Richard F. (1982), *Reminiscences of a Viennese Psychoanalyst*. Detroit: Wayne State University Press.

Stern, Daniel N. (1985), *The Interpersonal World of the Infant*. New York: Basic Books.

Stern, Daniel B., Mann, Carola H., Kantor, Stuart and Schlesinger, Gary (eds) (1995), *Pioneers of Interpersonal Psychoanalysis*. Hillsdale, NJ: The Analytic Press.

Stolorow, Robert D. and Atwood, George A. (1991), 'The Mind and the Body', *Psychoanalytic Dialogues*, v. 1, pp. 181–95.

Strouse, Jean (ed.) (1974), *Women & Analysis. Dialogues on Psychoanalytic Views of Femininity*. New York: Dell.

Sullivan, Harry Stack (1924), 'Schizophrenia: Its Conservative and Malignant

Features', *American Journal of Psychiatry*, v. 4 (old series, v. 81), pp. 77–91.

Sullivan, Harry Stack (1925), 'Peculiarity of Thought Processes in Schizophrenia', *American Journal of Psychiatry*, v. 5 (old series, v. 82), pp. 21–86.

Sullivan, Harry Stack (1929), 'Discussion. A. A. Brill, Schizophrenia and Psychotherapy', *American Journal of Psychiatry*, v. 9 (old series, v. 86), pp. 538–41.

Sullivan, Harry Stack (1937), 'William Alanson White. 1870–1937', *American Journal of Psychiatry*, v. 17 (old series, v. 93), pp. 1480–2.

Sullivan, Harry Stack (1953), *The Interpersonal Theory of Psychiatry*, Helen Swick Perry and Mary Ladd Gawel (eds), with an introduction by Mabel Blake Cohen. New York: Norton.

Sulloway, Frank J. (1979), *Freud, Biologist of the Mind*. New York: Basic Books.

Sutherland, John D. (1989), *Fairbairn's Journey into the Interior*. London: Free Association Books.

Suttie, Ian D. (1935), *The Origins of Love and Hate*. Republished in 1988. London: Free Association Books.

Swales, Peter J. (1982), 'Freud, Minna Bernays, and the Conquest of Rome. New Light on the Origins of Psychoanalysis', *New American Review*, v. 1, pp. 1–23.

Swales, Peter J. (1983), *Freud, Martha Bernays and the Language of Flowers*. New York: privately published. British Library shelf mark: YL.1987.a.440.

Swales, Peter J. (1986), 'Freud, His Teacher and the Birth of Psychoanalysis', in Paul E. Stepansky (ed.), *Freud, Appraisals and Reappraisals. Contributions to Freud Studies*, v. 1. Hillsdale, NJ: The Analytic Press, pp. 3–82.

Swales, Peter J. (1987), 'Freud, Katharina and the First "Wild Analysis"', in Paul E. Stepansky (ed.), *Freud, Appraisals and Reappraisals. Contributions to Freud Studies*, v. 3. Hillsdale, NJ: The Analytic Press, pp. 81–164.

Swales, Peter J. (1989a), 'Freud, Cocaine and Sexual Chemistry: The role of cocaine in Freud's conception of the libido', in Laurence Spurling (ed.), *Sigmund Freud. Critical Assessments*. London: Routledge, pp. 273–301.

Swales, Peter J. (1989b), 'Freud, Fliess and Fratricide: The role of Fliess in Freud's conception of paranoia', in Laurence Spurling (ed.), *Sigmund Freud. Critical Assessments*. London: Routledge, pp. 302–30.

Swales, Peter J. (1989c), 'Freud, Johann Weier and the Status of Seduction: The role of the witch in the concept of fantasy', in Laurence Spurling (ed.), *Sigmund Freud. Critical Assessments*. London: Routledge, pp. 331–58.

Tansey, M. J. and Burke, W. F. (1989), *Understanding Countertransference*.

From Projective Identification to Empathy. Hillsdale, NJ: The Analytic Press.

Taylor, W. S. (1928), *Morton Prince and Abnormal Psychology*. New York: D. W. Appleton.

Theweleit, Klaus (1989), Chapter 2, 'Male Bodies and the "White Terror"', in *Male Fantasies*. Cambridge: Polity Press.

Thompson, Morton (1951), *The Cry and the Covenant*. London: Heinemann.

Thompson, M. Guy and Thompson, Sharada (1998), 'Interview with Otto Nathan Will Jr.', *Contemporary Psychoanalysis*, v. 34, pp. 289–304.

Thornton, E. M. (1983), *Freud and Cocaine: The Freudian Fallacy*. London: Blond & Briggs.

Timms, Edward (1986), *Karl Kraus, Apocalyptic Satirist. Culture and Catastrophe in Habsburg Vienna*. New Haven, CT: Yale University Press.

Tomlinson, Craig (1996), 'Sandor Rado and Adolf Meyer', *International Journal of Psycho-Analysis*, v. 77, pp. 963–82.

Trevarthen, Colwyn (1993), 'The Function of Emotions in Early Infant Communication and Development', in J. Nadel and L. Camaioni (eds), *New Perspectives in Early Communicative Development*. London: Routledge.

Triarhou, Lazaros C. and del Cerro, Manuel (1985), 'Freud's Contribution to Neurology', *Archives of Neurology*, v. 42, pp. 282–7.

Tucker, Beverley R. (1936), 'Speaking of Weir Mitchell', *American Journal of Psychiatry*, v. 93, pp. 341–6.

Turkle, Sherry (1978), *Psychoanalytic Politics. Jacques Lacan and Freud's French Revolution*. New York: Basic Books.

Tylim, Isaac (1996), 'Psychoanalysis in Argentina: A Room with a View', *Psychoanalytic Dialogues*, v. 6, pp. 713–27.

Upson, Henry S. (1888), 'On gold as a staining agent for nerve tissues', *Journal of Nervous and Mental Disease*, v. 13, pp. 685–9.

van der Kolk, Bessel A. (ed.) (1987), *Psychological Trauma*. Washington: American Psychiatric Press.

Van Eeden, Frederick (1893), 'The Theory of Psychotherapy', *The Medical Magazine. A Monthly Review of Medicine, Surgery and Allied Sciences*. (London), v. 1, pp. 232–57.

Van Helden, Albert (ed.) (1989), *Sidereus Nuncius by Galileo Galilei*. Chicago and London: University of Chicago Press.

Waelder, Robert (1960), *The Basic Theory of Psychoanalysis*. New York: International Universities Press.

Walton, George L. (1908), *Why Worry?* Philadelphia: J. B. Lippincott.

Walton, George L. et al. (1910), 'Discussion [of Putnam (1910)]', *Journal of Nervous and Mental Disease*, v. 37, pp. 630–9.

Wasserman, Isidor (1950), 'Zarys charakterologii socjainej', *Zdrowie Puliczne*, v. 12, pp. 189–219.

Wasserman, Isidor (1958), Polish Review, A Letter to the Editor, *American Journal of Psychotherapy*, v. 12, pp. 623–7.

Watling, E. F. (trans.) (1947), *Sophocles. The Theban Plays*. Harmondsworth: Penguin.

Watson, G. N. (1979), 'Beauty and the Quest for Beauty in Science', *Aesthetics and Science. Proceedings of the International Symposium in Honor of Robert R. Wilson, April 27, 1979*. Fermi National Accelerator Laboratory, Batavia, Illinois.

Weigert, Edith (1939), 'Discussion on Psychoanalysis', reprinted in *Psychiatry*, v. 46, May 1983, pp. 186–92.

White, William Alanson (1909), 'The Relation of the Hospital for the Insane to the Medical Profession and to the Community', *Bulletin of St Elizabeths Hospital*, no. 1, pp. 7–11.

White, William Alanson (1913), 'Eugenics and Heredity in Nervous and Mental Disease', in William Alanson White and Smith Ely Jelliffe (eds), *The Modern Treatment of Nervous and Mental Diseases by American and British Authors*. Two volumes. London: Henry Kimpton, pp. 17–55.

White, William Alanson (1916), *Mechanisms of Character Formation*. New York: Macmillan.

White, William Alanson (1924), 'Primitive Mentality and the Racial Unconscious', *American Journal of Psychiatry*, v. 4 (old series, v. 81), pp. 661–6.

White, William Alanson (1925a), 'Notes on Suggestion, Empathy and Bad Thinking', in *Problems of Personality. Studies Presented to Dr Morton Prince, Pioneer in American Psychopathology*. London: Kegan Paul, Trench & Trubner.

White, William Alanson (1925b), 'Presidential Address', *American Journal of Psychiatry*, v. 5 (v. 82, old series), pp. 1–8.

White, William Alanson (1926), 'Review of *Group Psychology*', *Psychoanalytic Review*, v. 13, pp. 377–8.

White, William Alanson (1935), *Outlines of Psychiatry*, 14th edn. Washington DC: Nervous and Mental Disease Publishing Co.

White, William Alanson (1936), *Twentieth Century Psychiatry. Its Contribution to Man's Knowledge of Himself*. New York: Norton.

White, William Alanson (1937), 'Review of *The Origins of Love and Hate*', *Psychoanalytic Review*, v. 24, pp. 458–60.

White, William Alanson (1938), *The Autobiography of a Purpose*. New York: Doubleday.

White, William Alanson and Jelliffe, Smith Ely (eds) (1913), *The Modern*

Treatment of Nervous and Mental Diseases by American and British Authors. Two volumes. London: Henry Kimpton.

Whyte, Lancelot Law (1960), *The Unconscious Before Freud*. Republished in 1979 with an introduction by Arthur Koestler. London: Julian Friedmann.

Willett, John (1978), *The New Sobriety. Art and Politics in the Weimar Period 1917–1933*. London: Thames & Hudson.

Willett, John (1984), *Brecht in Context*. London: Methuen.

Williams, Linda Meyer (1994), 'Recall of Childhood Trauma: A Prospective Study of Women's Memories of Child Sexual Abuse', *Journal of Counselling and Clinical Psychology*, v. 62, pp. 1167–76.

Williams, Meg Harris and Waddell, Margot (1991), *The Chamber of Maiden Thought. Literary Origins of the Psychoanalytic Model of Mind*. London: Tavistock/Routledge.

Williams, Raymond (1979), *Politics and Letters. Interviews with New Left Review*. London: New Left Books.

Winnicott, D. W. (1962), 'A Personal View of the Kleinian Contribution', in D. W. Winnicott (1976), *The Maturational Processes and the Facilitating Environment*. London: The Hogarth Press, pp. 171–8.

Winnicott, D. W. (1964), 'Review of *Memories, Dreams, Reflections*', *International Journal of Psycho-Analysis*. v. 45, pp. 450–5.

Wittels, Fritz (1924), *Sigmund Freud. His Personality, His Teaching and His School*. Translated by Eden and Cedar Paul. London: Allen & Unwin.

Wolf, Ernest S. (1988), *Treating the Self. Elements of Clinical Self Psychology*. London: The Guilford Press.

Wollen, Peter (1991), 'Bitter Victory: The Art and Politics of the Situationist International', in Elisabeth Sussman (ed.), *On the passage of a few people through a rather brief moment in time: The Situationist International 1957–1972*. Cambridge, MA: The MIT Press, pp. 20–61.

Wolpert, Lewis (1992), *The Unnatural Nature of Science*. London: Faber & Faber.

Woolley, H. C. and Hall, R. D. (1925), 'Non-medical Workers and the Mental Hospital', *American Journal of Psychiatry*, v. 82 (old series), pp. 411–14.

Yalom, Irving (1974), 'Review of *Group Psychology and Ego Analysis*', in Norman Kiell (1988), *Freud Without Hindsight: Reviews of His Work 1893–1939*. New Jersey: International Universities Press, pp. 469–83.

Yang, Chen Ning (1983), *Selected Papers 1945–1980 with Commentary*. San Francisco: W. H. Freeman.

Young, Robert M. (1985), *Darwin's Metaphor. Nature's Place in Victorian Culture*. New York: Cambridge University Press.

Young, Robert M. (1986), 'Freud: scientist and/or humanist', *Free Associations*, v. 6, pp. 7–36.

Young, Robert M. (1997), 'UKCP/BCP Split: An Account', *The Psychotherapist*, no. 9, UKCP, London, pp. 6–7.

Young-Bruehl, Elisabeth (1988), *Anna Freud. A Biography*. New York: Summit Books.

Zinn, Howard (1980), *A People's History of the United States*. New York: Harper & Row.

Zulueta, Felicity de (1993), *From Pain to Violence. The Traumatic Roots of Destructiveness*. London: Whurr Publishers.

Acknowledgements

The publishers and author are grateful to the following for permission to reprint copyright material:

To Addison-Wesley for permission to reprint from *Anna Freud. The Dream of Psychoanalysis* by Robert Coles, Reading, MA: Addison-Wesley. To Harvard University Press for permission to reprint from *The Complete Letters of Sigmund Freud to Wilhelm Fliess, 1887–1904*, by Jeffrey Moussaieff Masson (trans. and ed.), Cambridge, MA: Harvard University Press, Freud material copyright © by Sigmund Freud Copyrights Ltd., editorial matter and translation copyright © 1985 by J. M. Masson; to reprint from *The Correspondence of Sigmund Freud and Sándor Ferenczi* edited by Ernst Falzeder and P. Giamperi-Deutsch, translated by Peter T. Hoffer, Cambridge, MA: Harvard University Press, Freud material copyright © 1992 E. Brabant, E. Falzeder and P. Giamperi-Deutsch; translation copyright © 1993 by the President and Fellows of Harvard College; and to reprint from *The Complete Correspondence of Sigmund Freud and Ernest Jones 1908–1939*, edited by R. Andrew Paskauskas, introduction by Riccardo Steiner, Cambridge, MA: Harvard University Press, Freud correspondence © 1993 by Sigmund Freud Copyrights Ltd., Jones correspondence © 1993 by the Estate of Sir Ernest Jones, editorial matter copyright © 1993 by R. Andrew Paskauskas by arrangement with Mark Paterson and Christine Barnard, introduction copyright © 1993 by Riccardo Steiner. To International Universities Press, Inc. for permission to reprint from Hermann Nunberg and Ernst Federn (eds) (1962, 1967, 1974, 1975), *Minutes of the Vienna Psychoanalytic Society*. Vol. 1:1906–1908, Vol.2:1908–1910, Vol.3:1910–1911, Vol.4:1911–1917; and to reprint from Norman Kiell (1988), *Freud Without Hindsight: Reviews of His Work 1893–1939*. To Mr Leonardo La Rosa of Niedeck Linder AG, Zurich, for permission to quote from an unpublished letter by Carl Jung. To Princeton University Press and Routledge for permission to reprint from

William McGuire (ed.), *The Freud/Jung Letters*, translated by Ralph Mannheim and R. F. C. Hull, copyright © 1974 by Sigmund Freud Copyrights Ltd. and Erbengemeinschaft C. G. Jung. To Sigmund Freud Copyrights, The Institute of Psycho-Analysis, The Hogarth Press, Basic Books and W. W. Norton and Company, Inc., for permission to reprint material from the *Standard Edition of the Complete Psychological Works of Sigmund Freud* (1955), translated from the German under the general editorship of James Strachey, in collaboration with Anna Freud, assisted by Alix Strachey and Alan Tyson, twenty-four volumes, London: The Hogarth Press. To The Hogarth Press and Basic Books to reprint from Ernst L. Freud (ed.) (1960), *The Letters of Sigmund Freud, 1873–1939*, translated by Tania and James Stern, London: The Hogarth Press, copyright © 1960 by Sigmund Freud Copyrights Ltd. To The Hogarth Press and Basic Books to reprint from *Sigmund Freud: His Life and Work* (three volumes, 1953, 1955, 1957), London: The Hogarth Press; and to reprint from Ernest Jones (1959), *Free Associations: Memories of a Psychoanalyst*, London: The Hogarth Press. To Rutgers University Press for permission to quote from Nancy Caro Hollander, *Love in a Time of Hate. Liberation Psychology in Latin America*, copyright © 1997 by Nancy Caro Hollander. To the Society of Authors as agents of the Strachey Trust for permission to quote from the correspondence of James and Alix Strachey.

I am grateful to the following colleagues for taking the time to respond to my queries on aspects of psychoanalysis and its history: Gwen Douglas, Luise Eichenbaum, Barbara Everall, Betsy Faulconer, John Forrester, Ilse Gubrich-Simitis, Jeffrey Masson, Peter Milford, Carolyn Morrissey, Elke Mühlleitner, Uwe Peters, Jacqueline Rose, Andrew Samuels, Peter Schoenberg, Ann-Louise Silver, Edward Shorter, Stuart Sutherland, Peter Swales, Professor Eleasar Weissbrot.

For help with German translations I am indebted to Heidi Ferid, Hilde Schoenfeld, Gisele Ruppin and Gudrun Wiborg. Riccardo Steiner, Jill Duncan and Linda Carter-Jackson made it possible for me to make very efficient use of the archive held at the Institute of Psychoanalysis in London. Robert Butler and Nigel Cochran facilitated my access to the letters of Martha Freud held at the Albert Sloman Library of the University of Essex. Fred Bauman and Marvin Kranz at the United States Library of Congress extended themselves both at a distance and on my visit to the Library to consult the psychoanalytic archive held there. Tom Roberts at the Sigmund Freud Copyrights Ltd. handled my repeated queries about sources, permissions and rules of engagement with the Freud archives with patience and good humour as well as directing my attention to the Brautbriefe archive at the University of Essex. Michael Molnar, Erica Davies and Keith Davies of the Freud Museum in London were unfailing sources of support and information. Andy Metcalf made available his interviews with Jock Sutherland. Stephen Mitchell very generously took the time to make photocopies for me of his extensive correspondence with Merton Gill. Gisele Ruppin worked miracles as my teacher of German. Gudrun Wiborg of the University of Kiel was my overall consultant on German translations as well as helping me to obtain sources in German not available in London.

I have had valuable conversations with Ellinor Fairbairn Birtles about Ronald Fairbairn, Sir Richard Bowlby about John Bowlby, Kit Fortune about Sándor Ferenczi, Brett Kahr about Donald Winnicott, Caroline Pick about belief, Roy Porter about psychoanalysis and psychiatry, Morty Schatzman about the seduction theory, Valerie Sinason about the seduction theory, Mark Solms about past and present neuropsychology, David Smith about the philosophy of science and psychoanalysis and Susan vas Dias about Anna Freud.

I was privileged to be a member of a psychoanalytic study group with Sally Berry, Margaret Green, Susie Orbach and Tom Ryan, whose depth and breadth of clinical experience was an anchor for a project that could have easily taken leave of its clinical roots. I had the benefit of a good exchange of letters with Bob Hinshelwood on the work of Melanie Klein and with Deborah Luepnitz on the work of Jacques Lacan. I thank them both for engaging with me on theoretical issues that should be more widely discussed in the literature. Mark Solms gave me the benefit of a considered reading of my account of Freud's career as a neuroscientist. Brett Kahr brought his knowledge of the literature and personalities of psychoanalysis, as well as his sharp theoretical views, to a critical reading of most of the manuscript. Colleagues and trainees at the Centre for Attachment-based Psychoanalytic Psychotherapy made me discipline my thinking for the purposes of teaching. Andrew Franklin helped shape the project in important ways in its earliest stages. From New York, Wendy Wolf at Viking Penguin made a number of valuable suggestions for cuts and additions that strengthened the book. Jane Robertson did a fine professional job of copy-editing the manuscript. Derek Johns helped me through the many stages of this project in ways large and small. Margaret Bluman was an editor divine in her patient restraint in dealing with a long, difficult project. And Susie Orbach read everything with a practised eye and pen. The book would not have been possible without her.

Index

INDEX

histology 33–4
Hitler, Adolf 13, 104
Hitschmann, Eduard 99, 113, 128
Hobsbawm, Eric 16
Hoch, August 146, 147, 155
Hofmannsthal, Hugo von 98
Hollander, Nancy 262, 263, 264, 270
Holmes, Jeremy 229
Holt, Robert 190–91
homosexuality 91, 96, 101
Horn, Ferdinand 24
Horney, Karen 187, 188, 212, 246–7, 249, 272
Horthy, Admiral Miklos 204, 205
Hug-Helmuth, Hermine 196, 246
Hughes, Athol 230, 233, 234
human subjectivity 254–8, 260–61
Hungary 200–207
Huxley, Thomas Henry 93
hypnoid states 85, 89–90
hypnosis 44–5, 59, 130
transference 140
hysteria 2, 40–62
childhood sexual abuse 65–92
displaced neural excitation 64
Freud's interest in 35–9
Freud's theories 65–92
literature 287
orthodox theories 72
psychoanalytic treatment 139–41
psychogenic origins 52–3, 56–62
symptoms 36, 40–41
treatment by Breuer and Freud 3, 40–62, 145
hysterogenic points 72

I Ching 138
id 189, 190, 233, 260
Illinois Eastern Hospital for the Insane, Kankakee, Illinois 154
impotence 112
Industrial Revolution 8, 9, 58, 283–4
Institute of Contemporary Psychoanalysis 187
Institute of Psychoanalysis, London 198
Institute for Social Research, Frankfurt 266
insulin shock therapy 163, 174
International Congress of Medicine, Budapest (1909) 103

International Psychoanalytic Association 106, 175, 254
International Psychoanalytical Congress
(1922) 247
Budapest (1919) 275
Nuremberg (1910) 110
Oxford (1929) 236
Salzburg (1908) 107, 109
Weimar (1911) 147
International Society for Medical Psychology 103
Internationalist Mental Health Team 9–10, 269
interpersonal theory (Sullivan) 176, 181, 192
interpretation, analytic 51, 102–3
Isaacs, Susan 221
Israels, Hans 87, 91
Iversen, Leslie 281

Jackson, Michael 15, 16
Jacobson, Edith 97, 267
James, William 145, 146, 151, 215
Jameson, Kay Redfield 278
Janet, Pierre 59–60, 85, 147, 148, 168
Jászi, Oscar 201, 205–6
Jeffrey, William 188
Jekels, Ludwig 128
Jelliffe, Smith Ely 29, 146, 152, 154, 157
Freud on 157
on lay analysis 175
and White 164–5
won over to psychoanalysis 155–6
Joffe, A. A. 97
Johns Hopkins University Medical School, Baltimore 149
Phipps Psychiatric Clinic 155
Johnson, Terry 81
Jones, Ernest 40, 51
American Psychoanalytic Association 149
analysis of Riviere 230–31
on Anna Freud v. Melanie Klein 211
autobiography 97
biography of Freud 18–19, 26–7, 29, 47, 56, 88, 128
British Psycho-Analytical Society 220
correspondence with Anna Freud 230–32, 234
correspondence with Sigmund Freud 103, 115, 147, 202–3, 215, 217–18, 230–31
correspondence with Jung 127

Jung on 156
and Klein 213–14, 219
on Meyer 157, 290
on Prince 156–7
on Putnam 157
support for Edith Jacobson 267
in USA 147, 151
on White 164
Jones, Gwenith 214
Jones, Katherine Jokl 214
Jones, Mervyn 214
Journal of Abnormal Psychology 146
Journal of the American Medical Association 145
Journal of Nervous and Mental Disease 164
Julia (film) 267–8
Jung, Agathli 196
Jung, Carl 93–129
American Psychopathological Association membership 148
American visitors to 146–7
chance 138
child psychoanalysis 196
and Freud 12, 93–113, 119–29, 148
impression of Jones 156
psychoanalytical theory 273–4
religion 119–20, 138, 273
on sexual abuse 82
split with Freud 12, 93–113, 119–29, 148
transference 134–5, 138–9
the unconscious 134–9
visit to United States 147
word association tests 120, 146, 147
juvenile delinquency 210

Kahane, Max 100
Kahr, Brett 74, 242
Kahn, Loe 290
Kapp, Wolfgang 20, 207
Kardiner, Abram 174, 188
Karl I, Kaiser 199
Karolyi, Count Mihayl 200, 202
Kausen, Rudolf 78
Kendrick, Walter 211, 214
Kennedy, Florence 250
Kepler, Johann 190
Kesey, Ken 173
Kiell, Norman 55, 59, 80
Kinderseminar, Vienna 210
King, Pearl 219, 222, 223, 225, 229
Klein, Arthur 195
Klein, Donald 277
Klein, Erich 195, 206, 209, 242

Sutherland, J. D. 235
Suttie, Ian 291–2
Suttie, Jane 291
Swales, Peter 18, 51, 52, 87
Symposium on Child
  Psychoanalysis, Innsbruck
  (1927) 211, 214, 234
Syrski, Simon 27

talking cure 3, 10, 48–50, 54–62
Taneyhill, G. Lane 149
Tardieu, Ambroise 74
Tavistock Clinic 242
Taylor, W. S. 153
Tedesco, Baron Eduard von 51
Temple, Shirley 15
Thaw, Harry K. 165
thiothixine 183
Thompson, Clara 187, 188, 189,
  249
Thompson, M. Guy 158
Thompson, Sharada 158
Thurston, John Mellen 165
Thurston, Lola Purman 165
Titchener, Edward Bradford
  147–8
Tomlinson, Craig 188
torture 10, 261–4, 269–70
Tourette's syndrome 60, 89
training analysis 133, 149, 223,
  236
transference 12, 130–43, 249
translation problems 287,
  289–90
Trenton State Hospital, New
  Jersey 173–4
Trevarthen, Colwyn 226
Triarhou, Lazaros 29
Trist, Eric 225
Trömner, Ernst 103, 104
tuberculosis 31–2
Tucker, Beverley 145
two-person psychology 252
Two Year Old Goes to Hospital
  (film) 224

unconscious 2, 134–9, 189
United States
  communism 191
  medical institutions 157–8
  psychiatry 3
  psychoanalysis 13, 144–92
University of Vienna 22–32, 82,
  95, 140, 190
Upson, Henry 34

Urban (Urbantschitsch), Rudolf
  von 40
Uruguay 261–4, 269

Van Der Kolk, Bessel 54
Van Helden, Albert 62
Vanity Fair 148
Verrall, A. W. 230
Vienna 259, 265
  anti-Semitism 104–5
  University 22–32, 82, 95, 140,
    190
  Wednesday Psychological
    Society 100–102, 107–12,
    130
Vienna Psycho-Analytic
  Association 268
Vienna Psychoanalytic Society
  97, 113–15, 210
Viennese Medical Society 4
violent disaster 9
von Lieben, Anna (Cäcilie M.)
  51–4, 56–7, 89, 98
von Lieben, Leopold 51

Waelder-Hall, Jenny 187
Walker, May 224
Wallace, Alfred Russel 58
Walton, George Lincoln 150–51
Washington-Baltimore Society
  187
Washington Psychoanalytic
  Society 149
Washington School of
  Psychiatry 181, 188, 191
Wasserman, Isidor 99
Watson, James Dewey 58
Wednesday Psychological
  Society 100–102, 107–12,
  130
Weier, Johann 87
Weigert, Edith 174
Weill, Kurt 118
Weiss, Nathan 60–61
Weldon, Fay 4
Wellcome Museum for the
  History of Science, London
  199
Wertheimstein, Josefine von 51,
  98–9
White, Stanford 165, 291
White, William Alanson 145–6,
  149, 152–4, 156–7, 185
  on anxiety 227
  on Freud 169, 290

on Jones 290
on lay analysis 176
Outlines of Psychiatry 153
partnership with Jelliffe
  164–5
psychoanalysis 159–69
St Elizabeths 170
Why Worry? (Walton) 151
Whyte, Lancelot 2
Wilberforce, Samuel 93
Will, Otto 158
William Alanson White Institute
  181, 188, 189
Williams, Robin 245
Wiltwyck School for Boys, New
  York 97–8
Winnicott, D. W. 135, 195,
  216–17, 241–4, 272, 273,
  276
  feminism 249
  and Melanie Klein 194, 195,
    223, 228, 242–3
  parent–child relationship 227,
    241–3
  and Riviere 217, 242–3
  two-person psychology 252
witchcraft 71, 87
Wittels, Fritz 18, 102, 110
women
  emancipation 245
  question the primacy of men
    249–50
  role in psychoanalysis 13,
    245–71
Woolf, Leonard 211
Woolf, Viriginia 211, 213
Woolley, H. C. 176
Worcester Hospital for the
  Insane, Massachusetts 154
Work, Hubert 170
Wright Brothers 11, 15
Wriston, William 58

Yalom, Irving 166
Yorke, Jim 274
Young-Bruehl, Elisabeth 210,
  215, 235, 244

Zasulich, Vera 265
Zentralblatt 113–14
Zinnemann, Fred 267
Zinner, Friedrich 25
Zodiac Group 187
zoology 27
Zulueta, Felicity de 240

FOR THE BEST IN PAPERBACKS, LOOK FOR THE

In every corner of the world, on every subject under the sun, Penguin represents quality and variety—the very best in publishing today.

For complete information about books available from Penguin—including Puffins, Penguin Classics, and Compass—and how to order them, write to us at the appropriate address below. Please note that for copyright reasons the selection of books varies from country to country.

In the United Kingdom: Please write to *Dept. EP, Penguin Books Ltd, Bath Road, Harmondsworth, West Drayton, Middlesex UB7 0DA.*

In the United States: Please write to *Penguin Putnam Inc., P.O. Box 12289 Dept. B, Newark, New Jersey 07101-5289* or call 1-800-788-6262.

In Canada: Please write to *Penguin Books Canada Ltd, 10 Alcorn Avenue, Suite 300, Toronto, Ontario M4V 3B2.*

In Australia: Please write to *Penguin Books Australia Ltd, P.O. Box 257, Ringwood, Victoria 3134.*

In New Zealand: Please write to *Penguin Books (NZ) Ltd, Private Bag 102902, North Shore Mail Centre, Auckland 10.*

In India: Please write to *Penguin Books India Pvt Ltd, 11 Panchsheel Shopping Centre, Panchsheel Park, New Delhi 110 017.*

In the Netherlands: Please write to *Penguin Books Netherlands bv, Postbus 3507, NL-1001 AH Amsterdam.*

In Germany: Please write to *Penguin Books Deutschland GmbH, Metzlerstrasse 26, 60594 Frankfurt am Main.*

In Spain: Please write to *Penguin Books S. A., Bravo Murillo 19, 1° B, 28015 Madrid.*

In Italy: Please write to *Penguin Italia s.r.l., Via Benedetto Croce 2, 20094 Corsico, Milano.*

In France: Please write to *Penguin France, Le Carré Wilson, 62 rue Benjamin Baillaud, 31500 Toulouse.*

In Japan: Please write to *Penguin Books Japan Ltd, Kaneko Building, 2-3-25 Koraku, Bunkyo-Ku, Tokyo 112.*

In South Africa: Please write to *Penguin Books South Africa (Pty) Ltd, Private Bag X14, Parkview, 2122 Johannesburg.*